# DISPLACEMENT : HOW TO FIGHT IT

Allan —
It is a beautiful book.
All in all, I'd rather
have worked with
Troxler.
Fondly,
Chan

This community handbook is dedicated to the memory and spirit of Wayne Baron, coordinator of the 1979 San Franciscans for Affordable Housing initiative campaign, whose death at age 28 took from us all a real fighter and a fine person.

## ADVISORY COMMITTEE

Hazel Bonner, *South Dakota*
David Bryson, *California*
Jack Cann, *Minnesota*
Felipe Chavana, *New Jersey*
Sylvia Lohah, *Colorado*
Ellsworth Morgan, *New Jersey*
Florence Wagman Roisman, *D.C.*
Andrea Saltzman, *California*
Paula Scott, *D.C.*
Mawina Sowa, *Massachusetts*
Steve St. Hilaire, *New Jersey*
Frances Werner, *California*
Rose Wylie, *Pennsylvania*

Allan Troxler

# DISPLACEMENT: HOW TO FIGHT IT

Chester Hartman
Dennis Keating
Richard LeGates

with Steve Turner

**Book design by Allan Troxler**

A publication of the Legal Services
Anti-Displacement Project

# AUTHORS

Chester Hartman holds a PhD in City and Regional Planning from Harvard University, and has taught there, as well as at Yale, the University of California-Berkeley, Cornell, and the University of North Carolina-Chapel Hill. He has been active in community housing struggles in the Boston and San Francisco areas and chairs the Planners Network, a national organization of progressive planners. His books include: *Housing and Social Policy* (Prentice-Hall, 1975), *Housing Urban America* (Aldine, 1980), and *Yerba Buena: Land Grab and Community Resistance in San Francisco* (Glide, 1974).

Dennis Keating is a lawyer and planner who teaches at the University of California-Berkeley and New College of California Law School. He is consultant to government agencies and housing groups at the local, state and national levels, and is the author of numerous publications on planning, housing and community development issues.

Richard LeGates is an Associate Professor of Urban Studies at San Francisco State University. As a lawyer and planner he has worked with many community groups involved in displacement struggles.

Steve Turner was a community organizer for several years in the Philadelphia area before becoming Executive Director of Urban Planning Aid, Inc., in Boston. Since 1973, he has worked as a freelance writer and editor. He was a contributing author to *No Nukes* (South End Press, 1979) and *Men in the Middle* (Spectrum Books, 1981), and is the author of *Night Shift In A Pickle Factory* (Singlejack Press, 1980).

Allan Troxler has worked as artist and organizer with groups such as Urban Planning Aid, Oregon Citizens Against Toxic Sprays, the Institute for Southern Studies and, most recently, Our South, a catch-all project for gay/lesbian politicking in central North Carolina.

# ACKNOWLEDGEMENTS

The extent of our debt and gratitude to those who have helped us put this guide together is enormous. Without their aid in providing information, through phone conversations, mailings, and personal visits, our task would literally have been impossible. Naturally, not all the materials we received could be incorporated into the book, but our understanding of the issues and selection of materials comes out of everything we gathered during the year and a half we worked on this project.

The following persons helped us by providing materials (identifications are those at the time of our contact): Thomas Alexander (Massachusetts Executive Office of Communities and Development), Stuart Andrews (Palmetto Legal Services, Columbia, SC), Buck Bagot (Bernal Heights Community Foundation, San Francisco), Susan Bain (National Urban Coalition, Oakland, CA), Helen Bean and Diana Bilovsky (North of Market Planning Coalition, San Francisco), Harold Berk (Community Legal Services, Philadelphia), Melinda Bird (Legal Aid Bureau, Frederick, MD), Barbara Blanco, Chuck Elsesser, Sandra Pettit and Warren Shakin (Los Angeles Legal Aid Foundation), Lou Blazej (San Francisco Dept. of City Planning), David Bloom, John Fox and Chuck Weinstock (Seattle Displacement Coalition), Paul Bloyd (Working Group for Community Development Reform, Washington, DC), Shuble Boling (Director of Housing Code Enforcement, Chatham County, GA), Michael Bonique, Rich Cagan, Ben Campbell, Jim Elam and Barry Rose (Richmond, VA), Peggy Borges and Van Buneman (Rural America, Washington, DC), Douglas Brooks and Jane Califf (Anti-Displacement Committee of Boerum Hill/Gowanus, Brooklyn), Ken Brown, Ed Donavan, Sylvalia Hyman and Joann Yawitz (United South End Settlements, Boston), Carol Brusegar Minneapolis Tenants Union), Don Bryant (Lawyers for Housing Los Angeles), Paul Burke, Carla Cohen, Larry Dale, Conrad Egan, Debra Greenstein, Judy Kossy, Bert Mason, Joe Guggenheim, Clyde McHenry, Tim Miles, Jan Opper, John Pickering, Alex Pires, Robert Ryan, Patty Stalling, Michael Stegman and Andy Udris (HUD, Washington, DC), Susan Carroll (Legal Aid Society of Minneapolis), Annette Rubin Casas (Inquilinos Boricuas en Acción, Boston), Bill Cavallini and Neil Rohr (Simplex Steering Committee, Cambridge, MA), Harriet Cohen (New York City), Marilyn Cohen (National Housing Law Project, Berkeley, CA), Rick Cohen (Rick Cohen & Associates, Hoboken, NJ), John Crowder (San Francisco Housing Authority), Fern Dannis (Dept. of Planning & Community Development, Alexandria, VA), Henry DeBernardo (North Philadelphia Revitalization Coalition), Armand Derfner (Charleston, SC), Louise Elving (Greater Boston Community Development), Marilyn Fedelchak (National Family Farm Coalition, Washington, DC), Sharon Feigon and Judy Kuskin (Seattle Tenants Union), Jeannie Fewell (City Planning Department, Charleston, SC), Theodore Fillette (Legal Services of Southern Piedmont, Charlotte, NC), Michael Fischer and Evelyn Lee (California Coastal Commission), Gregory J. Friess (Colonial Village, Inc., Reston, VA), Kathy Gannett (All-City Housing Organization, Boston), Chuck Geisler (Rural Sociology Dept., Cornell University), John Gilderbloom (Foundation for National Progress, San Francisco), Susan Gill (Philadelphia Corporation for Aging), John Goss (Legal Aid Society, Tidewater, VA), Clarence Green and Peggy Jones (South Philadelphia Inner City Improvement Association), Michael Harney (San Francisco Housing Coalition), Bill Harrington (Philadelphia), Betty Hepner (Office of Community Development,

Cambridge, MA), Patrick Hornschemeier (Legal Aid Society of Cincinnati), Tom Hutchinson (Univ. of California, Berkeley), Ilene Jacobs and Lee Reno (National Housing Law Project, Washington, DC), Pat Jenny and Carol Meek (Berkeley Planning Associates, Berkeley, CA), Idealla Jones (Housing Director, City of Savannah), Roy Jones (Camden Citizens Coalition), Michael Kane (All City Housing Organization, Boston), State Rep. Mel King (Boston), Gretchen Klimoski (Ohio Historical Society, Columbus), Michael Krysz, Bill Orrick and Elizabeth Youngerman (Savannah Legal Services), Dan Lauber (Evanston, IL), Charles Laven (Urban Homesteading Assistance Board, NYC), Bricker Lavik (Legal Aid Society of Minneapolis), Paul Levy and Thomas Massaro (Philadelphia Office of Housing & Community Development), Peter Marcuse (Div. of Urban Planning, Columbia University), John Mason (Cambridge-Somerville [MA] Legal Services), Chuck Matthei and Ted Shen (Institute for Community Economics, Boston), Nancy Maurer (Neighborhood Legal Services, Charleston, SC), Maurice McCrackin (Community Church of Cincinnati), Terry McLarney (Massachusetts Law Reform Inst., Boston), Jeff Miller (Neighborhood Development Corp. of Elizabeth, NJ), Marie Nahikian (District of Columbia Dept. of Housing & Community Development), Walter Park (Duboce Triangle Housing Alliance, San Francisco), Roger Powell, II (District of Columbia Department of Finance and Revenue), Vincent Quale (St. Ambrose Housing Aid Center, Baltimore), John Richard (Corporate Accountability Research Group, Washington, DC), Dick Schramm (National Consumer Cooperative Bank, Washington, DC), Ron Shiffman, Brian Sullivan and Pat Swan (Pratt Center for Community Development, Brooklyn, NY), Jim Shoch (Gray Panthers, San Francisco), Marty Strange (Center for Rural Affairs, Walthill, NE), City Councilman John Street (Philadelphia), Robert Stumberg (Harrison Institute for Public Interest Law, Washington, DC), Michael Swack (Economic Development Strategies, Somerville, MA), Madeline Talbott (Detroit ACORN), Carole Wagan (North Shore Community Action Programs, Salem, MA), Charles Warner (Common Space, Minneapolis), Seth Weissman (Hyatt & Rhoads, Atlanta), Frances Werner (National Housing Law Project, Berkeley, CA), Ann Wheelock (Boston), Marshall Whitely (Washington, DC), Sue Wilson (University of North Carolina), Erica Wood (Legal Research and Services for the Elderly, Washington, DC).

We apologize to anyone whose help we may inadvertantly have neglected to acknowledge in this lengthy "thank you note."

We are particularly grateful to those who took the time to read and comment on our initial draft (some of whom also had earlier furnished materials to us). Their help was extraordinarily valuable, and we hope it is reflected in the major changes and improvements we made, based on their comments. Emily Achtenberg (Citizens Housing & Planning Association of Metropolitan Boston), Joan Blackburn (National Association of Neighborhoods, Oakland, CA), Kate Crawford (National Low Income Housing Coalition, Washington, DC), Joe Giloley (National Association of Neighborhoods, Washington, DC), Marie Kennedy (University of Massachusetts, Boston), Marsha Simon (Washington, DC), and Michael Stone (University of Massachusetts, Boston) all gave us comments on the draft as a whole. The following persons commented on specific sections of the draft: Peter Behringer (Multi Family Housing Services, Baltimore), David Bryson and John Calmore (National Housing Law Project, Berkeley, CA), Jack Cann (Cedar-Riverside PAC, Minneapolis), James Chapman (Avery Anti-Displacement Clearinghouse, Chicago), Bruce Dale (New York City Housing Preservation and Development Department), Fred Feller (San Francisco Neighborhood Legal Assistance Foundation), George Gould (Community Legal Services, Philadelphia), Jorge Hernandez (Inquilinos Boricuas en Acción, Boston), Robert Kolodny (Columbia University), David Madway (National Housing Law Project, Berkeley, CA), Fred Ringler (People's Firehouse, Brooklyn, NY), Dennis Rockway (Camden Regional Legal Services, NJ), Florence Wagman Roisman (National Housing Law Project, Washington, DC), Joel Rubenzahl (Community Economics, Oakland, CA), Tony Schuman (New Jersey College of Architecture), Steve St. Hilaire (Hudson County Legal Services, NJ), Joe Szakos (Inez, KY). Frances Werner, staff attorney with the National Housing Law Project, provided useful last-minute first aid to our final page proofs, in helping update material made obsolete by very recent actions of the Administration and Congress.

Our Advisory Committee was extremely helpful in the original formulation of the work agenda, in their comments on the first draft, and in many other ways. The Metropolitan Council on Housing of New York City (Jane Benedict), *Shelterforce* (Jody Stollmack and Woody Widrow), *City Limits* (Susan Baldwin and Tom Robbins), *Disclosure* (Vera Benedek), Liberation News Service (Michael Skurato) and *City Life* (Mark Hoffman and Kathy McAfee) kindly allowed us to use their graphics files.

The many persons who typed our draft materials deserve an especial thank-you for their prompt, patient, and accurate work: Katherine Castro, Kathleen Clifford, Pat McPeak and Lucy Mandoriao of the National Housing Law Project, Berkeley, CA; Pat Coke and Mollie Felton of the Department of City and Regional Planning, University of North Carolina-Chapel Hill; Beryl Glover of Chapel Hill, NC; Michael Hillary and Ira Peppercorn of Cambridge, MA; and Anne Turner, Lowell, MA.

We also are grateful to the Center for Urban and Rural Studies of the University of North Carolina-Chapel Hill, the Center for the Study of Public Policy, Cambridge, MA, and the Institute for Policy Studies, Washington, DC, for providing us with office space at various points in our work. Alan Houseman, Director of the Research Institute for the Legal Services Corporation provided much needed support. The National Housing Law Project's Berkeley and Washington offices and their staffs were invaluable sources of support throughout our work.

The authors divided their tasks as follows: Chapters 4, 5, 6, 9 and 14 were originally drafted by Dennis Keating, who also provided research materials for other chapters. Chapters 3, 12 and 13 were originally drafted by Richard LeGates. Chapters 1, 2, 7, 8, 10, 11, 15, 16, 17 and 18 were originally drafted by Chester Hartman, who then edited all the materials into a first draft, which was reviewed by the Advisory Committee of the Legal Services Anti-Displacement Project and by the commentators acknowledged above. Steve Turner then took the commentators' responses, and, working with Chester Hartman, produced a second draft, on which he, Chester Hartman, Allan Troxler and Carl Wittman did final copyediting. Chester Hartman and Allan Troxler assembled the graphics and Pat Ford helped with pasting up.

C.H., D.K., R.L.
October, 1981

Library of Congress Catalog Number 81-82321
ISBN: 0-9606098-1-4

Typeset by Individual Types, Durham, North Carolina

Printed by the Banta Company, Menasha, Wisconsin

Published by the National Housing Law Project, Berkeley, California

This report was prepared as part of the Legal Services Anti-Displacement Project. The opinions expressed herein are those of the authors and do not necessarily represent opinions or policy of the Legal Services Corporation or the United States Government.

---

*Copies of* Displacement: How To Fight It *are available from the National Housing Law Project, 2150 Shattuck Ave., #300, Berkeley, CA 94704. The price is $7.50 per copy. Mail orders must be prepaid, and $2.50 per copy must be added for postage and handling. California residents add 6% sales tax (6.5% for BART District residents). Bulk orders of 5-19 copies receive a 15% discount. Larger discounts are available on orders of 20 copies or more.*

# Introduction

*Displacement: How To Fight It* is one of several products that have been prepared as part of the Legal Services Anti-Displacement Project. At a national meeting of Legal Services attorneys and their clients, held in Silver Spring, Maryland, in November, 1977, displacement was identified by the clients as their number one priority concern for national level research and coordinated action. Subsequently, the Research Institute of the Legal Services Corporation funded the Project to produce a series of studies/strategy papers/guidebooks.

This guidebook, written for community organizations and their advocates, is being released at a time when the problem of displacement has reached epidemic proportions. As our earlier study, *Displacement,* showed, a conservative estimate is that 2½ million Americans are being forced to move from their homes and neighborhoods each year, from all causes. It is also being released at a time of transition with regard to the government's housing and community development programs. The Administration and Congress currently are considering budgetary and program changes that may have serious impact on the displacement problem, as well as on some of the strategies outlined in this handbook. Unfortunately for displacees, these changes will probably serve to exacerbate the problem of forced moves. Cutbacks in authorizations for Section 8 and Farmers Home Administration housing subsidies, Section 312 rehabilitation loans, public housing modernization funds, and Community Development Block Grants can only harm the poor. Raising the proportion of income public housing tenants must pay, from 25% to 30%, will likely force many persons to move to overcrowded slums, in order to keep their housing costs down. Threatened elimination of the National Consumer Cooperative Bank and the Legal Services program will take away important anti-displacement protections. Cutbacks in VISTA, CSA and ACTION funds will rob communities of organizers whose work often is essential to effective anti-displacement strategies. Congressional moves to pressure cities into abandoning local controls over housing costs — under the threat of loss of federal aid — can only spell more displacement.

It is important that those concerned with the displacement problem keep abreast of changes in programs and authorizations, and fight to retain and expand those approaches that have served and can serve to keep people from having to move against their will.

# Chapter 1

## "WE NO MORE HOME"

Allan Troxler

The cops and bulldozers arrived at daybreak. Led by State Deputy Attorney General Edwin Wilson, 75 or more armed officials — city and state police, Coast Guardsmen, state park guards — had come to destroy a community.

Clement Apolo, 57, a disabled World War II veteran living on $257 a month, watched for a while, then as the giant bulldozers came closer to his own home he began to cry. "Might as well die, now it like this," he stammered in the familiar Hawaiian pidgin. "It hurts me right here," and he gestured to his heart. "The hell with it, man. They are going to take me in a pine box outa here."

Another 110 frightened, angry people, mostly native Hawaiians, huddled in their makeshift homes or scurried about in a desperate effort to halt the inevitable. Those who resisted most were arrested and handcuffed — 12 men and six women.

Clement Apolo seemed serious about dying in his small shack. Friends rushed inside with him. The radio was blaring the national anthem. A few minutes later, he emerged with his wife, Annie, 61, both sobbing. And then the bulldozer was there. "Where we going?" he screamed into the TV camera. "We no more home."

[These] families have simply joined the thousands of other dispossessed Hawaiians in this tropical paradise, where they, the first people of this land, are consigned to desperate poverty and a makeshift existence on public beaches, in state parks and in remote inaccessible areas . . .

With little or no income and faced with the highest housing costs in the nation . . . they are refugees in their own land, victims of a world of asphalt and tourism and condominiums.

San Francisco *Examiner*, May 5, 1980

Displacement in Hawaii. Displacement in Maine, California, Kansas, Georgia, Kentucky, New Jersey, you name it. *Displacement* is just a calm word for a frequent and shattering experience: people losing their homes against their will. The term describes what happens when forces outside the household make living there impossible, or hazardous, or unaffordable. The fact of displacement is a grotesque and spreading feature of life for lower-income people in the United States. It also means a process by which they are engineered out of their traditional neighborhoods, to make way for new occupants deemed more "desirable" because of the color of their skins, the taxes they will pay, or the "life style" they lead. And it describes a rapid whittling away of society's stock of low- and moderate-income housing.

The Hawaii story above is a dramatic example of one of the country's least publicized major calamities. *Displacement afflicts some 2½ million Americans each year.* Beyond that statistic, some 500,000 lower-rent units are lost each year, through conversion, abandonment, inflation, arson and demolition. And the great majority of displacees are the very people most likely to be harmed by the process: low-wage and welfare households, single-parent families, beleaguered minorities, the

fixed-income elderly. It happens in cities, suburbs, farm towns, everywhere. The cause might be condominium conversion, abandonment by the landlord or withdrawal of city services, a Corps of Engineers project, highway or hospital expansion, code enforcement, or the rent-raising that goes along with "gentrification" and "revitalization." The list even includes acts of God, such as windstorm and flood. But the real main sources of the problem

## Each year displacement afflicts some 2½ million Americans, and some 500,000 lower-rent units are lost.

are acts of profit-seeking humans, blended in with the work of planners, administrators and legislators who give higher value to the interests of the wealthy than to the shelter needs and neighborhood attachments of people with smaller pocketbooks.

Displacement has its open and ugly side, when occupied lower-rent units are destroyed for profit or converted to higher rent use, and their residents evicted. It also has a less obvious side, in which vacant housing gets the same treatment: no one is being directly displaced, but displacement is definitely underway. People who did live there were displaced when the units went off the market. And every one of those units that is permanently removed from the lower-rent housing stock increases the squeeze of rent inflation and other displacing pressures on the growing low- and moderate-income population, which must compete for a shrinking supply of housing. And since neither the private sector nor the government is adding much to this supply these days, the squeeze gets ever tighter. Whatever the cause

of displacement, lower income displacees are shoved out — almost always without assistance or compensation — into a housing market which is shifting its dwindling resources increasingly toward meeting the needs and desires of the wealthier segments of society. Urban displacement victims find themselves dealing with governments mainly concerned with "revitalization" — getting upper-income people, especially white professionals and business types, to live, play and shop downtown — which are encouraging real estate investors to profit from the process. In rural areas the comparable government concern may be with economic development, especially for energy production, which tends to get priority over the needs of those displaced along the way.

Woolaroc Museum, Bartlesville, Oklahoma

*Cherokees, Creeks, Choctaws, Chickasaws, Seminoles, Shawnees, Delawares, Senecas and some fifty other tribes were forced by an act of Congress to travel the "Trail of Tears" to the Great American Desert, and destruction.*

3

This has been a long-term pattern in the United States, even though the form and accompanying rhetoric may have changed over the years. In some senses, one can say that much of our country's history has been built on the principle of displacement: Native Americans starting in the 17th Century, Mexicans from our Southwest during the 19th Century, right through removal (and internment) of American citizens of Japanese ancestry from the West Coast during World War II and on into the urban renewal ("Negro removal" as it was then dubbed) program of the 1950s and 1960s. What may be different now is that the government's role is more subtle and behind-the-scenes, that on the surface at least it's nothing but "the market" at work. Yet as neighborhood markets shift toward the moneyed folks, others get dumped out to scramble for reduced housing opportunities, at escalating prices. That scrambling, as government sees it now, is basically just a part of life in the private market system, and a welcome one at that. A February, 1979 HUD Report to Congress on displacement shows how the wind is blowing. "Although the Federal Government must be sensitive to the needs of those persons who might be adversely affected by the implementation of federal programs, and by private revitalization," said HUD, "it must also make sure the beneficial effects of those programs are not lost."

In government language, an "although" like that means "this is unimportant."

The Legal Services Anti-Displacement Project strongly disagrees. *Moving people involuntarily from their homes or neighborhoods is wrong.* Regardless of whether it results from government or private market action, forced displacement is characteristically a case of people with

## CAUSES OF DISPLACEMENT

Abandonment
Accidental fire
Airport construction or expansion
Arson
Code enforcement (including overcrowding)
Conversion of rental apartments to condominiums
Demolition to make way for new housing
Demolition for safety or health reasons
Foreclosure
Highway or transit construction or expansion
Historic area designation
Institutional expansion (universities, hospitals, etc.)
Military base expansion
Natural disaster (flood, hurricane, tornado, earthquake, etc.)

Partition sales
Planning and zoning decisions (including decisions still in process which "leak" to real estate industry)
Public building construction
Redlining
Rehabilitation (private market)
Rehabilitation (publicly aided)
Renovation of public housing
Rising market prices and rents
Rising assessments and tax rates
School construction
Urban renewal
Withdrawal of private services from neighborhood or structure

*Compiled by Washington consultants George and Eunice Grier in a 1978 study conducted for HUD*

out the economic and political power to resist being pushed out by people with greater resources and power, people who think they have a "better" use for a certain building, piece

of land, or neighborhood. The pushers benefit. The pushees do not.

The Anti-Displacement Project also regards it as *fundamentally wrong to allow removal of housing units from the low-moderate income stock, for any purpose, without requiring at least a one-for-one replacement.* Demolition, conversion, or "upgrade" rehab of vacant private or publicly owned lower-rent housing should be just as vigorously opposed as when those units are occupied. Reducing the supply of *potentially* available housing generates additional inflationary pressures in the remaining supply, which in turn generates displacement.

Some will argue with such absolute positions, and will put forth examples where displacement is "truly in the public interest," or "necessary for the greater good," or even helpful to the types of people being displaced. Building a new public transit line, for instance, to make getting to work or shopping simpler. Or tearing down a few houses to enable construction of a larger low-income housing development. Even in such instances, however, experience tells us that involuntary displacement can be avoided by rerouting or replanning, or by making relocation opportunities so attractive — in terms of meeting people's housing, economic, and community needs — that the move becomes voluntary. (See for example the illustration from Atlanta on page 171.)

We are aware, however, of the difference that can exist between basic ideals and the reality of local struggles. We put forward the twin goals of absolute defense of the "right to stay put" and absolute requirement that there be one-for-one (or more) replacement of lower-rent units withdrawn from the market, realizing that many local groups will not be able to win such demands. For them, the anti-displacement battle may turn into a fight to get all they can to compensate for the pains and costs of dislocation, or to enable some residents

*After midnight at the entrance to the ladies' room of Penn Station, New York City.*

Ann Marie Rousseau © 1980

to remain. But the push toward basic goals is always important. While a generous moveout agreement may solve the immediate problems of some displacees, the suffering of the larger population will only increase until the line is somehow drawn — no more forced displacement, no more loss of lower-rent housing.

As it stands now, displacees typically go into worse housing situations, often at higher rents. And sometimes they go into no homes at all — into the streets. A front page story in the March 8, 1981 New York *Times* reports a just released study by the Community Service Society of New York which estimates there are 36,000 homeless men and women in that city, whose shelter is bus and railway stations, sub-

ways, steam tunnels and packing cases.

Even government statistics, flawed by a severe undercount, find 500,000 households — about 1.4 million people — being involuntarily displaced each year. About half of these households are inside, half outside metropolitan areas. These figures, appearing in the Census Bureau-HUD Annual Housing Survey (the only source of "hard" official numbers nationally), record only about half the real toll. Left out, for instance, are moves caused by increased rents and ownership costs, even though those probably represent the main type of involuntary displacement in today's tight housing market, and even though, in most areas where displacement is going on, that pinch has been

5

caused by government policies which encourage profiteering and reward housing speculation. Nor does the Annual Housing Survey include so-called "indirect," "secondary" or "hidden" displacement — that which results from private actions taken in response to nearby government projects, or rulings, or investments. The official tally also ignores multiple involuntary moves by the same household within the same year.

Our estimate, based on data available for individual cities and the work of scholars and consultants in the housing field, strongly indicates that the official figure must, conservatively, be doubled in order to give an accurate picture. Our July, 1981 report, *Displacement,* documents in detail the extent, causes and impacts of the problem nationally and in selected cities. Get a copy by writing us at 2150 Shattuck Ave., #300, Berkeley, CA 94704.

And of course, no statistics record the pain and anxiety of displacement conflicts around the country, nor the wide variety of political and geographic settings in which they take place.

● In San Francisco, the Tenderloin — a mixed hotel, residential and red-light area that is home to 20,000 low-income people, one-third elderly — is being coveted by the city's "number one industry," tourism. Three huge hotel structures are planned for construction. Although the luxury hotels are to be built on vacant or non-residential land, the ripple effects of "touristification" will be enormous. Organized community pressure has brought about a precedent-setting agreement to protect at least some existing residents from these pressures (see page 194), but in the long run

Alexander / Studio 53

*One of Atlantic City's proposed casinos purchased this entire block for their project. A lone resident refused to sell, even after an offer of over $1 million, plus lifetime free residence in the new hotel. After she turned the offer down, construction went ahead around her.*

the neighborhood's future seems to belong to the tourist industry.

• Tenants in Charleston, South Carolina, are being evicted by the College of Charleston Foundation, a private funding source created to get around slow state government processes for acquiring real estate — processes which include some displacement assistance provisions. The land is being bought for a state college, but because the Foundation is "private," the evictees will receive none of the relocation rights, protections or aids the state would provide. A protective lawsuit is underway.

• In Atlantic City, New Jersey, "the casino boom" is substituting hotels, high-cost shops, and high-cost housing for long-term resident households. Speculation near the beachfront has raised market values so high that resident retirees can't afford quadrupled tax bills. In Black and Hispanic neighborhoods, landlords are forcing tenants out by stopping maintenance, then bulldozing the buildings and selling the land. Dozens of small stores have disappeared along the boardwalk, victims of commercial lease costs rising into the stratosphere. Soon, says one local official, "it will be very difficult to build houses [here] except for the very rich." Meanwhile, at least ten other states are eyeing legalized casino gambling, and displacement results in those states will be similar.

• In Big Paint Creek Valley in Eastern Kentucky, the Army Corps of Engineers created a reservoir that took 12,600 acres (many of them never flooded), 230 occupied dwellings and many businesses. Relocation funds were insufficient to replace existing land-holdings for most residents in an escalating real estate market. Small farmers particularly lost their live-lihoods. Families used to supporting themselves on the land, through gardening and raising animals, were sent into crowded housing projects. Mental breakdowns and family breakups resulted.

• Various well publicized (plus lots of not so well publicized) nuclear reactor accidents, toxic chemical spills, and toxic waste dumpings, which put places like Three Mile Island and Love Canal on the map, have caused the temporary or permanent displacement of thousands of families. Such incidents and revelations can only increase.

**No statistics record the pain and anxiety of displacement conflicts around the country, nor the wide variety of political and geographical settings in which they take place.**

And so it goes, all over. In Salt Lake City, the Mormon Church tries to evict 42 tenants, many of them elderly women, some residents of 30 years' standing, so as to convert two buildings to office space. In New York, the gentrification on Columbus Ave. surges onto Amsterdam Ave., the next street over, spreading young whites and fancy stores into a low-rent, ethnically diverse neighborhood, tripling property values, pushing the traditional residents out. In Detroit, to save poor General Motors the pain of renovating its own Cadillac factory, the city plans to raze several hundred houses and businesses in a stable, racially-mixed neighborhood for a new plant site. Residents are fighting the plan, but the nation's sixth largest city and the world's largest manu-facturing corporation make for two very big opponents.

But the vast power of the displacers doesn't necessarily dictate the outcome. Organized residents of Cambridge, Massachusetts, for instance, have maneuvered the world-famous Massachusetts Institute of Technology to a standstill for nearly a decade in its efforts to develop the former Simplex Wire and Cable Co. site — with potentially powerful ripple displacement effects on the community — while denying area people a role in the planning process. At this writing, that battle continues. And so do similar conflicts all across the map.

It is for that combat, nationwide, that this book is designed. This is a manual on how to *fight* displacement. Our intent is to describe what kinds of things *work* (or can work) in resisting displacement, or derailing it, or at least winning the maximum concessions, in payments, assistance and replacement housing. This book is written for use by community groups and those giving them technical assistance (lawyers, planners, organizers, architects, etc.) In large part, also, it has been written *by* community groups. We have travelled extensively around the country, talking with people involved in the displacement problem, reading what they have written, observing what they have done. The result, laid out in the following chapters, is a compilation drawn from that wide-ranging experience.

Realistically, what lies before us — in each individual case and in the national effort — is a hard struggle. Not too many community groups have won their battles with displacement. *But we learned, while putting this guide together, that displacement can be successfully*

7

*fought.* The ingredients for the best defense and offense seem to be these:

• analyzing and understanding the forces causing the displacement

• studying the opposition and the opposition's plan in order to find vulnerable points

• acting militantly and politically to attack those weak points

• linking local efforts in city-wide, statewide, and finally national strategy and organization

There is no simple formula, let alone a guaranteed-or-your-money-back promise of success. Among other things, each community has its own individual problems and context, and what works in one place may be very different from what works in another.

This book offers experiences and ideas pulled together from the best of what groups around the country have tried and thought of to date in fighting displacement. It is not a laundry list: we have analyzed the various strategies and have selected, in our judgment, the ones most likely to head off displacement. We have attempted, also, to catalogue the types of in-

Louis Dunn

formation that proved useful in typical anti-displacement fights, and to indicate where and how to get such data.

In other words, this manual is intended as a starting point, a back-stop, a reference. But it is also an invitation. Displacement is a national problem, a powerful issue, and it is tied in directly with many other aspects of what is wrong with our housing system. We hope that local groups fighting to save their homes and their neighborhoods will also raise their sights toward a larger scope of action — the pressure that is needed to win the *right* to decent, safe, secure, affordable housing for us all.

---

To make this book publishable, useable, and less than ten pounds in weight, we have had to compromise between including all relevant detailed information here vs. referring readers to other sources for further facts. We have tried to incorporate enough detail to support each premise and tactic discussed, offering resource references and organizational contacts for those who want to explore the topics further. The most important references are incorporated into the text, and at the end of each chapter is a unified listing of these, plus subsidiary references. *We urge readers to use these references: write people, phone them, or if travel money is available, arrange a visit from or with groups who've already been through it.* There is nothing like comparing experiences and ideas for improving strategies and learning from the past. Send away for the reports, studies and ordinances listed: we've tried to include as much information as possible about how to order them. And by all means remember libraries, the best public means of access to statutes and regulations, law journals, other

periodicals, and books that either are too expensive to order or no longer are available. Law libraries at local law schools and in your courthouses, small libraries in HUD Area Offices (see Appendix A for addresses of these offices), and libraries at local colleges and universities — particularly city planning and urban studies libraries, where such programs exist — are places you generally can go to read materials and photocopy them for future reference. Librarians there can show you how to find materials you want. Don't be intimidated. Information is a key weapon in the anti-displacement struggle, and community groups should make every effort to arm themselves properly.

Our Legal Services Anti-Displacement Task Force, as well as similar networks established by other organizations such as the National Urban Coalition and the National Association of Neighborhoods (see page 213 for how to contact them), are all available to help link individual struggles with each other and provide whatever assistance we can. And be sure to contact your local Legal Services or Legal Aid office for further help.

If you want to contribute some further ideas and experiences, please contact us at the Legal Services Anti-Displacement Task Force, 2150 Shattuck Ave., #300, Berkeley, CA 94704, (415) 548-2600. If we get enough new material, we will try to put out a revised, second edition of this manual.

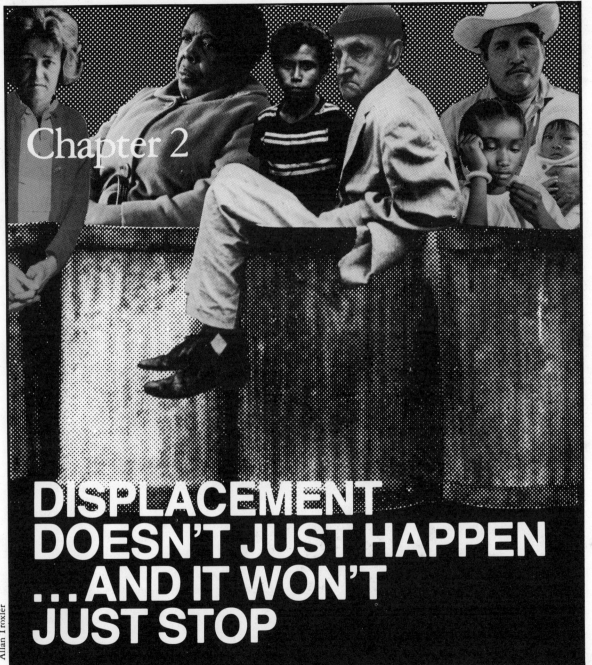

Chapter 2

Allan Troxler

# DISPLACEMENT DOESN'T JUST HAPPEN ... AND IT WON'T JUST STOP

"Displacement can only intensify as long as housing is maintained and produced as a commodity, as an investment first, and not as our basic human right."

*from "Toward a Housing Platform for the People of Boston," All City Housing Organization, Boston, Mass.*

Although the complexities of local displacement situations may make each one appear unique, in reality most of these situations are produced by the interaction of a common array of forces, policies and institutions, all of which are familiar mainstays of the current housing market.

The larger picture comes into focus when we look at two community groups located at opposite ends of the country. As we noted in our July, 1981 report, *Displacement,* the most accurate and realistic studies of displacement are done on the local rather than national level. Materials prepared by Seattle's Freemont Public Association (FPA) and Boston's All City Housing Organization (ACHO) contain powerful and similar analyses — although based on local evidence separated by 3,000 miles — of the cause and effect of displacement.

According to FPA, Seattle is pulling in more residents now than it is losing. The newcomer households "are characteristically younger, more affluent, and less likely to have children" than traditional residents. Why are they there?

Seattle is in the process of changing from a manufacturing-based economy of regional impor-

tance to a service-based city of national and international significance. This trend reflects Seattle's new economy based on trade with the Pacific Rim, Asia and Alaska, tourism, and its emergence as the financial and administrative center for one of the country's fastest growing regions. The investment capital fueling this growth comes from every corner of the globe.

The physical changes stimulated by this are manifested in very obvious ways. The Port of Seattle now ranks first on the West Coast in container capacity. Downtown office space has expanded by two million square feet between 1968 and 1977. Building permits have been obtained or construction begun on another 4.7 million square feet. This includes 10 office towers, 6 hotels and 3 condominiums. Nine of these structures will be over 30 stories (currently there are four such buildings). *Since 1960, 18,000 housing units have been lost in the CBD [central business district] as a result of private actions, urban renewal and code enforcement.* [Emphasis added.]

During the last four years (1975-1979), . . . the total number of households has increased by more than 22,000. This is attributable to the creation of a substantial number of new households and to the increasing numbers of people who have been attracted to the Pacific Northwest. The prospects of the strong and booming local economy and the much-touted "livability" have drawn people from across the country to relocate in Seattle . . . These trends have dramatically increased the demand for housing. . . .

Displacement pressures are also being felt in the older single family neighborhoods in the central core of the city which have been the homes for low and moderate income families, minorities, and elderly. As in-city living has become a preferred lifestyle for the more affluent, these neighborhoods have felt pressures from the increased demand for their resources. . . . Condominium conversions, rent increases, and the demolition of affordable units to make way for new condominiums and office space all contribute to the erosion of affordable housing. The average price of new market rate housing ($70,000 for a new single family house) is out of the range of the average household, let alone low income households. The few options that remain for homeownership by moderate income people are diminishing as speculation and escalating

property values become more widespread, and as costs of home maintenance and rehabilitation increase.

In the supply/demand economics that are supposed to underlie the "free market" system, of course, this growing need for additional, affordable housing should be met by an increase in units. But in Seattle, FPA describes a grotesque, opposite response by the market — one that almost every community organization around the country will recognize.

In the face of a rental vacancy rate that has dropped over the last two years to 1.7%, the affordable rental housing stock has actually decreased as apartments have been converted to condominiums and single family rental units have been sold to owner-occupants. In addition to this, because most of Seattle's land is already developed, much of the new construction that is occurring and planned is only possible if existing structures (often affordable rental housing) are demolished. . . . The housing shortage has reached crisis proportions, and there is a growing number of people who do not have the resources to compete for the limited housing supply. . . . [This has had a] severe impact on low and moderate income individuals who are most vulnerable to displacement pressures, and the communities that have historically been comprised of these types of people are being disrupted as social networks are destroyed. . . . *Almost 20% of all the households that moved during the past five years were forced to move. 27% of the lower-income households that moved and 34% of the elderly households that moved were displaced.* [Emphasis added.]

. . . Neither reinvestment nor displacement pressures are confined to one or two neighborhoods in Seattle. The shortage and high cost of housing is being felt in all areas. . . . The "trickle down" theory of housing supply does not work in these situations where the demand for all types of housing in all neighborhoods — even that which has traditionally been considered less desirable — continues to exceed the supply. Under current market conditions, few housing opportunities exist for those people who have limited resources with which to compete for what is available. . . .

Now take a 3,000 mile hop to the shores of Massachusetts Bay, and find . . . very little difference. Even though Boston's population is shrinking, not growing, ACHO, a coalition of tenant organizations and community groups, states flatly that "The major problem facing Boston's tenants and homeowners is 'displacement.' " Why? The city is being transformed, says ACHO, "from a manufacturing and trade center to a producer of high-grade services. Displacement has thrived on the City's inability to deal with the resulting rapid change." Among other things, notes ACHO, poor education and vocational training in the city, plus race and sex discrimination in employment, have ensured that outsiders will make up much of the upper-echelon labor force this new economy requires. But this sad fact, says ACHO, fits right in with the designs of state and city officials, and their companions in the community of corporations and banks.

"It is the policy of government and of financial institutions," says ACHO, "to 'reclaim' the cities for middle- and upper-income people who will work as managers, administrators,

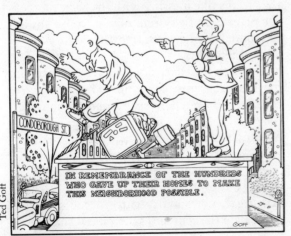

IN REMEMBRANCE OF THE HUNDREDS WHO GAVE UP THEIR HOMES TO MAKE THIS NEIGHBORHOOD POSSIBLE.

Ted Goff

and professionals in Boston's health, education, insurance, finance and governmental sectors." Most working-class neighborhoods around the city center, ACHO asserts, have suffered rent increases, property value hikes, and other displacement pressures resulting from the so-called "upgrading" as these new high-salaried workers — led and milked by real estate speculators — move in.

The invasion by a professional class has created a housing demand not easily met. This demand has contributed to condominium conversion, luxury rehabilitation, and inflated property values. . . . As a result [of the city's concept of a "spine" of high-density buildings from downtown to the Fenway], thousands are being kicked out of their Back Bay, South End, or Fenway homes. City policy favors the smooth return of upper-income people under the guise of expanding the tax base. But as institutions expand and special tax agreements are handed out, the City ignores the shrinkage of housing stock, of open space, and of the tax base itself. . . .

A second form of displacement is a result of "disinvestment." This occurs when banks (through "redlining"), landlords (by "milking" property to get quick profits with minimum investment) and government (by withdrawing essential services) force a neighborhood, often a Black or Third World community, to deteriorate. Apartments that aren't burned for a profit become uninhabitable, and the community breaks up.

And then — adding insult to injury — government operations which are supposed to aid low-income people often directly cause displacement. ACHO reports that the Boston Housing Authority has gone into court receivership largely because of "displacement, promoted by the city, that has left 6,500 [public housing] units vacant due to neglect and withdrawal of services." An outrageous result of this dereliction of duty, says ACHO, is that one of the Authority's major projects — Columbia Point, located on the harbor shore near a new University of Massachusetts campus and

the new John F. Kennedy Presidential Library — is going to be "upgraded" to higher income use.

Similarly, in the city's Southwest Corridor, development plans ostensibly designed to benefit surrounding working-class communities, largely Black and third world, now appear to be aimed as much at "upgrading" as anything else. The Corridor is a miles-long strip of open land blasted out years ago (with much displacement) through mixed residential-industrial territory. The highway intended to go on the cleared land was fought and defeated by surrounding communities. Now, as part of a neighborhood-oriented recovery approach, the city plans to relocate a transit line — which presently clogs nearby streets with elevated trestles and poor service — into the corridor. But, says ACHO, "The proposed new station stops are near desirable parcels," and improved conditions created by convenient transit and other aspects of the recovery plan "will enhance development potential that, without protection, will displace present residents."

## "We are mere pawns to be moved around by government and business policies that put profit before people."

"Displacement is not an accident," concludes ACHO, adding that Boston's city administration and banks and real estate interests have promoted gentrification opportunities in brochures and TV programs such as the "This Old House" series. "They have not said," however, ACHO angrily points out, "where they intend the displaced poor, elderly, or working people to move. But the only place left to go is out of the city. We are mere pawns to be

TO: THE MAYOR, THE BOSTON REDEVELOPMENT AUTHORITY AND THEIR SYCOPHANTS, THE COMMITTEE FOR NORTH HARVARD ST.

FOR NINE YEARS: WE HAVE RESISTED YOUR EFFORTS TO FORCIBLY EVICT US FROM OUR HOMES. BY YOUR ACTIONS YOU HAVE FAILED TO ACHIEVE YOUR GOAL: THE TOTAL DESTRUCTION OF OUR NEIGHBORHOOD. YOU HAVE DENIED US THE RIGHT TO BE FREE AND SECURE IN OUR OWN HOMES. YOU CANNOT MORALLY WIN HERE, AND NO RATIONALIZATION ON YOUR PART CAN JUSTIFY YOUR ACTS OF THEFT AND BRUTALITY. YOU VALUE MONEY AND BUILDINGS MORE THAN PEOPLE'S FREEDOM. THIS LAND IS RIGHTFULLY OURS, AND YOU KNOW IT! WE SHALL DEFEND IT WITH OUR LIVES!

## WE STILL WON'T MOVE!
## TO HELL WITH URBAN RENEWAL!

JULY 4, '69 IN MEMORIAM: TO ANNIE SORICELLI AND OTHERS WHO HAVE DIED IN DEFENSE OF THEIR HOMES

*In the 1960s a small neighborhood of single-family homes in Boston's Allston neighborhood, right across from Harvard's football stadium, put up a long and gallant fight against the bulldozers. Boston's mayor was trying to use urban renewal powers to reward a big political contributor who wanted to erect a luxury high-rise. They weren't able to save their homes, but their protest did result in moderate-income, rather than luxury, housing being built on the site.*

moved around by government and business policies that put profit before people."

FPA comes to much the same conclusion in its analysis:

If current trends are allowed to continue unchecked, the result could be the total erosion of the city's affordable housing supply. Seattle may become a place where retired people, low income households and even moderate income families cannot afford to live decently, and where population diversity would be lost over the long run. As private market forces make it more and more difficult for neighborhoods to provide a variety of housing opportunities, we will see more demands placed on our social service system. The demand for subsidies for housing and other basic needs can be expected to increase dramatically. This trend is already exemplified by the overwhelming need for and use of emergency shelter and food bank services in Seattle. As of January, 1979, the Seattle Housing Authority reported there were 2,473 people formally on their waiting list. There was no estimate of how many people were too discouraged to even get on the list.

This painful situation is not just an East-West Coast phenomenon. Communications with anti-displacement groups in other types of cities, in other areas of the country, make it clear that the pattern of forces operating in Boston and Seattle prevails — with slight variations — across the continent. (See, for instance, the excellent 46-page study "Indianapolis: Downtown Development For Whom?" [1980], available for $1.00 from the Indiana Christian Leadership Conference, Box 18160, Indianapolis, IN 46218).

Why is this so? ACHO points out that "Housing for people with low or moderate incomes has not been 'profitable' on its own, without government subsidy, since the Second World War." Rising costs of land and financing particularly have seen to that. But unlike transportation, retirement, education, and other areas, government has not moved to take over the costs of making the housing system work. Partly that is due to the heavy pressure of the real estate industry, which enjoys the money it can make from the shortage. But partly also it reflects the fact that ownership and marketing of real estate is the oldest, most hallowed form of capital accumulation in the war chest of private enterprise. To mess with that seems like messing with the basic roots of the private profit system, and government is too fond of that system to institute fundamental reforms.

So, with the exception of certain too-small, too-late programs, government has stuck with the profit-driven delivery system for housing. Inevitably, that has meant shrinkage of the housing stock at the low-moderate income levels, and, for the profit-seeking property owner, a need and opportunity to get more money out of the limited supply that is left. Making the commodity scarce, of course, helps to escalate the rent and sales rates. And then who can buy? Only the folks with money. Hook that up with the fact that municipal governments desperately need more tax revenue, but can't raise tax rates for fear of the political consequences, and mayors and city councillors begin to long for property values to go up so that the tax take will rise with them. Who can pay those taxes? Only the folks with money. And so we arrive at the self-serving, arrogant official point of view expressed in a recent New York *Times* Magazine article entitled "The New Elite and the Urban Renaissance": "Urban experts and politicians are beginning to understand that only the middle and upper classes — not the poor — can rebuild cities."

## Whereas nearly 70% of American families could afford single-family housing in the 1950's, fewer than 15% can afford it now.

The "free market," a myth propped up by subsidies, protections and tax breaks, actually works against meeting the nation's housing needs, and is in the process of producing a major social disaster. The housing subsidies provided by the income-tax system through deduction of mortgage interest and property tax payments — the overwhelming portion of which goes to upper-income homeowners — is over five times the amount of direct federal housing subsidies spent to help lower-income people. The current housing market system has brought us the displacement problem, and is responsible for the fact that ever higher proportions of Americans can't buy or rent a decent place to live, where they want to live, at costs they can afford.

For a closer-up look at the picture, ACHO offers the following analysis of how today's worsening situation has developed.

Recent economic and social developments have exacerbated the natural tendency to undersupply. High costs of land, of materials, and of borrowing money have pushed the cost of constructing a new residential unit in a multi-family building to well over $40,000 in Boston. At today's interest rates, and with Boston's property taxes, this price would require a family spending an affordable 25% of its income for housing to make $30,000 per year, whether they buy the unit as a condominium or rent it from a profit-minded landlord. Since few can afford new housing, it's not surprising that Massachusetts' housing production has plummeted. From a peak of 55,000 housing starts in 1973, the annual volume of housing starts in this state has remained between 20,000 and 22,000. Only 9,000 housing starts are forecast for 1980, with a projected direct loss of 15,000 jobs. State figures indicate an annual housing shortfall of 22,000 units, and a cumulative shortfall of 420,000 units by 1985. People cannot escape this pressure by staying in old housing, for in this time of shortage the working of the "free market" will force prices for old housing toward the unaffordable "replacement cost" of new housing, regardless of structural value. Rental housing will disappear. People can't escape by moving out of the State, for a nationwide shortfall of one-million housing units is forecast for 1980 alone. Home ownership is not the solution. Whereas nearly 70% of American families could afford single-family housing in the 1950's, fewer than 15% can afford it now. Costs of single-family housing have dramatically risen from a national median price of $23,400 in 1970 to $64,000 in 1979.

High interest rates also make refinancing less desirable for a landlord, thus removing the leverage [a term which describes an owner's ability to use very little of his/her cash to own housing, by borrowing the vast majority of capital needed] that once made owning real estate worthwhile. Today, the only way a landlord can capture the increase in equity and "market value" from a building is to sell it. Since other landlords no longer find it worthwhile to own rental housing, the apartments must be foisted off as condominiums onto unwary buyers.

Conversion to condos entails little capital investment, shrinks the rental market, and yields big profits for owners, converters (who are now often "big business" without experience in housing), and banks. "Buy now or move" ultimatums cause immeasurable disruption and generally double the cost of housing for those who reluctantly buy.

But with the high cost of building new housing, the rising cost of old housing, and the decreased incentive to profit-minded landlords to own rental housing, there is now an unprecedented increase in the number of people looking for homes. The "baby boom" generation is now coming of age and forming households, with a 50% increase in households nationwide predicted from 1970 to 1990. The increased demand for housing, the dwindling supply, and the cost of new construction have helped produce a housing crisis where the moderately well-off feel forced to buy condominiums or houses they don't really want, and where the poor are forced into substandard housing or out of the city altogether.

Speculators and financial institutions stimulate displacement. Developers and lending institutions benefit most from mortgage structures and spiraling interest rates that dilute ownership. Decisions made on the basis of profit potential prompt high financing charges, which are the fastest-growing component of housing costs. Thrift institutions lack funds for sufficient housing credit, since inflation has cut into savings deposits used by these banks to replenish the supply of credit. Investors find short-term loans at rising interest rates more profitable than long-term housing loans at fixed interest rates. An increasing dependence on commercial credit further tightens the mortgage money supply, and sends interest rates skyward.

Without the acquiescence of the government, however, these economic forces could not lead to the level of displacement occurring in Boston today.

### GOVERNMENT POLICY AND THE HOUSING CRISIS

Since housing is not "profitable" without direct subsidy or tax breaks from the government, governmental policy is crucial in determining the state of housing. Governmental housing policies have subsidized suburban growth at the city's expense, tolerated discrimination, and permitted the banking and real estate industries to develop self-serving policies.

13

FHA and Veterans' Administration mortgage insurance stimulated a continued increase of homeownership. These guarantees revived the post-depression housing market through expanded credit. The present national mortgage debt, encouraged by tax deductions, of $700 billion, documents the overextension of homeowners to the delight of the banking industry.

The 1949 Housing Act called for "a decent home and suitable living environment," but provided few ways to achieve this goal. Under the guise of urban renewal, this program allowed developers to convert sites occupied by the poor into commercial, civic, and luxury residential buildings. Nationwide, over one-half million low-income households were displaced to costlier, substandard housing, in areas often slated for future clearance.

The 1968 Housing Act reaffirmed the intent of the 1949 measure and recognized the neglect of lower-income families. Nonetheless, special interests continued to profit at public expense. Sections 235 and 236 of the 1968 Act were subsidy programs designed to enable low-income families to purchase or rent a decent home on the private market. By many accounts, these programs were drafted in accordance with [the wishes of] the National Association of Home Builders. People stretched their budgets to meet Section 235 guidelines, only to purchase, unknowingly, substandard homes. Excessive maintenance and repair costs caused widespread default on mortgage payments. The U.S. Commission on Civil Rights charged the FHA with using Section 235 to perpetuate segregation of housing. By the early seventies, the 1968 Act was debilitated by scandal and economic recession.

The purpose of the 1966 Model Cities Program was to eradicate poverty and blight with the help of citizen participation. Unfortunately, only 8% of its funding went for housing. The Nixon administration, declaring its intent to get out of the housing business, reshaped these programs by decentralizing power to local government. The ensuing concentration of power in city halls supported gentrification and political favoritism.

Federally-subsidized highways strangled inner-city communities. These roads accelerated suburban expansion. Demolition not only removed housing stock, but also contributed to the decay of

nearby neighborhoods as fear of highway clearance discouraged investment. Land-taking weakened the tax base, and frequently occurred in minority communities. Building the highways also moved jobs out of the city. Unable to relocate at old sites, many businesses migrated outward. Marginal firms folded. New industries generally located outside the city. If not for the highway moratorium, 5,000 more households and 5,000 more jobs would have been displaced from Boston by completion of the

Inner Belt, Interstate 95, and other roads. Unable to join the flight to suburbia, the minorities, elderly and poor were left behind to face unemployment and withdrawal of public services.

Though urban development policies now supposedly seek balanced growth through curtailment of suburban sprawl and investment in depressed areas, the intended beneficiaries are displaced. With government front money, banks and corporations have used their financial and managerial

Robert Zimmerman / The Montclarion

resources to protect and expand their profits, prestige, and influence. Community Development and Urban Development Action Grants can jeopardize neighborhood stability and deny resources to affected communities. Upper-income people can subvert the intent of "community development corporations" by forming corporations that further their own interests at the expense of residents of the community who have low or moderate incomes. Despite HUD guidelines to revitalize poor neighborhoods and local economies, UDAG funds have favored downtown development.

Declining federal assistance forces city officials to use [local tax] resources to attract funds for neighborhood revitalization. Such practices displace long-term residents and threaten the vitality of communities, since local property taxes fall the heaviest on those least able to afford them. Governmental complicity with big business has given Boston the highest property tax rate of any major American city. Unless property tax relief occurs, the escalating assessments from gentrification will displace all but the rich from the urban core. At the same time, though, "Proposition 13 fever" threatens basic human services. [This was written before the 1980 passage of Massachusetts' Proposition 2½, an East Coast version of Proposition 13 which seems to be doing exactly what ACHO envisioned. See the related discussion of property tax relief on pages 97-99.]

No government policies or programs adequately confront displacement. Skyrocketing housing costs are ignored. Reforms have been thwarted by the real estate industry with the acquiescence of the government. Comprehensive policy is derailed by the back-and-forth flow of personnel between government and the housing industry. Insistence on guaranteed profits by special interests, at each step of implementing a program, sabotages the program. In essence, government policy has encouraged the shortage of low- and moderate-cost housing.

As ACHO and FPA analyses also show, the overall effect of government policies at all levels is to increase, rather than prevent displacement. Even outside the area of encouraging (or planning) gentrification, government tax and regulatory policies are what make housing speculation so possible and profitable (see Chapter 4 for more detail on the speculation process and how to combat it).

But it is wrong to lay responsibility for displacement on the government alone. The larger message from the FPA and ACHO materials, and from the analyses of other groups, is that the major forces causing displacement are indeed *market* forces—profit-seeking and profitability, the availability and flow of investment capital, etc. It's just that government mostly nourishes that market on the ownership side, rather than regulating it for consumers on the demand side. So government actions and refusals to act have become powerful market forces themselves. In the end, the combination of the social policies of government and the profit interests of private capital merge. Each becomes largely the agent of the other. And together they create displacement.

The combination is strong, and hard to fight. But as the following chapters will show, this merger of government and the private profit sector can sometimes be forced apart in the housing field, can sometimes be blocked or outmaneuvered, or even made to retreat. The power and will to resist is essential to effective anti-displacement strategies.

Basically, to face the displacement problem squarely means facing the profit system squarely. *Intervening in the market* is at the heart of the effective anti-displacement strategies we've catalogued. The basic theme is *control:* trying to maximize people's control over their own lives and communities. The focus is on mechanisms and strategies that can counter the outside powers, institutions and people who want our neighborhoods and are manipulating them for new social designs or for profit. We have to devise alternative methods and institutions for producing, owning and managing property. Enough examples already exist — effective, successful neighborhood-based, non-profit and publicly directed forms of housing control — that we can say with confidence that alternatives to the present profit system in housing are possible.

The challenge posed by the threat and reality of displacement can lead us to see the necessity and wisdom of making fundamental changes in how the society treats homes and communities. For a look at the kind of housing and urban policy that would put people and their needs *first* — in our view, the most basic anti-displacement strategy of all — we suggest

**Enough examples already exist — effective, successful neighborhood-based, non-profit and publicly directed forms of housing control — that we can say with confidence that alternatives to the present profit system in housing are possible**

a reading of ACHO's "Housing Platform," contained in Chapter 18. This document offers an approach to the displacement problem which community groups — in order to avoid facing local struggles over and over again — should think about and begin to push.

*For those who would like to get in touch with them, the Freemont Public Association is located at 3410 Freemont Ave. N., Seattle, WA 98103, and the All City Housing Organization is reachable through Kathy Gannett, 38 Lindsay St., Dorchester, MA 02124.*

# Chapter 3

# GETTING AND ANALYZING DISPLACEMENT DATA:
## SAN FRANCISCO'S DUBOCE TRIANGLE HOUSING ALLIANCE

Allan Troxler

## "We don't have power, so we need information."

*Duboce Triangle Housing Alliance Member*

The quote above is right on target. It isn't so much that information creates power (although sometimes it does that, as when researchers discover secret schemes, or find that laws are being broken). Good information is a big help to anti-displacement groups in designing their counter-attacks, focusing their energies, and adapting their strategies and tactics to the changing situations they confront.

In the maze-like wilderness of housing information, however, doing effective research for action can be frustrating for organizations unused to the process. The purpose of this chapter is to show how good information can be found, and how it can be used, in fighting displacement. The example we'll look at is the Duboce Triangle Housing Alliance (DTHA), an impressively hard-working organization in the city of San Francisco. DTHA has been active in struggles to limit rental housing speculation, block conversion of residential units to commercial space, limit rent increases, and help tenants in the Triangle neighborhood obtain rent reductions.

DTHA has dug deeply into information on the neighborhood it is trying to save. The lessons the Alliance has learned about research work are offered here as guidance, and encouragement, to other neighborhood groups trying to understand the dynamics of displacement.

## THE NEIGHBORHOOD
## AND THE ALLIANCE

One side of the Duboce "triangle" is Market Street — San Francisco's main commercial artery. The neighborhood is a prime location, an easy fifteen minute bus ride from the financial district. It is compact, filled with attractive and physically sound Victorian buildings. It has good open space (two parks), and one of the best climates in a city whose neighborhoods have widely varying "microclimates." Not surprisingly, Duboce Triangle has been "discovered" and is gentrifying rapidly.

The neighborhood has seen lots of changes, but never this kind — until recently. According to one long-term resident of the area, interviewed for the DTHA Newsletter, the area was a working-class Scandinavian and Irish neighborhood when she was born just after World War I. At that time one of San Francisco's produce markets was located on what now is the site of a huge Safeway supermarket.

Physical decline set in. Widespread illegal conversions and crowding to house war workers during World War II speeded up the process. Another resident recalls that by the time he arrived in the late 1960s many of the area's residents were poor and the buildings weren't in good shape. By this time the population of the Triangle was a mixture of races (Black and Hispanic residents were prominent), incomes, household types — both families and singles — and lifestyles, with a burgeoning gay community spilling over into the area from nearby.

Things began to change in the late 1960s, when the Triangle was declared a Federally Assisted Code Enforcement area. Low-interest federal loans, coupled with code enforcement and public improvements, began to give the area a new look. The Triangle had become ripe for gentrification, and the 1970s saw massive additional private reinvestment, skyrocketing sale prices and rents, and dramatic alterations in the composition of the neighborhood.

In 1978, responding to the situation, the Duboce Triangle Housing Alliance formed. An existing group, the Duboce Triangle Neighborhood Association, consisting largely of liberal homeowners, had been established for many years. But the Association's non-profit tax status prohibited lobbying and the other forms of political activity intended by the Alliance's founders — who were mostly younger, less affluent renters, further to the left politically than the leadership of the Association. While all members of the Alliance were members of the Neighborhood Association, the Alliance was established with a separate identity and mission.

The main impetus for forming the Alliance was the eviction of a female-headed household on welfare. A small group of DTHA founders came together to try to keep the family in the neighborhood. The effort failed, but the struggle, and growing consciousness of the broader dynamics of housing pressure on the Triangle, soon involved the new Alliance in a broad range of activities with greater impact.

The core of DTHA consists of about half a dozen activists, with a wider support group of about 25 workers. Additionally, the Alliance can turn out more than a hundred followers for marches and important city political meetings. The DTHA newsletter and other mailings reach every one of the nearly 1,700 households in the Duboce Triangle neighborhood.

## THE NEED FOR RESEARCH

In the Spring of 1978, trying to get a handle on how to develop the best lines of resistance, DTHA began systematic analysis of conditions that were causing displacement in the Triangle neighborhood. At that time the principal concern was housing speculation. DTHA knew that outside speculators ("flippers") were purchasing Duboce Triangle properties and turning them over rapidly, at inflated prices, with little or no physical improvement. Residents' comments indicated rents were rising fast. And the population was obviously changing. Neighbors were moving away, and fewer and fewer children were playing in the streets. But hard information was needed in order to focus on what exactly was happening, and to plan how to fight back. So DTHA set out to document the rise in sales prices of housing, the increase in rents, the ways in which the neighborhood's population mix was changing, and the role the City had played in the situation through code enforcement and other programs. The Alliance was particularly eager to get proof that speculation and rent increases were related, and that rent hikes in the Triangle were not justified by the amount of owners' expenditures on their buildings.

This is the way DTHA's research proceeded.

## USING THE CENSUS

The first information source examined was the detailed reports of the U.S. Census. DTHA found the Standard Metropolitan Statistical Area (SMSA) volume, in this case San Francisco-Oakland, of the *Census of Population and Housing* most useful. Figure 1, from that volume, illustrates some of the detailed housing and population material the Census can provide: type of tenure (owning or renting), vacancies, condition of units, unit size, crowding, house value, rent paid, and race of occupants. In addition, special Census tabulations

Table H-1. **Occupancy, Utilization, and Financial Characteristics of Housing Units: 1970**

SAN FRANCISCO—OAKLAND, CALIF.,
SMSA H—45

| | Tract 0166 | Tract 0167 | Tract 0168 | Tract 0169 | Tract 0170 | Tract 0171 |
|---|---|---|---|---|---|---|
| All housing units | 2 702 | 2 556 | 3 521 | 1 688 | 1 814 | 3 731 |
| Vacant – seasonal and migratory | – | – | – | – | – | – |
| All year-round housing units | 2 702 | 2 556 | 3 521 | 1 688 | 1 814 | 3 731 |
| **TENURE, RACE, AND VACANCY STATUS** | | | | | | |
| Owner occupied | 259 | 301 | 218 | 250 | 552 | 837 |
| Cooperative and condominium | – | – | – | – | 5 | 11 |
| White | 139 | 127 | 91 | 201 | 522 | 622 |
| Negro | 102 | 137 | 102 | 20 | 6 | 130 |
| Renter occupied | 2 206 | 2 059 | 3 092 | 1 370 | 1 188 | 2 707 |
| White | 1 294 | 776 | 1 689 | 1 101 | 1 127 | 1 964 |
| Negro | 782 | 1 180 | 1 265 | 149 | 34 | 591 |
| Vacant year-round | 237 | 196 | 211 | 68 | 74 | 187 |
| For sale only | – | 4 | – | – | 1 | 7 |
| Vacant less than 6 months | – | ... | ... | – | – | 3 |
| Median price asked | – | – | – | – | – | $35 000 |
| For rent | 159 | 124 | 153 | 49 | 54 | 152 |
| Vacant less than 2 months | 136 | 103 | 136 | 36 | 49 | 130 |
| Median rent asked | $126 | $101 | $102 | $130 | $176 | $139 |
| Other | 78 | 68 | 58 | 19 | 19 | 28 |
| **LACKING SOME OR ALL PLUMBING FACILITIES** | | | | | | |
| All units | 151 | 191 | 312 | 125 | 17 | 166 |
| Owner occupied | 8 | 4 | 7 | 2 | 3 | 9 |
| Negro | – | 2 | 4 | 1 | – | – |
| Renter occupied | 119 | 142 | 250 | 107 | 12 | 135 |
| Negro | 27 | 70 | 49 | 10 | – | 23 |
| Vacant year-round | 24 | 45 | 55 | 16 | 2 | 22 |
| For sale only | – | – | – | – | – | – |
| For rent | 20 | 17 | 32 | 10 | 1 | 18 |
| **COMPLETE KITCHEN FACILITIES AND ACCESS** | | | | | | |
| Lacking complete kitchen facilities | 115 | 148 | 264 | 134 | 19 | 162 |
| Access only through other living quarters | 16 | 4 | 12 | 1 | – | 9 |
| **ROOMS** | | | | | | |
| 1 room | 130 | 176 | 346 | 134 | 41 | 202 |
| 2 rooms | 360 | 345 | 963 | 155 | 128 | 344 |
| 3 rooms | 736 | 725 | 1 022 | 402 | 422 | 856 |
| 4 rooms | 695 | 576 | 583 | 321 | 416 | 770 |
| 5 rooms | 350 | 348 | 358 | 400 | 436 | 693 |
| 6 rooms | 262 | 215 | 153 | 217 | 236 | 475 |
| 7 rooms | 95 | 108 | 65 | 37 | 68 | 190 |
| 8 rooms | 42 | 36 | 17 | 15 | 38 | 99 |
| 9 rooms or more | 32 | 27 | 14 | 7 | 29 | 102 |
| Median | 3.7 | 3.6 | 2.9 | 4.0 | 4.3 | 4.1 |
| All occupied housing units | 2 465 | 2 360 | 3 310 | 1 620 | 1 740 | 3 544 |
| **PERSONS** | | | | | | |
| 1 person | 885 | 953 | 1 629 | 601 | 660 | 1 178 |
| 2 persons | 750 | 698 | 921 | 515 | 707 | 1 233 |
| 3 persons | 367 | 313 | 340 | 210 | 202 | 528 |
| 4 persons | 193 | 163 | 177 | 111 | 104 | 278 |
| 5 persons | 119 | 94 | 94 | 90 | 38 | 174 |
| 6 persons or more | 151 | 139 | 149 | 93 | 29 | 153 |
| Median, all occupied units | 2.0 | 1.8 | 1.5 | 1.9 | 1.8 | 2.0 |
| Median, owner occupied units | 2.3 | 2.3 | 2.2 | 2.1 | 2.0 | 2.3 |
| Median, renter occupied units | 1.9 | 1.7 | 1.5 | 1.9 | 1.7 | 1.9 |
| Units with roomers, boarders, or lodgers | 336 | 206 | 216 | 189 | 172 | 356 |
| **PERSONS PER ROOM** | | | | | | |
| 1.00 or less | 2 249 | 2 182 | 3 049 | 1 498 | 1 702 | 3 366 |
| 1.01 to 1.50 | 142 | 126 | 167 | 76 | 24 | 112 |
| 1.51 or more | 74 | 52 | 94 | 46 | 14 | 66 |
| Units with all plumbing facilities – 1.01 or more | 199 | 160 | 241 | 114 | 38 | 167 |
| **VALUE** | | | | | | |
| Specified owner occupied units¹ | 72 | 99 | 57 | 72 | 300 | 441 |
| Less than $5,000 | – | – | – | – | – | 1 |
| $5,000 to $7,499 | – | 2 | – | – | – | – |
| $7,500 to $9,999 | 1 | 2 | 1 | – | – | – |
| $10,000 to $14,999 | 2 | 7 | – | 7 | 7 | 15 |
| $15,000 to $19,999 | 8 | 12 | 8 | 13 | 29 | 43 |
| $20,000 to $24,999 | 8 | 16 | 9 | 18 | 52 | 59 |
| $25,000 to $34,999 | 31 | 37 | 19 | 22 | 88 | 119 |
| $35,000 to $49,999 | 20 | 15 | 9 | 11 | 81 | 163 |
| $50,000 or more | 2 | 9 | 5 | 1 | 43 | 41 |
| Median | $30 500 | $28 100 | $27 400 | $24 400 | $32 000 | $33 600 |
| **CONTRACT RENT** | | | | | | |
| Specified renter occupied units² | 2 204 | 2 056 | 3 077 | 1 366 | 1 188 | 2 707 |
| Less than $30 | 7 | 21 | 14 | 8 | 5 | 7 |
| $30 to $39 | 7 | 14 | 11 | 4 | 1 | 11 |
| $40 to $59 | 71 | 65 | 254 | 62 | 15 | 58 |
| $60 to $79 | 159 | 255 | 416 | 144 | 38 | 200 |
| $80 to $99 | 307 | 366 | 691 | 229 | 97 | 274 |
| $100 to $149 | 1 169 | 911 | 1 361 | 638 | 374 | 1 237 |
| $150 to $199 | 401 | 323 | 252 | 218 | 361 | 648 |
| $200 to $249 | 50 | 55 | 27 | 42 | 146 | 154 |
| $250 or more | 11 | 28 | 18 | 7 | 135 | 82 |
| No cash rent | 22 | 18 | 33 | 14 | 16 | 36 |
| Median | $124 | $117 | $104 | $119 | $158 | $133 |

**Figure 1.** Information provided by the Census. The Duboce Triangle neighborhood is Tract 0169.

of Black and Hispanic residents provide particularly detailed information for minority areas. The social and economic data contained in this Census volume may be just as valuable to neighborhood groups as the housing data.

Census data are sorted and listed in various ways — from tables for the country as a whole down to others for individual blocks. DTHA found the listings for *census tracts* to be the most useful unit of analysis for studying displacement at the neighborhood level. Census tracts are drawn by the Census Bureau to include roughly 4,000 people and to conform as nearly as possible to natural neighborhood boundaries. (Census tract data are not, however, available for non-metropolitan areas, which are not "tracted." In these areas there are instead "enumeration districts" of about 800 people, data for which have not been available in printed form, although regional planning agencies often have acquired the data in raw form, on computer tapes. Starting with the 1980 Census, enumeration district data will be printed, although the Census Bureau has not as yet announced its policy on cost and availability.) As it happens, the Duboce Triangle neighborhood consists of exactly one census tract. Other neighborhoods which overlap census tract boundaries may have to go to block-level data, which makes using the Census more difficult.

Also starting with the 1980 Census, a new "Neighborhood Statistics Program" was introduced, specifically designed to help neighborhood groups. The Census Bureau will compile the data it has collected according to neighborhood boundaries, providing that they do not overlap with any other neighborhood for which statistics are being specially compiled, that there is some kind of official recognition of the neighborhood, and that a mechanism exists whereby the neighborhood has advisory representation at city hall. The last two criteria may be met in fairly simple fashion. However, to participate in the program the formal request and application had to be submitted by June 30, 1981, and these neighborhood breakdowns probably will not be available before the end of 1981 and perhaps not until the Spring of 1982. Doubtless the program will be continued in subsequent censuses and could be a really useful tool for neighborhood groups. For further information, contact Joanne Eitzen, Decennial Census Division, U.S. Dept. of Commerce, Washington, D.C. 20233.

The U.S. Census is conducted every ten years. (Congress in 1976 authorized an additional mid-decennial Census — 1985, 1995, etc. — but has not yet appropriated funds for it. In all likelihood the next Census will be in 1990.) At the time DTHA began its work, in 1978, the 1970 Census was quite stale. Now 1980 Census data are, or shortly will be, available in many public libraries, in city and county planning departments, and in most college libraries as well. Groups analyzing displacement will be able to contrast 1970 and 1980 Census data to get good evidence of the changes which have occurred over the last decade.

Reference librarians at any library can advise on the location of the nearest detailed Census data (smaller libraries often have only the summary reports), and reference staff at libraries housing the Census reports you need can point out the correct volumes and help find the relevant census tracts for your neighborhood.

## USING REALDEX

Another source of basic data the DTHA found useful was the San Francisco volume of the *Realdex*. The Realty Index Corporation prepares similar real estate listings for every major city. *Realdex* provides information on a building-by-building basis: the address number, block and parcel; number of stories in the building and type and year of construction; the number of units, rooms and bathrooms and total square footage of the building; information on recent sale prices and amount of mortgage loans; and the name and address of the owner of record. Since the *Realdex* is updated annually, it is also much more current than the Census after the first year of the decade. The *Realdex* is usually available at public libraries, at city assessors' offices, and in some local real estate firms, savings and loan offices, title insurance companies, and law firms.

## MULTIPLE LISTING SERVICE

Since the key concern was housing speculation, DTHA wanted to dig into sales and sale price information. One obvious beginning point was to monitor local real estate brokers' ads and newspaper listings of property for sale in the neighborhood. But this was quite inefficient. An improvement on this method was to use the *Multiple Listing Service* (MLS). This is a volume put out for real estate brokers which lists current properties for sale in an entire sales area, such as a city, usually on a weekly basis. In San Francisco, the MLS is several hundred pages long, but it is broken down by area. So it was easy for DTHA to find all properties for sale in the Triangle area in this one source. The MLS is not usually available in libraries, but may be looked at in real estate brokers' offices.

Of course, properties sold by owners without realtors' services never reach the MLS. This may be particularly true of "bargains" in a gentrifying area. But by looking at back issues of the MLS, the DTHA got a good idea of trends in the volume of sales and asking prices. *Be careful,* however: the MLS in many areas lists *asking price* rather than actual sales price, and actual sales prices may be lower. In other areas, the MLS lists both asking and final price.

Even better than the MLS in some places are trade publications such as Massachusetts' *Banker and Tradesman,* which gives all property sales, prices, mortgages, etc., listed by area and address, for the period the publication covers. Reference librarians can advise on whether and where such a publication exists in your area.

## CITY AND COUNTY RECORDS

To add to data from the Census, *Realdex,* and MLS, the Alliance then turned to city records of ownership and assessed property valuation. Every unit of government (county, city, town) that levies a property tax has assessment records. Property transfer records are usually kept by county governments. The content and format of the records varies greatly from place to place, as does the name of the office where these records are kept (Registry of Deeds, Hall of Records, etc.)

In San Francisco, the Assessor's Office has computer print-outs showing basic ownership and assessment information on all properties. Since these records are compiled block by block, it was easy for DTHA to get information on the Triangle neighborhood. *Deeds* for individual properties are also available as public records, and these provided detailed information on sales history, sale prices, financing, and other items of interest useful in tracing speculation.

At first, DTHA thought that *assessed valuation* figures would show pretty well how housing prices have gone up. Further research showed this not to be the case. The assessed value of real property is supposed to be a fixed percentage — which varies from state to state — of so-called true, or "fair market," value, which is determined by comparing a given property to comparable properties in the area. Thus, in California, where assessed values are supposed to be set at 25% of fair market value, a building worth $100,000 should, in theory, be assessed at $25,000. But DTHA found things didn't really work that way in the Triangle. First, according to Alliance members' calculations, the market values listed by the assessor were artificially low — only about 50-60% of actual market value of the units at the time research was being done. Second, they found that assessments were very uneven. Buildings that had not changed hands recently were generally assessed at a much lower percentage of actual market value than buildings that had changed hands recently. The technical and political reasons for such low and spotty assessments — which occur in most cities (if not all) — are many and complex. But the fact is that assessed valuation often cannot be taken as a fair indication of a property's real market value.

But the Assessor's records did provide another clue — one which ultimately paid off when the sales records in the Assessor's Office were compared with transfer-tax notations on the deeds of the buildings sold. Happily, the deeds were right next door, on microfilm, in the Recorder's Office.

The transfer tax is levied by most cities on all real estate sales. San Francisco, during most of the period under study, took one-half of one percent (or 1/200) of the *actual sales price.* So by multiplying the amount of the transfer tax by 200, DTHA could finally determine the real price at which a building had been sold (except, of course, sales that had been rigged or dishonestly reported). And if a building had been sold more than once, the transfer tax at the different times of sale was indicated. So, by looking at buildings which had been sold frequently, the DTHA at last had what it wanted: a solid basis for showing speculative profits.

## USING THE SPECULATION DATA

This information was put to immediate and effective use. DTHA identified five buildings which had been sold four to five times since 1970, with little money spent on improvements (this information also is noted on the deed), and with an enormous inflation of sales prices. One building which sold for $22,000 in 1970 had just been sold for more than $100,000. The Alliance prepared a leaflet identifying the properties and the information on how much they had been sold and resold for. More than 100 angry neighborhood residents then demonstrated in front of each building, accompanied by local media. One inflated property was immediately taken off the market. DTHA is sure that its research and use of data on individual buildings has dampened speculation in the neighborhood.

After completing the five initial case studies and acting on them, DTHA began putting together systematic information on the volume of sales and the amount of price rises in

the Triangle over a ten-year period. Here are two of the tables they prepared with this infor-

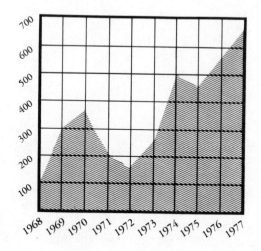

**Figure 2.** Houses sold in the Duboce Triangle / 1968-1977

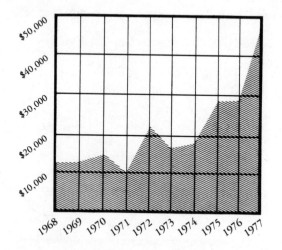

**Figure 3.** Average price of a unit (apartment or single-family house) in the Duboce Triangle / 1968-1977

mation, showing the rise in yearly sales activity and increases in the average selling price of dwelling units.

This sort of information was distributed widely in the neighborhood to raise people's awareness of the extent of housing speculation. It was also used effectively in testimony at hearings by the City Board of Supervisors on a range of rent control and related issues.

## MAKING EVEN BROADER USE OF THE DATA

But DTHA did not stop there. It seemed that all the information gathered in researching speculation would be useful for other issues as well, especially if integrated correctly. So Alliance members designed a computerized system that combined the group's research data for every dwelling unit in the neighborhood. The data base thus created has been expanded and used over and over in a variety of situations: working for rent rollbacks, blocking conversions of apartments over stores to commercial uses, and electoral campaigning on housing questions.

Most impressive among these additional uses of the data base was DTHA's dealings with the effects of Proposition 13. This notorious measure gave most landlords tremendous savings through property tax reductions. All over California, tenant groups demanded to share this property-owners' windfall through rent rollbacks, but frequently were outmaneuvered because they didn't know how much the landlord had gained from the tax cut. In the Duboce Triangle, however, even before the Assessor had informed landlords of the amount of their Proposition 13 benefits, DTHA had put out a memo to tenants of each rental unit in the neighborhood, detailing the precise annual and monthly tax savings the new law bestowed on that unit. The information enabled effective negotiations for maximum rollbacks.

## SURVEYING CHANGES IN POPULATION AND RENTS: DOOR TO DOOR

Another step in DTHA's information gathering efforts was a door-to-door survey to get better information on several subjects, particularly rents and population changes. The survey had the additional purpose of expanding and strengthening contact between DTHA members and neighborhood residents, and it came about mainly because the Alliance found difficulties in getting needed facts any other way.

Useful data on rents are hard to come by in printed sources. The Census collects rent information, but not frequently enough nor in great enough detail for effective use in neighborhood organizing. The 1970 Census contains aggregate information on the ranges of rent within a census tract — see Figure 1 — but gives no unit-by-unit listings. And the Census Bureau's Annual Housing Survey collects rent data for a nationwide sample of 77,000 households, but the information is not broken down in a way that can be used on a neighborhood basis. One other source of rent data is the Multiple Listing Service described above. For properties which are on the market, the MLS often, although not always, provides figures on rents current tenants are paying. But these may be overstated as a sales promotion device. Aside from newspaper ads, the only other way to obtain rent information is by asking the people who live there. Careful com-

parative tabulation of rent figures given in newspaper ads between two points in time can provide a useful indicator of changed rent levels. While the method is not super-scientific — not all classified ads give addresses or rent levels, rents asked are not necessarily rents obtained, and not all available apartments are advertised in newspapers — such a survey is relatively easy to carry out, using current newspapers and public library holdings of old papers, and sometimes may be the best or only information available.

Data on population characteristics are more available in reference sources than rent information, but tend to go out of date quickly. Had the 1980 Census been available, it would have given DTHA good information on the makeup of the neighborhood by race, income, occupation, and family composition. But the same types of information in the 1970 Census were too old to be relevant by 1978. Other sources DTHA could have used include the R.L. Polk *Directory* and school district data, both described later in the chapter. However, door-to-door interviewing would yield information more complete and accurate than either of those, so DTHA members designed a survey that checked population characteristics along with rent levels. The care they put into thinking it through and carrying it out was rewarded with a response rate of about 70% — extremely high for such an operation.

## CONDUCTING AN EFFECTIVE SURVEY

DTHA experience offers several pointers on effective surveying techniques. Interviewers, for instance, were quick to identify themselves as from the neighborhood (they displayed organizational emblems on their clipboards),

rather than from some government agency, pollster firm or collection outfit. They kept the interviews short: about six minutes from start to finish unless the person being interviewed obviously wanted to volunteer more information. They put sensitive questions, such as those about income, last in the interview.

Most interviewers in inner city neighborhoods have found that more people are at home during the evenings but that people are more willing to talk during the day. Many respondents are reluctant to talk to strangers at all after dark. Phone interviewing might have been possible, but that would have prevented the community contact DTHA wanted. Neighborhood groups have learned from experience that mailed questionnaires usually don't work: they tend to wind up in the waste basket.

## WHAT THE SURVEY SHOWED

The door-to-door effort yielded excellent information, and when the new data were compared with Census, and other, figures for 1970, a good picture emerged of the changes associated with displacement in the Triangle. Interviews showed that the median rent in 1978 (*median* means half the people are paying more than that amount, half less) was $287.50, compared to the 1970 Census figure of $119.00 — a 141% increase. By contrast, the survey found a mere 48% increase in residents' real median income — that is, take-home pay adjusted for inflation — during the same period. In terms of population shifts, 1970 Census figures listed about 21% of the Triangle's population as laborers and service workers; door-to-door checking revealed that figure had dropped to 9% by 1978. During the same period the proportion of professional workers rose from less than one-fourth to more than one-third of the entire population of the Triangle. The survey also documented a large increase in residents aged 25-34 years (the young professionals), and a decrease in number for children, the elderly, and the near-elderly. Surprisingly, the racial mix of the neighborhood remained about the same.

## THE DANGERS OF NEIGHBORHOOD CLASSIFICATION SCHEMES

Finally, DTHA looked into the relationship between government actions and displacement in the neighborhood. As noted, the entire Duboce Triangle had been designated a Federally Assisted Code Enforcement area in the late 1960s. DTHA believes that gentrification and displacement in the neighborhood would have happened anyway, but that the government's decision to classify the Triangle as a "deteriorated, but high potential" area, and to inject low-interest federal rehabilitation loans and grant money, had a major impact in speeding up that process.

How city planners choose to classify neighborhoods would be a matter of little concern if the classifications were merely descriptions. In fact, classification usually is followed by action — or withdrawal of services. If a neighborhood is unfortunate enough to be written off as so severely deteriorated that aid would be wasted on it, the prophecy may become self-fulfilling. "Triage" has become a popular government strategy. The word originated in World War I in the French medical practice of separating casualties into three groups: those requiring little or no treatment, those whose condition is apparently so hopeless treatment

would make little difference, and those for whom treatment makes the difference between life and death. In today's urban terms it means that officials only pump resources into communities they consider salvageable. (See further discussion of triage in Chapter 8.)

Some neighborhoods have fought back against being classified in this fashion. For example, when the city of Milwaukee developed a six-step index of "Relative Residential Status (RRS)," residents generally greeted the scheme with suspicion and hostility. One group in a "RRS IV" zone ("market beginning to falter") angrily demanded reclassification. Eventually the city withdrew the designation and classified the neighborhood as a new, seventh category area: "Special Study," or as one resident put it, "specially ornery."

*The people of the Duboce Triangle Housing Alliance have discovered that there is more to organizing a neighborhood than surveys and figures, so they go caroling at Christmas, have a Valentine's dinner and take kids around at Halloween. But for seven years now, the big community event has been the Neighborhood Association Street Fair. It takes some fifty people to plan and coordinate the jumbo barbecue and potluck — one covered dish offering gets you one meal ticket — the booths and craft displays, and the noon-to-six entertainment, all by Triangle residents and close friends — gospel choirs, fiddlers, rock bands, tap dancers and clowns. Cars are cleared from a two block area, the streets are cordoned off and upwards of 2,000 folks converge for this "totally nonpolitical" affair, as one organizer describes it. Which, of course, is the point.*

Walter Park

## INVESTIGATING THE FATE OF DISPLACEES

Where displaced households go and what happens to them are very important questions for anti-displacement efforts, both in terms of forming national policy, and in shaping local activists' responses to neighborhood situations. If displacees are resettling nearby, for instance, the important issue may be repeated displacement. If they have to move far away, the important issues may be transportation costs and loss of community. If they are having to double up with other families, crowding and illegal conversions will be major concerns. If minorities are moving to single-race ghettoes or suburban pockets of poverty, the focus may be increasing segregation or the dispersal of minority political power. And if higher shelter costs result from any of these situations, the main issue, especially for people on the margin, will be how little money is left for the other necessities of life.

The trouble is that tracing displacees to interview them is difficult, time-consuming, and complicated. Consequently, many anti-displacement groups conclude that their energies are better spent on more promising work — as did the research-skilled Duboce Triangle Housing Alliance, which reluctantly decided that the study it had wanted to do would take too much time and effort. Nonetheless, some work is going on in this field, and the Anti-Displacement Project hopes other groups will undertake more.

A recent review of studies which have tracked displacees, undertaken as part of the Anti-Displacement Project, suggests some common patterns which are likely to occur (see the report by Richard LeGates and Chester Hartman, cited on page 26). A substantial number of displacement moves — perhaps as many as one-third — are likely to be from one building to another within the same neighborhood. Another substantial percentage of displacees will probably cluster near the old neighborhood. Both of these tendencies often lead to displacement a second and third time as gentrification spreads.

Most displacee studies thus far tend to reflect the experiences of higher-income people who are usually easier to find, including among them many who report an improvement in their housing conditions and resulting satisfaction. The fate of lower-income displacees is not so well documented. But the evidence available strongly suggests that they end up with more crowded and lower quality shelter. Most important, virtually every displacee study has found that rents increase, sometimes quite dramatically, after the move. In some studies, increased racial segregation of displacees has been documented.

For groups intending to attempt research on what happens to displacees, the experiences of one such project, focused on the Hayes Valley neighborhood of San Francisco (coincidentally just a half-mile from the Duboce Triangle), is instructive. The elaborate and well funded project is being performed under HUD contract by a consulting firm, the National Institute for Advanced Studies (NIAS), 1133 15th Street NW, Washington, D.C. 20005.

The displacee research process has three basic steps: getting a list of people who have left a neighborhood (outmovers) during the time period under review (not all outmovers are displacees, of course); finding their new addresses; and contacting them for information on their new situations. None of these steps is easy.

In searching out who has left, NIAS found that the best source of information is the *Polk Directory*, published mainly for use by private firms in mail advertising, door-to-door sales, and market analysis. A *Polk Directory* is compiled annually for each of 300 cities, and copies of the directory for your locality are generally available at public libraries.

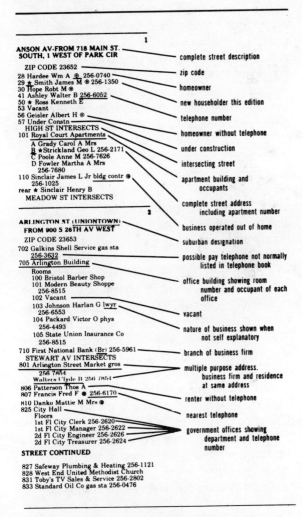

Figure 4. Information provided by the *Polk Directory*

23

Figure 4 shows the contents of a sample page — with explanations — from a *Polk Street Directory* (which is just one part of the total Directory). The Street Directory contains the name and address of every resident in the reported area, plus additional information of interest, and is updated each year. Importantly, people new to an address that year are marked with a star in the *Polk Directory,* so NIAS found that by noting all new movers in a given year, and checking the name of the residents at the same address the *previous* year, they could get a pretty good list of outmovers in that previous year. Working backwards a year at a time they were able to assemble names of several thousand outmovers from a small neighborhood over a ten-year period.

This sort of list, however, is far from perfect. Polk information is often gathered by relatively untrained and low-paid personnel, and it frequently contains errors, omissions, and misspellings. And since the *Polk Directory* is primarily intended for marketing, the publishing company does not expend enormous effort to obtain precise information for low-income areas which have little purchasing power. For such neighborhoods, and for others with substantial transient or non-traditional family populations, the Polk margin of error is very large. Among other things, since no one is required to respond to the Polk surveyors, refusal to give information, or to give correct information, creates a general problem for the directories. This aspect of the data accuracy question may be more serious for lower-income households and areas, where fears about the consequences of giving information to strangers are often greater, and well founded.

Walter Park

Another annual household-by-household directory is the *Haynes Directory* — put out in competition with the *Polk Directory* — and also available in public libraries in most cities. The *Haynes Directory* contains essentially the same information as the *Polk Directory,* and may be used for cross-checking the rival publication, or as an alternative source or supplement.

Some other sources of information on outmovers include:

**Voter registration lists.** These are not inclusive, since they contain information only on currently listed voters, and high percentages of people do not register, or aren't eligible to. Generally, however, they are quite accurate as to spellings and actual addresses.

**School records.** In San Francisco the school district maintains extensive computerized information on each school-age child. Since one-third of the city's school children move each school year, the records must be kept up to date. The city is under a court desegregation order, so school records contain accurate data on race. Use of these records, however, involves privacy issues. School officials may justifiably want to save parents and children from unwarranted access to their contents. Displacement researchers may not be able to overcome this barrier, but if the records are available they are frequently useful.

**Church records.** Studies have shown that people frequently maintain church affiliations after they have moved. Church records or informal information from ministers may be useful, although ministers may not want to divulge information about their parishioners.

Once the list of outmovers is assembled, the next step is to locate them at their new addresses, often a monumentally difficult task.

NIAS found that the Polk Directory itself was one source for finding new addresses for outmovers. In another section of the Directory there is an alphabetical list of all city residents, updated annually. This and the local phone directory are beginning points for tracing people who relocate within the same city, as most displacees apparently do. Here are some other suggested ways:

• A search through phone directories of nearby localities can net some of the people who moved out of the city.

• A call to old phone numbers might help since outmovers may have operator intercepts referring callers to their new number.

• A letter sent to the outmover at the old address, marked "do not forward" and requesting Post Office Form No. 1478, will sometimes produce a new mailing address from the post office. Check this possibility with your local postmaster.

• People displaced by public action or programs may be traceable through government relocation files.

• Former landlords and apartment house managers or neighbors may be able to provide information on where outmovers have gone.

## CONCLUSION

It is hard, often boring and frustrating to do the kind of backup research that anti-displacement work requires. But it is harder still to do without that research. One of the messages emerging clearly from a review of anti-displacement struggles around the country is that good information is one of the most important requirements for fighting back effectively. The evolving research and analysis program of the Duboce Triangle Housing Alliance, sum-marized in this chapter as an example of the kind of effort put forth by a number of anti-displacement groups, shows the vital contribution good data can make. And DTHA's work also reveals the most basic research step of all: get it started. Imagination, carefulness, and persistence are the ingredients needed to keep it going and make it work.

## REFERENCES

Key sources of information on neighborhoods and their residents are city *Realdexes* published for major cities by the Realty Index Corporation of Florida and available at public libraries, city and county assessors' offices, and at some real estate, lending institution and title insurance company offices. *Realdexes* contain information on individual city properties, including the name and address of the owner; the number of stories the building has and type of construction; number of rooms, bathrooms, and total square footage; age of construction; and frequently, sales and mortgage data also.

In some metropolitan areas, the weekly *Lusk Real Estate Guide* can be found, which lists sales by address and includes information on date sold, name of seller and buyer, sales price, amount, rate and term of mortgage, and who provided the mortgage. The sales data contained in the weekly Guides are also compiled into an annual *Lusk Real Estate Directory.*

The *Polk Directory* and the *Haynes Directory* (available in most public libraries) contain current (annually updated) names and addresses of every resident in the city, plus other data such as whether or not the individual is a new resident at that address and his/her occupation.

The U.S. Census Bureau's *Census of Population and Housing* volume on detailed characteristics (also available at many public libraries) provides information every ten years on housing and population characteristics at the census tract level. The 1980 Census will provide fresh detailed data on housing conditions, but as we move along in the 1980s that information will increasingly become stale. A practical guide to how to work with census data is *U.S. Census Data for Political and Social Research,* by Phyllis Carter (Washington: American Political Science Association, 1976). This compact volume describes the content of various census volumes and contains case studies of how to work with the data. It may be obtained from the American Political Science Association, 1527 New Hampshire Avenue NW, Washington, DC for $2.50.

The Census Bureau's new Neighborhood Statistics Program will compile data according to neighborhood boundaries, a very useful tool for community groups. There are some requirements that must be met, and all requests for these tabulations had to be submitted by June 30, 1981 (unless the Bureau decides once again to extend the deadline). For further information, contact Joanne Eitzen, Decennial Census Division, U.S. Dept. of Commerce, Washington, DC 20233.

The Annual Housing Survey, carried out by the Census Bureau and HUD (also available at local libraries, usually about two years after the survey year) provides more up-to-date information, but is based on a sample and is useful only for larger-scale (city, metropolitan area, regional and national) description and analysis of changes. The AHS can provide a picture of overall changes in housing conditions, costs and environmental concerns that can help provide a context for situations in specific neighborhoods. For a guide on how to use the AHS, see *Housing in America: The Characteristics and Uses of The Annual Housing Survey* (1980), by John Goering, available free from HUD, Product Dissemination Office, Washington, DC 20410.

A review of recent city-level studies on displacement, *Displacement,* by Richard LeGates and Chester Hartman (1981) is available for $2.50 from the Legal Services Anti-Displacement Project, 2150 Shattuck Avenue, #300, Berkeley, CA 94704. This review may suggest questions to ask and patterns to look for in analyzing displacement in your neighborhood.

Another useful recent review of the displacement problem is *Displacement: Where Things Stand* (1981), by George and Eunice Grier, available for $5.00 from the Grier Partnership, 6532 E. Halbert Rd., Bethesda, MD 20034.

Rolf Goetze's books *Building Neighborhood Stability* (1977) and *Understanding Neighborhood Change* (1979), both available from Ballinger Book Company, 2350 Virginia Avenue, Hagerstown, MD 21790, while not strongly anti-displacement, contain useful discussions of market dynamics and the role of media in affecting the way neighborhoods are perceived and classified. Goetze also has prepared an information bulletin for HUD titled "Neighborhood Monitoring and Analysis: A New Way of Looking at Urban Neighborhoods and How They Change" (1980), available free from the Office of Policy Development and Research, HUD, Washington, DC 20410.

An excellent guide to analyzing neighborhood ownership patterns and landlords' returns on investment is Urban Planning Aid's *People Before Property,* by Michael Stone (Cambridge: 1972). This useful volume is available from the Midwest Academy, 600 W. Fulleton Ave., Chicago, IL 60604, and in some university planning school libraries or the libraries of community organizations.

The *Neighborhood Planning Primer* (1980) prepared under a HUD contract, gives the essential steps involved in neighborhood planning: identifying and researching neighborhood issues; formulating goals, objectives and strategies; collecting, analyzing and graphically presenting data; creating and implementing neighborhood plans. It's available for $4.75 from the Superintendent of Documents, Government Printing Office, Washington, D.C. 20402; specify GPO Stock No. 023-000-006-44-8.

The Neighborhood Information Sharing Exchange, funded by HUD, is a network for neighborhood groups, city officials, private businesses, and lenders designed to share solutions to community revitalization problems. It also publishes a monthly newsletter, *The Exchange.* Its address is 1725 K St. NW, #1212, Washington, DC 20006, with a toll-free number, (800) 424-2851.

A special issue (September/October, 1981) of *Conserve Neighborhoods,* the newsletter of the National Trust for Historic Preservation, titled "Organizing Guide: Ideas for Bringing Your Neighborhood Together" is available free from the National Trust, 1785 Massachusetts Ave. NW, Washington, DC 20036.

The Duboce Triangle Housing Alliance may be reached c/o Walter Park, 170 Noe St., San Francisco, CA 94114, (415) 621-0389.

Related discussions of neighborhood struggles for which background research has been the starting point may be found in the sections on arson in Chapter 5, on the Home Mortgage Disclosure Act and Community Reinvestment Act in Chapter 10, and on the Community Development Block Grant Program in Chapter 12.

Chapter 4

# REGULATING SPECULATION TO PREVENT DISPLACEMENT

Allan Troxler

## THE MYTH

To make money and to survive, the private developer must convert less highly valued to more highly valued real estate, making everybody richer as a result. To paraphrase Adam Smith, the private developer in seeking his own interest promotes society's even though this was not part of his intention . . . In the process, the city's housing stock will have been upgraded and the city's tax base increased. All of us consumers will benefit, as we do from the availability of new or upgraded housing anywhere in the urban area.

*Stanford University Economics Professor Richard Muth, in the San Francisco* Chronicle, *January 30, 1978*

## THE REALITY

Speculation is real and widespread in the city of San Francisco . . . [It] has increased in the last few years and rapid turnover of property . . . is pushing up the entire housing market. [There is a] huge inflationary surge. . . . The effects are citywide and the number of neighborhoods directly impacted is increasing. . . . It is a myth that speculation is at least accompanied by substantial rehabilitation. We cannot find the building permits to justify this.

*Research report by Public Interest Economics-West and the San Francisco Housing Coalition, 1977*

*Speculation* is the driving force behind most private market housing displacement. The word means exactly what it seems to mean: investing, or manipulating an investment, with the intent to make big (bigger, biggest) unearned profits. It represents one of many ugly contradictions within the mainstream economic system — a basic market practice which operates destructively on society by accelerating inflation, distorting housing investment priorities, diverting capital away from needed new construction, and, of course, displacing people who can't afford to pay the blown-up rents and prices that give the speculators their profits.

In a word, housing speculation is a pretty rotten game people play. And even though attacking it means confronting a powerful component of the private enterprise system, speculation is coming to be seen as such a danger to the housing needs of the majority of American people that local attempts to regulate it are beginning to flower.

Speculation can be seen at work in condominium conversion; in slapdash rehabilitation work followed by steep rent or sales price hikes (or those even less tolerable increases that come with no renovations at all); in demolition of

housing so the property can yield a higher return; in arson for profit; even in disinvestment — abandonment or intentional deterioration — that yields a tax shelter or sets the stage for gentrification. These variations of the basic profiteering assault on housing all require different sorts of response from anti-displacement groups, and are discussed separately in subsequent chapters. But the most direct and well-known form of housing speculation is "flipping" — the purchase and quick resale of property at jacked-up prices, with few, if any, improvements made in the process. Variations of that kind of speculation are the main focus of this chapter.

In the case of flipped rental housing, rents escalate rapidly because sales prices are based on a multiplier of the building's rent roll. Displacement of tenants with low or fixed incomes is inevitable, since they will not be able to afford the resulting increases in rent. In

> **Often, buildings are sold and resold within a few weeks or months, for huge profits, with little or nothing being spent to improve the property.**

homeowner neighborhoods, speculation helps push sales prices out of moderate-income reach, and inflates property tax levels up to the point where low- and fixed-income owners may have to sell out. In rural areas, price-bidding for farmland by flippers and long-term investors alike keeps most beginning farmers out of the market, while rising property taxes and land rents drive marginal operators off their farms.

The current wave of speculation, which began in the late 1970s, poses a particular threat to people living in urban neighborhoods, where older housing is being rehabbed and sold to young professionals, in fringe areas, and in farming regions.

Various legal efforts to regulate or quash speculation have been tried or considered around the country. Those discussed in this chapter include:

- eliminating speculation incentives currently in the tax laws
- taxing profits from speculation
- regulating lenders who provide capital to speculators
- regulating speculative landlords and home purchases
- development rights purchase and land bank programs for farmland

In many situations, however, direct action may be the most appropriate first step. Chapter 3 recorded the success of San Francisco's Duboce Triangle Housing Alliance in slowing gentrification-related speculation through research, demonstrations and media exposure. Quite often, speculators are people, or institutions, who don't want it known that they are as greedy as they are, and the embarrassment of public attention may scare them away. Also,

© King Features Syndicate, Inc., 1977. World rights reserved.

hopes for quick flipper profits may be dampened by the appearance of pickets and demonstrators. A building whose hard-pressed tenants take to the street is a building that won't readily sell for an elevated profit.

The long-term solution to the problem of speculation lies in altering or controlling the profiteering drive of the real estate market. In that effort, imagination, militancy, and persistence are the key ingredients.

## THE MECHANICS OF HOUSING SPECULATION

If you're one of the fortunate 10% of the population who has spare capital to speculate with, you've got lots of choices. The stock market is an institution entirely devoted to speculation. Or you can sink your money into hog bellies, grain futures, gold, silver, art, a prizefighter, a racehorse.

But many choose real estate instead, because it is among the most profitable forms of speculation in the United States. Real estate is especially attractive to speculative investors because they can "leverage" a small investment into the ownership of very valuable property. A single building can be bought, for instance, by borrowing most of the purchase price, and then that building can be used as collateral to borrow more money to buy more buildings. This practice is known as "pyramiding." In inflationary periods like the late 1970s, notable for tight local housing markets characterized by low vacancy rates and the declining production of new rental housing, real estate speculation has proven increasingly popular.

Newspaper stories on the speculation game abound. A San Francisco *Chronicle* feature, "Secrets of a Real Estate Speculator," quotes one Bill Greene as follows: "One of my rules of thumb is that I never buy anything unless I can sell it in a week for a profit of $10,000. . . . I once bought a house that was covered with yellow-and-black siding. . . . I paid $18,000 for it, put on wood shingles right over the siding, and sold it in a couple of weeks for $40,000." Greene's "latest project is teaching classes — charging students $250 a pop — on how to become a real estate tycoon. A recent session of Greene's tycoon class drew 250 would-be barons to a downtown hotel. Some of his graduates, Greene reports, are already on their way to becoming real estate millionaires." (Greene has also just been convicted for failing to pay income taxes, it should be noted.) A recent *Wall Street Journal* feature on an ex-social worker turned speculator in Philadelphia ("she turned from patching up broken homes to patching up broken houses") describes a typical deal: "One of her early coups was a burned-out shell that cost her $1500 in 1975. She replaced electrical wiring, the furnace and the wood stairs. She held it for four years, renovated a few other houses on the block and sold it for $69,500."

Greed, however, is not usually invoked in defense of speculation. As the quote from Professor Muth at the beginning of the chapter shows, there is strong, if misbegotten, support for speculation because of its supposed benefit to cities. People who take this line — and many of them are wealthy and influential (no surprise) — oppose regulation of speculation, and they have won most of the battles so far. They point to the upgrading of property that speculation is alleged to bring — increased market value and taxable value of buildings and farmland due to supposed improvements. What could be better? An improved property stock *plus* an increasing tax base.

For the most part, however, this line of reasoning is a self-serving attempt to justify the profits of speculators and the unregulated market system in general, and to downplay the costs for displacees victimized by the market process. As we have noted, much of the "increased value" of speculated properties has nothing to do with improvement. Often, buildings are sold and resold within a few weeks or months, for huge profits, with little or nothing being spent to improve the property. When repairs are made, they often are merely cosmetic and rarely justify the sharply inflated resale prices. And when a big rent or price increase does actually represent serious renovations, who really benefits? The answer, obviously, is those who had the most housing choices to begin with.

The assertion that speculation increases the municipal tax take is questionable, too. Widespread city tax abatement policies designed to encourage rehabilitation tend to cancel out potential increased revenues. So do the demands for additional expensive city services that usually come along with higher-income, politically influential new residents. And the spread of tax limit laws — such as California's Proposition 13 and Massachusetts' Proposition 2½ — caps cities' abilities to capitalize on property value increases in any case.

Moreover, any revenue gains to municipalities from speculative property value increases involve substantial and inequitable decreases in the federal tax take. Big loopholes have been lobbied into the Internal Revenue Code to benefit speculative investors, and with each new purchase a high proportion of the "increased value" — the creation of which is supposed to aid the general treasury — runs out through these holes and into the speculators' pockets. Mortgage interest payments are deductible from income tax for speculators the same as for homeowners, for instance. And since almost the total amount of mortgage payments in the early years of payback consists of interest charges, speculators simply write off a large percentage of their finance costs to Uncle Sam. Additionally, there is the notorious "accelerated depreciation" provision, giving housing preferential treatment with respect to the supposed eventual effects of aging and natural deterioration. So even though a building is actually *appreciating* in value and returning a profit, the speculator gets to register a hefty amount of paper "loss" on tax returns in each of these accelerated depreciation years. This is what is called a tax shelter: the non-existent but deductible "loss" is allowed to offset and cover an equal amount of taxable income, making that amount into tax-free money. Under complex deals arranged by tax lawyers and accountants, these tax shelters can be syndicated (divided into shares and sold) to limited partners, so that people with lots of otherwise taxable earned income — doctors, dentists, etc. — can shield some of that income from taxes. The ability to create and use this tax shelter undergirds much speculative housing activity.

This same kind of speculation support also makes itself felt in the countryside. "I handle tax-sheltering housing too," says one Northern Vermont realtor, "and in terms of tax shelters I'd rather have a dairy farm. Every two weeks you get a milk check. You don't have to chase rents. There are no tenant problems, and only a few employees." And, of course, the farm and its equipment qualify for accelerated depreciation just like a flipper's newly-bought building in the city.

The uncollected income taxes from all these loopholes add up to one major point: *private speculation is publicly supported.* But while those who profit from speculation benefit as a result, those who are displaced and the society as a whole do not. Displacees pay directly in higher living costs, disruption of their lives and reduced housing options. Overall, we get a reduction of the moderate-cost housing and farm stock — exactly what we don't need — and inflated rents and prices for everyone, as the combined effects of swollen profits and increased scarcity of affordable land and housing hit home.

It is important to be familiar with the motivations and techniques of real estate speculators, not to mention the variety of ways property can be owned and financed, and the tax, and other, advantages each one offers.

**A 1977 San Francisco study found that the average price of properties sold within one year of their previous transfer had increased an incredible 115%.**

The best available guide for community groups on such subjects is Urban Planning Aid's *People Before Property: A Real Estate Primer and Research Guide,* by Michael Stone. This book contains good basic explanations of real estate mechanics, sources of information on ownership questions, and tells in detail how to do relevant research. It was written for use in Massachusetts, but most of the information is adaptable to other states. More conventional sources of information on real estate investment include textbooks such as *Real Estate Investment Analysis and Taxation,* by Alan Cerf and Paul Wendt, and *Real Estate Investment and*

*Finance,* by Stephen Roulac and Sherman Maisel. Both should be available through libraries and bookstores.

## SNAPSHOTS OF SPECULATION

Chapter 3 told how the Duboce Triangle Housing Alliance documented speculation in one San Francisco neighborhood. Larger studies also have been done in that city, in other places where regulation of real estate speculation has been proposed, and in farm territory all over the country. Side by side, this collection of reports outlines a national picture in which speculation, and the displacement it causes, are increasingly visible, everyday features of American life. The various studies (all referenced at the end of this chapter) also offer a valuable set of closeups of what speculation looks like.

Washington, D.C., for instance, the only city that currently has a tax on real estate speculation, reviewed residential property turnovers during 1972-74. Of 8,367 properties examined (row houses, flats, and semi-detached buildings), 1,798 (21%) were sold twice within the two-year period, *with the increased price on the second sale averaging 50%.* The rapid turnover properties were concentrated in particular neighborhoods.

A 1977 San Francisco study (conducted by Public Interest Economics West and the San Francisco Housing Coalition) found that the average price of properties sold within one year of their previous transfer had increased by an incredible 115%. For those properties sold within two years of previous transfer the price increase averaged "only" 65%. Meanwhile, the annual rise in the housing component of the Consumer Price Index for the area was a mere 10%.

In Madison, Wisconsin, Coact Research, a public interest research firm, looked into "rapid turnover" (defined as property bought and resold within three years) during 1977-78. The research found that rapid turnover rental buildings were gaining in value faster than non-rapid turnover buildings, even though they were twice as likely to have code violations. Tenant transiency in these buildings was particularly notable.

Szep / Boston Globe

The Seattle Office of Policy Planning, analyzing property sales between 1976 and 1978, found considerable speculation in single-family and rental housing. Short-term multiple sales accounted for 5-10% of all sales during this period, with rates of return far exceeding the average for long-term sales.

In San Diego, the California Public Interest Research Group (CALPIRG) studied speculative transfers between 1976 and 1978. Using a definition of speculation that included multiple sales within a period of two years and eight months, high profits, and the absence of significant improvements or renovation prior to sale, CALPIRG found that 19% of property transfers citywide during the period were speculative. It concluded:

> Speculative transactions were widespread in San Diego and they have a negative impact on the local housing economy. Inordinately high profits, averaging up to 380% annual profit, rapid turnover (averaging under one year), and the noticeable lack of any physical improvements are clear signs of the existence of housing speculation. The fact that a substantial portion of the housing stock is subject to speculative investment artificially inflates the level of demand, and therefore inflates both rental rates and the costs of homeownership.

Meanwhile, in rural areas of the country, federal government data show that speculative investment has intruded in farm territory as powerfully as in urban housing, and the effects, although not as large in terms of total numbers displaced, are just as great when measured proportionally. (See pages 109-111 for related materials on the displacement of small farmers.)

The U.S. Census showed that by 1974, about 40% of all farmland was already owned by non-farmers. A U.S. General Accounting Office survey of farm sales in the late 1970s found that non-local investors were responsi-

*"Mister, do you know the difference between your tractor and a bulldozer? . . . Profit."*

ble for about 40% of all farm purchases on a continuing basis. The pressure of this speculative bidding for farms has pushed cropland prices to the point where land rents and taxes, even in non-developing areas, are too high for marginal farmers.

It appears, moreover, that the pressure will only increase. A 1979 U.S. Department of Agriculture study, *Structure Issues of American Agriculture,* which projected a continuing decline in the number of small farms, pointed out that changes in tax laws "have made . . . farm assets increasingly more attractive than other assets," adding that between 1960 and

1978 the value increase of such investments "surpassed the effects of inflation by a wide margin." Unbeknownst to most city dwellers, rural territory has become a speculators' heaven, as investor-serving *Forbes* magazine noted in an October, 1979 article headlined "How ya gonna keep 'em away from the farm after they've seen . . . $3,500 an acre?"

One result, of course, from this speculative activity in rural areas is increasing numbers of small farm families probably headed for towns or cities to compete for the shrinking supply of available housing.

## ELIMINATING SPECULATIVE INCENTIVES IN THE TAX LAWS

Most cities already tax real estate transfers, but this tax is not intended to control speculation. It is typically small, intended only to cover the administrative costs of title recording and to raise a modest amount of additional revenue.

The federal and state governments also tax real estate transfers, but their taxes too are revenue-raising devices not intended to deter speculation. In fact, these tax laws are presently structured to *encourage* speculation.

Unlike "ordinary" income (from salaries, interest and dividends, etc.), profit from residential real estate which is held for at least one year is considered a "capital gain." Instead of being taxed at normal graduated federal income tax rates, real estate speculators who wait the required year are exposed to a maximum long-term capital gains tax rate of only 28%. Speculators often time their buying and selling so as to maximize benefits from capital gains treatment, but frequently the profits from quick flipping are so attractive as to outweigh the preferential tax treatment. Speculators also have developed ways of deferring federal taxation of profit from sales through tax-free "exchanges" in which owners trade buildings. This preferential treatment is an addition to other tax advantages available to property owners such as "depreciation" allowances, discussed above.

Elimination of the incentives for investment and speculation in real estate that currently exist in federal and state income tax legislation would be preferable to legislating a local anti-speculation tax. A local tax merely offsets, at least in part, existing federal and state tax loopholes. However, the prospects for anti-

Ken Alexander / San Francisco Examiner

speculation reforms at the federal and state levels are dim. In fact, existing tax benefits which make real estate speculation profitable seem likely to be expanded.

So, until a national anti-displacement movement develops, any tax reforms regarding speculation probably will have to come through local government, which, by taxing away speculative profits, can shrink or nullify the tax breaks speculators now enjoy.

## TAXING SPECULATION: THE WASHINGTON, D.C. STORY

Putting a punitive tax on real estate profiteering is a difficult undertaking. The craftiness, power and connections which put pro-speculation benefits into existing tax laws must be met and overcome. But the task is not impossible. The District of Columbia City Council adopted an anti-speculation tax in 1978, although the law is much weaker than was desired by its advocates. The legislature of the farm-based state of Vermont passed a special tax in 1973 to help protect its rural land from uncontrolled gobbling and subdivision by the winter sports and tourist industries. In 1978, the citizenry of Santa Cruz, California, adopted an anti-speculation tax, initiated by the Santa Cruz Housing Action Committee, by a 53-47 margin, only to have it ruled invalid when the state's infamous Proposition 13 required any new taxes to get approval of two-thirds of the voters.

Sweeping anti-speculation legislation was proposed in the District of Columbia in 1975, but the City Council rejected it. The idea was reintroduced in a new version in 1977, as The Residential Real Property Transfer Excise Tax, but as it evolved under Council consideration it was considerably weakened. Now in effect,

the law applies only to structures with fewer than five units and within that limit contains no less than 18 exempt categories. The most significant of these are exemptions for structures that are the principal residence of a seller (even if there are rental units in the building as well), and for rehabilitated properties sold with a two-year warranty on the rehab work — an exemption added at the urging of developers. Thus the law has no impact on the displacement caused by (or "justified" by) even minor rehab in gentrifying areas. And in fact, because of that exemption, it may even encourage such displacement.

The law applies a sliding scale of taxation to property transfers, based on the length of time the property has been owned and the amount of profit made on the transaction (more details on this provision are contained in the next section). Within 30 days after a transfer, sellers must file appropriate tax forms and proceed to pay the tax.

The law also focuses on property "dealers" — persons who transfer three or more properties within 30 months. Dealers are required to buy annual licenses, at a cost of $25-$100, depending on the number of transactions made, and to post a $2,500 bond. Non-compliance by dealers can result in fines or loss of license, and voiding of any transfers they may have made.

One of the problems with the law is the number of different agencies its implementation and enforcement require. Transfers are listed with the Recorder of Deeds. Dealers' licenses are issued by the Real Estate Commission. Tax forms and payments are handled by the Department of Finance. And three other local agencies are involved as well. This bureaucratic maze obstructs efficient implemen-

tation, but still does not explain why the law was simply not enforced for almost a year after its passage.

A status report on the law, issued in late 1980 by the D.C. Department of Finance and Revenue, revealed many shortcomings, primarily attributable to poor enforcement procedures. Basically, people selling property were ignoring the law, in large part due to the fact that "administration of the speculation tax was virtually non-existent. No staff was assigned to administer the tax, a few poorly designed forms were available, and there was no follow-up at all to assure taxpayer compliance. In short, taxpayers may have assumed that the lack of adequate administration of the tax meant that they could successfully avoid filing of the tax forms." In light of this dereliction, it is amazing that, according to the report, as many as 30% of the transfers of properties covered by the law actually were accompanied by filing of the required forms. Among the 3,117 returns filed in the two-year period, all but four claimed exemption or that they owed no tax because they had sufficient expenses, under the terms of the law, to offset any taxable gains. To point out the obvious: a law is no better than its enforcement.

The D.C. government will be looking to strengthen the law in 1981, and recent steps have been taken to administer the current law competently. A full-time employee has been assigned to administer the speculation tax, aided by students from the University of the District of Columbia. Tax bills are being sent out, and follow-up steps are being taken to ensure payment. And claims of exemption and offsetting expenses are being investigated rather than simply being accepted at face value. One of the legislative changes to be sought is the requirement that sellers file the tax forms at the same time the deed is being recorded, rather than within 30 days. This is expected to significantly increase compliance, as sellers and buyers may be worried that failure to comply with the law will cloud the title transfer.

In this muddle of poor enforcement, it is hard to say whether this weakened law has had much impact on Washington's displacement problem. Washington also has ordinances regulating rents and condominium conversions, each of which helps put a brake on speculation (see Chapters 5 and 9). An anti-speculation tax will clearly have a stronger net effect in concert with such laws than it will by itself. And overall reduction in speculation is certain to reduce displacement, even if some of the causes escape regulation.

## DRAFTING A LOCAL ANTI-SPECULATION TAX

Probably the best first step for an anti-displacement group interested in developing such a law is to enlist a lawyer, or a community-oriented research group familiar with federal, state and local real estate tax laws and real estate financing in general. Progressive tax reform organizations, public interest research outfits, and consumer groups all can be helpful in designing such laws. If you need information on where to find them, write Ralph Nader's Tax Reform Research Group, 215 Pennsylvania Ave. SE, Washington, DC 20003, or the Public Interest Research Group, 1346 Connecticut Ave. NW, Washington, DC 20036.

The second important step is to find out what forms of local taxation are allowed under state laws. It probably will take special author-

ization of the state legislature to permit a local tax on speculators' income, for instance. But existing authorization for local excise taxes often allows for taxing the property transaction itself.

Again, an anti-speculation tax by itself will not end speculation. But it will have political effect on the market beyond the range of its economic deterrence: it is a signal to investors that the climate may be changing. And in concert with other residential property regulatory laws, especially rent, eviction and demolition controls, and condominium/coop conversion restrictions, an anti-speculation tax could be a considerable aid in reducing displacement.

Based on local experiences around the country, the following are the main considerations in drafting such a law:

**Defining speculation.** Usually, property subject to the tax is defined as that which is sold more than once within a short period (usually three to five years). The definitions of a real estate "sale" or "transaction" and "sellers" or "dealers" must be carefully worded in order to discourage evasion.

**Coverage.** Usually, only residential property is covered. And within that category some types of ownership and property transfer situations may be exempted from the anti-speculation tax:

**Homeowners** are usually treated differently than absentee landlords. (Federal and state income tax law now allows them to postpone any tax on the capital gain from the sale of their principal residence so long as they invest within 18 months in another house which becomes their principal residence.) Therefore, the law could exempt any profit made by owner-occupants.

**Elderly Homeowners.** Federal tax law now permits any homeowner 55 years or older to permanently exempt from federal taxation any profit made on

the sale of his or her principal residence up to $125,000 on a one-time basis. This tax shelter is designed to enable elderly homeowners to treat this profit as tax-free retirement income. Similarly, a local anti-speculation tax might want to give the elderly special treatment.

**Owner-Occupant Landlords.** Landlords who are also the owner-occupants of small (usually two-, three-, or four-unit) buildings may also be exempted, just as they are often exempted from rent controls (see Chapter 9). The rationale for this may be the assumption that owner-occupants are less likely to be speculators, or the feeling that small owners ought to be allowed to build up a "nest egg," or simply political expediency — to reduce opposition to passage of such a law.

**Government Agencies and Non-Profit Housing Sponsors.** Residential property owned by a governmental agency is exempted because its transfer is not considered speculative, and it may not be subject to a local tax anyway. Housing owned by non-profit sponsors may also be exempted.

**Gift Property.** The transfer of residential property through gift or inheritance is exempted because this is not typically speculative.

**New and Rehabilitated Housing.** The sale of newly constructed and substantially rehabilitated housing may be exempted so as not to discourage new construction and rehabilitation. But any rehabilitation exemption must be carefully considered — as noted in the case of Washington, D.C., such an exemption may leave a serious source of displacement untouched.

In general, exemptions must be carefully considered and narrowly defined, within the bounds of state and local laws and political realities, lest the law become meaningless. While there may be some reasonable basis for exempting small owner-occupant landlords and homeowners from speculation controls, such exemptions tend to undermine the very effort, since a large portion of the housing stock is in these categories. The "benefits" for every such owner exempted are counterbalanced by higher prices and rents that the 1-4 new occupant households of each of these properties must pay in order to allow exempted owners to reap their speculative profits.

**Taxable profit.** In order to tax speculative profit, the profit to be taxed must be defined. Usually, the basic figure before exemptions is the difference between the purchase and sale prices, assuming that the sale is what is called an "arms-length" transaction at a fair market price. (An arms-length transaction means that the buyer and seller are not colluding to set an apparently below-market, fraudulent price in order to evade the tax.)

Exemptions from this figure may include the value of any improvements (rehabilitation or additions) if their cost can be documented. The point in so doing is not to discourage improvement of the existing housing stock, including installation of energy-efficient systems such as insulation and solar retrofitting. Such deductions may be restricted to situations where owners have not already recovered their investments through rent increases.

Additionally, it has been suggested that all or part of the general inflationary rise in area housing values may be exempted from the tax in order to avoid assessing supposedly non-speculative profits. This is a somewhat contradictory exemption, however, as housing speculation is one major cause of that general inflation. Moreover, at the steep inflation rates of the last several years, simply holding a property for the inflationary increase becomes a form of speculation — producing displacement just like any other form. If it is not deemed desirable to treat all forms of profit equally, a compromise might be to allow some inflationary profit to remain untaxed and tax everything above that level. The law passed by the Santa Cruz voters dealt with this issue by exempting from the tax altogether any prop-

erty the owner sold for no more than a 3% annual increase over the price that owner paid for it.

Subtracting applicable exemptions from the basic profit figure yields the taxable profit — which is then taxed at the appropriate rate.

**Rate of taxation.** The rate of taxation set in a given locality must reflect the basic purpose of the tax: to discourage speculation in order to preserve the low- and moderate-income housing stock, prevent displacement, and stabilize neighborhoods.

As noted, the District of Columbia uses a sliding scale tied to the length of time the property has been owned, and the amount of profit made on the sale. Profits from properties sold within six months after purchase are taxed at a rate ranging from a maximum of 97% (if the profit is 300% or more) to a minimum of 5% (if the profit is 16% or less). The longer the holding period and the lower the profit, the lower the tax rate. For example: if property is held at least 2½-3 years, then the maximum tax rate is reduced to 84%, if the profit is 300% or more; the minimum tax rate of 5% applies to properties sold at a profit of 56-59%; and any profit less than 55% is not taxed at all.

The Santa Cruz legislation would have taxed all properties held for less than four years; after four years, the tax would not have applied. It also used a variable tax rate that declined the longer the property was held: 25% of the total sales price for properties held one year or less, 23% for properties held one to two years, 21% for properties held two to three years, and 18% for properties held three to four years. As noted above, if the owner chose to sell at a non-speculative price — defined in the law as no more than a 3% annual increment — the sale was exempt from the tax.

A proposed San Francisco ordinance, which also exempted the cost of improvements, would have imposed a similar but stiffer variable tax rate — 80% of the profit for properties

35

held for one year or less, 60% for one to two year holdings, 30% for two to four year holdings, and 15% for properties held four to five years.

## HARDSHIP APPEALS

The Santa Cruz initiative and the proposed San Francisco ordinance established appeals boards to hear hardship appeals from owners. Only resident owners (not absentee landlords) could appeal the tax. Grounds for reduction or waiver of the tax were sales necessitated by relocation of the seller because of employment, a change in the owner's marital status, a change in the number of occupants, an unavoidable loss in income, or other similar compelling circumstances beyond the control of the seller. The allowance of hardship appeals to deal with non-speculative transfers provides flexibility necessary to administer an anti-speculation tax.

## TAX REVENUE

The revenue generated by an anti-speculation tax can either go into a city's general fund or be placed in a special fund to be used for housing-related purposes. If the tax successfully deters speculation by reducing short-term transfers, however, it will not produce much revenue.

To sum up: getting a local anti-speculation tax passed and enforced is difficult, but not impossible. Alone, however, such a law will not effectively combat speculation. It is most effective when combined with the controls on rents, evictions, demolitions and condominium/coop conversions described in Chapters 5 and 9.

## REGULATING LENDERS WHO PROVIDE CAPITAL TO SPECULATORS

Since real estate speculators are so dependent on borrowed money, institutional lenders could make speculation much more difficult by either refusing to lend at all to speculators or by imposing strict conditions on their loans (for example, demanding higher than normal downpayments or forbidding short-term resale). But federal regulatory agencies such as the Federal Reserve Board and the Federal Home Loan Bank Board would have to impose such policies, because banks and other lenders presently profit handily from speculation, and in their own ways encourage it.

**Institutional lenders could make speculation much more difficult by either refusing to lend to speculators or by imposing strict controls on their loans.**

Congress may have opened the door to pressure for exactly that sort of regulation. A "sense of Congress" resolution (Sec. 603) in the 1980 Housing and Community Development Act states that "lending by federally insured lending institutions for the conversion of rental housing to condominium and cooperative housing should be discouraged where there are adverse impacts on housing opportunities of the low- and moderate-income and elderly and handicapped tenants involved."

The distinction between displacement caused by general housing speculation and that caused by condo/coop conversions, which may be described as a specific subform of housing speculation, is minimal. The chairs of the House Banking, Finance and Urban Affairs Committee, and of the Senate Subcommittee on Housing and Urban Affairs have already contacted the federal agencies which regulate financial institutions (including the Comptroller of the Currency and the Federal Deposit Insurance Corporation in addition to those already mentioned) to inquire how they intend to respond to this sense of Congress. Anti-displacement groups seeking to control speculation may wish to build on this congressional initiative. Added strength in such an effort may come from the implementing regulations of the Community Reinvestment Act (see page 102), which requires assessment of whether a lending institution's policies "promote efforts to assist existing residents in neighborhoods undergoing a process of reinvestment and change."

These beginning steps by Congress may help the anti-displacement movement, if they are used imaginatively and forcefully.

## REGULATING SPECULATIVE LANDLORDS

An alternative to taxing profits and restricting loans to speculating landlords is to regulate rent increases. If landlords cannot automatically pass on their inflated speculative costs to tenants, then speculation becomes unprofitable.

Several California cities have included anti-speculation clauses in their rent control legislation (see Chapter 9). While it is too early to measure the impact of this aspect of rent control on speculation in these cities, clearly the speculative fever which characterized the pre-rent control period has cooled. A solid rent control law incorporating anti-speculative provisions is more effective than an anti-speculation tax. But one important limitation to this strategy is that any units exempted from the local rent control ordinance also would be exempted from the anti-speculation provisions. As indicated in Chapter 9, substantial portions of the housing stock have been categorically exempted from most of the newer rent control ordinances.

## REGULATING SPECULATIVE HOME PURCHASES

In many areas, the price of single-family housing has escalated even faster than rents. In these circumstances, speculators — always flexible — have invested in the homeowner market. Typically, house-buying speculators acquire the property, rent it out, or even live in it for a short term while awaiting the price increase that will give them their profit, and then sell. This pattern showed up widely in California, for instance, in the late 1970s.

An approach to regulating speculation in single-family housing is to control resale prices. The basic mechanism for this tactic usually is a legal "covenant," or agreement, by the purchaser to sell at a controlled price.

Several suburban communities which have adopted long-range growth management plans restricting housing development have also instituted what is called "inclusionary" zoning. This means that developers can be awarded "density bonuses" allowing them to build more units than the normal zoning permits if they reserve a certain percentage (usually 10-15%) of their units for moderate-income purchasers. But that opens the door for speculators and others to buy these below-market units and then resell them at market prices, reaping a windfall profit. To prevent this,

some localities have decided also to place controls on resale prices.

Resale controls have been enacted by Boulder, Colorado, Palo Alto, California, and the California Coastal Commission. Their intent is to allow moderate-income families continuing access to single-family housing where the escalation of housing prices would otherwise make it impossible for them to move or remain.

**If speculation could be stopped or controlled, much of the displacement described in this handbook would end or markedly decrease.**

Boulder passed its resale control ordinance in May, 1980. It applies to all housing developed under the city's 1977 growth management law, which requires that 15% of the units built on specially annexed land be set aside at prices affordable by moderate-income households. When the original buyers of these moderately-priced units sell, the maximum they can charge is the original price plus the cost of any improvements and a percentage equal to the increase in Boulder's median income from the time of purchase to the sale. This is intended to ensure the availability of homes in Boulder that moderate-income families can afford, although nothing in the ordinance requires that such homes be sold to a buyer who actually has a moderate income.

Resale controls are being considered for houses constructed by private developers financed through tax-exempt mortgage revenue bonds. Many states and cities have used this financing method to reduce housing costs, since they can raise money for mortgage lending by selling these bonds at a below-market

interest rate (see page 103). As noted there, Congress recently passed legislation designed to halt abuses in the use of this financing method to aid upper-income purchasers (in large part because the Treasury was losing so much money from wealthy purchasers of these tax-exempt bonds). Unfortunately, the new legislation places no restrictions on the incomes of purchasers. It only limits the price of the housing financed this way and requires that in multi-family buildings 10-15% of the units be rented out at Section 8 income levels. States and localities presumably could add their own resale restrictions, in order to prevent speculators and others from turning these tax break subsidized homes and apartments into luxury housing. Any time the government offers private developers or borrowers some kind of benefit, such as low-interest loans, it has the right — indeed, the obligation — to get back in return some guarantee that the housing produced by the bargain will benefit households that really need assistance.

The idea of resale controls as an anti-speculation device, while new, has a good deal of promise. Some of the same principles are embodied in limited-equity housing cooperatives and community land trusts (see Chapter 16). Imaginative use of this approach by community groups which are sponsoring subsidized housing development might well curb displacement.

## RURAL REMEDIES: PURCHASE OF DEVELOPMENT RIGHTS AND LAND BANKING

Speculative attacks on rural property have provoked various efforts to preserve this land for agricultural purposes, enable moderate-income families to have access to farms, and halt displacement from rural areas. A nation-wide listing and evaluation of such programs appears in the volume on "current efforts to protect agricultural land" of the *National Agricultural Land Study,* listed at the end of this chapter.

One approach is for the state and/or local government to purchase the "development rights" to the land — pay farm owners the difference between the potential development value and the agricultural value of their land, in exchange for which a deed restriction is executed permanently forbidding resale of the land for anything but agricultural purposes. A good model of this approach is Massachusetts' Agricultural Preservation Restriction Program, enacted in 1977 with the help of farm advocacy groups in that state. (Further information on this law is available through William King, Land Use Administrator, Department of Food and Agriculture, 100 Cambridge St., Boston, MA 02202.)

Another approach is land banking, such as that established in 1972 by the Social Democratic Government of Canada's Saskatchewan Province. The Land Bank Commission there uses public funds to buy farms and farmland on the open market, then turns them over to qualifying farmers — who must have income of $10,000 a year or less and no more than $60,000 in assets — on life-time leases, with options to buy after five years. (See also the section "Protecting Small Farmers From Displacement," on pages 109-111.)

# CONCLUSION

If speculation could be stopped or controlled, much of the displacement described in this handbook would end or markedly decrease. Powerful interests support it, however, and many persons mistakenly see themselves as beneficiaries of the process, when as consumers of housing they are damaged by it equally. While housing and land speculation are regarded by some as an integral part of the "free enterprise system," when that freedom for some produces social costs for the majority — in the form of higher housing costs, lesser availability of housing, and vast amounts of displacement — it is time to put some brakes on the system. Effective anti-speculation measures must become a key element of a comprehensive anti-displacement strategy.

# REFERENCES

## RESEARCH AND WRITING ON HOUSING SPECULATION IN SPECIFIC AREAS

**San Diego:** *Speculation and the Housing Crisis: A CALPIRG Investigation of Real Estate Speculation in San Diego,* January, 1980, available for $2.50 from the California Public Interest Group, 3000 "E" St., San Diego, CA 92102.

**San Francisco:** *Speculation in Real Estate Markets: A Primer on Tax Policy Alternatives,* available from Public Interest Economics-West, Room 406, 1095 Market St., San Francisco, CA 94103.

*Real Estate Speculation in San Francisco,* available from the San Francisco Housing Coalition, 409 Clayton St., San Francisco, CA 94117.

**Seattle:** *Seattle Displacement Study,* October, 1979, available from the Seattle Office of Policy Planning, City Hall, Seattle, WA.

**Madison, WI:** *Residential Property Turnover Study: A Report to the City of Madison,* June, 1979, available for $4.50 from Coact Research, 1121 Univeristy Ave., Madison, WI 53715.

**Washington, D.C.:** "Restoring the City: Who Pays the Price?" by Carol Richards and Jonathan Rowe,·, is an article in the Winter, 1978 issue of *Working Papers for a New Society,* a periodical published at 186 Hampshire St., Cambridge, MA 02139. The article describes the forces at work in the unsuccessful first attempt to push through anti-speculation legislation in Washington, D.C. If local libraries do not subscribe, a back copy of this issue can be obtained from the magazine for $2.50.

"A Report on D.C. Law 2-91, The Residential Real Property Transfer Excise Tax," October 27, 1980, available from the D.C. Department of Finance and Revenue, Washington, D.C., evaluates the dismal record of this law during its first two years and puts forth recommendations for amending it and improving its administration.

**California:** "Curbing Real Estate Speculation in California," an article in Volume 8 of the *Golden Gate Law Review* (1978), describes the Santa Cruz anti-speculation ordinance in greater detail, plus a proposed San Francisco law which the city's Supervisors refused to pass, and a novel temporary anti-speculation ordinance aimed at single-family housing enacted by Davis, California. The article should be available for reading or copying at most law libraries.

## INFORMATION ON RURAL LAND SPECULATION

*National Agricultural Land Study,* conducted by the U.S. Department of Agriculture and the Council on Environmental Quality, is available from the National Agricultural Land Study Group, New Executive Office Building, 722 Jackson Place NW, Washington, DC 20006. The volume most relevant to land preservation and displacement covers "current efforts to protect agricultural land." A 20-page *Executive Summary* identifies and abstracts the component volumes.

*Foreign Investment in U.S. Agricultural Land — How It Shapes Up,* Comptroller General of the United States, U.S. General Accounting Office, July 30, 1979, document number CED-79-114. A report on 18 months of research into farm sales around the country that reveals very interesting material about patterns of *domestic* speculation in farmland (since foreign investment, as the research discovered, is relatively slight). Available from the GAO's Document Handling and Information Services Facility, P.O. Box 6015, Gaithersburg, MD 20760.

*Structure Issues Of American Agriculture,* U.S. Department of Agriculture, November, 1979 (Agricultural Economic Report 438). A comprehensive review of the evolving status of the agricultural economy, including considerable amounts of data and analysis on trends in land ownership, farm displacement, etc. Available free from the Economics and Statistics Service, U.S. Dept. of Agriculture, Washington, DC 20250.

*A Time to Choose: Summary Report on the Structure of Agriculture* is available for $5 from the Superintendent of Documents, U.S. Government Printing Office, Washington, DC 20401.

*New Directions in Farm, Land and Food Policies: A Time for State and Local Action* (1981) is an excellent 320-page collection of materials put out by the Agricultural Project of the Conference on Alternative State and Local Policies, available to community groups for $9.95 from the Conference, 2000 Florida Ave. NW, Washington, DC 20009.

*Vermont Land Gains Tax Study,* by R. Lisle Baker, Environmental Law Institute, 1346 Connecticut Ave. NW, Suite 600, Washington, DC 20036. The study reviews and evaluates the impact of a 1973 state law passed to combat speculation prompted particularly by tourism, vacation homes, and the winter sports industry.

## UNDERSTANDING AND RESEARCHING SPECULATION

*People Before Property: A Real Estate Primer and Research Guide,* by Michael Stone of Urban Planning Aid (1972). An excellent guide to carrying out real estate research and understanding real estate finance, and comprehending causes and effects of speculation. Written for use by community groups. Focus is on Massachusetts, but most information

can be adapted to other states. Available from the Midwest Academy, 600 W. Fullerton, Chicago, IL 60614.

An updated, more nationally focussed version of this guide, with a particular emphasis on anti-arson work, titled *Research: A Manual For Arson Analysis and Property Research,* is available for $5 from Urban Education Systems, 153 Milk St., Boston, MA 02109.

Two useful textbooks are: *Real Estate Investment Analysis and Taxation,* by Alan Cerf and Paul Wendt (McGraw-Hill, 1979, 2nd edition); and *Real Estate Investment and Finance,* by Stephen Roulac and Sherman Maisel (McGraw-Hill, 1976).

General starting points for assistance in speculation research and drafting anti-speculation measures are the Public Interest Research Group, 1346 Connecticut Ave. NW, Washington, DC 20036, and Ralph Nader's Tax Reform Research Group, 215 Pennsylvania Ave. SE, Washington, DC 20003.

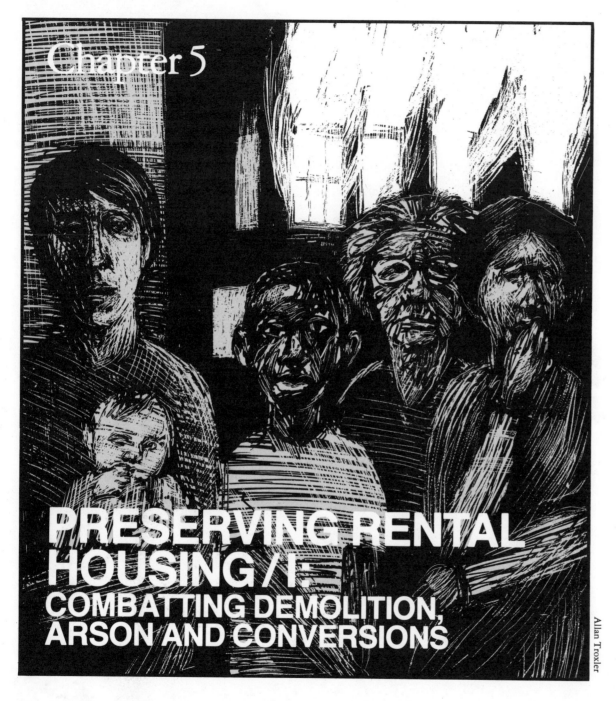

Chapter 5

# PRESERVING RENTAL HOUSING / I:
## COMBATTING DEMOLITION, ARSON AND CONVERSIONS

Allan Troxler

he most dangerous forms of displacement are those that compound their own effects — by removing rental units from the market at the same time they remove renters from the units. Demolition is one of these multiple troubles. Arson for profit is another. Conversion of apartments to condominiums or involuntary coops is a third.

Even a quick review of the effects of these profiteering processes—especially condo/coop conversion — raises scary questions about the future supply of rental housing. It's a case of market contradictions coming full circle to feed upon themselves: demolition, arson, and conversion make money for speculators by *shrinking* the availability of shelter for rent, and the more they shrink it, the more money they generate.

For the rest of us, this reduction of units — even if they're vacant when they're knocked down or torched — means that rents climb faster in the housing that's left, that we have to compete for shelter, and that we are ripped off financially and psychologically in the bargain.

Any systematic trimming of the housing stock creates displacement all up and down the ladder. It is worst, however, at the levels occupied by older people and poor people.

But demolition, conversion, and arson don't just operate through a big, society-wide squeeze: they also put lots of tenants directly out on the street. This chapter takes a look at the impact of these forms of displacement, and at ways and means organizations around the country have used to combat them.

## HOUSING DEMOLITION

The big urban renewal and highway bulldozers of the 1950s and '60s are mostly gone. Private demolition is now a far greater cause of displacement than the publicly sponsored version, although much private demolition activity is supported and triggered by public programs and policies, ranging from the development incentives in tax laws to the ripple effects of government investment and expenditures.

Bigger profit for property owners is almost always the motive of demolition. Creation of higher-density or upper-income housing, for instance, or the substitution of commercial for residential use, are typical reasons triggering the demolition of existing rental housing. Often too, owners will choose to tear buildings down when ordered to bring the property up to minimum code standards, rather than spend the money needed to fix them.

In many areas tenants have organized successfully to prevent or restrict demolition, or to make owners provide replacement housing

S. Pines / Shelterforce

or relocation benefits to displaced residents.

Berkeley, California, led the way in April, 1973, when voters opposed to high-density speculative development in low-density areas passed a ballot initiative called the Neighborhood Preservation Ordinance (NPO). Berkeley's NPO requires developers who demolish apartment buildings with four or more units to replace at least one-fourth of the units destroyed with low- or moderate-income housing. Even this limited replacement requirement has virtually ended the demolition of rental housing in Berkeley.

Santa Monica, California voters went much further. In April, 1979, an initiative there which established an elected rent control board (see Chapter 9) also banned housing demolition unless the board — which has charge of demolition permits too — makes *all* the following factual findings:

● the unit is not occupied by low- or moderate-income tenants

● the rent level is beyond that which can be afforded by low- or moderate-income tenants

● removal of the unit will not adversely affect the supply of rental housing, and

● the landlord cannot make a fair return on investment from the existing unit (note that "fair return" is a very different standard from "profit maximization")

Exceptions are allowed if the affected units are uninhabitable, or new rental housing units will be built, at least 15% of which will be affordable by low-income tenants. Santa Monica's sweeping housing protection initiative has also virtually ended displacement caused by housing demolition — and, as described later in this chapter, is having significant impact on condominium conversions too.

For information on Berkeley's NPO, write the City Attorney's office, 2180 Milvia St., Berkeley, CA 94704. For information on Santa Monica's demolition/condominium conversion/rent control law, contact the Santa Monica Rent Control Board, 1685 Main Street, Santa Monica, CA 90401.

In June, 1980, Seattle, Washington passed a relatively weak demolition control law. Owners there must obtain a demolition license, the fee for which is a sliding-scale percentage of the estimated replacement cost of the building. The rate is 3-20%, depending upon the type of district zone in which the building is located — the higher the density, the higher the fee. License fees are paid into a Housing Replacement Fund, to be used to subsidize low-income housing production. Single-family homes are exempted, however. The intended new land use must also be approved before a demolition permit is given; a developer can't simply tear down a structure, put in a parking lot, and wait for a hot opportunity. Owners must provide relocation assistance to tenants displaced by demolition: low-income tenants, for instance, are entitled to $1,000 in relocation benefits. While Seattle has not prevented displacement due to demolition, the law is at least a healthy step forward, in that it recognizes a public interest in protecting and replacing the housing stock, requires private displacers to give relocation compensation, and puts limits on what a private owner can do with his property if housing demolition is involved. (For information on Seattle's Housing Preservation Ordinance, contact the Seattle Displacement Coalition, 619 N. 35th St., Seattle, WA 98103.)

An important lesson stands out in the comparison of the Berkeley, Santa Monica, and

Bulletin Populaire / LNS

Seattle approaches to regulating housing demolition. *If the only barrier to demolition is dollar penalties and relocation assistance payments, developers will probably absorb these as a cost of business and will continue to demolish lower-rent housing because alternative uses are so profitable.* Only when the development process is directly restricted, or construction of lower-income replacement housing is required as a condition for allowing removal of units, is speculative demolition actually halted.

Historic preservation and housing planning laws may sometimes be invoked to oppose demolition that will displace poor tenants and destroy rental housing (see discussion on pages 162-167).

Direct political pressure also works in appropriate situations. For example, elderly poor tenants in Los Angeles recently persuaded the City Council to prohibit the demolition of their low-rent building for the construction of luxury condominiums. The City Council based its decision on the requirement of the Housing Element of its General Master Plan which calls for the city to provide all of its citizens the opportunity to live in affordable housing. Fighting demolition displacement on a building-by-building basis in this way is hard, but can be done.

## ARSON FOR PROFIT

The purposeful, criminal burning of rental housing has grown in recent years into a major cause of displacement, and of housing loss. The growing wave of torchings each year is exacting a terrible toll: tens of thousands of residential units, mainly in lower-income neighborhoods; an estimated 700 deaths and 10,000 injuries to occupants and firefighters; and multiple millions of dollars in lost municipal tax revenues.

But arson makes big money for some people. The estimated annual toll of property damage from criminal burning is $1.5 billion, most of which is recovered from insurance companies by property owners.

Arson typically wipes out absentee-owned housing. Sometimes it occurs because of vandalism, or revenge, or extortion, or pyromania, or attempts to cover up other crimes. But more frequently, it's the building's owners who arrange it, and the motive is speculative profiteering. Mostly it's done to get the insurance payoff ("selling out to the insurance company"). But arson also offers a quick, cheap way to clear a site for development, or to remove buildings protected by historic preservation restrictions, or to get rid of a property once it has been depreciated for tax purposes. Insurance awards give owners tax-free cash to use for other investment, an excellent source of real estate investment funds when conventional mortgage sources dry up in periods of "tight money." It is revealing that arson rates tend to go up when the economy goes down.

Usually, the target of a total burnout is a

vacant building, often emptied by an earlier, smaller fire set to drive the tenants out. But even a long-vacant building that burns is characteristically only the final chapter in another kind of displacement — that which results from disinvestment, withdrawal of maintenance and services. And any way you approach it the end is the same: removal of housing from the market.

Of most concern to anti-displacement groups are the fires intended to force people out and cause neighborhood change. (See also our discussion of withdrawal of city firefighting services in Chapter 8.) Speculators may use arson to remove stable tenants and trigger "blockbusting," or to empty properties to facilitate remodeling or condo conversions, or to capitalize on rent control laws that permit unlimited increases upon change of tenancy (see discussion of "vacancy decontrol" on page 86). Further, burnt-out buildings torched for insurance profits are a neighborhood blight that can lead to greater disinvestment.

Whole neighborhoods can be decimated by arsonists. In the Bushwick section of Brooklyn, for example, 1,140 multiple dwelling buildings — *one-third of the entire housing stock* — were lost to arson in a single year. The process is described in the magazine *Dollars and Sense:*

> [Real estate speculators] begin by selling property back and forth between combinations of associates, family members, and even loyal secretaries, at gradually rising prices. This allows the property to be insured each time at a higher value, and ultimately at a level considerably above its true market value. (Dummy corporations are sometimes employed to further obscure the nature of these sales.) While all this is going on, landlords will "milk" the building, putting off needed repairs and neglecting to pay taxes. This causes the true value of the building to deteriorate further below the insured value and

makes life miserable for the building's tenants. When the building is finally torched, the profit will be considerable.

Among the big losers are city governments, which are denied tax revenues, not only once the building is burned down but earlier as well, since buildings slated for arson are usually way behind in their taxes. A recent New York *Times* series on arson concluded that in that city "arson is costing tens of millions of dollars in revenue that, a generation ago, would have been anticipated by the city as an annual source of guaranteed income."

Arson is a difficult problem to deal with, in part because the profit potential is so high, but also because law enforcement is relatively ineffective. According to the U.S. Fire Administration, arrest rates are 9%, conviction rates 2%, incarceration rates 0.7%. Moreover, insurance companies mostly refuse to take forceful preventive measures: it is easier for them to make quick settlements, and pass on losses to all customers in the form of rate increases. Besides, both agents and underwriters find overinsurance generally profitable.

## FIGHTING ARSON

### COMMUNITY ORGANIZATION, RESEARCH AND ACTION

The strongest defense so far developed against the perils and displacement of arson — and it is quite effective — is strong community and building organization, backed up by good research and a willingness to act. Fires rarely occur in buildings with strong tenant organizations, and alert community organizations can quickly deal with abandoned buildings before the arsonists get to them. The outstanding example of this multi-pronged approach is Boston's Symphony Tenants Organizing Pro-

ject (STOP), which put a halt to a heavy arson assault on its neighborhood around Northeastern University and the Fenway, developed a research program now being used by community groups and fire marshals around the country, and sparked an investigation which resulted in the arrest of a large gang of arsonists.

STOP got started after fires in 29 of the neighborhood's 74 buildings, all in a two-block area, had left five persons dead and 600 homeless. Organizers leafletted, called local meetings, allied with nearby neighborhood groups and sought information from the city, converting local anger and anxiety into an

Metropolitan Council on Housing

anti-arson campaign. Neighborhood awareness and watchfulness grew. Meanwhile, other activists began to research the fires: identifying owners, tracing the recent history of property transfers, etc. Patterns began to emerge for buildings with fires of "suspicious origin." Similarities appeared as to when, where, and how the fires started, and how each of the buildings was operated. Rapid and frequent resale of the property, always at escalating prices, showed up. In fact, a whole set of "predictors" emerged from the torched buildings: tax delinquency, previous structural fires, code violations, liens and other claims against the property, ownership by certain landlords (although accurate ownership records were hard to come by), and heavy over-insurance.

Armed with this research, STOP demanded an investigation. The City was unresponsive, but the State Attorney General followed STOP's lead. The media began to give the issue attention, and the fires suddenly stopped. Within six months, the Attorney General, several jumps ahead because of the community's work, indicted 33 people on charges of arson, fraud, bribery and murder. The cast of characters revealed the web of professions that make for an efficient arson ring: lawyers, retired fire captains, a former lieutenant in the State Fire Marshal's office, real estate agents and their friends and relatives.

Since then, experience elsewhere has only confirmed the fact that the widespread arson in our cities involves well organized rings of conspirators, able to call on "fire brokers" and other "professionals" in the business. A recent 19-month undercover investigation in New York City, for instance, exposed one of the largest arson-for-profit rings ever uncovered in the U.S., involving two arsonists who have admitted responsibility for 46 fires, and 13 landlords who owned more than 400 buildings in an intricate maze of at least 45 corporations.

## CHANGING THE PROPERTY INSURANCE SYSTEM

Laws that make it harder for an owner to take the insurance from a torched building and run will work strongly against arson for profit. Some localities now have ordinances enabling them to attach liens for back taxes to insurance awards. Another more basic approach is suggested by Gelvin Stevenson, an economist writing in the September 11, 1977 New York *Times:*

. . . The fundamental problem of the industry in approaching the arson-for-profit problem lies in the nature of property insurance in the United States. It insures the financial interest and not the physical structure. The insurance industry is now neutral on whether the claim is reinvested in the damaged property or not. And this is a key to a far-reaching and powerful arson prevention strategy. If paid claims were automatically reinvested in the damaged property, the financial incentive for arson-for-profit would disappear.

New York State recently passed a weak law allowing local governments the option to try to put Stevenson's suggestion into practice.

**If paid claims were automatically reinvested in the damaged property, the financial incentive for arson-for-profit would disappear.**

Another approach would be for localities to pass laws placing liens on fire insurance claims to cover the costs of repairing or selling burned-out buildings. This could be particularly useful in repairing the damage of small fires promptly, to prevent moveouts and further destruction. Since a frequent pattern, as mentioned above, is the use of a small fire to drive out tenants, followed by a full-scale conflagration, such laws are important steps.

Further reform possibilities include transferring unsafe buildings to community or city ownership, before or after fires occur, by means of eminent domain (government land-taking, with compensation) and tax sales. Stevenson points out that insurance companies are permitted, under the terms of their policies, to repair fire damage in lieu of paying claims, but they almost never do so. Governments unwilling to act more firmly might at least put pressure on local insurers to do this, or at least to stop overinsuring risky buildings. A recent potentially influential housing court decision from Boston required the owner of a residential hotel badly damaged by an arson fire to restore the units to habitable condition and make efforts to find former occupants and resettle them in the renovated units. The court held that a tenant's occupancy rights are not ended merely by virtue of an intentional fire temporarily destroying the habitability of the unit.

For groups wanting further information about arson, we recommend the following sources:

● *Arson: The Federal Role in Arson Prevention and Control* (1979) is a report submitted to Congress by the U.S. Fire Administration that offers one of the best overviews of the problem, and contains a section on relevant state and federal law reforms. It is available free from the Federal Emergency Management Agency, Washington, D.C. 20472. The U.S. Fire Administration also puts out a periodic *Arson Resource Bulletin,* available free from the same address.

● Urban Education Systems is a non-profit group set up by some of the activists in the STOP group, whose work is described above. They have available an *Arson Action Guide* (free); *Research, A Manual for Arson Analysis and Property Research* ($5); and *Tools: A Handbook for Anti-Arson Programs and Laws* ($5). Write them at 153 Milk Street, Boston, MA 02109. They have received an LEAA grant to coordinate a National Arson Prevention and Action Coalition, bringing together community-based organizations from across the country into regional councils to work on arson research and prevention, and will be holding East Coast, Midwest and West Coast regional conferences during 1981.

# CONDOMINIUM AND INVOLUNTARY COOPERATIVE CONVERSIONS

The displacement of tenants as a result of the conversion of apartments buildings into condominiums and involuntary cooperatives has recently become an issue of national concern. A wave of "condomania" has swept a great many urban areas, resulting in the conversion of 260,000 apartments between 1977 and 1979, and the phenomenon is expected to continue. Government estimates are that 1.1 million units will be converted by 1985 unless public regulation or the unavailability of mortgage funds gets in the way.

In New York City and a few other places, the main conversion scheme is the full-equity or stock cooperative (see page 177 for an explanation of the difference between this and a limited-equity cooperative). But the distinction between this type of coop and condominiums is slight, the process of conversion is essentially the same, and the effects are equally bad. In a condominium, individual apartments are owned outright by different owners. In an imposed coop, each tenant buys a share in a corporation which owns the whole structure. *Coops pushed on tenants by landlords should not be confused with limited-equity coops that tenants may voluntarily adopt to save their housing.* These are discussed in Chapter 16.

The basic reasons for the upsurge in condo/coop conversions are simple and powerful: high profitability, and strong market demand. First, despite the lucrative profits landlords can receive from the cash flow, tax benefits and appreciation in value of rental properties, it is usually much more profitable to sell an apartment as a condominium than to lease it out. Rapidly rising operating costs, often increasing faster than renters' abilities to afford them, plus, in some localities, landlords' reduced ability to treat tenants arbitrarily (because of rent and eviction controls), help convince landlords that selling their properties is more profitable.

45

Second, condo/coop converters have a ready market, especially in places where housing is tight and vacancy rates are low. Condos and coops are expensive, but even so they are generally cheaper than single-family detached houses, have lower operating costs than such houses, and still offer the tax advantages of home ownership. Established tenants who cannot afford to buy (and the escalation of monthly payments caused by the changeover typically is enormous) are usually easily replaced by young couples, single professionals, well-heeled retirees — or by speculators and investors, who buy, push the price up even further, and sell again. In particular, condos offer first-time buyers an opportunity to get on the home ownership escalator.

There is some controversy about the actual impact of condo/coop conversions. A 1980 HUD study entitled *The Conversion of Rental Housing to Condominiums and Cooperatives,* for instance, concluded that the net effect on availability of rental units is less than it appears, because some tenants buy their units, and those new buyers who had been renting elsewhere free up the rental units they previously occupied. But even subtracting these offsetting effects, the fact is that conversions reduce the supply of rental units while helping to inflate rents for those remaining. That ripple-effect rent escalation reflects both increased demand pressure on the shrinking rental unit supply, and the magnetic upward pull on competitive rent levels resulting from the high cost of buying into coops and condos. It produces further hardship and displacement all down the line.

The HUD study, and the way HUD is publicizing it, tends to play down the broad-scale impact of conversions, in much the same

way HUD is downplaying the displacement issue generally in its recent studies and reports on the subject. HUD stresses that only 1.3% of the nation's entire rental stock has been converted to date. But since condo/coop conversion is concentrated in certain cities and neighborhoods so far — it promises to spread — the conversion rate in those areas is considerably higher. The proportion of rental housing already converted in Denver is 8.8%; in Houston, 7.3%; in Washington, D.C., 6.9%; in Chicago 5.4%; and in some previously stable neighborhoods of those cities *a third or more* of the rental stock has already been converted. These figures have special significance in light of the already tiny vacancy rates for decent rental housing in most cities—even a relatively small number of conversions makes things far tighter than they already are, by raising rents and increasing the difficulties of finding a place to live for everyone.

The HUD study did show, however, that for the majority of residents of buildings that get converted, things get worse. Those who can't buy, and who stay as tenants of investors or speculators who purchase their apartments, have to pay much higher rents for the same unit. Tenants who buy their own unit pay on the average 36% more per month (although some of this may be offset by the tax advantages of home ownership), and half say they did not want to buy but felt they had no choice. Those who move — the great majority — do indeed find it difficult to get a new place, and usually incur rent increases in the process, in addition to moving expenses. Not surprisingly, the elderly, racial minorities, families with children, and the poor among these displacees have the hardest time.

Also, the HUD study undercuts the condo/coop converters' justification for their actions. Typically, says HUD, few building improve-

Chicago Rehab Network / redrawn by Allan Troxler

*"There's no room. We're going condo!"*

ments are made during conversion, and conversion does little to improve a community's tax base.

## FIGHTING BACK

In localities were there has been extensive condo/coop conversion activity, resistance has been growing. The range of responses stretches from direct action to some fairly well-developed laws, all outlined below. In a growing number of places, anti-displacement groups and their allies have pushed local governments to declare a temporary moratorium on conversions while alternatives are studied. In Fort Lee, New Jersey, the community pressure was strong enough to get a permanent ban on conversions passed (although the courts later ruled this unconstitutional). Always, the first step in dealing with any threatened condo/coop conversion is organization: organizing the tenants within the building, and making connections with other area housing and community groups concerned about the impact of conversions. Whether it's picketing, pushing for new laws, or negotiating with developers, well-organized tenants will always come out better off.

## NEGOTIATING CONCESSIONS

In places with no or weak laws regulating condo conversions, negotiating with the converter is an important tactic. Concessions won this way are nothing to be sneezed at. They might include lowering the sales price for all units, paying moving costs and relocation bonuses, extending time for tenants to move, or even reserving some units for low- and moderate-income tenants.

Negotiating for concessions is actually another term for squeezing the converter's pro-

fits. It's possible — even though many of the concessions listed above are quite costly to the developer — since speed is one of the important factors in the most lucrative forms of conversion. The converter's objective is to sell all the units in a building as quickly as possible and move on to other conversion projects, tying up borrowed capital as briefly as possible. So substantial concessions often will be made simply to avoid delays. (Usually professional converters rather than existing landlords carry out the conversion, because of the different ways that tax laws treat "business profits" as opposed to "real estate appreciation.")

Another important factor in negotiating is militancy. As in the Duboce Triangle neighborhood, where pickets set back embarrassed speculators (see Chapter 3), tenants who demonstrate outside their converted buildings can make the prospect of living there grim for potential condo/coop buyers. Tenants at a Bethesda, Maryland, conversion site, for instance, picketed so relentlessly for five months that the converting firm was forced to give in on important concessions. Needless to say, negotiating for concessions works best when tenants operate collectively rather than individually.

The foremost thing to remember in negotiating for concessions is that converters' profits in the coop/condo business are typically *huge,* often running 100% of investment and more. There is always plenty of room to squeeze.

Two good short guides are available which explain in detail how tenants can organize against condo conversions: *Condominium Conversion Organizing* (1979), available for $3 from the Santa Barbara Rent Control Alliance/Housing Action Project, P.O. Box 2166,

Santa Barbara, CA 93120; and *Going Condo: A Tenant Survival Manual* (1980), available for $3 from the California Public Interest Research Group, 3000 "E" Street, San Diego, CA 92101.

## FEDERAL, STATE AND LOCAL LEGISLATION

The strongest strategies thus far to *prevent* the displacement caused by condo conversions take the form of regulatory legislation, passed as a result of community pressure in various places around the country — despite stiff opposition from the real estate industry. Up to now, the best laws have been created at the local level, where tenants can bring the greatest political pressure to bear. Federal and state legislation is much softer, reflecting the weak political standing of tenants with Congress and state legislatures.

Following Congressional hearings on condo conversions in 1979, and a protest demonstration by tenants on the steps of the United States Capitol in October, 1979, Congress passed the Condominium and Cooperative Conversion Protection Act of 1980 (Title VI of the 1980 Housing and Community Development Act). But the Act does nothing to prevent the displacement of tenants. It merely expresses the sense of Congress that states and localities should act so that tenants receive adequate prior notice of a conversion, and guarantees tenants the first right to purchase their units. This of course does nothing to protect tenants who cannot afford to purchase and therefore will face eviction. There is little prospect that Congress will regulate condo conversions in the near future.

Elements of other federal legislation and regulations, however, give anti-displacement groups some potential weapons in fighting condo/coop conversion. As discussed in Chapter 4, Section 603 of the Housing and Community Development Act of 1980 stated the "Sense of Congress" that lending for conversions should be discouraged "where there are adverse impacts on housing opportunities of the low- and moderate-income and elderly and handicapped tenants involved." And implementing regulations of the Community Reinvestment Act (see Chapter 10 for fuller explanation of this law) contain as an assessment factor "Whether the [lending] institution's policies promote efforts to assist existing residents in neighborhoods undergoing a process of reinvestment and change." By tying this sense of Congress resolution to the CRA regulations, anti-displacement groups have a lever to use on the lenders who finance conversions.

Finally, the Federal Home Loan Bank Board has a rule that purchasers of units converted with loans from federally regulated lenders must use those units as their residence. The rule is intended to prevent speculative converters from acquiring the units and jacking up prices. A 1980 Congressional investigation revealed that the largest condo converter in the country was systematically violating this rule by forging borrowers' loan applications. Tenant groups able to spot this sort of shenanigan can cause a fair amount of trouble for the converters they are dealing with.

Almost half of the states have passed condo conversion legislation. (State legislation is detailed in Chapter XI of the 1980 HUD study cited above.) The Uniform Condominium Act, approved in 1978 by the American Bar Association, embodies the approach recommended by Congress and is likely to serve as the model for most future state regulation of condo conversions. The Act does not prevent displacement, and so further state or local action is needed. One real danger of the Uniform Condominium Act, however, is that the courts may hold that passage of the Act by a state preempts stronger local ordinances. A Maryland court has already invalidated a more stringent Montgomery County ordinance regulating condo conversions because that state has adopted the Uniform Condominium Act. The message is clear: community groups should oppose passage of the Uniform Condominium Act by state legislatures unless it is modified to include strong anti-displacement provisions, or has wording attached that clearly enables stronger local action.

A few states do have legislation which limits displacement. New York's is about the best, although powerful challenges have limited its coverage. Real estate industry lobbying there prevented renewal of a 1974 statewide condo and coop conversion law in 1977. The resulting local option version now applies only to New York City and three neighboring suburban counties. This law permits an owner to convert a building under an "eviction plan" or a "non-eviction plan." Under the eviction plan, 35% of the tenants in occupancy must agree to purchase their apartments before the building can be turned over to the new cooperative corporation, and the plan must either be put into effect or abandoned within six or eighteen months of presenting it to the tenants (depending on whether they are protected under the city's rent control program or its weaker rent stabilization program). Under the non-eviction plan, only 15% of tenants in occupancy must buy their units before the plan is declared in effect, but those who don't buy cannot be evicted. Under the eviction plan, those living in rent controlled units who don't buy can stay for two years (unless at least 80% of current tenants have bought their units, in which case they can be evicted immediately); those living in rent stabilized units can stay the latest of three dates: one year after the conversion plan was accepted for filing, the effective date of the plan, or the expiration of their lease (unless it has a 90-day cancellation clause). Under either plan tenants over age 62 whose household income is under $30,000 a year, and who have resided in their apartment at least two years, cannot be evicted. Such lifetime lease provisions were recently upheld by a New York court.

The District of Columbia recently enacted legislation in effect giving elderly tenants (households whose head is 62 years or older) with incomes under $30,000 a year lifetime tenancies, in order to protect them against forced purchase of their rental units.

Connecticut and Michigan have recently passed condo conversion controls which give limited eviction protection, but not lifetime leases, to elderly and handicapped tenants.

According to Chapter XII of HUD's 1980 condo study, 54 localities had enacted condo conversion control ordinances by early 1980. The strongest form of condo conversion control that exists in the U.S. is in Santa Monica, California, where the same elected board which regulates rents, evictions, and demolitions must also pass on condo conversions. The rent control board applies the same standards to proposed condo conversions as to proposed demolitions: Are tenants low- or moderate-income people? Are the rent levels affordable by low- or moderate-income tenants? Will conversion adversely affect the supply of rental housing? Can the landlord make a fair return without conversion? "Yes" answers to any of these questions can result in denial of a permit.

Other local laws vary considerably in purpose and in their impact on displacement. (Reports cited at the end of this chapter give detailed descriptions to allow comparison and choice of the most appropriate local models). Among the approaches they offer, the following seem best suited to prevent displacement:

• Banning conversions totally unless the rental vacancy rate is above what is generally considered "healthy" — so that the conversions do not further aggravate an existing shortage of rental housing.

• Requiring prior approval by some proportion of the present tenants before conversion is allowed. As noted above, 15-35% tenant approval is required in New York City and other parts of New York State, and in some cities a higher percentage is mandated (40% in San Francisco, for instance). Where possible, community groups should push for a far higher consent figure — say 75-80%, together with lifetime leases and other protections for the minority who do not wish to purchase their units. "Commitment to purchase" is also a better standard than "approval," since developers can, and often do, purchase a tenant's "approval" with a relatively small cash payment.

• Imposing an annual ceiling on the allowable number of conversions, either by setting an absolute number or relating the ceiling to the number of newly constructed rental units. This puts pressure on the real estate industry to create housing, rather than just creating profits for themselves by manipulating the existing housing supply.

• Requiring converters to build replacement rental housing so that the existing rental housing stock is not reduced. Replacement housing should be started or completed prior to conversion taking place, to ensure that it gets built. A far less desirable alternative is to require converters to contribute a fee to a fund for future housing development, since it is unlikely that much housing will get developed quickly through such fees.

• Prohibiting or limiting the eviction of existing tenants, at least those who are poor, elderly, or handicapped, by requiring lifetime or long-term leases at controlled rents (unless the converters provide comparable replacement housing). However, if only certain types of tenants — the elderly, for example — receive these eviction protections, landlords likely will discriminate against such people by refusing to rent to them in the first place, in order to eliminate a future barrier to conversion.

## OTHER LEGISLATIVE OPTIONS

If it proves impossible to persuade localities to ban or limit condo conversions, then pressure can shift toward enactment of regulations and programs that give at least some of the present tenants a better chance to purchase their own units or continue living there. This can be done by:

• Giving existing tenants a "first right of refusal" and providing technical and financial assistance to organized tenants to purchase their buildings as limited-equity cooperatives rather than condominiums (see related materials on coops on pages 65 and 176-184).

• Subsidizing purchases made either to lower income tenants (using Community Development funds for a downpayment, for example) or to public housing agencies for rental to eligible tenants. California's Department of Housing and Community Development and its Housing Finance Agency both provide subsidized apartment purchase loans to low- and moderate-income tenants facing displacement as a result of conversions. (Further information on this program is available from California's HCD, 921 10th St., Sacramento, CA 95814.)

The state of Massachusetts recently introduced a small-scale demonstration project, under which local housing authorities can purchase condominium units in order to allow low-income elderly tenants to continue living there (vacant units also can be purchased for rental to eligible low-income elderly households). For more information, contact the Office of Policy Development (attn: Thomas Alexander), Executive Office of Communities and Development, 100 Cambridge St., Room 1404, Boston, MA 02202.

• Limiting the price of all or some of the converted units to make them affordable to existing tenant occupants and other lower income households. This approach is illustrated in the "inclusionary zoning" provision adopted in 1979 by the California Coastal Commission, which regulates development in the state's seacoast areas. Charged with protecting, encouraging and sometimes providing low- and moderate-income housing, the Commission will approve conversions only if the owner agrees that at least 1/3 of the units will remain as low- and moderate-income housing, either through a rent subsidy program (such as Section 8) or a sale program with prices set at levels lower-income people can afford, including resale restrictions of the type described on pages 36 and 37. In the three years this legislation has been on the books, nearly 500 low- and moderate-income units have been assured under approved conversion plans. Another 4200 units of new low- and moderate-income housing have been incorporated into developers' plans through these zoning provisions. (Information on these regulations is available from the Commission at 631 Howard St., San Francisco, CA 94105.) Similar "inclusionary zoning" and resale restrictions can also be passed on the local level by amending the local zoning ordinance, although, as with all such ordinances, enforcement can be lax unless community groups put on the pressure. Such inclusionary mandates need not involve public subsidies: they can be accomplished either through an "internal subsidy system" — raising some prices, lowering others — or at the simple "cost" of converters taking a lower profit.

If tenants must move, then local governments should be pressed to require converters to provide comparable replacement housing and pay all tenant relocation costs, at least equal to federal relocation assistance standards (see Chapter 15 for a discussion of federal and state Uniform Relocation Act benefits).

If local government refuses to regulate condo conversions at all, tenants can fight back politically. Condo conversions have become a major political issue in local elections. For example, in the San Francisco Bay Area city of

Emeryville in September, 1979, tenants organized a successful recall of two City Council members who voted against a proposed ordinance requiring 50% tenant approval for condo conversions. The ordinance would have restricted the conversion of a 1,247-unit luxury apartment into condos by a major Canadian condo developer. (Unfortunately, however, despite the successful recall election, the condo conversion eventually went through).

**Government estimates are that 1.1 million rental units will be converted to condominiums by 1985 unless public regulation or the unavailability of mortgage funds gets in the way.**

Finally, current federal and state tax codes generally encourage and assist the conversion process, just as they do with other forms of speculation. (A useful discussion of this issue appears in *Condominium Conversions: Possible Changes in Federal Tax Laws to Discourage Conversions and Assist Rental Housing,* by Richard Bourdan, available free from the Congressional Research Service, Library of Congress, Washington, DC.) So the same kind of federal, state, and local tax reforms described in Chapter 4 as useful in combatting speculation could also dampen profiteering from condo/coop conversions.

## LEGALITY OF CONDO CONVERSION CONTROLS

So far, there have been relatively few legal challenges to ordinances regulating condo conversions, but attacks will probably increase as stricter control measures are passed. Tem-porary bans on conversions, for instance, generally have been upheld. But several have been invalidated, and, as noted above, an attempt by Fort Lee, New Jersey, to rule out condo conversions permanently was declared unconstitutional. Laws giving lifetime leases to tenants who don't want to buy have been upheld.

Quite recently, a unanimous Supreme Court in Massachusetts upheld an ordinance passed by the City Council in Cambridge — where 2300 units, 8% of the city's privately owned rental stock, have been converted over the last two years — allowing the city's rent control board to deny certificates of eviction to people who buys condos converted from the stock of rent-controlled apartments. No displacement is allowed, even when buyers want to occupy converted condos themselves. The Cambridge law, similar to the one in Santa Monica, gives the rent control board discretion to withhold a "unit removal permit" if an overall housing shortage exists in the city, if there is hardship for the specific tenants involved, and if the landlord has taken no steps to ameliorate these conditions. The court held that the "property rights" of condo purchasers did not encompass eviction of current residents and that anyone purchasing a condominium unit after the date the Cambridge City Council passed its ordinance was sufficiently on notice of the restricted eviction rights. Since the Cambridge ordinance does not ban condo conversions outright, as did the overturned Fort Lee ordinance, other cities may find the courts more willing to uphold this form of regulation, particularly given the precedential Massachusetts ruling. The question of whether a city that does not have rent control can adopt such a law is still open (the Massachusetts court held that the condominium eviction restric-tion was an integral part of the city's rent control ordinance) — all the more reason to enact such controls on a comprehensive basis. Further information on the Cambridge ordinance and the supreme court ruling is available through John Mason, Cambridge-Somerville Legal Services, 24 Thorndike St., Cambridge, MA 02141. (A useful discussion of the constitutional theories that have been used to challenge condo conversion controls is contained in the article "Condo Conversion Is a Religious Experience," by David Madway in the May/June, 1980, issue of the *Housing Law Bulletin,* available free from the National Housing Law Project, 2150 Shattuck Avenue, #300, Berkeley, CA 94704).

## OTHER TYPES OF CONVERSIONS

In older central cities especially, there are many buildings in commercial districts that contain apartments, usually above street level storefronts. These apartments are usually considered "non-conforming" uses under local zoning laws but are allowed to remain in use.

If commercial "revitalization" begins, these units are all too likely to be eliminated by conversion to stores or offices, since commercial rents are generally higher than residential rents. This happens especially when a new owner purchases a building to renovate it for commercial purposes.

Displacement of tenants through this process can be prevented by regulation. For example, Berkeley, California, amended its zoning ordinance to allow its Planning Commission to grant permits for conversions from residential to commercial use only if such a conversion does not conflict with the Housing Element of the city's General Master Plan. If a commercial conversion will displace low- and moderate-income tenants and eliminate affordable rental housing units, then the Planning Commission can deny the permit or require the owner to provide relocation assistance to the displaced tenants. San Francisco has also acted to prohibit further conversion of residential space to commercial use, above the ground floor, on several commercial streets in neighborhood business districts where the conversion process was reducing the neighborhood housing supply. (For further information on the San Francisco approach, write the city's Planning Department, 100 Larkin Street, San Francisco, CA 94102).

While this type of regulation may protect tenants living in legally permitted units along commercial strips, it doesn't help residents of mixed-use areas zoned residential-commercial, or of illegal, substandard apartments. If landlords decide to convert such units or evict the tenants, they are defenseless. Broadening a local anti-conversion law's coverage to include rooms and apartments which are well established but technically illegal, or which do not conform to local codes, should be considered as an additional goal for anti-displacement groups.

New York City's "loft war" presents a somewhat different problem with regard to conversion of technically illegal living units. Tens of thousands of New Yorkers live in converted former manufacturing and commercial loft spaces. Many are artists for whom large, unobstructed live-work space is an ideal solution to their needs. When they originally moved in, the buildings were virtually unrentable, due to the departure of manufacturing trades from the city. Many of the spaces are illegal, in terms both of zoning and the landlord's failure to have a certificate of occupancy. Tenants frequently took long-term leases and installed basic amenities themselves — bathrooms, kitchens, heat and hot water.

Now that "loft living" has become very trendy, the landlords who at first welcomed the pioneers with open arms want them out so they can convert to fancy apartments and condominiums. And they're using the standard harassment techniques — shutting off essential services, raising rents astronomically, etc. The tenants, who technically are there illegally, have no recourse to city protective laws and agencies.

The loft tenants have organized, however, and got the state legislature to pass a temporary "moratorium" tenant protection law in November, 1980, as part of an Omnibus Loft Bill, which requires landlords of loft buildings with three or more residential units to offer one-year leases, at a maximum 11% rent increase — compared with the 200-300% increases they had been demanding — despite the "illegal" status of the lofts. While the tenants' rights portion of the bill expires on June 30, 1981, it can be anticipated that the organized loft tenants will demand permanent protection.

A related issue is what are referred to in some locales as "in-law apartments" — small units, sometimes in a basement or garage, that may technically be in violation of the zoning ordinance or housing code, but which provide useful and needed living space. In some cases, they were originally constructed for relatives but now are rented out to others. In neighborhoods zoned single-family, the addition of a second unit to the structure may violate city ordinances, and because the units often have been squeezed into space not originally intended for living, ceiling heights may be slightly too low or there may be minor violation of other code standards. In some cities, there have been moves to legalize these technically illegal units or actually encourage creation of new "in-law apartments." The mayor of San Francisco recently proposed such legalization/encouragement as one way of increasing that city's ultra-short housing supply (for further information, write the Mayor's Office, City Hall, San Francisco, CA 94102); and a provision to this effect was included in San Francisco's Affordable Housing Initiative (see Appendix B, Title VII[E][1].

## REFERENCES

### DEMOLITION

Rent/Eviction/Demolition/Conversion Control in Santa Monica: For more information, write the Santa Monica Rent Control Board, 1685 Main St., Santa Monica, CA 90401.

Seattle's Housing Preservation Ordinance: For more information, contact the Seattle Displacement Coalition, 619 N. 35 St., Seattle, WA 98103.

Berkeley's Neighborhood Preservation Ordinance: For more information, write the City Attorney's Office, 2180 Milvia St., Berkeley, CA 94704.

### ARSON

*Arson Action Guide* (free)
*Research, A Manual for Arson Analysis and Property Research* ($5)
*Tools: A Handbook for Anti-Arson Programs and Laws* ($5)
All available from Urban Education Systems, 153 Milk St., Boston, MA 02109. This group is a non-profit operation set up by some members of STOP, the Boston organization which led the way in fighting arson.

"Stopping Arson," by Sheridan Tatsuno, an article on Boston's STOP organization, appeared in the July, 1979 issue of *Planning,* available through the American Planning Association, 1313 E. 60th St., Chicago, IL 60637, or may be read or copied at most local planning departments.

*Arson: The Federal Role in Arson Prevention and Control* (1979), report submitted to Congress by the U.S. Fire Administration, available free from the Federal Emergency Management Agency, Washington, DC 20472. Offers good overview of the problem.

*Arson Resource Bulletin,* periodical published by the U.S. Fire Administration, available free from the Federal Emergency Management Agency, Washington, DC 20472.

## COMMERCIAL CONVERSIONS

San Francisco's restrictions on conversions of residential to commercial property: For more information, write the Planning Department, 100 Larkin St., San Francisco, CA 94102.

## CONDO/COOP CONVERSIONS

### OVERVIEW

*The Conversion of Rental Housing to Condominiums and Cooperatives* (1980), a HUD report, available free from HUD User, P.O. Box 280, Germantown, MD 20767. Debatable conclusions, but contains highly useful background information, and catalogue of current state and local legislation.

A good critique of the HUD study, by Tufts University sociologist Peter Dreier, appears in the September/October, 1980 issue of the magazine *Working Papers,* and is available as a reprint for 25¢ from the magazine at 186 Hampshire St., Cambridge, MA 02139.

*A Reader on Condominium Conversions and Housing Development,* edited by Rachel Bratt, Peter Dreier and Steven Kaye, is available for $3 from Dept. of Urban and Environmental Policy, Tufts Univ., Brown House, Medford, MA 02155.

Congressional hearings on the condo conversion problem were held March 30-April 1, 1981, by the House Subcommittee on Commerce, Consumer and Monetary Affairs. Copies of the hearing transcript should be available shortly (free) by writing to the Subcommittee's Chair, Congressman Benjamin Rosenthal, at the House Office Bldg., Washington, DC. The Subcommittee is planning a second round of hearings in the Summer of 1981.

Another good Congressional compilation of condominium materials is "Condominium Housing Issues," hearings before the U.S. Senate Subcommittee on Housing and Urban Affairs, on S.612, held June 28, 1979. Copies are available free from the Subcommittee.

### STATE & LOCAL REGULATIONS

*Condos, Co-ops and Conversions: A Guide on Rental Conversions for Local Officials* (1979), by Jennifer Soloway, available free from the California Office of Planning and Research, 1400 Tenth St., Sacramento, CA 95814.

*Condominium Conversion Controls* (1979), by the Urban Consortium, available free from Public Technology, Inc., 1140 Connecticut Ave. NW, Washington, DC 20036.

"Condominium Conversions — the Number Prompts Controls to Protect the Poor and Elderly," by Daniel Lauber, a good introduction to the issue, appears in the April, 1980 edition of the *Journal of Housing,* available for reading or copying at most HUD Area Office libraries; local housing authorities and redevelopment agencies also may have subscriptions.

New York's existing laws and proposed reforms on condo/coop conversions: a detailed description appears in Volume II of the *Final Report* (1980) of the New York State Temporary Commission on Rental Housing, available from Two World Trade Center, Room 6735, New York, NY 10047.

*New York Magazine,* in its March 31, 1980 issue, published a 17-page "Co-oping Guide" — focused largely on New York City, where condo conversion takes the legal form of coop conversion, but useful

for other areas as well. It is available for $1.50 by writing their Circulation Dept., 755 Second Ave., New York City, NY 10017; write "Co-op" on the envelope.

For a copy of the District of Columbia ordinance giving lifetime tenancies to elderly residents of buildings being converted, write the D.C. Dept. of Housing and Community Development, 1133 N. Capitol NE, Washington, DC 20002.

For further information on the Cambridge ordinance preventing buyers of condominiums from displacing their occupants, and the recent Massachusetts Supreme Court decision upholding this ordinance, write Cambridge-Somerville Legal Services, 24 Thorndike St., Cambridge, MA 02141, attn: John Mason.

California Coastal Commission's "Inclusionary Zoning" restricting condo conversions: For more information, write the Commission at 631 Howard St., San Francisco, CA 94105. The California Legislature effectively repealed this provision, unfortunately.

California's program of subsidized apartment purchase loans to low- and moderate-income tenants facing displacement in condo conversions: For more information, write the Department of Housing and Community Development, 921 10th St., Sacramento, CA 95814.

### TENANT RESPONSE

Good, short guides giving details on how tenants can organize against condominium conversions are:

*Condominium Conversion Organizing* (1979), Santa Barbara Rent Control Alliance/Housing Action Project, P.O. Box 2166, Santa Barbara, CA 93210, $3.

*Going Condo: A Tenant Survival Manual* (1980), California Public Interest Research Group, 3000 "E" St., San Diego, CA 92102, $3.

*Condominium Conversion: Options for Tenants and Rental Market Protection* (1979), especially Chapter II, "State/Local Legislative Alternatives," is available from the National Council of Senior Citizens, 1511 K Street, NW, Washington, DC 20005. A useful reference, especially for local legislation.

A two-part series titled "Condomania," by John Atlas and Peter Dreier, appearing in the March, 1980 and June, 1980 issues of *Shelterforce,* a national housing movement newspaper, is available for $3 from 380 Main St., E. Orange, NJ 07018.

## OTHER SOURCES

"The Regulation of Rental Apartment Conversions," volume 8 of the *Fordham Urban Law Journal* (1980), page 507 ff., available for reading or copying at most law libraries.

"Condo Conversion Is A Religious Experience," by David Madway, is a useful discussion of the constitutional theories that have been used to challenge condo conversion controls. It appears in the May/June, 1980, issue of the *Housing Law Bulletin,* available free from the National Housing Law Project, 2150 Shattuck Ave., #300, Berkeley, CA 94704.

Current information on condo/coop conversion litigation and regulations can be found in the *Community Association Law Reporter,* published by the Community Association Inst., 3000 S. Eads, Arlington, VA, available at most law libraries.

*Condominium Conversions: Possible Changes in Federal Tax Laws to Discourage Conversions and Assist Rental Housing* (1980), by Richard Bourdan, is available free from the Congressional Research Service, Library of Congress, Washington, DC.

## LOFT CONVERSIONS

For further information on New York City's "illegal" lofts and efforts to protect their occupants, contact the Lower Manhattan Loft Tenants, Box 887, Bowling Green Station, New York City, NY 10004. A useful article on how the 1980 Omnibus Loft Bill was passed in the New York State Legislature appears in the January, 1981 issue of *People's Housing News,* available from People's Housing Network, 198 Broadway, New York City, NY 10038.

Chapter 6

# PRESERVING RENTAL HOUSING / II:
## SINGLE ROOM OCCUPANCY RESIDENTIAL HOTELS

Robert Wersan /*City Limits*

Low-rent residential hotels, often called SROs (for Single-Room Occupancy), are the bottom of the housing ladder, and are also one of the most painful — and fought-over — parts of the displacement problem.

SROs are for people who don't have the money or the family support to live anywhere else, especially the single, pension-dependent elderly. And when these people are displaced, as increasingly is happening, they have no place else to go. The growing number of "shopping bag ladies" and "derelicts" on the streets of most cities, for instance, is a direct result of the reduction of SRO rooms. As noted in Chapter 1, New York City now has an estimated 36,000 people whose shelter is bus and train stations, steam tunnels and packing cases.

SRO hotels are concentrated in urban areas, especially cities where migratory labor is or has been a significant part of the workforce, and where immigrants enter the United States. These hotels rent both to transient tenants on a daily or weekly basis, and to pensioners and others on a long-term basis. Limited house-keeping services are sometimes provided. Often, SRO housing is substandard. And when small room sizes and lack of amenities are taken into account, the rents for these units are not really so cheap. Nevertheless, in the face of a critical and continuing shortage of subsidized housing for the poor, SROs are an irreplaceable source of much-needed housing. (A useful general reference is the 57-page information paper, "Single Room Occupancy: A Need for National Concern," 1978, prepared for and available from the U.S. Senate Special Committee on Aging, Washington, DC.)

*Man sleeping on a bench, covered by three boxes, around midnight. Herald Square, New York City.*

## THE PROBLEM

The marginal resources and seeming powerlessness of SRO tenants makes them very vulnerable to displacement, and in recent years both public and private development projects — not to mention speculative conversion by SRO owners themselves — have had just that effect. New York City and San Francisco are places where the problem has already grown big enough to warrant official study, which is to say that a whole lot of people have already been hurt. Other cities are undergoing the same process.

A recent New York City study revealed that the number of low-rent ($50 per week or less) SRO hotel units declined from 50,000 in 1975 to 28,000 in 1978. (More recent New York data show that between July, 1979, and September, 1980, alone, 50 SRO hotels, containing 8,577 rooms, were lost.) The study found:

> The chief reasons for the disappearance of this housing resource are inflation and economic development. In the last year and a half 28 hotels raised their prices, charging more than $50 per week for their rooms, which put them above our definition of lower-priced hotels and out of the price range of the poor. In this same period of time 18 hotels closed, most planning to convert to apartments. Since 1975, 70 lower-priced hotels have closed. Eight additional facilities presently are in the process of closing, and more have plans to do so.

This study predicted that, if this trend continues, lower-priced hotels would be "extinct" in New York City by 1984:

> What all this means is that the low-income individual needing furnished accommodations in New York City will soon not be able to find a place to live. The New York City lower-priced hotel is an endangered species. New sources of housing accommodations for their displaced populations must be provided.

The 28,000 SRO tenants threatened by displacement in New York City are welfare recipients, pensioners, and minimum wage workers. (The report, *The Diminishing Resource: Lower-Priced Hotels in New York City,* 1979, is available through the Office of Crisis Intervention Services, NYC Human Resources Administration, 250 Church Street, New York City, NY 10013).

San Francisco's SRO housing stock is similarly threatened. A San Francisco City Planning Department study revealed that between 1975 and 1979, 5,723 of the city's 32,214 SRO units disappeared. In the city's Tenderloin District, it is estimated that in 1979 alone ten hotels containing 1,192 SRO units were being converted into tourist hotels. Tourism has become San Francisco's major industry, and hotels catering to tourists are far more profitable than SRO establishments.

New York and San Francisco experiences show that displacement pressures on SROs can come from many directions. Happily, they also show that organized tenants and support groups can fight back effectively. Indeed, some of the fiercest displacement battles in the country have taken place over the issue of SRO housing. The following brief cases give examples of the range of threats to SROs, and of how those tenants responded.

SRO hotel districts are a favorite target for publicly-sponsored downtown redevelopment clearance projects. For example, the Yerba Buena office and convention center project in central San Francisco displaced 4,000 retirees because of the demolition of SRO hotels. But tenant and community resistance and litigation against this wipe-out resulted in a surprising amount of recovery: about half the units torn down were replaced, and subsidized for permanent low-rent occupancy by federal and state sources *and the city's hotel tax,* with the tenants' organization acting as developers and managers of much of the new housing.

Another threat to SRO units is publicly-subsidized rehabilitation through HUD's Section 8 and similar programs.

In New York City, rehab through the "J-51" tax-abatement subsidy program (explained on page 161) since 1975 has resulted in conversion of many SRO hotels into luxury rental housing. Tenants have been displaced without receiving relocation benefits or replacement housing from private developers.

Tenant organizers see this displacement of SRO tenants as a key step in the gentrification of Manhattan's entire Upper West Side, especially the area surrounding Columbia University, which owns many of the SRO hotels that are being converted. (For information on community resistance to the conversion of SRO hotels in this area, contact the Morningside Tenants Federation, 501 West 121 Street, New York, NY 10027).

In rehab projects using federal Section 8 funds, HUD's so-called Minimum Property Standards require separate kitchens and baths, rather than allowing the congregate type of facilities most SROs provide (and which are allowed under HUD's public housing program for the elderly). Fear of displacement because of the renovation of SRO hotels under Section 8-type programs led area residents and neighborhood groups represented by Legal Services attorneys in San Francisco's Tenderloin District to oppose subsidized rehabilitation.

Privately sponsored demolition of SRO hotels for more profitable use is also commonplace. The struggle of poor, predominantly Asian-American tenants to prevent destruction of the International Hotel, located on the edge between San Francisco's Chinatown and its downtown financial district, was a stirring chapter in this continuing war of profit against human need. It took over ten years for developers finally to evict the nearly 100 tenants, with as many as 5,000 people at times protesting the planned demolition. The midnight eviction was finally carried out, only by using

400 police and sheriff's deputies to break through the crowd of 2,000 protecting the residents.

The International Hotel Tenants Association first sought to purchase and rehab their hotel. They then tried to have the San Francisco Housing Authority take it by eminent domain for use as public housing. Community pressure forced the Authority to begin condemnation proceedings, and to ante up a $1.3 million loan from the city's Community Development Block Grant funds. But the courts eventually ruled this taking illegal, because the Housing Authority was planning to sell the rehabilitated hotel back to a tenant development corporation. (This was definitely a class-biased piece of judicial reasoning, since that is what redevelopment agencies do all the time — take private property to convey it to a private developer. It's just that that process, which the courts almost never interfere with, usually involves taking poor people's property and giving it to well-heeled entrepreneurs and corporations).

While the International Hotel residents failed to save their building, their ten-year struggle inspired other tenants in downtown SRO hotels to organize to protect and improve their housing, and to propose a housing development plan which may eventually produce low-rent units, along with other uses, right on the former site of that hotel.

Tragically, poorly maintained SRO hotels have all too often been destroyed by fires which have killed or maimed elderly and handicapped residents. Arson for profit, discussed in Chapter 5, has increasingly been a motive for this abominable form of displacement.

Rachelle Resnick

# STRATEGIES AND RESPONSE

## GETTING SOME BREATHING SPACE: A MORATORIUM ON SRO CONVERSIONS

In San Francisco, opposition to the conversion of SRO hotels led to a temporary moratorium in November, 1979 — the first such stoppage in the United States. It came about through efforts of the Gray Panthers, Legal Assistance to the Elderly, and various neighborhood groups. The moratorium was then extended through December, 1980, in order to permit consideration of permanent regulatory SRO hotel conversion legislation.

Developers, however, successfully evaded the temporary ban in various ways, and the city failed to provide vigorous enforcement. What the SRO owners set out to do was manipulate San Francisco's weak rent stabilization ordinance, enacted in June, 1979. This law allows landlords to charge whatever rents they want if controlled units are "voluntarily" vacated. In many SROs whose conversion was halted by the moratorium, owners began reducing essential services — turning off elevators and utilities, for example.

Tenants fought back. They picketed and demonstrated, sued to restore essential services, and to win damages for the traumatic distress caused by reduction of those services, and successfully petitioned the San Francisco Rent Stabilization Board to reduce controlled rents to compensate them for illegal service cuts. The anti-displacement effort received very sympathetic coverage from the local media, which heavily publicized the brutal tactics employed by some hotel owners to force tenants to leave. This media exposure was critical in making enforcement of this mora-

Rachelle Resnick

*The following photographs suggest the diversity of the International Hotel tenants, and their indomitable spirit.*

torium, plus basic regulation of SRO hotel conversions, into major issues. However, in the interim considerable damage had already taken place. An October, 1980 study by the North of Market Planning Coalition revealed that 2,374 SRO units in San Francisco's Tenderloin District were wrongfully converted during the moratorium, following illegal evictions largely carried out through harassment and intimidation of tenants.

## GETTING A PERMANENT BAN

But the community effort paid off. Just before the moratorium extension ran out, the San Francisco Board of Supervisors (city council) unanimously passed a permanent ordinance which essentially freezes the minimum number of residential units in the city's hotels at the level it was on November 23, 1979 — the date the Board adopted its original moratorium.

Under the ordinance, hotel units used for residential purposes as of the moratorium date must be registered with the city, are permanently designated as residential units, and can be converted only if the owner builds new residential units to replace those converted, or places in the city treasury sufficient funds for the city to build new units. Penalties for violating the law — and private parties can bring suit against owners suspected of such violations — are not criminal but civil; they include payment of stiff damages in addition to all attorneys' fees.

The effectiveness of the SRO anti-displacement campaign waged by citywide and neighborhood housing groups is revealed in the startling support for this path-setting ordinance from Supervisors who normally back real estate interests down the line. It was also illustrated in a quote from the Chamber of Commerce's city hall lobbyist in the next day's San Francisco *Examiner:* "It's almost a motherhood issue. There is really a definite need for that kind of housing in those areas." (For a copy of the ordinance, write the San Francisco Gray Panthers, or Legal Assistance to the Elderly, 944 Market Street, San Francisco, CA 94102).

(Unfortunately, just as this guidebook was going to press, the San Francisco Board of Supervisors, bowing to pressure from the real estate industry, modified the ordinance they had just recently passed, weakening its protective features substantially. The two groups cited in the above paragraph can provide details on the new ordinance and the political muscle that led the city to back down from its original strong stance.)

Neighborhood groups and churches in the Tenderloin have also moved to protect their district from "touristification," through rezoning or "downzoning." They have filed an application with the Planning Department to change the zoning in a 25-block area from the "downtown general commercial" category to the "neighborhood commercial" and "mixed residential-commercial" categories. They also are seeking to reduce building height limits in the central part of the area from 80-230 feet (7-25 stories) to 80 feet. And as a third step, they are asking the Planning Department to create a special use district in the core of the Tenderloin, in order to limit the number of

Eric Stein

tourist enterprises, parking lots, and non-residential uses above the ground floor (see related discussion on page 194). Under city ordinances, what is requested in rezoning applications of this type is put into effect for a year on an interim basis, pending Planning Department study, preparation of environmental impact reports, and final decision by the city. (For further information on this rezoning move and the hotel-neighborhood agreement outlined in Chapter 17, contact the North of Market Planning Coalition, 295 Eddy St., San Francisco, CA 94102.)

## NUTS AND BOLTS OF PRESERVATION STRATEGIES FOR SRO HOUSING

As the San Francisco experience shows, there is no substitute for an aroused and organized community when it comes to campaigning for anti-displacement protection. And

Rachelle Resnick

another message from the situation is that media coverage can be an important part of the effort: it's sad but true that displacement creates the kind of human interest stories that the press and TV feed on, and those stories can highlight displacement issues, make important political points, and garner citywide support for effective regulation and preservation.

The components of such protection ideally would include these:

### RENT CONTROL: A FIRST STEP

In order to prevent the conversion of low-rent SRO units into high-rent housing or tourist hotels, rents in residential hotels must be controlled. New York City has long controlled residential hotel rents under its rent control and rent stabilization legislation.

### CONVERSION CONTROLS: A NECESSITY

If residential hotel rents are controlled, hotel owners may try to convert the buildings to other, non-controlled uses — for example, transient tourist hotels — displacing low-income residents in the process. Regulation of such SRO hotel conversions can be done in a way similar to the regulation of housing demolition and condominium conversions described in the previous chapter. Key features of effective, comprehensive conversion control legislation include these:

● Recognition of SRO residential hotel units as an endangered housing resource.

● Registration of all existing SRO units.

● Restriction of conversions until there is a normal vacancy rate.

● Replacement of converted SRO units on a one-for-one basis.

- Relocation assistance to displaced tenants by hotel owners who are permitted to convert.

San Francisco's new ordinance is the first in the nation to embody major elements of this approach. Further information on what a more inclusive law might look like, and strategies to get there, is available from the Hotel Conversion Task Force, North of Market Planning Coalition, 295 Eddy Street, San Francisco, CA 94102.

Rachelle Resnick

## REFORMING DANGEROUS PROGRAMS

In New York City, proposals have been made to alter the city's "J-51" tax abatement program for rehabilitation (see page 161), which makes conversion of SRO hotel units into apartments highly profitable. These reforms include:

- Allowing use of J-51 abatements for SRO rehab too, instead of restricting the program to conversions to apartments.

- Denying J-51 tax benefits to developers and owners who illegally harass and evict SRO tenants.

- Requiring J-51 beneficiaries to provide relocation benefits to displaced SRO tenants.

For further information on New York City SRO legislation, contact the Office of SRO Housing, Mayor of New York, 51 Chambers Street, Room 1201, New York, NY.

## NONPROFIT SRO REHAB: PRESERVING THE RESOURCE

In Portland, Oregon, code enforcement and demolition have threatened SRO hotels in the revitalizing downtown area. Several have been saved through the intervention of nonprofit service agencies, which assumed ownership and management. However, because the owners had been operating them illegally as slum tenements, subsidized rehab is necessary to bring the hotels into compliance with housing and health codes.

A difficulty arose, however, in that HUD regulations regarding congregate living facilities, discussed earlier, put a penalty on use of Section 8 rehabilitation and Community Development Block Grant funds to bring the taken-over hotels up to health and housing code standards: many units would have had to be ripped out to make room for the required separate bathrooms and kitchens.

But the Burnside Consortium, a neighborhood organization opposed to displacement, has gotten HUD permission to use Section 8 funds on a trial basis to maintain congregate living patterns in rehabilitated SRO hotels. (For information, contact The Burnside Consortium, 110 N.W. Third Avenue, Portland, OR 97209).

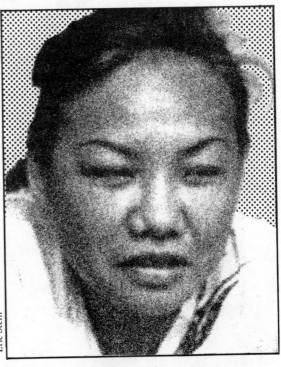

Eric Stein

The Seattle Displacement Coalition (mentioned in Chapter 18) is attempting to persuade the city to subsidize similar SRO rehab by private developers in order to prevent displacement and the loss of congregate housing.

The California Department of Housing and Community Development and California Housing Finance Agency are currently developing special rehab standards and subsidy programs for SRO hotels occupied by low- and moderate-income persons. (For further information, contact the California Department of

Housing and Community Development, 921 10th Street, Sacramento, CA 95814.)

HUD is currently studying SRO housing conditions, and, as noted, is also funding experimental SRO hotel rehabilitation demonstration projects in Oregon and Washington designed to minimize tenant displacement by allowing more flexible use of Section 8 subsidies and Section 312 rehabilitation loans, the latter of which are scheduled for termination under proposed Administration budget cuts. (Further information about the HUD study, which should be released soon, is available from their Office of Policy Development and Research, Washington, DC 20410.)

Rachelle Resnick

# REFERENCES

## THE SRO SITUATION

"Single-Room Residential Hotels Must be Preserved as Low-Income Housing Alternative," by Sheryl Lincoln, an informative article on the subject, appears in the July, 1980 *Journal of Housing,* available for reading or copying at most HUD Area Office libraries. Local housing authorities and redevelopment agencies may have subscriptions.

"Single Room Occupancy: A Need for National Concern" (1978), a useful general reference prepared for and available from the U.S. Senate Special Committee on Aging, Capitol Bldg., Washington, DC.

"Residential Hotels: A Vanishing Housing Resource" was the title of a conference, held June 11-12, 1981, in San Francisco, sponsored by the Governor's Office of Planning and Research and the California Department of Housing and Community Development. Copies of the papers presented there and the conference proceedings are available through the Governor's Office of Planning and Research, 1400 Tenth St., Sacramento, CA 95814.

## SAN FRANCISCO TENANT RESPONSE TO SRO DISPLACEMENT

"San Francisco's International Hotel: Case Study of a Turf Struggle," by Chester Hartman, about the strong and significant but ultimately losing battle to keep this SRO property for its tenants, appears in the May/June, 1978 issue of the magazine *Radical America,* available for $1.00 from P.O. Box B, North Cambridge, MA 02140.

A film on the International Hotel, called "Manongs: Tenants of the International Hotel," will be available in early 1982. Inquiries should be addressed to the Asian American Media Center, 275 15th Ave., San Francisco, CA 94118.

*Yerba Buena: Land Grab and Community Resistance in San Francisco* (1974), by Chester Hartman et al., the story of a lengthy and complex struggle against SRO displacement from downtown revitalization, is available for $10.84 from New Glide Publications, 330 Ellis St., San Francisco, CA 94102.

A model, comprehensive anti-conversion ordinance for SROs: write the Hotel Conversion Task Force, North of Market Planning Coalition, 295 Eddy St., San Francisco, CA 94102.

San Francisco's SRO Preservation Ordinance: for a copy of the law and information on the campaign that produced it, write the Gray Panthers or Legal Assistance to the Elderly, 944 Market St., San Francisco, CA 94102.

Frances Werner and David Bryson, attorneys with the National Housing Law Project, have recently received a grant from the Administration on Aging to put together a packet of legal and organizing materials on how to preserve SROs, based on an analysis of the San Francisco experience. They can be contacted at 2150 Shattuck Ave., #300, Berkeley, CA 94704.

## SROs IN NEW YORK

*The Diminishing Resource: Lower-Priced Hotels in New York City* (1979), a study revealing the economic dynamics and developmental trends in SRO housing, is available through the Office of Crisis Intervention Services, NYC Human Resources Administration, 250 Church St., New York, NY 10013.

"Salvaging SRO Housing," by Susan Baldwin, is a useful article in the April, 1981 issue of *City Limits,* a housing magazine available from 424 W. 33 St., New York, NY 10001.

Community resistance to SRO conversion in Upper West Side, Manhattan: for more information, contact the Morningside Tenants Federation, 501 W. 121st St., New York, NY 10027.

## EXPERIMENTS IN SRO REHAB

Experimental Use of Section 8 Funds for rehab of SRO units: for information, contact the Burnside Consortium, 110 N.W. Third Ave., Portland, OR 97209.

A major HUD study on SROs and HUD's policy and programs in this area is due to be completed shortly. Write their Office of Policy Development and Research, Washington, DC 20410.

California's new special rehab standards and subsidy programs for SRO hotels: for more information, contact the Department of Housing and Community Development, 921 10th St., Sacramento, CA 95814.

Marc Jahr / *City Limits*

Chapter 7

# DEALING WITH DISINVESTMENT AND ABANDONMENT

> **"Vacant, boarded houses are not a neutral force. They lead to the destruction of neighborhoods and do active violence to the people who must live near them. They are not just symbols of physical decay, they are monuments to moral, economic and political evil. More than this, they are a taunt, a jeer in the face of the homeless."**
>
> *from a poster distributed by the Columbia Heights Community Ownership Project, a neighborhood land trust in Washington, D.C.*

So far this manual has dealt with active kinds of displacement, when owners and speculators *use* property in ways that make their tenants move. But there is another side of the problem, equally big and harmful, that results from owners' *disuse* of their property: letting buildings run down, withdrawing services, cutting down maintenance, and finally abandoning them.

*Disinvestment* is the dry but appropriate word for this process, when landlords discard what they've invested in buildings that no longer return the profits they want.

Every city and most large towns are now blighted to some degree by housing abandonment — and are suffering the rent inflation that inevitably comes when people who were in those houses have to leave and compete with everyone else for the shrinking rental options available. In many major urban areas, in fact, disinvestment is among the primary causes of displacement.

Housing abandonment must be understood as a product of a central feature in the mainstream economy: the costs of making an "attractive" profit by operating a property often exceed the amount of money tenants in low-income neighborhoods (where abandonment almost always happens) can pay. Particularly in a time when fuel prices and other aspects of inflation are heavily outstripping low-level incomes, the poor are not a profitable market in real estate.

Put another way, the profit system in housing *cannot* serve the poor, and abandonment is one of the biggest and ugliest proofs of that fact.

It is also a proof of something else: for people with money, the market system is structured to work almost as well in reverse as it does for the normal, expansionist form of investment. And that is why, even while the property is going to ruin, disinvestment can still be a profit-making proposition.

Sometimes the abandonment process is relatively innocent, as such things go: a small-time landlord gets in over his/her head, starts cutting back on maintenance and tax payments in order to sustain a cash flow, and ends up with a property saleable only at below-market prices, and burdened by municipal liens. Solution? Abandonment.

But typically, the full disinvestment-abandonment process occurs under a series of owners, each of whom has neglected the property to a greater or lesser degree, leaving each new owner with the cumulative neglect of the past. Frequently, however, this seemingly "natural" progression really represents a conscious operating strategy of abandonment.

Unscrupulous landlords may buy buildings with very little cash down (using several mortgage loans), make no repairs, pay no property taxes, get behind in fuel and utility bills, and just collect rent moneys — using some to pay off the loans, and pocketing the rest. (A recent Washington *Post* story on Elmwood Apartments, a 52-unit complex in Southwest Washington described by city housing officials as one of the worst examples of "walkaway" property abandonment by a landlord in the city, documented that the owner had run up $100,000 in unpaid utility bills, $28,000 in unpaid water and sewer bills, and $12,000 in back taxes). After two or three years of this type of operation, code inspectors and property tax officials finally come down on the delinquent operators with demands for repairs and payments, "or else." Then the landlords — who are really *disinvestment speculators* — simply walk away from their buildings, leaving a mess of run-down units and unpaid bills behind them that the city and others must account for. Sometimes there is a terrible final touch: arson. They have the building torched and collect the insurance, perhaps killing and injuring people in the process. (For further discussion of the arson problem, see Chapter 5.)

Abandonment by owners and speculators can be encouraged or amplified by a larger institutional form of abandonment: "redlining" by banks and insurance companies, in which mortgage money and insurance coverage are withheld from whole neighborhoods judged to be in decline (see "redlining" discussion on pages 101 and 102). Or there may be municipal disinvestment in the form of withdrawal of city services (for the story of how one neighborhood fought such official abandonment, see Chapter 8). Often racism is at play, with minority neighborhoods being treated even more irresponsibly and destructively than white neighborhoods of equivalent income levels.

Whatever the cause, whatever the approach,

abandonment always involves tax delinquency, which makes the property available for quick and inexpensive government acquisition. This is one cause for hope — short of major changes in the housing system — in trying to undo the work of disinvestment.

Another source of hope is the inventiveness and energy of people who need housing, and who have come up with various ways, sometimes bold and unconventional, for reclaiming the wasted resources of disinvestment. Some of the most dramatic of these (as in the Philadelphia experience documented on pages 68-71) target and reoccupy vacant, boarded-up buildings. But in many situations, the insiders, tenants in buildings likely to be abandoned, have found ways to take over on their own, as the landlord is on the way out. Toward the end of the abandonment trail, when the landlord has even stopped attempting to collect rents (often because angry tenants have begun rent-withholding, sometimes under legally established procedures available in some states), tenants have banded together, pooled their rent money and begun operating the building themselves.

This chapter will examine the various responses to housing abandonment that have evolved in two major cities which have suffered badly from it: Philadelphia, with its two- and three-story row houses, and New York, with its four- to six-story tenements and big apartment blocks.

The experiences of groups in these two cities will show that while there are no magic solutions, there *are* some productive ways to proceed. And as always, they will show that organization, preparedness, and militancy are among the most important ingredients in effectively fighting back.

## NEW YORK CITY'S EXPERIENCE

Walkaway property abandonment by landlords who feel they cannot make a profit on their buildings occurs in many cities, but New York City has by far the most abandoned buildings (although it does not have the high-

Marc Jahr / City Limits

est *rate* of abandonment among U.S. cities). So it is not surprising that one finds there the greatest number of programs and groups set up to deal with this problem, some of which perhaps can serve as models for other cities.

The tax delinquency/abandonment pattern became so common in New York several years ago that the city changed its laws to require foreclosure against a property after only a year of unpaid taxes, rather than having to wait three years, as had been the case. Waiting three years had meant the city was losing potential money and that salvageable, often occupied property was deteriorating rapidly. (Recently, however, the city has begun again to delay the takeover of tax-abandoned buildings, citing lack of funds to support direct city ownership and operation of such units.)

Through what are known as *in rem* proceeding — the legal process under which the city moves against a property delinquent in its taxes — New York has taken over large numbers of abandoned properties. As of September, 1979, the city owned some 11,700 residential buildings containing some 166,000 dwelling units — nearly 6% of the city's entire housing stock, and enough units to house the entire population of Buffalo — mostly acquired through *in rem* proceedings. This extensive municipal acquisition happened largely because of pressure from community groups seeking to prevent the loss of valuable housing resources.

The majority of the units in city ownership are vacant. But an estimated 4,100 buildings, containing 35,000 units and housing perhaps 125,000-150,000 persons, were occupied when acquired.

New York City, like other cities, traditionally has not wanted to hold on to the properties it acquired under tax foreclosure proceedings. It lacked housing management capabilities and rejected any notion that the city ought to be directly in the housing business (beyond the public housing operations of the housing authority, in most cities an entity legally distinct from the city government itself). So periodically it held auctions to sell city property to private investors — meaning speculators, for the most part. "Buy a Piece of New York City," urged one advertising announcement. "It's your opportunity to obtain, for as little as $100, the best possible hedge against inflation . . . Real Estate."

Needless to say, properties purchased at these auctions were not bought by people seeking to provide low-income housing or fix up the structures for those currently occupying them. Worse, if no purchasers were found, the city would simply demolish the structures and hold on to the vacant lots until some other use or purchaser was found. Community groups saw the auctions and demolitions as merely official participation in the disinvestment/displacement process. So demands began to grow for the city to cease the auctions, and cooperate instead in establishing programs that would keep the buildings in use as low-rent housing.

## THE COMMUNITY'S IDEA: CITY AS HOUSER OF LAST RESORT

Trying to find effective ways to combat abandonment, anti-displacement groups were pushing the city toward the role of "houser of last resort" — toward taking responsibility for ensuring decent living conditions when the private market abdicates this role. That is not a concept that New York, or any city, would gladly embrace, particularly at a time of fiscal

constraint. But forceful pressure from neighborhood residents won some important concessions in that direction, especially in the area of city-backed programs for community control, improvement, and eventual ownership of the disinvested housing.

A range of creative ownership and management alternatives has been introduced, some by community groups on their own initiative, others by the city government and neighborhood groups working in tandem. No less than

Marie Thurman / City Limits

**Under New York's Community Management Program, nearly two dozen established neighborhood organizations each manage several buildings in their areas.**

six official "alternative management programs" are currently being supported by the city, in most cases in response to activities spontaneously begun by community groups, which in turn were reacting to the poor management record of the city itself as owner of these properties. For a good handbook describing these programs, get a copy of *The Alternative Management Programs: A Housing Resource Guide* (1980), put out by the Community Service Society of New York, 105 E. 22nd Street, New York City, NY 10010.

Under these programs, management of about 8% of the city's *in rem* buildings has already been assigned to community organizations; to associations of tenants in a building (who can manage the building themselves or hire an outside manager responsible to them); to court-appointed receivers; or to private real estate firms with good management performance records. Since most of the *in rem* buildings are in need of major repairs, the management programs also build in rehabilitation loans and grants, using local and federal sources — Community Development Block Grant funds, federal Section 312 low-interest loans, emergency repair funds, etc. Some of them also contain training components aimed at developing tenants' capacity to manage, and eventually own, their buildings.

## TENANT INTERIM LEASE PROGRAM

Under this program, the city's agreement with an *in rem* building's tenant association requires that tenants undertake training in management skills, for which the city has contracted with the Urban Homesteading Assistance Board (UHAB), a city-wide, non-profit technical assistance organization. In this program the city also provides building condition surveys, cost estimates for repairs, and financing assistance in making needed repairs. Eventual sale of many of these buildings to their tenants is likely.

## RECEIVERSHIP PROGRAM

Under the receivership Program, court-appointed receivers are allowed to use rents to make needed improvements and repairs.

## COMMUNITY MANAGEMENT PROGRAM

Under the Community Management Program, nearly two dozen established neighborhood organizations each manage several buildings in their areas, and the city provides grants of anywhere from $2,500-$20,000 per unit for repairs and major systems replacement and rehabilitation (new roof, plumbing/electrical/heating systems, new windows, etc.)

## "MANAGEMENT IN PARTNERSHIP"

Under a variation of the Community Management Program known as the Management in Partnership Program, an experienced management group is paired with a local group that has expressed interest but has no experience or track record. The "senior partner" works with and trains the local group over a two-year period, moving toward eventual independent management by the "junior partner," and again upgrading and repair funds are made available to supplement rental income.

Under all these programs, the city's goal is to dispose of these buildings as soon as is feasible, rather than retaining them in public ownership.

## VOLUNTARY COOPS AND SWEAT EQUITY

Other important community and community-city approaches to recovering abandoned housing in New York City are "sweat-equity" (self-help) rehabilitation, and formation of tenant cooperatives. New York has a lot of housing coops, spanning the range from huge to tiny, and from those that combat displacement to those that cause it (the latter are featured in Chapter 5). A more general discussion of tenant-formed coops as an anti-displacement tactic appears in Chapter 16.

## VOLUNTARY COOPS

The use of cooperatives as an anti-displacement approach by low-income people in New York dates mainly from the early 1970s and is directly related to the disinvestment/abandonment phenomenon. As noted, in many occupied but landlord-abandoned buildings, tenants pool resources and rent money and provide essential services for themselves, in effect taking on the rights and responsibilities of the departed landlord. This decision-making and common work often set the stage for actual transfer of ownership to a legally formed cooperative association of the existing tenants.

One 1973 New York City survey identified 12 projects with 700 units that had been converted from rental to cooperative status in this manner, with an additional 25 projects containing 1,400 units in the process of conversion/rehabilitation, and another 100 projects with more than 6,000 units which had either received preliminary approval for public financing to convert or were actively seeking such approval.

"At the outset, there was no public program for coop conversion," according to Columbia University researcher Robert Kolodny. But tenant pressure pushed the city to adapt programs designed for other purposes to coop conversion. As Kolodny puts it, municipal action

. . . came primarily in response to the demands of tenants who had sustained their buildings for a period themselves but who needed the financing to upgrade the buildings and the leverage to gain permanent control of them at nominal cost. Virtually all of the city's various "receivership" and emergency repair programs for distressed housing and several municipal loan programs for rehabilitation were pressed into service, along with those federal programs that lent themselves to such efforts. Various rules, regulations, and routines had to be bent and adapted, and even then they did not always fit these unusual ventures.

There has been no systematic followup evaluation of these early 1970s New York City coop conversions. It is generally known that some fell on hard times after a few years. This is attributable in large part, however, to New York City's severe fiscal crisis and the Nixon Administration's 1973-74 total moratorium on all federal housing programs, which together pulled the rug out from under many of the programs essential to the success of the coop conversions. By the time the programs were restored many of the projects had already gone "belly up." But Kolodny concludes that, "While there is no comprehensive information on them, it is apparent that at least a few of the coops are doing well. All the basic indicators of effective management are there: low vacancy rates, limited turnover, long waiting lists, good building maintenance, and general resident satisfaction." Virtually all the ones that succeeded were groups of "working class and welfare-dependent minority households whose housing alternatives were narrowly limited."

Cooperative conversions clearly have an important place in the box of tools community groups should turn to in fighting disinvestment. In conjunction with demands on the city for quick tax foreclosures and resource assistance necessary to make conversions work, the process is well suited to recovering carefully considered specific buildings, depending on their condition and the will of those living in the building.

But coop conversions should not be oversold. As Kolodny notes, their success depends in most instances on outside support which the tenant group may not be able to control or depend on: technical assistance, rehab funds, tax abatements, etc. They are not *the* answer to displacement problems, they are only one of the answers.

## SWEAT EQUITY

The New York experience also sheds light on the value of self-help, or "sweat equity," rehabilitation, which attempts to reduce housing costs and salvage abandoned buildings by using community residents' own labor. The process may include hiring outside contractors for the more complex parts of a rehab job, but a parallel purpose of self-help rehab is training community residents in construction work so they can compete for private sector jobs in the building trades.

New York City has had a number of self-help housing projects (some supported by HUD demonstration grants), all involving major "gut" rehab of abandoned buildings. They have been combined with the cooperative ownership and self-management programs in order to reduce costs further and ensure resident control throughout. Under some of the earlier programs, labor was donated, and most of the participants lived on income from welfare payments, but later programs saw the need to provide wages for resi-

dent workers, often through CETA funding. Rehabilitation trainees sometimes were persons who planned to move into the completed units, sometimes other neighborhood residents. The Urban Homesteading Assistance Board has been an important source of support for this work, providing technical and organizing assistance, moral support and publicity, as well as working to make city programs more adaptable to the needs of the self-helpers.

Researcher Robert Kolodny has also ana-

lyzed New York's "Sweat Equity" experience, and has identified the following prerequisites for success: a committed neighborhood-level sponsoring group; a pool of labor willing to work at low wages in return for training and/or housing benefits; user-control throughout (including ownership and management); ability to acquire the building, often a shell, at a nominal cost; property tax exemption or abatement; subsidization of labor costs through grants; low-interest rehab loans; and

*City Life / Vida Urbana*, Boston

technical assistance. In short, getting everything together is no piece of cake.

In fact, Kolodny's analysis suggests real limits on sweat equity as an anti-displacement tool. In the first place, by mid-1978 only 13 projects with 171 total dwelling units had been completed and occupied. About an equal number were either in the midst of rehab or had received preliminary loan approvals. The job training aspects have run into problems, in part because of difficulties coordinating housing and CETA programs, in part because high unemployment in the construction industry has made it difficult to parlay self-help training experience into full-time construction work. Additionally, sweat equity takes considerably longer than conventional rehab, although the quality of the work has proven high. Also, the lower labor costs attributable to self-help have not reduced rehab costs all that much, and there still is the problem of inadequate resident incomes to meet ongoing housing costs. While sweat equity serves well in some areas and under some conditions, it is a problematic approach to solving disinvestment-caused displacement problems of lower income people. (For more information contact UHAB in New York, and look at Robert Kolodny's book, both cited in references at the end of this chapter).

## SOME PHILOSOPHICAL AND POLITICAL ISSUES RAISED BY THE NEW YORK EXPERIENCE

The various New York City programs and approaches described above result from a basically *temporary* involvement by the city government in the situation. Under pressure from neighborhood groups, the city simply uses its powers and resources to effect transfer of ownership or management control from the private owner to the tenants themselves, or to private nonprofit groups working to provide people with decent housing. Although some backup support continues, for the most part the initial grants and abatements are a short-term kiss-off, and the new tenant owners are left in the long run to the mercies of a market which has already proved it can't provide housing at their income levels. The real need, say many housing activists, is a restructuring of that market, with government taking a *permanent* housing role. Homefront, New York's Citywide Action Group Against Neighborhood Destruction and For Low-Rent Housing, criticizes the cooperative/sweat equity approach this way:

> By working through these programs, communities implicitly accept the proposition that tenants must solve their own housing problems. Government programs are only temporary measures to help them internalize the illusion that they can "compete" in the private market without help. . . . To the extent that they believe they must learn to survive in the market, they do not demand the replacement of an exploitative market by government-provided housing. . . . The most serious problem with these programs . . . is that they place most of the responsibility for housing improvement on individuals and local communities, which have the least resources, and get the government (which has the resources) off the hook.

The housing cost structure of the private profit-oriented economy is always a barrier to neighborhood groups. The debt service (mortgage principal and interest payments) on rehab loans for one sweat equity group on the Lower East Side consumes 65% of the rent roll. Neighborhood groups are put in the position of landlords — humane ones, but nonetheless landlords who must make decisions about property and tenants according to the dictates of the private market in which they operate. In one instance reported by Homefront, a homesteading group was forced to evict two of its laborers who had contributed thousands of sweat hours to renovate their building, because they couldn't keep up with the rents. As rising operating costs continue to outstrip tenants' incomes, the likelihood of such evictions increases. The programs, Homefront's report concludes, "are set up primarily to take buildings off the City's hands, and perhaps even more importantly, to develop the capability and philosophy of private ownership among community housing organizations. . . ." Homefront adds, moreover,

> . . . The professional management ideology which is representative of the City's cost-benefit accounting mentality has pushed community organizations into the role of enforcer of government interests. Community groups are often caught between the enormous pressure from the Housing Development Administration to complete an imposed deadline and the reality of working with unskilled workers needing careful instruction in acquiring construction skills. Since the communities have little control over the project, due to their reliance on HDA funding, they have been penalized for attempting to be considerate of tenants requiring special rent payment agreements.

Homefront's critique also finds that the programs are all very small, far too small to make a real dent in the city's housing problem.

> Government subsidies to non-profit tenant or community owners — tax-exempt mortgage financing, mortgage insurance, interest reduction, tax abatements and purchase price reduction — are similar to subsidies given to profit-making owners. By their very nature, these forms do not distinguish between profit and non-profit ownership. Consequently, pressure for government aid to housing results in massive aid to the private market as a whole, with the for-profit sector, because of its political clout, grabbing the lion's share.

Homefront — and others — suggest that broader changes are needed in the housing system, at the neighborhood, citywide, and national levels — aimed primarily at replacing profit-oriented, private-market decisions and allocations with social control over the financing, production, distribution and management of housing.

What Homefront urges is a more fundamental thrust that recognizes the private market's inability to provide decent housing for low-income people, and focuses energies on "a broad struggle to force the government to take over, own and maintain more housing, under tenant control. . . . Public ownership with tenant control is the only . . . way to get a significant amount of housing for low-income people, because it is the only serious alternative that does not rely on the private market and mortgaging, and keeps rents in line with income." The full Homefront report, *Housing Abandonment in New York City,* is available for $5.00 from Tony Schuman, 56 W. 22nd Street, New York, NY 10010.

## THE PHILADELPHIA STORY: HOMESTEADING ON HUD

In many cities, a lot of properties built or "rehabbed," usually in the shoddiest way under various HUD programs, have been abandoned. And since HUD provided the funds or guaranteed the loans, HUD then has become the owner of these derelicts. While, generally speaking, HUD gets back its owner-abandoned multi-family structures through mortgage default with tenants still in them, when it comes to single-family homes, the federal agency has amassed a truly huge pool of vacant, mostly run-down structures. In their boarded-up state, they are a blight — by the hundreds, even thousands — in St. Louis, Detroit, Baltimore, Newark, and many other cities. But as potentially useable housing, they are also a valuable community resource.

For its part, HUD generally has done nothing about these buildings — has just let them sit. Sometimes it has made efforts to sell them or fix them up, but "budget constraints" have always prevented any solid solutions.

In Philadelphia, people got tired of waiting. A group called the North Philadelphia Block Development Corporation began what they called the "Walk-In Urban Homesteading Program" — inspired, bold direct action to put tenants back into some of HUD's idle houses in that city. They were led by Milton Street, a first-rate organizer, later elected to the Pennsylvania State Assembly, and then State Senate, by his North Philadelphia district.

### "We have to get angry. You got to act a little crazy to put a stop to this."

Milton Street, quoted in *North City Free Press,* Dec. 14, 1977

At the time, there were 40,000 abandoned buildings in Philadelphia, many of them HUD's. In Black North Central Philadelphia alone, HUD owned some 5,000 vacant residences.

Beginning in April, 1977, Milton Street began organizing people to use his "passkey" — a pair of metal clippers — to get in and occupy buildings. The takeovers were usually single-family homes. Street's organization screened potential occupiers, and those chosen signed an informal agreement to fix up the buildings and make them habitable. People moved in and immediately began to improve their homes.

Needless to say, the outcry from public officials was loud and anguished. They were concerned about "ownership rights" and "property rights" and they didn't want federal and local government agencies to look bad. "When a person takes the law into his own hands and commits such illegal acts," said Philadelphia's City Council President George Schwartz, "then this is the beginning of anarchy." And Patricia Harris, HUD Secretary at the time, visiting Philadelphia for some ribbon cutting ceremonies, declared that Milton Street's people "have no greater right to take a vacant house than a vacant auto." Harris charged that the walk-in homesteaders were "no better than shoplifters, who grab a piece of merchandise off the shelf, claiming it should not be left unused." HUD threatened, and in several cases carried out, evictions of some of the families occupying the unused homes.

But official outrage met a surprising amount of hostility from the public, and the press as well. A Philadelphia *Daily News* editorial from January 6, 1978, slammed back at Secretary Harris' denouncement of the homesteaders:

HUD is a slumlord. Only HUD doesn't want to be bothered with tenants. Homes lie unoccupied and gradually become useless. People need housing. That is supposed to be HUD's business, putting people into homes instead of keeping them out.

HUD should do something about these homes it owns. If it cannot, it must find a way to get homes into the hands of private owners whose pride can help arrest the slide of our neighborhoods.

Mrs. Harris compares Street and his squatters to shoplifters. She is missing the point altogether, perhaps on purpose. Stores do not abandon their merchandise. They try to sell it. HUD contentedly sits back and does nothing at all, feeling that references to the legalisms involved will make the problem go away. It won't, even if Mrs. Harris prattles on forever about "whether we're going to deal with property in a lawful way . . . or let anyone walk in off the street and say, 'this is mine.'"

HUD's job is to provide housing for poor people and to keep the cities from further decline. That job is not being done. . . .

The public was getting a good education in the ironies, inconsistencies and illogic of how the system operates. Street's comment on Secretary Harris' comparison of vacant houses to vacant automobiles went as follows: "On the legal issue, we say that abandoned cars can be towed away and destroyed and we don't worry about owners. Then, I say, let's use the same approach on abandoned houses, but save the house, the neighborhood, and a family."

HUD fought back. Trying to soften the story of the eviction of some homesteaders, a Department spokesman told a Philadelphia *Bulletin* reporter that "evicted squatters are offered public housing." But a feature article on one of the evicted homesteaders from the same day's Philadelphia *Tribune*, the major paper of the city's Black community, reported ironically: "Ms. Jones [one of the evicted persons] explained that she had moved from the Fairhill [public housing] project, 11th and Columbia Avenue, out of fear that something would happen to her children. 'I couldn't sleep at night because I was scared that someone would break into my house,' she said."

"When they evicted the families," said Milton Street in another *Tribune* article, "they paid security guards to sleep in the houses overnight, and that just doesn't make any sense. They throw out people who need the houses desperately, and then they pay security guards to live in them. It's crazy, I tell you, just plain crazy."

The Philadelphia *Bulletin's* story on the eviction said: "According to Mrs. Sabree's neighbors, the house she and her family took over was in bad disrepair before the woman

moved in and fixed it up. It was the only abandoned house on a block of neat and well-kept houses."

A Philadelphia *Daily News* editorial (August 8, 1977), headed "Squatters' Rights" asserted:

Milton Street seems to be an expert at what no other government agency — city or federal — is very good at. And he is doing it without miles of red tape, bureaucratic forms, administrators, inspectors, lawyers and all the other things that make bureaucracy the monster it is.

He is putting people who need homes into houses that have stood vacant for far too long . . . Rather than doing battle with Street, the Rizzo administration and HUD should get behind the man and help him . . . We've heard a lot from City Hall and Washington bureaucrats and politicians about how much they want to provide housing for the poor. Here's a chance to see if they really mean it.

Meanwhile, in the quiet space behind the publicity war, HUD was beginning to compromise and surrender. The *Daily News* of February 5, 1979, noted that within 18

**"Words can't explain how I feel. We have plenty of room. We're happy. If people were allowed to get a home to fix-up, something that's theirs, there wouldn't be so much vandalism. I've told Mr. Street, anytime they need me, just call. I'll be there. Housing is the main issue for everyone and I won't forget how it was before."**

Fredenia A., whose family, along with some 100 others, received title to abandoned houses they illegally entered in the summer of 1977 as part of State Rep. Milton Street's 'walk-in homesteading program,' quoted in the *Philadelphia Daily News*

months of the supposed outbreak of "anarchy" in the city, "some squatters have quietly received titles to the homes they broke into." In fact, half of the 200 walk-in homesteader families got legal ownership of their new houses when HUD deeded them over through the city's Gift Properties Program (a program enabling owners of tax-delinquent properties to "donate" them to the city, in exchange for cancellation of the debt and some tax benefits). Fifty more homesteader families received conventional or FHA mortgages. Another 25 stayed in their houses under a rental agreement with HUD. Ten were evicted and decided not to return. And the remaining 15 cases dragged on in the courts.

The positive side of the picture was clear to anyone who looked. Needy households were in homes which HUD had been letting sit, and were fixing them up. The city was getting property taxes that HUD had not been paying. Neighborhoods were having eyesores and blighting influences removed. One of the women given title to her home by HUD was quoted in the *Daily News* as follows: "Words can't explain how I feel. We have plenty of room. We're happy. If people were allowed to get a home to fix up, something that's theirs, there wouldn't be so much vandalism. I've told Mr. Street, anytime they need me, just call. I'll be there. Housing is the main issue for everyone and I won't forget how it was before."

The irony of the whole affair is that a 1977 HUD study had already found that a giveaway policy would make sense in budgetary terms. The Philadelphia region led the nation in amount of HUD money lost by retaining abandoned houses, and according to a Philadelphia newspaper report on the study, "The numbers illustrate that taking a 100 percent loss by giving properties away at the time of acquisition would have compared favorably with the actual losses realized by holding the properties for resale."

The walk-in homesteaders dented HUD policy more than they reshaped it. But in Philadelphia city affairs, their brilliant initiative had effects far larger than the occupation of homes. Their action dramatized the city's housing crisis as nothing else in recent years had, and, together with other protest actions, brought about far-reaching changes, particularly in how the city was spending its Community Development funds. As the September 13, 1977 Philadelphia *Evening Bulletin* described it:

> The Rizzo Administration is planning to invest more than $2 million in federal and state money this year in a new housing program for the western area of North Philadelphia, City Hall sources said. The move is significant because earlier this year the city had intended minimal investment there, concentrating most of its housing money in six other neighborhoods. But the summer-long tactics of community activist Milton Street, breaking into and occupying vacant homes there, and political pressure by black members of City Council, have reportedly changed City Hall thinking.

A *Bulletin* story a few days later noted that, "Some high officials in the Rizzo Administration have conceded privately that Street was 'galvanizing city attention' on the problem of vacant houses."

The way such direct action is best carried out will vary from city to city, depending on the neighborhood situation, local politics, and many other factors. (Those who want to contact Milton Street for more information can write him at the State House, Harrisburg, PA 17102). But some of the more important lessons from the Philadelphia experience include these:

• Walk-in homesteading leaders need to make sure that the homes their campaign occupies are not already sold to another community family: mistakes on this issue can pit poor against the poor. HUD sometimes used this as a reason to reject the idea of walk-in homesteading altogether, even though the vast majority of the homes occupied were not already sold. At one point in negotiations with Street HUD gave the group a list of 38 homes in which it could place people, but included some that already had been sold. HUD claimed it was an error; others claimed it was an intentional ploy on the part of the agency to create problems for Street's group.

• It is important to establish good prior relations with neighborhood groups in the area where homesteaders are moving into abandoned homes. When the HUD list of 38 homes showed several in the Germantown area, Street met with the Southwest Germantown Association to explain the program and coordinate the two groups' activities. Following that meeting, the Association voted to support the move-ins.

• Wherever possible, block-wide rather than individual takeovers are more effective. Street felt such an approach, had it been possible, would have given strength both to the movement and to the neighborhoods. He also put forth the proposal that the government should establish neighborhood building supply depots to provide materials, technical assistance and other aids for the homesteaders.

• Walk-in homesteader campaigns should develop the capacity to coordinate as much as possible with related city functions, such as Philadelphia's Department of Licenses and Inspections, which tears down an average of 15 abandoned homes each week (at a cost of

$5,000 per home), and other city efforts such as the Gift Properties Program and the official Homesteading Program.

• Direct actions such as walk-in urban homesteading are most successful when bolstered by parallel actions and linked with other goals. Street's organization, for instance, dramatized its demands by picketing HUD's Washington headquarters, which led to an immediate meeting with Secretary Harris, and by sitting in at HUD's regional office in downtown Philadelphia. In November, 1978, responding to a HUD report which charged that the city's $63 million annual CD allocation was being spent in racially discriminatory ways, protesters blocked city bus and trolley lines at rush hour to demand further reallocation of city Community Development funds to nonwhite and lower-income areas. In late 1978, some 3,000 persons marched to the Gallery, a big new downtown shopping mall, to begin a boycott aimed at dramatizing the distorted priorities in use of federal urban aid funds. This fancy shopping complex had received $28 million in federal and local construction aid, while ghetto areas were starved for federal and local funds. Furthermore, in a city with a 44% Black population, only 2% of the Gallery's businesses were Black-owned.

But the most important lesson of all is that, under proper conditions, direct building takeovers are a highly useful strategy to combat disinvestment-related displacement. As a front-page story in the Sunday New York *Times* concluded: "Both city and federal officials concede that while it is illegal — breaking and entering and squatting — Mr. Street's way seems to work. It is preventing the sacking of abandoned housing that usually follows soon after the last tenant leaves."

Ben Achtenberg / Plainsong Productions

It's not a tactic for timid people. Most of the 200 persons who broke in and stayed during 1977 and 1978 were arrested at least once, then moved right back in. But the potential in such action for inspiring people, far and near, is great. The *Bulletin* reported that Street's venture "has attracted not only the attention of local and federal officials but social reformers across the nation. He has received inquiries about this form of urban homesteading from activists in Chicago, Washington, Houston and the West Coast."

Closer to home, walk-in homesteaders affiliated with the Puerto Rican Alliance began taking over abandoned homes in Philadelphia's Hunting Park section in the Spring of 1980. When HUD threatened to evict them, Alliance members sat in at Carter-Mondale

headquarters in Philadelphia to protest the eviction plan. North Philadelphia Congressman William Gray 3rd worked out an agreement whereby the sit-inners left when HUD announced it would back off from the scheduled eviction date, and that HUD's General Counsel would come to Philadelphia before the end of the week to negotiate a solution to the problem. The evictions, scheduled for May, were never carried out, and as of this writing the Puerto Rican Alliance is about to sign an agreement with HUD giving the formerly abandoned homes to their present occupants — a carbon copy of the victory won by Milton Street's group.

*Direct action — carefully conceived, planned, and implemented — is often a community's most useful tool.*

## REFERENCES

### NEW YORK'S PROGRAMS

*The Alternative Management Programs: A Housing Resource Guide* (1980), a description of New York City's experiments with community-based restoration of abandoned housing, is available for $1.50 from the Community Service Society of New York, 105 E. 22nd St., New York, NY 10010.

For information on management training in New York's resident-run abandoned housing reclamation projects, contact the Urban Homesteading Assistance Board, 1047 Amsterdam Ave., New York, NY 10025. UHAB is one of the most experienced community-oriented organizations in the country dealing with housing rehabilitation, self-help techniques and housing management, and is a valuable source of other information as well. UHAB also is involved in providing technical assistance to several other cities, including Hartford and Oakland, as part of a HUD demonstration project in multi-family homesteading.

*Multi-Family Housing: Treating the Existing Stock,* by Robert Kolodny (1981), an analytical report on experiments with reclamation of abandoned housing in New York, is available from the National Association of Housing and Redevelopment Officials, 2600 Virginia Ave. NW, Washington, DC 20037.

*Housing Abandonment in New York City* (1977), Homefront's 139-page analysis of the issues, focused on New York but applicable in many ways to other localities as well, is available for $5.00 from Tony Schuman, 56 W. 22nd St., New York, NY 10010.

### GENERAL REFERENCES

*Housing by People: Towards Autonomy in Building Environments,* by John Turner (Pantheon, 1977), and *Freedom to Build: Dweller Control of the Housing Process,* edited by John Turner and Robert Fichter (Macmillan, 1972), good general references on the subject, are available at many libraries or can be ordered by bookstores.

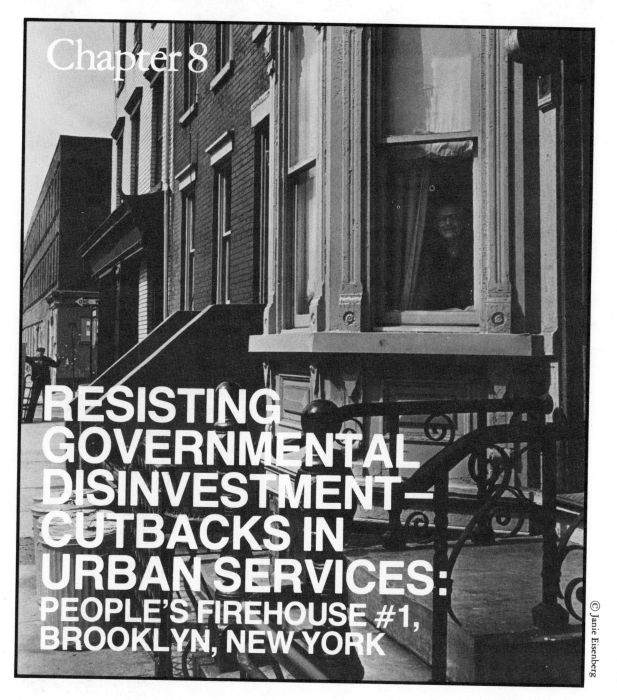

# Chapter 8

# RESISTING GOVERNMENTAL DISINVESTMENT— CUTBACKS IN URBAN SERVICES: PEOPLE'S FIREHOUSE #1, BROOKLYN, NEW YORK

© Janie Eisenberg

The previous chapter dealt with disinvestment by landlords and other forms of private market housing abandonment. But there is a parallel governmental type of disinvestment — often it goes right along with the private kind — that is, in its own way, even more frightening and dangerous. It shows up in urbanologists' terms such as "planned shrinkage" and "triage," a word which means, roughly, letting the worst-off die. Depending on the level of government involved, the concept can apply to a neighborhood, a city, even a whole region. But the core of the idea at all levels of application is this: *getting poor and non-white people out of central city and "impacted" areas as a means of relieving the urban fiscal crisis.*

It is an approach that signals government's admission of failure in the so-called "war on poverty." Now, the solution being proposed is not that we eliminate poverty, but instead that we eliminate concentrations of poor people within our cities by moving them out and around — rearranging the population rather than bringing about fundamental and needed changes. Under this approach there'll be all kinds of vacant land and structures to use for restoring the city's economic health: to provide jobs, housing, and services, that is, for the upper-income people who — as this policy would have it — ought to be replacing the city's poor. They pay more taxes, you see.

Probably the best way to describe the idea is to let some of its leading advocates speak up: First, Roger Starr (formerly New York City's Housing and Development Administrator, now an editorial writer for the New York *Times.*) In a 1976 article for the New York *Times* magazine, entitled "Making New York Smaller," Starr had this to say:

If the city is to survive with a smaller population, the population must be encouraged to concentrate itself in the sections that remain alive. This sort of internal resettlement . . . must be encouraged. . . . The stretches of empty blocks may then be knocked down, services can be stopped, subway stations closed, and the land left to lie fallow until a change in economic and demographic assumptions makes the land useful once again . . . Essentially, planned shrinkage is a recognition that the golden door to full participation in American life and the American economy is no longer to be found in New York. . . . We could simply accept the fact that the city's population is going to shrink, and we could cut back on city services accordingly, realizing considerable savings in the process.

The "encouragement" Starr speaks of is the focus of this chapter. William Baer, in an article titled "On the Death of Cities" (in *The Public Interest*, a leading journal for those espousing the anti-poor, anti-minority "planned shrinkage" ideology), puts it this way.

Financial ill health has forced cities across the U.S. to rid themselves of their least essential functions and cut back severely on more basic services so that the civic corpus might be saved. Decisions thus are being made that treat certain public functions as expendable, others not. The focus of triage in these cases is on paring away the least efficient services.

Phrases like "efficiency," "civic corpus," and "a change in economic and demographic assumptions" are thrown around as if they were scientific concepts on which everyone agrees. In reality they express mainly the perspective, values, and interests of the kinds of people who put forth such proposals. In his critique of such ideas, Queens College economist William Tabb points out that:

The fiscal crisis is caused by decisions based on private profit calculations and the failure of society through the political process to place social needs ahead of the imperatives of the market. . . . American social scientists are fond of denying that there is such a thing as class struggle. In the case of the New York fiscal crisis, they speak in value-neutral

terms of increasing efficiency. . . . Class conflict explains why crisis exists, why those in power choose the scapegoats they do, why they seek the "solutions" they do. Alternative answers that do not require the poor and the workers to bear the burden of the crisis must begin with an analysis that does not blame them for the existence of the crisis.

More recently, the Report of the President's Commission for a National Agenda for the Eighties made big headlines by proposing a large-scale, national version of triage, calling for reduced federal aid to the older cities of the Northeast and Midwest in favor of encouraging population shifts to the Sunbelt. In the Report's own words: "This transformation of older cities from centers of manufacturing and production to centers of services and consumption will require that their 'health' be defined at new, and often lower, levels of population and employment." The Commission calls for "vigorous government programs of assisted migration" as "older industrial cities . . . become scaled-down residential centers for households, defined by a narrower range of age, composition and income differences." In other words, bye-bye to poor people, large families, old folks, racial minorities.

Lest this be regarded as "just another government report," consigned to the shelves,

a page 2 story from the February 23, 1981 Washington *Post,* headlined "Administration Moves Abandon Ailing Northeast and Midwest Cities," has this to say:

The Reagan administration is moving swiftly to embrace the philosophy of a controversial presidential commission report issued last month that said national policy should not be designed to protect the declining economies of the Northeast and Midwest. . . .

In its first month, the Reagan administration has implicitly adopted that philosophy through its budget, tax and regulatory actions. By shrinking the role of the federal government and putting more reliance on the natural forces at work in the economy, the Reagan program is providing additional stimulation to the already booming Sun Belt while reducing or eliminating programs that have cushioned the economic decline in the industrial heartland. . . .

● Reagan's proposed budget cuts — from the elimination of public service jobs to the cap on Medicaid — will fall most heavily on northern states and cities, which have become increasingly dependent on federal grants.

● The administration's proposed increases in defense spending will be distributed more to the South and West, where there is a greater concentration of military bases and aerospace and electronics firms, than in the North and Midwest.

● The action to decontrol oil prices and the planned deregulation of natural gas will further stimulate the economies of the energy producing regions and drain more money away from energy consuming states.

Dan Stern / City Limits

• A commitment by Interior Secretary James G. Watt to develop additional water projects in the West to support the growing population will provide federal subsidies for one of the Sun Belt's most critical long-range problems, even during a time of budget austerity nationally.

• The administration's proposed changes in unemployment insurance and trade adjustment assistance, programs that now are greatly beneficial to northern states whose economies were built on basic industries like autos and steel, will force workers to accept new jobs more rapidly and might encourage migration to economically healthy regions of the country. . . .

Although Reagan's program provides no explicit endorsement of this philosophy, nor specific subsidy programs to encourage migration, his budget cuts will put additional strain on already weak regional economies, and the reduced aid to unemployed workers, the more stringent eligibility requirements for extended unemployment insurance and the new requirement that workers not be allowed to wait for jobs in their skills will place pressure on workers to find jobs—any jobs—more quickly, wherever they are.

## JOB DISPLACEMENT AND HOUSING DISPLACEMENT

The link between housing and employment is strong. A job paying decent wages is the only way, apart from presently inadequate government subsidy programs, that people can afford to live and stay in decent housing in neighborhoods of their choice. Housing displacement can lead to job displacement, if people are forced to move out of transportation range of their current employment. And job displacement can lead to housing displacement when plant closings and other employment cutbacks make it impossible or unwise for people to continue living in a given neighborhood, city, or even region. As several of the examples presented in this guidebook show, more far-sighted community groups include employment demands and programs along

with housing demands and programs. (See, for example, the material on Boston's Inquilinos Boricuas en Acción, pages 195-198; the resolution of the tourist hotel invasion into San Francisco's Tenderloin, page 194; and the construction jobs won by residents of the Marion Gardens public housing project in Jersey City, pages 122-127.)

While detailed discussion of the jobs issue is beyond the scope of this manual, we have listed several references at the end of this chapter for community groups dealing with this problem.

## LOCAL APPLICATIONS OF "PLANNED SHRINKAGE"

Withdrawal of municipal services is proving a key element in the application of "planned shrinkage" concepts. Many communities have found that a quick way for city officials to start depopulating an area chosen for civic abandonment, or for transformation to some "higher and better use," is to pull the plug on basic things such as fire and police protection, schools, garbage pickup, street cleaning and repairs — services that can make the difference between a healthy, safe, satisfying neighborhood and one that provides little to nothing in the way of basic community needs. As municipal support erodes people begin to move out "naturally." Presto: without having to use messy eminent domain powers or costly land acquisition, an entire area can be made "ripe for redevelopment." As a report by the Anti-Displacement Committee of Chicago's Heart of Uptown Coalition put it: "The city [works] hand-in-hand with property owners and developers to cut back health services, remove jobs from the community, and eliminate educational and recreational programs for children.

Take away the institutions and programs people depend on for health, housing, education and employment, and people tend to grow weak, give up, leave the city or literally die."

## PEOPLE'S FIREHOUSE: A BROOKLYN NEIGHBORHOOD FIGHTS BACK

One of the most basic of all city services, of course, is fire protection. In older neighborhoods particularly, with poor wiring and defective heating systems, fires have a greater chance of occurring. In crowded areas, particularly those with lots of old-time frame construction, fires spread more rapidly. And when "arson for profit" is rampant — in areas where landlords are taking the final steps to milk their properties — the need for good fire protection is all the more pressing.

The Northside section of Brooklyn fits most of those categories. It is a neighborhood of 12,000 people, part of the larger Williamsburg area. Some 60% of the housing stock in this densely populated area is wood frame construction with common walls to the adjacent structures. Most of the housing is so-called "old law tenements" built around the turn of the century; 40% of the housing was officially labelled as "deteriorating" or "dilapidated" in the 1970 Census. The neighborhood is zoned for mixed industrial and residential, and scattered throughout are true combustion horrors such as paint and chemical factories, lumber yards, and liquified natural gas tanks. Under the streets runs a jet fuel pipeline servicing JFK Airport. The population is three-fifths elderly, a large proportion of whom live above the ground floor. It's clearly a neighborhood for which good fire protection services are crucial.

But Northside is also an area that the city would like to use for new industrial development. So it was no accident that city service cutbacks during the 1970s "fiscal crisis" hit this neighborhood especially hard. The police precinct station was closed down in 1970. Sanitation services were cut by 50%. A well-baby clinic was shut down in 1975, and the

hard. To allow closing of the local fire station would be to sign the neighborhood's death warrant.

They met, they talked, they planned. And then they acted. On November 21, 1975, the day before the scheduled closing, some 200 neighborhood residents came down to the firehouse and held its men and engines hostage.

But five days later the city convinced the judge to dissolve his order. And then on Thanksgiving evening the city once again attempted to remove the fire engine and close the building. Paul Revere-like, neighborhood residents by the hundreds were summoned to surround their fire equipment, and they did — for 16 months — until the city finally agreed to restore these vital services in two stages. What happened in the intervening months, and thereafter, is a good example of highly effective community organizing, community self-protection, and how to move organizationally from one vital issue to an entire set of interrelated concerns.

During the period of occupation, residents and organizers ran the former quarters of Engine 212 as a "People's Firehouse," responding to fires in their own vehicles, collecting data, building up information with which to fight the city and prove that the decision to close 212 was wrong. They did research on Fire Department policy decisions, and studied the area's fire protection system, including hydrants and alarm boxes. And they used the firehouse building as a community service center, with a summer lunch program.

On the immediate issue of fire protection services, the neighborhood reluctantly agreed to a compromise city proposal to reopen the station on a scaled-down basis, as a so-called "utility unit," to respond only to a limited number of call boxes. But Northside kept the pressure on. From a store front opposite the station, activists monitored its performance carefully. They showed that because it was responsible for so limited a number of call boxes it was idle 98% of the time, that it was providing no service at all to the broader Northside community, that it was not even

© Janie Eisenberg

nearby Greenpoint Hospital was also closed in 1975, except for the emergency room. That same year the city announced it was closing Engine Company #212, located for 114 years in Northside — the last straw. The community realized it had to fight this one and fight it

The seizure lasted just a day, ending when the city agreed to cancel the closing for five days to allow the residents time to institute legal proceedings.

In court, Northside advocates obtained a temporary restraining order against the city.

given responsibility for such important back-up services as insuring that neighborhood hydrants were in working order: of the 300 hydrants in the area, fully 90 were either out of service or defective.

Beyond this fact-gathering and monitoring, the community kept up a barrage of protest actions: they held demonstrations at City Hall and Gracie Mansion (the mayor's official residence), visited the homes of the Fire Commissioner and Deputy Mayor, 70 strong, leafletted the 1976 Democratic Convention at Madison Square Garden, and burned effigies

of leading political figures from the firehouse flagpole. Their most dramatic protest gesture came the day after a fire destroyed three buildings a block and a half from the firehouse when three broken hydrants prevented fire-fighters from extinguishing the blaze promptly. A contingent of neighborhood residents, mainly older people, blocked morning rush hour traffic on the Brooklyn-Queens Expressway, a road built in the 1950s which divided the neighborhood in half and took some 2000 homes. They caused a monster traffic jam extending some 18 miles in both directions.

The city finally gave in. On June 17, 1978, newly elected mayor Edward Koch and other city officials formally reopened Engine Company #212 at its full prior service level. But in honor of the long struggle — and as a warning to the city — the strong community support organization which grew out of the hard fight kept the name "People's Firehouse."

The victory had been a costly one. In the 2½ years Engine Company #212 was closed, ten people died in fires in the officially disinvested neighborhood. But out of the struggle came an organization and set of programs that might just prevent Northside from becoming part of the city's shrinkage plan. People's Firehouse, Inc., is now an organization with a full time staff of 24 and dozens of volunteers, and an annual operating budget of some $100,000 ($1 million, if rehab moneys for the city-owned buildings they manage are counted).

Among the neighborhood services People's Firehouse now provides are:

**Neighborhood commercial revitalization:** facade renovation has been carried out on 33 buildings in two blocks of Bedford Avenue, the neighborhood's major commercial street.

**Fire prevention and anti-arson work:** hydrants are regularly monitored to make sure they are functioning; free smoke detectors are being placed in all city-owned structures and in homes where older people live; and research on arson prediction systems is being pursued — including computerized information data on tax arrears, building code violations, multiple history of fires and other predictors of arson. People's Firehouse, Inc. now is also making its fire prevention and anti-arson technical assistance services available to other communities through grants from ACTION and the city's Community Development Agency.

© Janie Eisenberg

77

**Housing preservation and rehab:** People's Firehouse is rehabbing six buildings, containing 72 units, under the Section 8 substantial rehab program. It manages eleven city-owned buildings, with 103 units. And it administers the receivership program (see Chapter 7) for five buildings the city has taken over under its so-called "7A Program." It also runs a landlord counseling service for building owners with maintenance and management problems they want to solve, a tenant counseling service for residents of buildings whose landlords are not interested in finding solutions for their maintenance and management problems, and a "tool lending library," funded by a bank, to assist self-helpers.

Beyond these services, People's Firehouse produces a widely read monthly neighborhood newsletter, educational materials on fire prevention and housing rehab in Polish, Italian, Spanish and English — the major languages in this multi-ethnic community, runs a lunch program, and serves as overall ombudsman for complaints about city services.

Lest a falsely optimistic picture be given, it should be realized that the battle to save Northside is not yet won. Other than the firehouse, the rest of the city services the neighborhood lost in the 1970s have not yet been restored. Pressure on areas of this type to "fold up and die" is still strong, coming from both the city and the private sector. The very research done around the closing of Engine Company #212 showed the kinds of forces that communities like this are up against: the 33 firefighting units the city closed in the 1972-75 period, for example, were primarily in working-class and minority areas. Since these neighborhoods already had an above average rate of fires and fire deaths, the plan

behind these closings could not have been to focus services where they are most needed. Instead, it seems almost certain that the city's actions trace back to analyses and recommendations by the Rand Institute in studies funded by HUD and — surprise! — the City of New York, analyses and recommendations that embody the "planned shrinkage" strategy.

As this chapter has tried to suggest, it is important to look at neighborhood displacement as part of a broader process of planned change in cities and regions. It isn't just housing abandonment. Withdrawal of vital community services may be the way in which an existing neighborhood is undermined and changed. The case of People's Firehouse in Brooklyn shows how a determined community can combat such municipal disinvestment, and how the fight can be expanded into a comprehensive neighborhood preservation strategy. And the ripple effects are already moving out from Brooklyn: in response to public service cutbacks mandated by Massachusetts' Proposition 2½ (see page 98). People's Firehouses #2-6 have recently been established in Salem, Somerville, Beverly, Malden and two Boston neighborhoods, all of which were scheduled for fire station closings. The first of these, in Boston's Charlestown area, received help from their Brooklyn predecessors, when two of the leaders from People's Firehouse #1 flew up to show a film documentary on their occupation and give "how to do it" advice.

# REFERENCES

## FISCAL CRISIS

Two recent films are useful aids in helping communities understand the fiscal crisis of cities. *Tighten Your Belts, Bite The Bullet* (48 minutes, color) focuses on Cleveland and New York City and shows the role the banks have played in producing layoffs of city workers and cutbacks in vital services. *Taking Back Detroit* (55 minutes, color) focuses on how several progressive elected city officials respond to that city's economic problems. Both are available from Icarus Films, 200 Park Ave. S., Rm. 1319, New York, NY 10003.

## JOB DISPLACEMENT

A useful general study is the book *Economic Democracy,* by Martin Carnoy and Derek Shearer (M.E. Sharpe, 1980), available through bookstores and libraries.

"Plant Closings: Fight Back" (1980) is a 31-page pamphlet published by the Citizens Labor Committee on Plant Closings, available from NAM, 3244 N. Clark, Chicago, IL 60657 for $1.50. The CLCPC is located at 3600 Wilshire Blvd., Suite 2200, Los Angeles, CA 90010.

*A Guide for Communities Facing Major Layoffs or Plant Shutdowns* (1980) is available from the Employment and Training Administration, U.S. Dept. of Labor, Washington, D.C.

*Employee Ownership in Plant Shutdowns: Prospects for Employment Stability* (1979), by Robert Stern, K. Haydn Wood and Tove Helland Hammer, is available for $4 from the W.E. Upjohn Institute for Unemployment Research, 300 S. Westnedge Ave., Kalamazoo, MI 49007.

Barry Bluestone and Bennett Harrison, *Corporate Flight: The Causes and Consequences of Economic Dislocation* (32 pages, 1980), $3.95.

*Plant Closings: Resources for Public Officials and Community Leaders* (85 pages, 1979), $4.95.

*Plant Closings Briefing Book: Issues, Politics and Legislation* (70 pages, 1980), $4.95.

All three of the above publications are available from the Conference on Alternative State and Local Policies, 2000 Florida Ave. NW, Washington, D.C. 20009.

## PEOPLE'S FIREHOUSE

For more information on the People's Firehouse struggle, outcome, and future, contact their storefront, 125 Wythe Ave., Brooklyn, NY 11211, (212) 384-9344, or their Housing and Community Development Office, 113 Berry St., Brooklyn, NY 11211.

"People's Firehouse #1," a 25-minute award-winning color documentary film, is available through Third World Newsreel, 160 Fifth Ave., Suite 911, New York, NY 10010. The rental charge is $50.

"The People's Fire House Fact Sheet," and "The Politics of Fire Protection and What This Means to the Survival of Communities in New York City," (1977), short papers by Firehouse Administrator Fred Ringler, are available free from the Workshop in Political Theory and Policy Analysis, Indiana University, 814 E. 3rd St., Bloomington, IN 47401.

# Chapter 9

# PROTECTING TENANTS:
## RENT/EVICTION CONTROLS AND OTHER LAW REFORMS

enants are most vulnerable to displacement: they are underprotected by the law, and the housing market increasingly ignores their needs. The wildly escalating price of single-family housing guarantees that today's renters (about a third of the nation's households, with much higher proportions in most cities) are in a permanent tenant class. And it is a class that can only grow. Deterioration, abandonment, demolition, and condo/coop conversions are trimming away rental housing stock faster than new construction supplies it. Figures developed by the National Low-Income Housing Coalition indicate that a half million housing units are lost to the lower income housing stock each year through these causes and

through inflation. Amidst the growing shortage, speculators shift as many units as they can toward the higher-income sector where the big profits are, further squeezing the low- and middle-income population in the process.

Nationally, by 1977, almost half of America's renters were paying more than one-fourth of their income for rent. While this has generally been the accepted guideline as the "proper" proportion of income households should devote to housing, it is clear that millions of U.S. families have incomes so low that they cannot take care of their other basic needs if they do in fact use 25% of their income for housing. University of Massachusetts housing economist Michael Stone has developed the concept of "shelter poverty," which takes the

minimum budgets published by the U.S. Bureau of Labor Statistics and adds up all the *non-shelter* expenditures required; comparing these with actual family income, he asks how much money is left over for housing, if the household spends all the government says it needs to spend for a minimum level of living with respect to other items (food, medical care, clothing, transportation, etc.) Using 1976 data, Stone found that for a family of four with income less than $7500 a year, *not a penny* can be spent for housing, if the family is to be able to afford these minimum non-shelter living standards. Only at about the $12,500 a year income level can the four-person household really "afford" to devote 25% of its income for shelter. So much for the standard

yardstick. Moreover, in almost all local rental housing markets, rents are rising faster than tenants' incomes. And as those incomes fall further behind inflation, the bottom layer of oppressed renters swells, until they arrive at the miserable and militant state of the squatters described in Chapter 7.

Short of major reforms in the national housing system, and sudden boosts in rental housing production—neither of which looks likely soon — legal controls on rent increases and evictions are about the strongest anti-displacement weapons tenants have. Growing tenant desperation and militancy are bringing about more widespread enactment of local controls of various sorts. Due to political reasons discussed in greater detail in later parts of this chapter, effective state and federal controls are much less likely.

This chapter examines some of the major features and flaws of rent and eviction controls in use around the country, and other aspects of landlord-tenant law reform as well.

## COMPREHENSIVENESS IS THE KEY

Early experiments with rent control have established that property owners will adopt a number of alternative, displacement-causing strategies to escape any attempt to regulate their profits. Condominium conversions, for instance. Falsified causes for eviction. Even demolition of housing when newly-constructed units are exempt (as they frequently are) from controls.

So a "package" of interlocked controls is the most effective strategy. In 1979, tenant pressure in Santa Monica, California, forced adoption of a comprehensive ballot initiative creating an elected board to regulate rents, evictions, condo conversions and demolitions. The board's activities have cut effectively into displacement. (See Santa Monica references in Chapter 5, or write the Santa Monica Rent Control Board, 1685 Main Street, Santa Monica, CA 90401.)

In terms of models, however, the most complete approach yet attempted to protect tenants was Proposition R, a 1979 legislative initiative by a coalition of housing-concerned organizations called San Franciscans for Affordable Housing.

Proposition R offered an ordinance (see Appendix B for full text) which laid out a comprehensive local approach to meeting the city's housing needs. The measure contained controls over rent increases, demolitions, and conversion of rental units into condominiums; required "just cause" for eviction of tenants from rent controlled units; controlled housing speculation through specific anti-speculative provisions in the rent control mechanism; and provided mechanisms for increasing the supply of housing (by shifting a portion of the hotel tax to a housing subsidy fund; creating a municipal bond program to assist in the development, rehabilitation and purchase of low- and moderate-income housing; shifting Community Development Block Grant funds to housing production; and using surplus city land and buildings for housing — all to be produced by neighborhood-based housing development corporations). The ordinance also would have speeded up processing of building permits, and would have encouraged so-called "in-law" apartments (small secondary units).

The ordinance was defeated 41% to 59%, in large part because several months before the election the city acted to head off Proposition R by passing weak rent control and condo conversion control ordinances. (An analysis of the Prop. R campaign may be found in a series of articles in the Fall, 1979, June, 1980 and February, 1981 issues of *Shelterforce,* available from 380 Main Street, E. Orange, NJ 07018.)

## ORGANIZATION FIRST

Drives for rent control and other forms of tenant protection have often served as catalysts that enabled a wide variety of organizations to coalesce and pull together. The 50-member San Franciscans for Affordable Housing coalition, for example, included organized labor, church bodies, the Democratic Party County Committee, gay rights groups, women's orga-

Merle Cunnington / *Valley News,* Van Nuys, California

nizations and civil rights advocates, in addition to housing and neighborhood groups from all over the city. The strength of the opposition — the real estate industry and its political chums — demands solid, broadly-based organization in order to win.

Victory is definitely possible. Since 1969, rent control laws, containing varying amounts of the related controls mentioned above, have been adopted by voters or legislatures in New York (New York City and several suburban counties), Massachusetts (Boston, Cambridge, and Brookline), New Jersey (more than 100 cities since 1973), the District of Columbia, and California (23 cities and counties, including Los Angeles City and County and San

**A package of interlocked housing market controls is the most effective strategy.**

Francisco, since 1978). Baltimore and Miami Beach both passed rent control by voter initiative, but courts (which in general have proved far more concerned with protecting landlords' profits than tenants' rights to live decently) declared both laws unconstitutional. Tenants have fought and are fighting for rent control in many other cities in which displacement has become a major issue, including Philadelphia, Chicago, New Orleans, Minneapolis, Seattle, Oakland, and San Diego.

At present, New Jersey and California have the fastest growing and most successful movements for local rent control. For information on the campaigns in these two pivotal states, contact the New Jersey Tenants Organization, P.O. Box 1142, Fort Lee, NJ 07024, and the California Housing Action and Information Network (CHAIN), 1107 Ninth Street, Suite 1017, Sacramento, CA 95814.

## PROTECTION OF TENANT ORGANIZATIONS

Generally, tenant unions are not legally recognized and protected. Few landlords have recognized tenant unions as legitimate bargaining agents for tenants. Fewer still have signed binding agreements with them. An interesting new approach to gaining legal ground for tenant organizations to stand on is the Madison, Wisconsin "Rental Relations Ordinance," which requires landlords to bargain in good faith with any legally constituted union established by their tenants. The law, passed in 1978, had a sunset clause and, by a 11-10 vote of the Madison City Council in April, 1981, was not renewed. The success of the ordinance during its short life is shown in the fact that during 1980, 22 tenant unions, representing more than 6,000 tenants, bargained collectively with their landlords. For more information on the Madison law, contact the Madison Tenants Union, 1045 E. Dayton Street, Madison, WI 53703.

## HOW RENT CONTROL INHIBITS DISPLACEMENT

Rent control is a basic anti-displacement protection because it can prevent landlords from arbitrarily pricing low- and moderate-income tenants out of neighborhoods where speculation and rent inflation are rampant.

### AN END TO RENT GOUGING

First, under a typical rent control law, exorbitant rent increases are prohibited. This can be done by any of several methods (see page 85); the choice and combination in each locality must be based on considerations of fairness, administrative efficiency, legality and political acceptability. Usually some general

formula or principles are established to cover all controlled units, and provision is made for hardship adjustments in individual cases. Setting these upper limits gives tenants some security and the ability to predict roughly how much their rents will rise, and so prevents arbitrary and massive rent increases. And it gives tenants a legal handle to fight out-of-line rent hikes.

### A BARRIER AGAINST SPECULATION

Because rents are controlled, real estate speculation is usually reduced. Speculators' profits are based upon the ability to freely increase rents after buildings are bought. Many rent control laws prohibit landlords from raising rents automatically merely because they have bought a building at a higher price. Nor are rent increases automatically given to cover increased mortgage costs when landlords refinance their properties in order to extract the building's increased market value in cash (unless the borrowed money is used for necessary capital improvements). Speculators thus are deterred from buying overpriced buildings through "leveraging" (that is, buying with a low downpayment and borrowing the remainder of the price) and then forcing the tenants to pay for the new mortgage through increased rents. For an example of this type of anti-speculation clause in a rent control ordinance, see Title IV, Section G of San Francisco's Proposition R, in Appendix B.

### REGULATING EVICTIONS, TOO

Laws to prevent unwarranted and retaliatory evictions are sometimes sought as separate reform goals. More frequently — and effectively — they are integrated into rent control ordinances, where they ensure that landlords have a hard time getting rid of tenants who refuse to pay illegal rent hikes, or who otherwise insist on their rights.

A variety of state and local prohibitions against retaliatory evictions are now on the books. But a more general and effective reform is what is called the "just cause" (or "good cause") eviction statute, which aims to guarantee tenants some real security of tenure. Under such laws, tenants cannot be evicted except for a specific just cause. Allowable causes are stipulated in the law and vary from place to place, but generally include: failure to pay rent; violation of the lease agreement; willful destruction of property; the landlord's wish to occupy the apartment or have a relative occupy it; the landlord's desire to demolish, convert, or rehab the building, etc. Further extensions of these rights can come through complementary regulations designed to preserve the rental stock from conversion and demolition, as discussed in Chapters 5 and 6. As noted there, the Massachusetts Supreme Court recently upheld unanimously a Cambridge ordinance permitting the city, under its rent control law, to withhold a certificate of eviction from the buyer of a condominium unit who wants to occupy that unit him/herself. Thus, under these conditions, an owner's desire to occupy his/her unit is not a just cause for eviction. In some instances, a distinction is made between just causes that are the tenant's doing (nonpayment, property damage, etc.) and those which are the landlord's doing (desire to use the property for other purposes, etc.), and when the landlord provokes an eviction, the law may require owners to give tenants more time to move or to assist with moving expenses. For an example of one set of "just causes" proposed by housing reformers and of

distinctions between how tenant-caused and landlord-caused reasons are treated, see Title VI, Sections A-C of San Francisco's Proposition R in Appendix B. "Just cause" eviction protections now exist for tenants throughout New Jersey, for all tenants in federally subsidized housing, and for most tenants living in localities where there is rent control.

## CONSIDERING RENT CONTROL? PREPARE FOR A HOT DEBATE.

Just let rent control be mentioned by local activists, and the heavy guns are wheeled out. Here is a short primer on the usual attacks against rent control, and data with which to counter them:

### It discourages new construction.

False. As described below, rent control ordinances usually are written to exempt new units. A 1978 study published by the California Department of Housing and Community Development found "no empirical evidence that rent control causes a decline in construction." And in any case we ought to be developing nonprofit, community-oriented housing delivery systems so we are not at the mercy of private developers' profit calculations to get our housing.

### It encourages landlords to undermaintain their buildings in order to preserve their profit levels, and it will inevitably lead to abandonment of unprofitable buildings.

False. And careful studies of places with rent control prove it. A doctoral dissertation on Brookline, Massachusetts, found that the percentage of the rent dollar spent on maintenance actually *increases* after passage of rent control; and data from Cambridge, Lynn,

Somerville, and Brookline (all Boston suburbs) show that permits for alterations, additions, and repairs increased 22-69% following adoption of rent control. Rent control laws often tie allowable rent increases to housing code compliance. All rent control ordinances allow a reasonable rate of return on investment and pass-through of the costs of necessary and reasonable maintenance and capital improvements. "Undermaintenance" is as rampant in cities without rent control — for example, Chicago, Detroit and Philadelphia. The problem is not rent control. It's irresponsible, profit-gouging landlords. And the answer is strict code enforcement, adequate rehab subsidies, and a shift in ownership and control of rental housing to nonprofit, community-oriented and public organizations.

### It leads to abandonment.

Another red herring. A nationwide survey by the National Urban League showed New York City was fifth in the rate of abandonment, behind four cities without rent control. A study by the Women's City Club of New

Chapter 9 / PROTECTING TENANTS

York concluded "rent control did not emerge as a reason for abandonment." The Temporary State Commission on Housing and Rents in New York City found: "Rent control can have little effect [on abandonment rates], for it is clear that it is the oldest, least desirable tenement housing which is abandoned — housing which is unable to produce substantially more income in a free market."

**It causes a decline in property tax revenues,** which are based on assessed values, which in turn are kept down by rent control; the tax burden thus falls increasingly on home-owners and business.

The 1978 California Department of Housing and Community Development study mentioned above, which compared a sample of 26 rent-controlled cities against 37 non-rent-controlled cities, all of them in New Jersey, showed an exact 25% increase in the tax base for both groups over the study period. There was no shift in the tax base, a finding corroborated in two later New Jersey studies.

**It will increase tensions between landlord and tenant.**

They've got to be kidding. All rent control does is require just treatment of tenants. It will not harm existing decent landlord-tenant relationships. The vast majority of tenants have no legal or economic power with respect to their landlords, and that is what maximizes tensions.

**It will lead landlords to discriminate against poorer tenants and displace them in favor of richer tenants.**

Landlords already discriminate without rent control. By giving tenants more secure tenure, rent control lessens such discrimination.

**It will lead to loss of rental housing from conversion and demolition.**

If accompanied by strong rental housing preservation regulations, as outlined in Chapters 5 and 6, this can't happen.

**It is too costly to administer and involves too much "red tape."**

False. Costs of administering rent control are usually no more than $10-$15 per unit annually, and are generally paid for by a registration fee from landlords. It therefore costs the general public and the city nothing. While any intervention in the "free market" does require an administrative mechanism, it is well worth the price. Consider the results if the same argument were applied to the Federal Aviation Administration, for example, which grounds unsafe planes, or the Food and Drug Administration, which keeps dangerous products off the market.

**It is philosophically wrong to intervene in the free housing market.**

Which side are you on? That's a "philosophy" the rich and powerful love. It not only is *right* to intervene in the free market, but fortunately it is done all the time. The real estate market already has building and housing codes that don't permit construction and operation of unsafe buildings, even though such buildings might be more profitable to their owners. And there are zoning laws that prevent an owner from building office towers or factories in residential neighborhoods, even though that might be very profitable indeed.

## DRAFTING RENT CONTROL LEGISLATION

There is no single "model" rent control act. Local rent control laws vary widely, reflecting the goals of their sponsors, local political situations, legal and administrative constraints, and related factors. In general, the issues involved in drafting a rent control law are quite complex, requiring more detail and space for explanation than this manual can provide — although a review of San Francisco's Proposition R in Appendix B is useful for this purpose. Groups wishing detailed technical information should consult "A Brief Guide to Drafting Rent Control Legislation," by W. Dennis Keating, contained in John Gilderbloom's *Rent Control: A Source Book.* Additionally, *Rent Control,* by the New Jersey Tenants Organization, focuses on New Jersey but can be helpful to groups drafting laws elsewhere. (See references at end of chapter for how to obtain these publications).

### EXEMPTIONS

It is worth noting here — if only to help understand the shortcomings of rent control — the several categories of rental housing that often may be exempted from rent control laws:

**New units** built after the passage of rent control (exempted so as not to discourage the construction of more rental housing).

**Apartments in small owner-occupied buildings** (usually up to three or four units). Such units typically are exempted to avoid problems caused by regulating landlords who may not keep careful records, and it is also argued, but is unproven, that owner-occupant landlords usually are not rent-gougers. Perhaps more important, small landlords may be a politically influential group whose opposition to the ordinance should not be triggered (although exempting these landlords also deprives their tenants of benefits, and thus a corresponding source of political support may be lost). To the extent that recent experience is a guide, the three most recent successful rent control voter initiatives (Berkeley and Santa Monica, California, and Baltimore, Maryland) all exempted small owner-occupied buildings.

**Units in hotels and motels** which are occupied for a short term (two to four weeks or less). On the other hand, *residential single-room occupancy (SRO) hotels* should be regulated because their tenants are not transient and need protection. (See Chapter 6.)

**Government-owned and operated (public) housing,** since such tenants already have effective rent controls. In addition, since 1976 HUD has preempted state and local control of rents for federally subsidized privately owned apartments, and has reserved the right to preempt rent control in federally insured privately owned apartments. HUD adopted this controversial preemption policy at the urging of the private real estate industry. It justifies the policy by claiming, without proof, that strong local rent controls may threaten the government's financial interest in preventing landlord default and foreclosure. This stance clearly ranks HUD's fiscal concerns over the needs of moderate-income tenants. Predictably, state housing finance agencies generally have followed HUD's lead, preempting local government's right to control rents in privately owned but state-insured and -subsidized apartments.

**"Luxury" apartments,** meaning those which rent for more than a specified high rent figure. This exemption is based on the assumption that wealthier tenants do not need to be protected against rent gouging. But as rent rates climb, a fixed "luxury" figure will soon become non-luxury. And large families and communal households may lose rent control coverage by paying "luxury" rents only because of their huge space needs.

**Rented single-family houses.** Such an exemption may be used to encourage owners to continue renting these units rather than selling them, which would reduce the available supply of rental housing.

## RENT ADJUSTMENT METHODS

As noted above, a variety of methods are available and have been used in different rent control ordinances to regulate rents. Many rent control laws include a maximum allowable annual percentage rent increase or empower a rent control board to determine this.

Some rent control laws tie rent increases to landlords' increased costs. Generally, landlords are allowed to pass on to tenants all normal and reasonable increased operating and maintenance costs and amortized capital improvements. However, mortgage debt financing costs and depreciation often are disallowed because the former represents "equity" to the landlord and the latter is not necessarily a real expense. Under New York City's Rent Stabilization system, rent increases are based on an operating cost index, a price index of selected landlord costs compiled annually by the Bureau of Labor Statistics.

Some rent control laws condition landlords' right to general rent increase adjustments on "substantial" compliance with local housing and health codes, and maintenance of existing or essential services.

A relatively simple but misleading rent increase standard is the Consumer Price Index (CPI), or the CPI Rent Index, issued bimonthly by the Bureau of Labor Statistics. Landlords argue they should be allowed to raise rents automatically by at least the CPI. But where a building is mortgaged, as almost all are, a significant part — frequently well over half — of the landlord's costs are fixed and do not vary as do other expenses, because mortgages are usually at long-term fixed rates. Therefore, a CPI standard in an inflationary economy provides a built-in windfall for most landlords.

The courts have generally held that rent control ordinances must guarantee landlords a "fair return on investment," but how to define this standard is a ticklish issue. "Fair return" formulas can be provided in the law itself, or the rent control board can be given power to determine the formula, with the law containing only general guidelines or factors to consider. There are several fair return formulas possible. One is to base fair return on the landlord's investment. Another is to allow a return on market (or assessed) value. While the latter is simpler, since it avoids some tricky questions, such as how to value the owner's own labor, it leads to circular results: present market value is based on a multiple of gross rents, whose excessive and exorbitant levels are the reasons for imposing rent controls in the first place. Use of market value as the base rewards speculation and leads to continuing excessive rent spirals.

In this regard, a March, 1981 court action giving the City of Santa Monica three months to revise its fair return formula from one based on landlord equity to one based on current market value is highly disturbing. If sustained, this precedent could have serious implications for the future of meaningful rent control. In hot housing markets especially (where rent control is most likely to be enacted), and because of heavy use of mortgage financing, the gap between the landlord's own investment and what the property is worth can be enormous. Using the current market value as a basis for investment return has to allow for extremely high rents. One would think the fair standard would be to allow return only on what the owner actually has invested, but, as noted above, the courts seem to take the landlords' side with distressing frequency.

In any case, even when the basis for computing a fair return is established, there still will be controversy over what percentage return on the investment represents "fairness."

Beyond that, a rent control law will have to allow for individual "hardship appeals," deviations from the standard formula which can be invoked by tenant and landlord alike to obtain modifications based on a particular set of facts. Generally, hardship rent adjustments should be allowed only if the landlord has fully complied with the rent control law and housing code; only if necessary and unavoidable landlord operating and maintenance costs are considered; and only if there is a ceiling placed on cumulative annual rent adjustments.

## FIGHTING VACANCY DECONTROL

One way the real estate industry regularly attacks rent control laws — both those being proposed and those already adopted — is to demand that "voluntarily" vacated apartments be automatically decontrolled, enabling landlords to demand the "market" rent from new incoming tenants. Controls on rent increases would either be permanently lifted, or would be re-applied for the duration of this new

tenancy, but starting at a new level set by whatever the market will bear. Landlords argue that they should be allowed to do this in order to offset their "losses" from controlled units by renting to tenants willing to pay higher rents.

Bea Oakes / Metropolitan Council on Housing

In reality, vacancy decontrol is simply a means to phase out rent control through tenant turnover. According to a recent study, funded by HUD, on anti-displacement strategies for San Francisco:

> If normal turnover patterns persist (and experience in other rent-controlled cities such as Los Angeles indicate that they do), then one-fourth to one-third of all rental units will become vacant each year. This means that the entire stock will decontrol on average of once every three or four years.

Over time, rents will increase at the same rate (and perhaps even more), although the big jumps will be imposed between tenancies rather than during the residence of a given tenant. For instance, after New York State forced New York City to add vacancy decontrol to its rent control laws in 1971, a state commission found that the monthly rent increases in newly vacated apartments averaged 52% more than those allowed for rent-con-

trolled tenants. A 1980 Los Angeles study revealed that the annual rent increases in 1979 for vacated units averaged 18%, compared to the 7% maximum allowed for rent controlled apartments. A San Francisco study showed that between October, 1979 and April, 1980, rents on vacated units rose 23%, compared with a 7% increase for controlled units. Landlords have been successful in persuading local governments in New York City, Los Angeles, Boston and San Francisco to adopt vacancy decontrol, despite organized tenant opposition. New York City tenants did win the repeal of vacancy decontrol in 1974, but this reversal has not yet occurred in the other cities mentioned.

Vacancy decontrol is a strong displacement threat to rent-controlled tenants, too. It gives landlords an incentive to get rid of them in order to charge new tenants whatever the market will bear. In theory, a "just cause" eviction clause (described above) protects tenants from illegal evictions and landlord harassment. But in practice, it is hard for tenants to prove that landlords are actually circumventing the law. For example, if a just cause for eviction is that a relative wants to occupy the apartment, the eviction will be granted. Only after moving out could the tenant discover that this event never occurred. Substantial penalties for such intentional evasions may be put in the law — Title VI, Section B(3) and B(4) of San Francisco's Proposition R, for instance, contains such a clause — but in reality few tenants will be inclined to go back and check once they have moved away, and in any event such illegal intentions are very difficult to prove. Anyone who thinks this concern about decontrol-related evictions is overblown need only check out the San Francisco experience: after the Board of Supervisors there adopted a weak form of rent control in 1979, containing "just cause" eviction protections along with vacancy decontrol, eviction actions increased by 28% within three months.

Vacancy decontrol also pits tenant against tenant within the same building: landlords undermine collective tenant consciousness and action by telling new tenants their rents are so high because they are "subsidizing" the older rent-controlled tenants. But the broader damage wrought by vacancy decontrol is that even where there is no immediate displacement impact, it reduces the supply of housing available to the poor and working people most vulnerable to displacement.

Vacancy decontrol in *any* form defeats the anti-displacement impact of rent control.

# COMMERCIAL RENT CONTROL

As the story about the gentrification of New York's Amstedam Avenue shows, quite often the businesses serving lower-income groups or particular nationalities are displaced right along with their customers.

Housing activists rarely grieve over the plight of business people: too often their respective goals conflict and preclude cooperation. Particularly in poor communities, many businesses have the image of rip-off establishments, peddling shoddy goods for all the profit possible.

But then, too, every community has businesses with a different image: useful, dependable, necessary, a welcome part of the fabric of neighborhood life. Their exodus can have a powerful effect on residential affairs, particularly when they are replaced by businesses that attract moneyed people who shop for houses

there too, while neighborhood residents must travel further and further to find stores that fill their needs and fit their budgets.

Most small business owners do not own the property in which they do business. They rent. And speculators target such properties with even greater gusto than apartments when gentrification is afoot, because of the massive profits to be made. A growing shortage of commercial space puts small businesses at the mercy of their landlords and at a severe competitive disadvantage against the financial institutions, securities offices, attorneys, corporations and other heavies who can outbid them for space.

A recent article from the *Village Voice* gives some New York City examples: a stationery store on the Upper West Side had its monthly rent raised from $1,500 to $8,000, so the owners sold their stock and went out of business; an Italian restaurant in the SoHo area had its rent hiked from $1,100 to $5,000 a month and then closed its doors; the non-profit New York Hospital Association had its midtown office rent raised from $6.50/square foot to $34/square foot.

Under nationwide World War II rent controls, commercial properties were covered along with residential units. In New York City, two City Councillors representing opposite ends of the political spectrum have just joined — on behalf of some two dozen small business and trade associations — to reintroduce commercial rent control. The act would allow a maximum 12% annual rent increase for space less than 5-10,000 square feet, depending on the type of business, and for the first time, commercial tenants would be entitled to a rent rebate if the landlord failed to provide adequate services. The law would

## Boom Changing Face of Amsterdam Ave.

[New York City's] Amsterdam Avenue in the 70's and 80's is beginning to catch the spillover of boutiques and restaurants from Columbus Avenue, its neighbor to the east, which itself underwent a major restoration in the last decade. . . .

While investors look forward to the big rents and increased property values of an improving neighborhood, others are concerned that the service businesses — delicatessens, shoemakers, locksmiths and cleaners — will be forced out.

And, although Amsterdam Avenue in the 80's still reflects a strong Spanish influence, rising rents are changing the avenue's ethnic makeup as more middle-class whites move in.

Some of the shopkeepers on Amsterdam had been chased off Columbus Avenue by the rising cost of commercial space. . . . "All the service businesses are going to be chased out," said Joseph Greenberg, the owner of the London Shade and Glass Company, a window repair and accessory business.

For Joel J. Rhodes, "Amsterdam is a hot area for stores." Mr. Rhodes, who runs the Joel J. Rhodes Real Estate Agency at 383 Amsterdam Avenue, is part owner of several properties on the avenue. "There is confidence here now," he said. "It's a flow. Nothing is stopping it. Amsterdam is going to get better. We're at the point where rents on Columbus Avenue are sky high and the more conservative businessman wants Amsterdam because the rents are more reasonable."

He and a partner paid $300,000 for two buildings at 76th and Amsterdam four years ago. He made $100,000 in repairs, rented one building to J G Melon, a restaurant, and the other to International Food, a supermarket chain.

"I've had offers of $1.2 million for the properties," he said. "You figure it out. That's quite an investment if I wanted to sell."

Apartment rentals on the avenue are also becoming more expensive. A one-bedroom apartment in a renovated tenement goes for about $500 a month, according to Mr. Rhodes.

Sally Goodgold, chairman of Community Board 7, speaking of the neighborhood's changing ethnic makeup, said: "There is no question that we're losing numbers. Amsterdam Avenue has traditionally been a low-rent, service avenue. If we lose Amsterdam, if it goes like Columbus Avenue, we are in danger of losing the ethnic diversity of the West Side."

*New York Times,* Sept. 28, 1980

apply stiff penalties to landlords who overcharge. A similar bill has been introduced in the New York State Legislature, with additional protections against arbitrary evictions. For further information on the New York City effort, write City Councillors Ruth Messinger or Bernard Gallagher, City Hall, New York City, NY. For information on the state legislation write State Assemblyman John Dearie, State Office Building, Albany, NY.

## LIMITS OF RENT CONTROL

It must be recognized that even a relatively strong rent control law offers only limited protection against the displacement of poor people. In the current economy, rent control can only end rent-gouging and slow down the rate at which rents are increasing. It cannot stop rent increases altogether. Rent control ordinances typically allow landlords to pass their own cost increases (property taxes, fuel and utilities, maintenance) straight through to tenants. And unlike public housing and other federal programs that subsidize rents, requiring tenants to pay no more than one-fourth of their income for shelter (going up to 30% under the Administration's new "budget cutting" proposals), rent control seldom ties rent levels to tenants' ability to pay. While rent control does place a ceiling on annual increases, tenants must still pay the permitted rent hikes, regardless of their income.

Median rents nationally increased 9.6% annually during 1973-1977, while tenants' incomes only increased 5.6% annually during that period. In New York City, where local rent control was weakened considerably after 1969 due to landlord pressure, 57% of tenants were paying more than one-fourth of their income for rent by 1978 (compared to 49% nationally in 1977), and 38% were paying 35% or more of their income on rent (compared to 30% nationally). Traditional rent control does not completely insulate tenants from the national trend of rents rising faster than tenants' incomes.

## THE RENT CONTROL BATTLEFIELD

Even though rent control gives tenants only part of the protection they need against displacement, the real estate industry has fought hard to kill each and every local ordinance that has appeared. In 1978, major developers formed a National Multi-Housing Council (NMHC) to coordinate their anti-rent control activities. The NMHC operates in collaboration with realtors (National Association of Realtors), homebuilders (National Association of Home Builders), landlords (National Apartment Association), and mortgage bankers (Mortgage Bankers Association). It provides legal, organizing, and financial assistance to local anti-rent control campaigns. It is lobbying the federal government to deny housing and community development assistance to municipalities where rent control is in force.

Congress came very close to passing legislation of this type in 1980. And at the time this book is going to the printer, a major battle to save local rent control from federal interference is raging. The Senate passed an amendment to the Housing Act, withholding Section 8 housing subsidies from localities with rent control measures that do not exempt newly constructed housing and do not permanently decontrol controlled units when they become vacant. Housing groups are actively lobbying to have Congress eliminate this amendment, which, apart from its pro-landlord bias, is totally inconsistent with the new Administration's philosophy of limiting federal intrusion into local affairs. Supporters of this amendment argue that rent control dampens private real estate development activities, and so Section 8 and Community Development funds ought not be invested where they can't stimulate maximum private market response. But the argument is false. Real estate development activities continue at high levels in places with rent control (look at Manhattan, the District of Columbia, Northern New Jersey). In fact, an even better case can be made for not wasting federal housing subsidies (Section 8 certificates in particular) in places where there is no rent control to keep "fair market rent levels" down, since such subsidies must cover the gap between market prices and what poor people can afford. Why not restrict federal housing

and community development funds to localities *with* rent controls? (For information on the movement to prevent federal restrictions on local rent controls, contact the National Tenants Union, 380 Main Street, E. Orange, NJ 07018.)

Where local movements for rent control are strong, the real estate lobby's tactic may be to go to the state legislature (through campaign contributions, entertaining by lobbyists, business connections, etc.) where they usually are quite influential, and push through a law stipulating that only the state, not localities, can pass laws controlling rents. This has happened already in Florida, Arizona and Washington.

Strong as the real estate industry is, however, it is not invincible. The tenant move-

LNS

ment dealt it a resounding defeat in June, 1980, when a California housing coalition defeated Proposition 10, the statewide "Fair Rent" initiative. This so-called "rent control" legislation was an effort by the real estate interests to end all local rent control except a toothless version acceptable to them. The intended act provided tenants with virtually no protection: it empowered cities and towns to regulate rents only if they allowed rent increases equal to the change in the Consumer Price Index, required vacancy decontrol, did not require landlords to register their units (which would have made enforcement all but impossible), and did not require just cause for eviction. Despite a lavish $6.9 million campaign by the landlords, who outspent tenants 38 to 1, Proposition 10 lost by a two-to-one margin. For information on how tenant groups fought this campaign, read *How We Won "No" on 10: CHAIN's Campaign Strategy — Local and Statewide,* cited at the end of this chapter.

Once rent control is enacted, landlords customarily fight it with every trick in the book: evasion, obstruction, and constant attempts to repeal. Their arsenal includes: refusal to register their units with the city (in order to bankrupt rent control boards, which usually are funded by registration fees); general non-compliance with the law; requiring illegal coercive agreements of tenants (for example: imposing various "fees" and "charges," which in effect are rent increases); litigation to have rent control declared illegal; lobbying to weaken or repeal rent control legislation; harassment of rent control boards; and even attempts to subvert a law once it has passed by taking over its administration. In Berkeley, where rent control board members are ap-

pointees of individual city councillors, one councillor opposed to rent control appointed a landlord who actually had brought suit against the ordinance. (Several California city attorneys have ruled that city councillors who own four or more rental units in that city cannot vote on rent control matters, since they have an illegal conflict of interest.)

Cidne Hart / LNS

## RENT CONTROL: A SUMMARY

Where tenant displacement is at issue, rent control is an essential element in an anti-displacement strategy. But the enduring opposition of the powerful real estate industry, plus rent control's own limitations, all make enactment and enforcement of comprehensive laws a difficult undertaking. Where it has been adopted, rent control has stabilized rents and neighborhoods without the disastrous consequences proclaimed by its opponents. Moreover, beyond its value in keeping rent increases down, rent control — by retarding speculative price increases and laying the groundwork for non-speculative resident control and/or ownership — is a vital step toward keeping open the possibility of a transition from market-controlled to consumer-controlled rental housing. (See related material in Chapter 16 on cooperatives and land trusts.) To be most effective, rent control must be an integral part of an overall, comprehensive anti-displacement strategy, whether it is proposed on a citywide, neighborhood, or building basis.

# OTHER TENANT PROTECTIONS

## WARRANTY OF HABITABILITY

The most important general concept developing today in reform of landlord-tenant law is what is known as the "warranty of habitability." This doctrine, which legislatures are adopting more and more, and courts are coming to accept, recognizes an implied obligation in tenants' leases, whether written or oral, that the landlord will provide a habitable apartment meeting the minimum requirements of local housing and health codes. If the landlord fails to provide a habitable apartment, then the tenant can demand that repairs be made, and can use this failure on the landlord's part as a defense in court against eviction attempts, or to justify withholding all or part of the rent. Some states and localities go further and specifically authorize rent withholding or so-called "repair and deduct" remedies, whereby tenants can use their rent to make

necessary repairs themselves, in instances where the landlord is not providing a habitable apartment. The concept of warranty of habitability comes directly from the field of consumer law, and attempts to apply to basic shelter some of the same protections one gets when buying a refrigerator or TV set.

## PROTECTION AGAINST DISCRIMINATION

In neighborhoods undergoing gentrification, there is usually rampant discrimination against the kinds of tenants most likely to be displaced. These "undesirables" are minorities, families with children, transients (for example, students), and, generally, low-income tenants. They have what speculators consider a "bad image." Speculative landlords prefer upper-income professionals who are able and willing to pay high rents, and perhaps will be interested in purchasing their units if the building is later converted to condominiums.

Laws have been passed in a few states and cities to prevent discrimination against tenants with children. These local acts supplement existing national and state legislation which makes refusal to rent illegal if it is based

on race, religion, sex, or handicapped status. However, anti-discrimination legislation has been notoriously difficult to enforce. Landlords are not required to give reasons if they refuse to rent or decide to evict. Discrimination is difficult to prove and typically involves lengthy and expensive litigation. Tenants bear the burden of enforcement when landlords refuse to rent to them, treat them arbitrarily, or try to evict them in a discriminatory manner. Nevertheless, the existence of anti-discrimination legislation can help deter some types of displacement. (A "Child Discrimination Packet" — including sample preventive legislation — is available from the National Housing Law Project. Instructions for getting it, plus other helpful references, are at the end of the chapter).

## PROTECTION AGAINST UTILITY SHUTOFFS

Law reforms in various places are beginning to cut down displacement caused by utility shutoffs that result when landlords stop payment — either as a final step in milking properties before abandonment, or as a strategy to force tenants out. Under Pennsylvania's new Utility Services Tenant's Rights Act, a two-tier notice system is required before gas, electric, or water service can be terminated. This requires utilities to notify tenants if landlords are seriously delinquent in their bills, and allows tenants to pick up utility services directly, without having to assume responsibility for previous arrears. Tenants can collectively retain utility service merely by paying for the last 30 days and can deduct these and future payments from rents otherwise due the landlord. And landlords cannot have service shut off unless they submit to the utility a sworn notarized statement that the units are vacant or that the tenants have agreed to the shutoff.

Washington, D.C. passed similar emergency legislation last winter, barring landlords from turning utility services off on their own in order to force tenants out. When a utility company receives such a request, it must notify the tenants, who then have time to get a court order permitting them to use rent moneys to pay any outstanding bills and keep service going.

Some useful court decisions have appeared in this area as well, such as a Seattle ruling that when landlords have not paid their water bills, the city's water department cannot terminate service to tenants without notice and a due process hearing. Information about these anti-displacement protections appeared in the August/September, 1979 *Housing Law Bulletin* and may be followed up through the National Housing Law Project, 2150 Shattuck Ave., #300, Berkeley, CA 94704.

A significant limitation in this area of protection, however, lies in the different kinds of companies supplying fuel. Gas and electric companies — publicly regulated, sometimes publicly owned — are relatively easy to make responsible for tenant protection. Smaller, private outfits that supply oil and coal are not.

## SHORTCOMINGS OF LEGAL STRATEGIES

Even where tenants have legal rights to prevent arbitrary evictions, these rights are hard to exercise. Experienced tenant lawyers, in Legal Services or in private practice, are hard to find, and threatened cutbacks in or total elimination of the Legal Services program

Ben Achtenberg / Plainsong Productions

compound this difficulty immensely. Judges often are hostile to tenants who attempt to defend themselves. Judges may be landlords themselves or closely allied with property-owning interests. Tenants often cannot afford to pay court fees, including jury fees, or to pay rent into "escrow" pending the outcome of their case, which means they are effectively denied access to the courts. Tenants may be unfamiliar with the court system and intimidated by the tactics of landlords and their lawyers, even though such tactics may be illegal. And there is growing use of sophisticated and often ruthless "professional" eviction services. The high proportion of tenants who are elderly, transient, non-citizens, illegal immigrants or lack proficiency in English make them a particularly vulnerable class.

Ben Achtenberg / Plainsong Productions

Moreover, making changes in land*lord* (the word itself is revealing)-tenant law — which dates from feudal times and retains much of the flavor of the Dark Ages — is hard. For the most part, the situation is governed by state constitutions and statutes governing what localities can do. And, of course, many state legislators, and local government officials, are themselves landlords, real estate brokers, lawyers or insurance agents, or get big campaign money from the real estate industry.

Nonetheless, pushing for change in landlord-tenant law remains a vital element in an overall anti-displacement strategy. Law changes are like footholds that help in the long, slow climb toward larger system change. And some reforms — even if they eventually get beaten down — are of tremendous aid in situations where displacement pressures otherwise would be overwhelming.

Overall, landlord-tenant law is moving slowly toward a more even balance between the rights of those who own and the rights of those who use property. Books like *The Rights of Tenants,* by Richard Blumberg and James Grow, and publications such as "Understanding Landlording," by CHAIN (2300 Foothill Drive, Oakland, CA 94601), can help local groups navigate the maze toward reform.

## REFERENCES

### RENT CONTROL: BASIC REFERENCES

*Rent Control: A Source Book* (1981), edited by John Gilderbloom, is a useful compilation for community groups. It contains "A Brief Guide to Drafting Rent Control Legislation," by W. Dennis Keating. Available for $7.95 from the Housing Information Center, Foundation for National Progress, Box 3396, Santa Barbara, CA 93105.

*Rent and Eviction Controls: An Annotated Bibliography,* by W. Dennis Keating (1976), is available for $5 from the Council of Planning Librarians, 1313 East 60th St., Chicago, IL 60637.

"Rent Control: A Practical Guide for Tenant Organizations," a useful reference, appears in Volume 15 of the *San Diego Law Review* (1978), available in university and court law libraries.

New Jersey's Rent Control Movement: for more information, contact the New Jersey Tenants Organization, P.O. Box 1142, Fort Lee, NJ 07024. They have published a guidebook called *Rent Control,* which focuses on New Jersey law but can be helpful to groups drafting laws elsewhere.

California's Rent Control Movement: for more information, contact the California Housing Action & Information Network (CHAIN), 1107 Ninth St., Suite 1017, Sacramento, CA 95814.

Massachusetts' Rent Control Movement: for more information, contact the Massachusetts Tenants Organization, 10 West St., Boston, MA 02111.

New York City's Rent Control Movement: for more information, contact the Metropolitan Council on Housing, 137 Fifth Ave., New York, NY 10010.

Santa Monica's composite rent/eviction/demolition/conversion controls: for more information, write the Santa Monica Rent Control Board, 1685 Main St., Santa Monica, CA 90401.

*Housing Law Bulletin,* published bi-monthly by the National Housing Law Project, 2150 Shattuck Ave., #300, Berkeley, CA 94704.

*Shelterforce,* a national tenants' movement newspaper, published quarterly, 380 Main St., East Orange, NJ 07018.

The National Tenants Union was formed in June, 1980, to coordinate rent control organizing at the national, state, and local levels. It can be contacted through *Shelterforce.*

*Fair Return Standards and Hardship Appeal Procedures: A Guide for New Jersey Rent Leveling Boards* (1981), by Ken Baar and Dennis Keating, treats in great detail the issue of how rents are adjusted. While written for New Jersey, it is of wider applicability. Available from the National Housing Law Project, 2150 Shattuck Ave., #300, Berkeley, CA 94704.

## RENT CONTROL: LOCAL CAMPAIGNS

San Francisco's Comprehensive "Proposition R" Housing Ordinance: An analysis of the campaign appears in the Fall, 1979 issue of *Shelterforce,* available from that organization at 380 Main St., E. Orange, NJ 07018. Further discussion of this campaign is contained in the June, 1980 and February, 1981 issues.

*How We Won "No" on 10: CHAIN's Campaign Strategy — Local and Statewide,* the story of the defeat of a real estate industry counterattack on rent control in California, is available for $1.75 from CHAIN, 2300 Foothill Boulevard, Oakland, CA 94601.

*ROOF Campaign:* An analysis of the November, 1980 Initiative 24 rent control campaign in Seattle is available for $2 from ROOF, 1133 23rd Ave., Seattle, WA 98122.

*Winning Rent Control in a Working Class City* (1980), an analysis of Baltimore's successful electoral campaign (subsequently overturned by the courts), is available for $2 from the Baltimore Rent Control Campaign, 2319 Maryland Ave., Baltimore, MD 21218.

## COMMERCIAL RENT CONTROL

Commercial Rent Control in New York City: for information, write City Councillors Ruth Messinger or Bernard Gallagher, City Hall, New York, NY.

Commercial Rent Control in New York State: for information, write State Assemblyman John Dearie, State Office Bldg., Albany, NY.

## RENT CONTROL: KNOW YOUR ENEMY

"How to Prevent and Defeat Rent Control," by James Webb, offers a look into the enemy camp, and a forewarning of tactics local campaigns will face. It appears in Volume 5 (1980) of *Real Estate Issues,* available in many public and university libraries.

The campaign to place federal restrictions on local rent controls: for information on how to counter this effort, contact the National Tenants Union, c/o *Shelterforce,* 380 Main St., East Orange, NJ 07018.

## RENTAL DISCRIMINATION AGAINST CHILDREN

A "Child Discrimination Packet" (including sample preventive legislation) is available from the National Housing Law Project, 2150 Shattuck Ave., #300, Berkeley, CA 94704, attn: Katherine Castro. Free to Legal Service people, $15 to others.

Further information is available from the Fair Housing for Children Coalition, P.O. Box 5877, Santa Monica, CA 90405, and from the Housing Rights for Children Project, 6501 Telegraph Ave., Oakland, CA 94609.

"Strategies to Combat Discrimination Against Families with Children in Rental Housing," by Larry Keating and Anne Keating, a case study of the (as yet unsuccessful) attempt to pass anti-discrimination legislation in Atlanta, is contained in *Planning to Meet the Changing Needs of Women,* edited by Mary Deal, available from HUD's Office of Policy Development and Research, Washington, DC 20410.

A HUD report, "Measuring Restrictive Rental Practices Affecting Families with Children: A National Survey" (July, 1980), is available from HUD's Office of Policy Development and Research, Washington, DC 20410.

## PROTECTION AGAINST UTILITY SHUTOFFS

See the August/September, 1979 *Housing Law Bulletin,* available from the National Housing Law Project, 2150 Shattuck Ave., #300, Berkeley, CA 94704.

## PROTECTING TENANT UNIONS

The Madison "Rental Relations Ordinance," requiring good faith bargaining with any legally constituted tenant union: for more information contact the Madison Tenants Union, 1045 E. Dayton St., Madison, WI 53703.

## MOBILE HOMES

Tenants' rights of mobile home owners on leased sites in mobile home parks: "Mobile Home Living: A Guide to Consumers' Rights," is available for 50¢ from Housing Advocates, Inc., 717 Citizens Bldg., Cleveland, OH 44114. It highlights Ohio law, but also offers a national overview.

## GENERAL REFERENCES

*Rental Housing: A National Problem That Needs Immediate Attention* (1979), a good information source on the housing crisis, in the government's own words, is available free from the U.S. General Accounting Office, Room 1518, 441 G St. NW, Washington, DC 20548.

*The Rights of Tenants,* by Richard Blumberg and James Grow, a good primer on law reform, is available for $1.95 from bookstores or from Avon Books, 250 W. 55th St., New York, NY 10019.

"Understanding Landlording," a good source of information on law and law reform, is available from CHAIN, 2300 Foothill Blvd., Oakland, CA 94601.

Chapter 10

PREVENTING DISPLACEMENT OF HOMEOWNERS

Ben Achtenberg / Plainsong Productions

U p to this point, we have mostly considered the plight of renters. But low- and middle-income homeowners, who make up a substantial portion of the nation's households, are also often imperiled. Homeownership is no guarantee of housing security any more, if it ever was. Sometimes displacement comes at the hands of speculators (see Chapter 4). Sometimes, as the Detroit story on page 100 shows, it is from government economic development policies. Sometimes, as the Kentucky story on page 107 relates, it is from public works projects that offer inadequate reimbursements and relocation assistance. Sometimes regressive property taxes are the cause. And sometimes it is greedy credit institutions that feed on the incomes of people already run down by inflation.

Whatever the cause, the result hurts the renter population as well as homeowner displacees, because former homeowners often become renters, and have to find their shelter in an already overcrowded market.

### Homeownership is no guarantee of housing security any more, if it ever was.

Of course, homeowners generally are in a better legal position to resist displacement than tenants. And when they do have to move, often they reap the inflated value of their property just as a speculator would — with equally harmful effect on the broader housing situation. This may make it hard for tenants and homeowners to work together effectively in anti-displacement campaigns. But tenants and homeowners should remember that homeowners' "profits" are largely imaginary. Usually they have to put their new-found wealth

*"I've called the family together to announce that, because of inflation, I'm going to have to let two of you go."*

Drawing by Joseph Farris; © 1974 / *The New Yorker Magazine*, Inc.

right back into the market to buy or rent a new place to live. In the end, only real estate brokers, speculators and mortgage lenders profit from inflation in single-family home prices.

For their part, homeowners should understand that effective anti-displacement programs will and should cool off the whole overheated housing market. If public funds go into supporting homeowners in gentrifying neighborhoods, there should be some corresponding controls placed on resale prices (see Chapter 4). And property tax breaks for elderly and lower-income homeowners should not be passed on automatically to others who may not need them.

In the end, the anti-displacement interests of low- and moderate-income homeowners and tenants are much the same. Hopefully the future will find them in the same movement.

This chapter will examine the main causes of forced displacement of homeowners, and some of the ways people can fight back.

# DISPLACEMENT THROUGH NEW TYPES OF HOME FINANCING

Change in the nature of home mortgages is making homeownership much more chancy at the same time that it makes lenders' profits much more certain. Since the 1930s, the traditional home mortgage in the United States has been the fixed-interest, "level payment" variety: a long-term loan at a pre-set interest rate, paid back in monthly amounts that remain the same over the life of the mortgage. (The components of the monthly payment vary over time, however, with the larger portion being interest at first, and only a small portion going to repayment of principal — a ratio that shifts in the other direction over the course of the mortgage). This kind of mortgage gives homeowners lots of security — they know that no matter what, the main part of the family's housing costs will not rise with inflation.

In recent years, however, with rising interest rates, lending institutions have become unhappy with this situation. Their long-term mortgage funds tied up at earlier, lower interest rates would be much more profitable if

Clay Bennett © 1981 / Fayetteville (N.C.) *Times*

subject to the new rates. So there has been a fairly rapid introduction of various new types of mortgages that permit lending institutions to take advantage of rising interest rates, at the expense of the average homeowner. Under these new mortgages, homeowners can find their monthly payments escalating soon after they sign the initial mortgage agreement. This shifts the balance of burdens and benefits so that banks and savings and loans get more profit, while homeowners pay more and consequently become more insecure about keeping up with house payments.

*"My ancient ancestors got a variable rate mortgage on it and nobody's been able to pay it off."*

## VARIABLE RATE MORTGAGE

The most common of these new home loan types is the "variable rate mortgage," in which lenders are allowed to change the interest rate periodically to keep up with changes in some overall economic index of interest rates. There may be some consumer protections, such as an upper limit on the amount the interest rate can

95

be raised (usually 2½%), the amount it can be raised each time (usually ½%), and the frequency of increases. Also, in the unlikely event interest rates go down, the borrower gets a lower interest rate. Customers often are induced to accept such mortgage terms, either because no options are available or because of sales gimmicks — such as making the initial terms for this type of mortgage more attractive than a conventional, traditional mortgage. But in the long run, and often in the short run, variable rate mortgages are not in the homeowner's interest. If they were, the lenders wouldn't be pushing them so hard.

## ROLLOVER MORTGAGE

Another variation is the "rollover mortgage," which is written for a short term — say, five to seven years — instead of the more usual 25-30 years. Monthly payments, however, are based on an assumed long-term amortization of principal, in order to keep payments low. The mortgage is renewed (rolled over) several times, with each renewal requiring a renegotiation at current interest rates. Any large increase in payments resulting from interest increases at the time of the rollover may outstrip the owner's ability to keep on paying. This type of mortgage caused homeowners great grief, and loss of their homes, during the Depression. With the rise of "non-institutional lenders," in particular sellers who in effect become mortgage lenders by taking the majority of the sales price in the form of a note secured by the house, these short-term mortgages are becoming increasingly prevalent.

## GRADUATED PAYMENT MORTGAGE

Yet another variation is the so-called "graduated payment mortgage," under which monthly payments in the early years — say, the first five years — start lower than they would be under a conventional, fixed-payment mortgage, then climb higher at a stipulated rate. The purpose of such mortgages is to get people with slightly lower incomes into the ownership market, under the assumption that their incomes will increase and they will be able to afford the climbing monthly payments. If their incomes do *not* rise fast enough, they are in trouble.

## REVERSE ANNUITY MORTGAGE

Another new mortgage form, tried thus far in only a few places, is the "reverse annuity mortgage." Elderly homeowners can borrow against the increased value of their home, particularly where the original mortgage has been paid off, and the proceeds of the loan are disbursed in monthly payments to cover the owner's general living expenses. These loans are written only for a short period, usually five years, and unless the lender is willing to write a new reverse annuity mortgage, the elderly homeowner must repay the loan, which often can be done only by selling the house and moving. This type of loan has real displacement dangers for people who have the bad luck to live longer than the short-term annuity period.

## SHARED EQUITY MORTGAGE

Under the "shared equity" mortgage, the homeowner, in exchange for getting a slightly lower interest rate, agrees to split profits with the lending institution, according to a set formula, when the house is sold. This arrangement is very different from the "equity participation" co-purchasing arrangement discussed in Chapter 17, in which the homebuyer gets the benefit of someone else putting up a portion of the original capital required to purchase the home, in exchange for splitting the profits. Under this "shared equity" mortgage, the homeowner gets little and the lender gives little, but the homeowner loses a lot of potential benefits and the lender reaps some handsome gains.

In all these new loan forms, it is almost a certainty that the homeowner will have to shell out considerably more in payments over the life of the mortgage. Accordingly, the trend may lead to a dramatic rise in default and foreclosure rates, as monthly interest payments climb under variable and graduated rates and rollover mortgages have to be refinanced at new, higher interest levels. Protections against foreclosure vary widely from state to state, and homeowners have to be alert to make sure lenders give them all the protections the law allows. A useful aid in this process is the three-part "Mortgage Foreclosure Primer," by David Madway and Daniel Pearlman, which appeared in the July, August and November, 1974 issues of *Clearinghouse Review.*

The forces creating these changes in the mortgage instrument are national in scope, spurred on by the powerful federal financial regulatory institutions — concerned more about the welfare of lending institutions than about the average homeowner, by the banks and savings and loans themselves, and by Congress. They are beyond the capacity of neighborhood groups to deal with locally in any effective manner. Until a larger movement appears that can deal with them, however, it remains important to understand how they affect displacement and neighborhood stability.

*"It's a breakthrough in home financing. Your parents put up the first $100,000."*

## DISPLACEMENT FROM PROPERTY TAX INCREASES

As neighborhoods "revitalize," various changes take place that can uproot current homeowners. One, of course, is property tax increases resulting from rising values and assessments. An elderly couple owns their home free and clear, having bought it decades ago and paid off the mortgage. Property tax assessments are low, based on low original sales prices, slow increases in value, and even slower reassessment practices. All of a sudden the neighborhood "takes off" and house prices start going wild. The tax assessor comes back through, hoping to capture some of this value in the form of higher tax revenues for the city. Since reassessments are based in large part on recent sales prices for comparable properties, the elderly homeowners get socked with a huge increase in their tax bill, perhaps $500-1,000 or more. The result: either severe financial hardship, or displacement, if the owners have to sell out, take their profits, and move to a rental unit or buy another home in a less costly area. (Such persons, who have not participated in the real estate market for decades, may also be totally unaware of financial realities and may wind up selling their home for far less than it is worth, and far less than they will need to secure replacement housing — see the section below on homeowner counselling.)

In order to prevent this sort of displacement, it is essential that some kind of property tax relief be provided to low- and moderate-income families in gentrifying neighborhoods. But this can't really be done without confronting the fact that property taxes, extremely regressive as they are, are a burden on lower-income homeowners everywhere. Tax-oriented anti-displacement strategies must come in the form of broad-scale relief. A subsequent section discusses the misguided direction the spreading "tax revolt" has taken, which sometimes *accelerates* displacement. What follows are examples of tax relief measures specifically designed to aid low- and moderate-income households.

### "CIRCUIT-BREAKERS"

This term comes from the field of electrical engineering, where the dangers from current overload are prevented through an automatic device that breaks the electrical circuit rather than allowing the overload. Applied to tax relief, it means that when the property assessment overloads the family income capacity, the property tax circuit-breaker provides automatic relief.

There are several basic variations of the circuit-breaker. (A good description of these variations is contained in a short study titled *Property Tax Circuit-Breakers: Current Status and Policy Issues,* available free from the Advisory Commission on Intergovernmental Relations, Washington, DC 20575.) They can be applied state-wide or locally. They can be applied to renters as well as owners, since renters in effect pay property taxes as part of their rent bill — for purposes of computing the tax, a given percentage of the rent bill, usually 20%, is assumed to be the renter's tax payment. They can apply to the elderly and disabled only, or to everyone, regardless of age or health status. They can be restricted to households under a certain income or apply to everyone regardless of income. Formulas used in computing circuit-breaker relief can — and do — vary widely, and benefits may come in several ways: tax credits, cash refunds or lower initial tax bills.

Most commonly, the overload level is determined by setting a maximum acceptable percentage of income a household should be expected to pay in property taxes (the percentage can vary by income level). In the District of Columbia, for example, households with annual incomes under $3,000 receive a tax credit (or cash refund, if the household has no local income tax obligation to which this credit can be applied) for 80% of a tax bill that exceeds 2% of the household's income; households with annual incomes over $5,000 receive tax credits, or cash, for 60% of a tax bill that exceeds 4% of the household's income. In other jurisdictions — Arkansas, Missouri, and Connecticut, for example — credit or refund is given for 100% of the tax obligation that exceeds a certain percentage of income, although in some states there is an upper dollar limit on the amount of the credit/refund. An

97

alternative formula is to refund a certain percentage of the property tax bill, no matter what its size, with the percentage refunded higher for lower-income households.

## RURAL "CIRCUIT-BREAKERS"

In rural areas, separate circuit breakers for farmland are an important addition, not only to assist farmers financially but to preserve farmland and open space. In Michigan, for example, farmers receive a refundable tax credit for property taxes that exceed 7% of household income. To obtain this relief, farmers must agree to keep their land as farmland for at least ten years, and if the agreement is not renewed, the farmer owes the last seven years' back taxes (without interest or penalty). Farmers' circuit-breakers of this type usually include an upper limit on beneficiaries, in terms of acreage, in order to restrict benefits to small farmers.

(For other tax-related anti-displacement protections for farmland, see Chapter 4.)

## "HOMESTEAD EXEMPTION"

An alternative to the circuit-breaker is the so-called "homestead exemption," in which the assessed value of owner-occupied homes is reduced by a certain specified dollar amount, sometimes for the elderly, sometimes for all owner-occupiers (in which case the elderly may be given a larger reduction in assessed value). Some states have both homestead exemptions and circuit-breakers. The advantage of the circuit-breaker mechanism is that it can pinpoint beneficiaries according to need, rather than giving equal benefits to households, regardless of need. Moreover, homestead exemption provides no benefits for renters, even though renters generally have lower incomes than homeowners and therefore have

greater need for tax relief. Another consideration is that in some states a constitutional amendment is required to introduce homestead exemptions, whereas the courts have held that circuit-breakers do not violate constitutional requirements for uniform treatment of all classes of taxpayers.

**The property tax, like the sales tax, is one of the most regressive taxes we have.**

Pressures for general property tax relief, as well as for circuit-breakers and other specific devices, will of course come from a far broader constituency than just those concerned with the displacement issue. Anti-displacement arguments and organizations can nonetheless play a major role in introducing such reforms, determining their specific form, and pushing them through. In particular, anti-displacement groups can aid greatly in supplying the progressive guiding principles needed to ensure that the explosive energies unleashed by property tax relief campaigns carry through to good results.

## GUIDING PRINCIPLES FOR PROPERTY TAX REFORM

The property tax, like the sales tax, is one of the most regressive taxes we have. Lower-income people pay a higher proportion of their income on housing than do upper-income people: the property tax therefore takes a larger proportional bite from people with lower incomes. Both for political reasons — that is, wider support — and in the interests of social justice, circuit-breakers and similar reforms should cover everyone who needs help, rather than singling out small classes of people with

particularly evident problems. And the formulas and systems proposed should be as progressive as possible, delivering greater relief to people with lower incomes.

## MAKE IT BIG ENOUGH

If displacement of homeowners from gentrifying areas is to be avoided, it is important that benefits under circuit-breaking mechanisms be large enough to offset rapidly escalating values and reassessments. The ACIR study cited above, which reports results from a 1974 survey of state governments, showed that the average beneficiary got a break of only $150 a year, and that in only three states did the average claimant receive $200 or more. By comparison, sudden reassessment increases in a gentrifying area can raise a household's tax bill many times the amount.

## LOOK OUT FOR MISGUIDED "TAX REVOLT FEVER"

Tax revolts are spreading widely throughout the country, most dramatically evidenced by California's Proposition 13, which passed overwhelmingly in 1978. Massachusetts' cousin to that, Proposition 2½, also passed massively in 1980. Similar bills are cropping up all over, and anti-displacement groups are certain to be involved in the campaigns that surround them.

Most of these major tax reform initiatives are actually corrupting the legitimate and powerful movement to ease the property tax burden. Wealthy people and landlords benefit most from Propositions 13 and 2½, and the "reform" in both cases rubs salt in that wound by endangering public services that lower-income people need and are least able to replace on their own: public transportation, clinics and hospitals, fire and police protection, libraries, public assistance payments, etc. Property tax relief should be progressive in and of itself, and also should be joined to other kinds of tax reform (on income tax, capital gains, etc.) that combine to shift the burden for necessary social costs to those who can afford them.

Additionally, it is clear by now that the guiding forces in the major "tax revolt" initiatives like Propositions 13 and 2½ are in fact big-money people whose real purpose is to line their own pockets. Proposition 13, for instance, has had a notoriously regressive outcome. It placed an absolute limit of 1% of market value on the amount of the annual property tax bill, and limited annual assessment increases to 2%, applying these rules to all kinds of property. The lion's share of benefits — $4.1 billion of the $6.4 billion in rake-offs during the first year — went to owners of factories, shopping centers, businesses, stores, and rental properties (where, most ironically, the benefits all went to the landlords and none to the tenants who really pay those property taxes.) The average homeowner got big relief, but at the price of giving the big property owners even bigger relief, and the renters none. Since one of the two initiators of Prop. 13, Howard Jarvis, was head of the Los Angeles Apartment Owners Association, this was not surprising.

The regressive nature of Prop. 13 will become even more pronounced as the years pass, due to its provision that properties can be reassessed up to current market value whenever they're sold. Since residential properties tend to change hands more frequently than commercial and industrial properties (particularly large ones — the Bank of America headquarters doesn't get sold very often), homeowners and renters will, over time, pay an increasingly large portion of the total property tax.

Overall property tax reform *is* needed in our cities and rural areas. Commendable efforts toward this goal include attempts to shift the burden away from residential property generally. Massachusetts' statewide Question 1, adopted in 1978, amended the state constitution to permit creation of what is known as a "split tax roll." Instead of having to tax all types of property at the same rate, the state now has four taxation categories, with preferential assessment ratios, plus homestead exemptions, for homeowners. The initiative campaign was carried out by a broad and unusual statewide coalition, including homeowners, consumer groups, seniors, minorities, unions, teachers, mayors, and even the American Legion. A central force in the coalition was a citizens' group called Massachusetts Fair Share, which had been working on tax reform issues for several years. Further information on their campaign is available from them at 304 Boylston St., Boston, MA 02116.

# HOUSING CODE ENFORCEMENT

Housing codes can present a displacement threat to lower income homeowners (and to renters as well — see pages 151 and 152). If housing code enforcement requires owners to make repairs they cannot afford, their only choice may be to sell their homes and move elsewhere. It is by no means unheard of for a city to use housing code enforcement as an intentional tool to force lower-income people out of an area targeted for development. It was done under the urban renewal program, to reduce the costs and difficulties of clearing land, and it is done today when "upgrading" is under way.

Housing codes had an honorable birth, invented by reformers a century ago to try to deal with the deadly tenements into which the historic waves of immigrants were stuffed. The codes were meant to ensure that everyone had shelter meeting at least minimum standards for health and safety.

But the codes don't accomplish that: millions of Americans continue to live in substandard, below-code conditions. Enforcement, in city and countryside alike, is always spotty, and often is guided by prevailing politics, with class and race discrimination and outright corruption frequently involved. Moreover, the codes, which vary from locality to locality, often contain questionable requirements not clearly related to health and safety, standards that can be interpreted in a highly subjective fashion.

Too often, the upgrading required — new wiring, for instance, or new plumbing — is more than lower-income owners can afford. Stretched out over a period of years, something that compassionate and regular code enforcement might have prompted, it could have been done. But under the gun of sudden inspection and quick deadlines, lower-income homeowners may have little choice but to sell and move. City planners know this.

It is important for neighborhood groups to differentiate between code enforcement operations (and related rehab programs) that work *against* displacement, as opposed to those consciously intended to uproot an established population, or those which unintentionally have the same effect. In the latter two cases, organized efforts are needed to modify the code enforcement and rehab effort, to make it more

Bob Buchta

## Reindustrialization Calling

Ann and Andrew Giannini have, they say, everything they want: a home they enjoy, neighbors who watch over one another, stores within walking distance. Mrs. Giannini, 69 years old, tends 65 rose bushes in her backyard, and Mr. Giannini, 71, looks after a splendid garden of corn, peppers, beans, lettuce, radishes and carrots, right here in this factory city.

But the Gianninis live in the path of a major project designed to preserve jobs for Detroit and to help revitalize the American automobile industry.

In June, the city announced a plan . . . to acquire and raze several hundred houses and businesses in the Gianninis' East Detroit neighborhood. By combining this 375-acre parcel with the Chrysler Corporation's huge abandoned Dodge Main plant to the north, in Hamtramck, the city would be able to provide the General Motors Corporation a 465-acre site for a new $500-million Cadillac plant.

Under present plans the site would be sold or leased to G.M. at prices comparable to those of open land in suburban or rural areas. . . . The Cadillac proposal illuminates the issues [underlying] reindustrialization — plant closings, job losses, sales slumps, tax concessions, decisions by corporations where to reinvest their capital. . . . When an appraiser knocked on the

Gianninis' door this summer, reindustrialization, it might be said, was calling. . . .

"I think we are so desperate for jobs we will do anything," argued Maryann Mahaffey, a member of the City Council. "We are trapped. The multinational corporations are doing the economic planning for the world. . . ."

For some of the residents of the highly ethnic, about half-white and half-black neighborhood . . . the logic of jobs and redevelopment and reindustrialization is not paramount. . . . Perhaps 300 [of them] have banded together under the Poletown Area Revitalization Task Force to fight construction of the plan or to insure that if their neighborhood is destroyed, they receive acceptable prices for their homes and assistance in finding new homes.

Thomas Olechowski, chairman of the Poletown Task Force, says that G.M. should refurbish the old Cadillac site and continue to use it. He contends that Detroit should avoid spending extensive public money to subsidize heavy, and, in his view, perhaps obsolete industry. . . .

[The Gianninis] reared six children in their home. It has carpets, and shelves for their books. Mr. and Mrs. Giannini often sit on their porch and take the air until far into the night. . . . "It may seem like a slum to some people," Mrs. Giannini said. "It's not. To us, it's home. . . . I thought as long as you got the title your home belongs to you for life."

*New York **Times**, Sept. 15, 1980*

Bob Buchta

humane. Such modifications might give people more time to remove violations, permit exemptions from "picky" requirements that do not relate to health or safety of occupants, and provide homeowners with assistance in meeting code standards. Low-interest loans, outright grants, free home repair services (see page 108) are all important ways of easing the burden of code enforcement. Insisting that neighborhood organizations play an advisory role in the enforcement program can also help to minimize displacement.

Concentrated code enforcement almost always requires additional inspectors, and in some instances neighborhood residents have been trained and hired as code inspectors for their own areas. This increases the chances that the enforcement operation will be sensitive to the human problems involved. (A description of one such program, in Paterson, New Jersey, is contained in the July, 1969 issue of the *Journal of Housing*.)

It is useful to know, too, that the right of housing inspectors to enter homes is not absolute: several leading court decisions have held that inspectors must secure a search warrant if homeowners do not wish to let them in. (For further information on this point, see "Differential Enforcement of Housing Codes — The Constitutional Dimension," in volume 55 of the Univ. of Detroit *Journal of Urban Law,* 1978, by Daniel Mandelker, Julie Gibb and Annette Kolis.)

One homeowner group, the Bois d'Arc Patriots, saw the displacement dangers of housing code enforcement, and successfully fought it off in the Sante Fe and Mt. Auburn areas of East Dallas, Texas. There, the largely retired homeowners formed block clubs to oppose the designation of their area for redevelopment.

Their first step was to oppose a city program to hire 40 temporary code inspectors for the area, which they rightly saw as the initial move towards displacement. By informing homeowners that they did not have to let inspectors on their premises, confronting city officials with direct opposition to this program, and generally educating and organizing the neighborhood around the impending redevelopment threat, the group was able to get widespread media coverage and force the city to draw back. A good videotape on the Bois d'Arc Patriots' resistance to the displacement/gentrification impact of Dallas' CDBG program is cited on page 140.

# WHEN THE MONEY DRIES UP: REDLINING, THE HOME MORTGAGE DISCLOSURE ACT, AND THE COMMUNITY REINVESTMENT ACT

A particularly perverse form of displacement occurs when lending institutions and insurance companies decide to withhold funds and services from neighborhoods that need them, or offer mortgages and insurance policies at discriminatory, often unaffordable rates, or on oppressive terms. This practice is called *redlining,* and it reflects the racist or class-biased assumption that particular low-income neighborhoods are worthless for investment purposes. Homeowners who need to make renovations to maintain their property — to meet code standards, for instance, or just to continue living there — can't get the loans they need. And if fire insurance is unavailable, even otherwise willing lenders will withhold investment funds. Even well-intentioned landlords can't get money to fix up their buildings. The result: accelerated deterioration, disinvestment, and displacement.

Two relatively recent federal laws help to make both redlining research and counter-attack possible. These are the Home Mortgage Disclosure Act and the Community Reinvestment Act.

## RESEARCHING REDLINING WITH THE HOME MORTGAGE DISCLOSURE ACT (HMDA)

Adopted by Congress in 1975, strengthened and extended in 1980, HMDA offers a way to get at previously unavailable data on mortgage lending patterns, data that can be used to document redlining. HMDA covers all federally-insured metropolitan area banks, savings and loan institutions, and federal credit unions — meaning the vast majority of real estate lenders. It requires them to report every year, by census tract or zip code area, the number, value, and location of real estate loans they have originated or purchased. The data must be submitted on a standard form which lenders must retain for five years and make available for viewing and copying on request.

At first, community groups encountered difficulty in piecing together these reports, dispersed as they were among the many lending institutions that might be operating in a given area. But this obstacle was overcome by the 1980 Housing and Community Development Act, which mandated the establishment of a central repository system for HMDA

Mortgage Loan Disclosure Statement
(Specimen Form)

101

Chapter 10 / PREVENTING DISPLACEMENT OF HOMEOWNERS

data in each metropolitan area. Additionally, this 1980 improvement requires compilation of aggregate census tract data on location, age of housing stock, income levels and racial characteristics of loan recipients for all reporting institutions within each metropolitan area. As of this writing, the central data repository system has not been established, although it likely will be in a very short time. To locate the repository for your area, contact the regional office of the Federal Reserve Board, the Federal Home Loan Bank Board, the Federal Deposit Insurance Corporation or the Comptroller of the Currency — any local bank or savings and loan can give you the address and phone number of these regional offices.

Thus, for the years since 1975, and particularly from 1980 onward, HMDA data make it possible to get a good picture of lending practices on a neighborhood-area basis for lending institutions suspected of redlining. (The 1980 Act also calls for a study of the feasibility of requiring HMDA-type information for small business loans as well, with a report and recommendations to be submitted to Congress by March 1, 1981. As of this writing, the report now is scheduled for submission later in 1981; copies will be available from the Federal Financial Institutions Examination Council, whose address is listed at the end of this chapter.)

Some community groups have analyzed mortgage lending in their neighborhoods in detail. A good how-to-do-it booklet, containing case studies of successful experience, is *Home Mortgage Disclosure Act and Reinvestment Strategies: A Guidebook* (1979), available free from HUD's Office of Policy Development and Research, Washington, DC 20410.

## FIGHTING BACK WITH THE COMMUNITY REINVESTMENT ACT (CRA)

This law, passed in 1977, takes HMDA a step further. CRA expands the service requirements for federally-supervised lending institutions to include an obligation to help meet local credit needs of the communities in which they are located. In other words, under CRA, banks and savings and loans must give to, as well as take from, the neighborhoods off of which they profit.

Community leverage under this law is not great, but can be useful. The pressure potential develops when neighborhood groups get enough data, such as HMDA figures, to convince — or threaten to convince — federal regulatory examiners that the community's credit needs are not being met. This tactic works best on those occasions when lenders apply to the federal agencies that regulate and insure them for permission to merge, expand, or acquire. Even the opening of an electronic teller machine requires such permission. Such transactions are so important to lenders that they often are willing to negotiate substantial concessions in order to eliminate any community opposition to their plans. In some situations, local groups have made good deals for their communities through CRA challenges. And in a few instances lenders actually have been denied the permissions they sought. Needless to say, even one such case reverberates loud and clear through the banking industry.

In San Bernadino, California, for example, a savings and loan agreed to open an inner city branch in exchange for the community dropping its CRA challenge to their application to open a suburban branch. In St. Louis, the

mostly Black Wellston Community Organization brought a challenge against a bank seeking permission to acquire a bank in Clayton, an upper-income suburb. With the St. Louis Federal Reserve Bank acting as mediator, the community got the bank to agree to make $1 million in improvement loans available to Wellston residents, establish more flexible loan terms and credit standards for Wellston borrowers, establish a job training and placement program in the community, provide housing counselling services for the community, begin an outreach program to market credit services in Wellston and inform real estate brokers that credit was available, and hire a community investment coordinator and a consultant to help obtain federal and state funds for reinvestment.

Of course, in gentrifying areas the problem is not credit starvation but too much money. (Some observers even think CRA may have backfired by letting loose a flood of loans to newcomers that winds up displacing current residents.) The CRA challenge tool therefore must be used carefully, and is appropriate only in certain well-defined situations. Where the community has a specific reinvestment strategy to put forth, one which identifies investment needs, sets investment goals, and selects a clear plan of action, chances are better that a CRA "victory" will aid the people now living in the area, rather than boosting a gentrification process. Some of the useful anti-displacement financing tools mentioned in other parts of this guide can be incorporated into such agreements: loans for limited-equity coop conversions (see pages 176-180), withholding funds from speculators (see page 36), equity participation (see page 193).

For further information on CRA strategies, contact the National Training and Information Center, 1123 W. Washington Blvd., Chicago, IL 60607. They publish a community reinvestment handbook, "Pass the Buck... Back," and with their affiliate, National Peoples Action, publish *Disclosure,* a newspaper which provides up-to-date information on HMDA and CRA activities by community groups and government agencies.

## DISPLACEMENT FROM TROUBLESOME NEW SOURCES OF HOUSING MONEY

One of the hottest housing finance ideas of the late 1970s was mortgage revenue bonds. In this approach, a state or city government borrows money by floating a bond issue, and then lends that money out for housing purposes. Because city and state bond interest is exempt from federal income taxes, these bonds can be sold at below-market interest rates: wealthy investors are willing to take a lower than market return on them because the income is non-taxable. So the money borrowed in this fashion then can be loaned out at lower interest rates. The idea became very popular with local and state governments, and in no time the market was flooded with such bond issues (which, ironically, served to drive up borrowing costs).

The approach is objectionable from the outset, because the price for this "cheap" housing money is letting rich investors avoid paying taxes. But it also has led to displacement and other disadvantages for lower-income people. In Minneapolis, for example, money raised from mortgage revenue bonds was lent to condominium buyers, actually fueling the displacement of several hundred households. In other areas, the funds have been used to finance luxury units or aid upper-income homebuyers and rehabbers.

Abuses of the program and loss of revenue to the U.S. Treasury led Congress to pass legislation in late 1980 restricting the use of these bonds. The new federal rules place upper limits on the amount of these bonds each state can issue and impose other restrictions that may make them less attractive to investors. But

they do little to decrease the displacement potential of new mortgage revenue bond issues. So anti-displacement groups in communities where mortgage revenue bond programs are being proposed should be on guard to prevent such programs from financing buyers and development that will force people out of their homes and neighborhoods. With enough local pressure, this approach — if it is to be used — can be employed primarily or solely to help lower-income buyers and rehabbers, through equity participation arrangements (see page 193) and low-interest rehab loans, to develop limited-equity coops, and to refinance lower-income homeowners' indebtedness so as to avoid displacement. (See page 155 for discussion of HUD's Section 223(f) refinancing program.)

## HOMEOWNER DISPLACEMENT THROUGH CRIMINAL RIP-OFFS

Various forms of homeowner ripoffs, by contractors, "home finance counsellors" and others, are becoming increasingly prevalent. Such unscrupulous activities, most often directed at elderly, poorly educated, and disabled persons, are on the increase in this inflationary period, largely due to the sharply rising value of homeowners' equity. (Equity is the homeowner's original downpayment and mortgage principal repayments, plus any increase in the value of the property beyond what is still owed on the mortgage.) For owners who bought a long time ago, particularly in areas that now are gentrifying, this equity may be quite large, as market pressures and inflation combine to lift the house price far above what it was originally bought and mortgaged for. Where the mortgage has been paid off, the

ASK ABOUT
MUTUAL FIDELITY'S NEW
"INFLATION FIGHTER"
HOME LOAN PROGRAM

Ken Alexander / San Francisco Examiner

KEN ALEXANDER 3-26

*"What it boils down to is, we don't lend you a dime, you just make interest payments."*

total equity may be several times the original investment.

The ripoff schemes — and there are several kinds — are designed to get possession of a house so that it can be sold, and the inflated equity taken away as cash. Typically, entire webs of salesmen, "counsellors," contractors, and finance companies are involved. Their quick-profit frauds not only cause forced relocation and severe financial loss to their victims, but also have strong destabilizing effects on neighborhoods.

Defrauding of homeowners is widespread, but is particularly prevalent in areas such as Southern California where home values have been rising especially fast. The material that follows is taken from accounts of such practices in the Los Angeles area. It gives the details of some of the more common fraud approaches. It also shows how effective action by investigative newspapers and Legal Aid lawyers can spur legislative and law enforcement response.

**The home repair scam** works like this: door-to-door salespeople come around, sometimes after an initial phone solicitation, selling paint jobs, burglar protection systems, air conditioning, drapes and carpets, termite extermination, plumbing/electrical/heating work, siding, fences, or whatever. Using well-honed sales pitches, they get around the "but we can't afford it" response by offering to do the work on credit. The contracts homeowners are pressured into signing have all kinds of damaging clauses, from hidden high interest charges to lack of protection against faulty work. Most dangerously, however, they are "lien sale" contracts — meaning that homeowners' failure to meet payments lets the crooks take the house as compensation. And since the payments are far higher than the salesperson promised, the likelihood of this happening is great.

In one case documented in court records, a woman was sold a burglar/fire/medical alert alarm system for a contract price of $2500 (the unit was later appraised as worth $600), to be paid for over ten years in monthly installments of $89.12 — adding up, with finance charges, to a total of $10,694.40, or nearly three-fourths of the home's assessed value. A month later, the woman died of a heart attack (the medical alert system didn't even work — among other hidden charges was a $10 monthly operating fee), and her heirs, a blind brother and a disabled sister, faced eviction because of non-payment on the alarm system loan. In a typical move, the alarm system firm sold the home to a finance company at a foreclosure sale held at the finance company's office.

Under California law, no court hearing was even required. And without a court hearing,

victimized homeowners have no chance to raise a defense to the foreclosure action, such as shoddy workmanship or the company's failure to live up to the terms of the contract. Often the contractor and finance company work hand-in-hand, sometimes sharing offices and company officers, the aim being not so much to sell the goods as to use the contract to gain ownership of the house through foreclosure proceedings, where there is virtually no competitive bidding. Unlike regular mortgages, where the lender generally is willing to work out terms to help a delinquent borrower, the operators of these schemes will foreclose as soon as the law allows and will not work out any arrangements to help the homeowner remain. Often those signing such fraudulent contracts don't even receive the legally-required default notice, which triggers a 90-day period during which the borrower still can pay the amount owed and avoid foreclosure.

Other deceitful practices include: not informing the borrower that default on the improvement contract would lead to loss of the home (or actually assuring the homeowner fraudulently that the opposite is the case); not even giving the homeowner a copy of the contract; altering the contract after it has been signed; and failing to notify homeowners of their right to cancel the contract within three days of signing it. Further confusion is added when the contract is sold to a finance company, in whose name the bills arrive, and the homeowner doesn't even recognize the company demanding the money. As the Los Angeles *Times* put it, "the sales tactics and subsequent actions of [these] finance companies . . . fly in the face of every modern consumer protection and truth-in-lending law."

The **"mortgage counselling" scam** runs something like this: when a homeowner gets behind in mortgage payments, the mortgage holder files a "Notice of Default and Election to Sell," which begins the 90-day period after which foreclosure and sale can take place to recover the money loaned. These notices must be recorded with the County Recorder and are open for public inspection. So-called "default counsellors," "home loan counsellors," even "foreclosure saviors" copy these notices and show up at the door of the hapless homeowner, offering help in loan management, working out repayment terms with the mortgage holder, budget management, etc. In practice, they do just the opposite: use every dirty trick in the book to ensure that the home will in fact be lost and that the "counsellor" will wind up owning it. The device generally used is a complicated and deceptive "sale-lease option plan," in which the "counsellor" in effect lends money to the homeowner to pay off the mortgage arrears, under a contract that gives the "counsellor" title to the home if even a single payment on the new loan is missed. Terms and interest rates on this loan are so deceptively stated, moreover, that homeowners are likely to miss payments — which is the goal of the scam in the first place.

Thousands of homeowners in the Los Angeles area have suffered loss of their homes and displacement due to the crooked activities of these "suede shoe operators" in the real estate field. (An exact figure cannot be stated, since many people are too embarrassed by the swindle to reveal it to their friends and neighbors or to government authorities.)

Concerted legal and media work started a rapid process of public exposure and concern that led to government protective action. A series of lawsuits filed by the Legal Aid Foundation of Los Angeles on behalf of clients who had been ripped off provided the beginning documentation for a hard-hitting series of articles, starting in early 1979, by Los Angeles *Times* reporter Henry Weinstein. Injunctive lawsuits were filed by the California Attorney General's consumer fraud unit to stop these practices, and the courts responded to these and the Legal Aid suits with a series of tough injunctions against the most notorious perpetrators of these operations. The crooks were forbidden from bringing foreclosure and eviction actions. Specific deceptive practices were halted, and profits from allegedly fraudulent real estate transactions were frozen until damage suits already filed could be adjudicated. (One of the ruses used by these operators is to move assets outside the county or state, and thus out of the reach of a court's jurisdiction, or to declare bankruptcy. A $8,000 judgment won by one homeowner against one of these swindlers still had not been collected four years later because of such tactics.)

A further step was taken by Los Angeles City and Los Angeles County, which separately set up homeowner fraud prevention projects, to protect owners against unethical contractors and foreclosure counsellors through honest counselling, including contractor and Legal Aid referrals. These projects also set out to force restitution to defrauded homeowners, and to get information for criminal prosecutions.

More thoroughgoing reform was brought about through state legislation triggered by all this exposure. During its 1979 session, the California legislature passed no less than six laws designed to deal with homeowner swindles. They require foreclosure sales to be carried out by persons having no interest in the outcome of the sale, a measure designed to prevent collusion and other shady practices which preclude competitive bidding. (A lobbyist for the California Association of Realtors was quoted as acknowledging that under prevailing practices someone "could hold a foreclosure sale in a telephone booth with his brother being the only bidder.") The new laws also prevent "foreclosure counsellors" from taking over any ownership interest in a counsellee's house, and eliminate other specific abuses by such operators. Prominent printed warnings are now required on lien-sale contracts, indicating that failure to meet payments can result in loss of one's home. The

> "Under prevailing practices, someone could hold a foreclosure sale in a telephone booth, with his brother being the only bidder."

laws strengthen the state's Contractor Licensing Law to put fraudulent contractors out of business, and permit easier recovery of damages. They also provide that contracts and notices to homeowners regarding foreclosure contain clearer statements of rights and remedies, that persons dealing in such foreclosures cannot "take unconscionable advantage" of a homeowner; and that unconscionable transactions may be rescinded within three years. More generally, they permit consumers to void any "unconscionable" contract. (Until 1979, California was one of only three states that did not have such a law.)

While these laws represent real progress in protecting homeowners against displacement and loss of assets, no one should be under the illusion that mere passage of laws means the end of the problem. Effective enforcement by local district attorneys and the Contractors Licensing Board will be a major hurdle. Evasion and loopholes started just weeks after passage of these laws. According to the same Los Angeles *Times* reporter, in a story headed "Large Lenders Allegedly Evading Homeowner Protection Law," several of the state's largest financial institutions immediately began using a new contract in home improvement sales that they maintain exempts them from the new reforms designed to curb abuses in the use of lien-sale contracts.

Even stronger legislation that would have abolished the use of lien-sale contracts for home improvement didn't make it through the California legislature because of intensive lobbying by the billion-dollar texture coating industry and financial institutions. Many of the major banks and savings and loans have a considerable behind-the-scenes role in these shady transactions, by purchasing lien-sale contracts from home improvement contractors, thereby supplying them with additional operating capital and a quick profit, while at the same time insulating themselves from direct participation in unethical and illegal practices. One of the bills that did pass contains a feature forbidding financial institutions from purchasing lien-sale contracts that have "reassignment clauses." These clauses provide that when a borrower falls behind in payments the contract is sold back to the home improvement concern. This law hopefully will make lending institutions choose more carefully when purchasing such contracts, which in turn should make contractors a little more concerned about overselling.

More information on these practices and what was done to halt them is available from the Legal Aid Foundation of Los Angeles, 3663 W. 6th St., Los Angeles, CA 90020.

# FIGHTING DISPLACEMENT THROUGH HOMEOWNER COUNSELLING

One effective approach to combatting displacement and destabilization in homeowner neighborhoods is to offer accurate information, informed counselling, and needed aid and advocacy services to people confused or threatened by changing neighborhood conditions.

A good model for this kind of operation is Baltimore's St. Ambrose Housing Aid Center (321 E. 25 St., Baltimore, MD 21218). St. Ambrose had been in operation since 1972, originally with assistance from the Baltimore Association of Catholic Charities and the State Housing Commission, and has helped some 1100 families remain in their neighborhoods or find and purchase affordable housing there. Some 70% of their clients are Black. Part of their work is outreach efforts to people in danger of displacement, to advise them of their best course of action, and to counsel those seeking to buy in their neighborhoods. The Center also buys properties, rehabs them, and sells them to people who will help stabilize the neighborhood, assisting them to find financing when necessary. The Center has established good relations with several local banks, which provide lines of credit for the acquisition and renovation work. And this access to capital, plus an intimate knowledge of the local real estate market, enables the Center to compete successfully with speculators at tax and other repossession sales. In some instances, St. Ambrose absorbs part of the acquisition and rehab costs in order to keep sales prices down and make it possible for lower-income people to move into the neighborhood. Because of the volume of the operation — a stock of about 50 homes is maintained, mostly bought in rundown condition, then refurbished — the Center has its own contractors on staff to do the renovation work. The staff numbers 16, and the annual budget (1979) is about a quarter of a million dollars, primarily from Catholic Charities and Community Development Block Grant funds. Almost a third of those the Center helps are single-parent households, with annual incomes in the $6-12,000 range; two-parent households who get assistance are likely to have somewhat higher incomes ($10-18,000 a year).

A further extension of St. Ambrose's operations is Charm Realty, a brokerage firm, which is self-supporting through sales commissions. Assisting with the buying and selling of homes puts the organization in a good position to influence who moves into the neighborhood and to insure stability and a good mix of income and ethnic groups and household types.

Another example of neighborhood-based and -oriented real estate brokerage services is the East Side Housing Action Committee (ESHAC) in the Riverwest area of Milwaukee. Residents there decided to fight the speculators by opening their own realty firm. A triggering incident was when a speculator convinced a family its home was worth only $17,500, and then resold it two months later for $33,000. The firm encourages homeowners to sell to owner-occupants rather than absentee landlords and speculators, and current renters are counselled so they can buy homes from their landlords or other homes in the area. ESHAC also runs "buyers clinics" at which loan officers from lending institutions, FHA staff people, and others knowledgeable about home-buying and homeowning advise prospective purchasers.

Like St. Ambrose, ESHAC was started with the help of a government grant (in this case, from the Wisconsin Department of Local Affairs and Development). The group was well established: at the time it opened its realty operation, it had grown in seven years from a tiny tenant group to 500 dues-paying members, a staff of ten, and an annual budget of $300,000. This fact helped to overcome the protests of the local private real estate industry to the opening of the brokerage operation. Among other activities, ESHAC has conducted a successful anti-highway struggle, transformed a failing supermarket into a grocery coop, founded a community credit union, and established the city's largest natural foods store.

ESHAC's housing listings come from regular realtor services, as well as from more informal, word-of-mouth sources within the neighborhood. As with St. Ambrose, the related activities of the organization feed naturally into its real estate brokerage activities. For further information contact ESHAC at 531 E. Burleigh St., Milwaukee, WI 53212.

Housing counselling services are available in many parts of the country to assist people who are considering home purchase, or who are having difficulties paying for or managing their current homes. HUD maintains a list of HUD-approved counselling agencies for homeowners and renters, primarily for people involved in HUD-assisted housing programs. Services are free (and according to HUD Washington officials, persons displaced as

# Uprooting Eastern Kentucky

*Geneva Sherman came from West Liberty, Kentucky, in the coalfields of Morgan County, to tell Congress of the wrongs done when the Army Corps of Engineers moved people away from the planned site of the Big Paint Creek Valley Reservoir. These are selected, condensed excerpts from her testimony.*

Rural people are very different from urban people in how they use the land. To Paint Creek people land is security. You can fall fall back on it whenever times are rough, not as an investment, but as a means to get by on. If these people have their land, they [can] raise from 30 to 90 percent of their food. They get fuel for heat right from their own property.

Lawrence Pierce / *Rural America*

Due to the coal boom in eastern Kentucky, housing has gotten so scarce the people couldn't find the land to even build a house on. . . . The land has literally been stolen.

The Corps has done absolutely nothing to examine the needs of these people before they came in to relocate them. The chief Corps of Engineers office in Washington was advised by mail that the Relocation Act program on Paint Creek was not good, and by return mail we received a letter stating that the program was good, due to the fact that less than five percent of the people were going to court. . . . [But] the people [here] have not obtained the skills or knowledge to deal with bureaucrats . . . in complicated legal rights issues. Most of all their experience with the bureaucracy has been one of acceptance of authority.

There was one particular case: Lazarus and Bessie Blevins, [who lived] on his brother's farm in a very good house, but the Corps said it was not decent, safe, or sanitary because it didn't have a bathroom. Lazarus and Bessie had 10 children. He could not read or write. . . . The Corps said : "Well, you can go to an apartment in town, because the low-income housing project had to rent to him."

Lazarus said, "I would rather be dead in hell than living in a housing project." That is the way he felt about it. He said, "I want a farm. . . . I lived on a farm, I need a farm."

So after many months of negotiation, Lazarus still didn't have a place to go. The Corps left him one night and about an hour later he completely cracked up and had a nervous breakdown. When he went to Eastern State Hospital, [Bessie] had to split her children up — the 10 children that had lived at home — among families.

Finally the Corps made the housing project manager give them housing. When Lazarus returned to his home, now in the housing project, his wife told me she was afraid to take him because he will go all to pieces. The doctors said he could crack up again at any time.

He never was the same. Spent most of his time at his brother's house on a farm, and four years after they moved him, he died.

a result of HUD actions are also considered as people "involved in HUD-assisted housing programs"). There are some 650 of these HUD-approved housing agencies nationally, both private non-profit and public bodies. They doubtless vary a great deal as to what services they offer, how competent they are, and how sympathetic they will be to displacees. Nonetheless, they are a resource community groups concerned with displacement might want to check out. For the names of HUD-approved housing counselling agencies in your area, write or phone your HUD Area Office (see Appendix A), directing the request to the Neighborhood and Consumer Affairs Representative.

## FIGHTING DISPLACEMENT WITH REPAIR AND MAINTENANCE AID

Another highly useful anti-displacement service for homeowners performed by some neighborhood groups is free, or at-cost, repair and maintenance services for low-income residents. This approach combats displacement caused either by deteriorating housing conditions, or the demands of housing code enforcement, by removing hazards and code violations without swamping the homeowner's budget. To date, most such programs have been restricted to elderly low-income homeowners, but expanding the support to single-parent households and lower-income homeowners generally would clearly be a useful further step.

One of the most successful efforts has been Detroit's Maintenance Central for Seniors, begun in 1975 with a federal grant through the Older Americans Act. The group now has a staff of 50 and an annual budget of nearly $3

million, through Community Development Block Grant and private — including foundation and business — funds. One of the nicer features of the Detroit program is its use of retired craftspersons wherever possible, to take advantage of their experience and skills and supplement their incomes. As the group's founder put it, "they know these older houses much better than those younger folks, because they built these kinds of houses in their younger days." They also conduct training classes for younger people. Some 600 repair jobs a month are carried out by Maintenance Central, and the group has expanded its work throughout the city. For more information about this Detroit effort, contact Maintenance Central for Seniors, 3750 Woodward Ave., Detroit, MI 48201.

Programs of this type exist in many cities, sometimes funded under the Community Development Block Grant program, sometimes through private sources. In late 1980, HUD financed a Home Maintenance and Repair Demonstration for the Elderly, modeled after the Baltimore Neighborhood Housing Services Program, in seven cities: Greensboro (NC), Cleveland, San Francisco, Cincinnati, Hot Springs (AR), Boston, and Philadelphia. (A list of demonstration program contacts in each of these cities appears at the end of this chapter.) Each is slightly different in terms of sponsorship, area of operation and eligibility, and all unfortunately limit themselves to non-major repairs. Further information about the HUD demonstrations and the broader project of which is is a part, which includes a survey of all such programs in the U.S., is available from the Division of Housing Management and Special Users Research of HUD's Office of Policy Development and Research.

Related to this are the so-called "weather-ization programs," usually funded by the Community Services Administration. Under these programs, insulation, weather stripping and storm windows can be installed, free, in order to reduce home heating costs for low-income elderly persons. Information on such programs is generally available from local anti-poverty agencies, although the new Administration has indicated it will seek to terminate this program or have it incorporated under Community Development Block Grants.

## SPECIAL ANTI-DISPLACEMENT AIDS FOR OWNERS OF HUD-ASSISTED HOUSING

Persons who are or became homeowners with HUD/FHA-insured mortgages, under the Section 235, 203(b) or 221(d)(2) programs, were displaced in large numbers during the 1970s due to the actions of the mortgage-holders and HUD. These programs were characterized by numerous scandals — from shoddy renovation work, to outright fraud by government appraisers (for which many were sent to jail), to financial shenanigans by mortgage lenders. The result was an enormous number of mortgage defaults and foreclosures as lower-income households were bilked into paying excessive payments, beyond either their means or what the home was worth, for "rehabilitated" properties that began to fall apart, sometimes within weeks after the family moved in.

Beginning in 1973, in Chicago, a long and complex series of lawsuits were filed on behalf of the approximately six million people living in such HUD-assisted housing. The court action was intended to stop this displacement, and to require the lending institutions and government agencies responsible for the situation to halt the process of fast foreclosures that was producing it. While the lending institutions managed to get themselves off the hook, the courts did hold HUD responsible for failing to properly supervise the actions of the lenders, and ordered HUD to take remedial steps. HUD then stalled on settling the case until 1976, when a federal judge threatened to cite the Secretary of HUD for contempt of court. The settlement, and its subsequent amendments, offer a useful variety of protections and assistance to people threatened by displacement in HUD housing, and also to those already wrongfully displaced.

The court settlement calls for HUD, under certain conditions, to accept assignment of a mortgage that is in default — that is, take over management of the mortgage, rather than foreclose on it and evict the occupants — if the default is due to circumstances beyond the borrower's control. If the homeowner can show a reasonable probability that, given a period of reduced or suspended payments of up to 36 months, she or he can resume full mortgage payments and pay off any arrears, then HUD must allow the household to remain and must hold off on eviction and foreclosure.

With the change of Administration in 1977, HUD first began to take the assignment program seriously, issuing handbooks to guide the process and training field staff. As a result, the rate at which HUD accepts applications from homeowners in default has risen from 8% to 25%. Following a two-year period of negotiations, HUD agreed to a procedure for mortgage assignment that gives fair treatment to persons who were denied their rights during the time (1976-77) when HUD was effectively ignoring its own settlement agreement. Persons whose applications were previously rejected can have their requests reconsidered. Persons who for good cause had never done so can now apply for assignment. If HUD determines they were wrongfully rejected for the assignment program, they can get their old house back, if it's still available, or get another home from HUD's inventory of foreclosed single-family homes. It is estimated that as many as 30,000 families who lost their homes through foreclosure under these programs may be able to get their houses back or get another house.

The negotiations, which ended in 1979, stipulated that during the 36-month forebearance period monthly mortgage payments can be reduced or entirely suspended, and in no case can a household's total monthly housing expense exceed 35% of its income. After the 36-month forebearance period, in what is known as the "reinstatement period," payment of the accumulated arrears (payments not made in the past) usually will be spread out over the remaining life of the mortgage, to reduce their immediate impact — and in some instances the life of the mortgage can be extended ten years. But the new monthly payments cannot be higher than those the homeowner had been making under the mortgage that was foreclosed. (By extending the mortgage term, monthly payments can remain the same, even with the addition of arrearage.)

As part of the 1979 negotiations, HUD also agreed to continue this assignment program in its present form at least through 1984, and after that it is required either to operate the same or an equivalent program to enable homeowners to avoid foreclosure during periods of temporary financial distress.

Since making the 1979 agreement, HUD has proposed an alternative way of dealing with its obligations, essentially by lending money to the homeowner to pay off his or her debts, rather than directly acquiring the mortgage. This program, known as the Temporary Mortgage Assistance Payment Program, has been passed by Congress, and HUD currently is drawing up regulations to govern its operation. This approach was devised to ease the federal government's budgetary burden—only the transition loan to the homeowner appears on the federal budget, rather than the entire amount of the mortgage acquired by HUD as insurer.

For further information about the remedies available under the HUD agreement, contact the Legal Assistance Foundation of Chicago, 343 S. Dearborn St., Chicago, IL 60604, attn: William Wilen; or the National Housing Law Project, 2150 Shattuck Ave., #300, Berkeley, CA 94704, attn: David Madway.

Further discussion of displacement from HUD housing may be found in Chapters 7 and 11.

## PROTECTING SMALL FARMERS FROM DISPLACEMENT

One class of homeowner really in need of displacement protection is the small farmer. From 1950 to 1974, the number of farms with less than 50 acres fell from two million to half a million. Each year, 1% of the nation's farm families lose their agricultural livelihood, and often their housing, to urbanization, land price inflation, property tax increases related to development, and competition from "factory farms." Everything from technology to tax laws to corporate diversification conspires to force small farmers off their land.

## From 1950 to 1974, the number of farms with less than 50 acres fell from two million to half a million.

In general, tax incentives favor the rich over the poor: provisions that shelter income from tax bites are worth more to those whose tax rates are higher; and the rich can more easily afford the professional assistance needed for maximum manipulation of tax breaks. Tax provisions which reward and aid investment in farm land, equipment, and such recent innovations as "hog factories" and "poultry factories" give investors a competitive advantage over small farmers, whose main inputs are their own labor and management-husbandry skills, which receive no tax subsidies. As economists Chuck Hassebrook and Marty Strange of Nebraska's Center for Rural Affairs describe it, "The trend toward bigger and fewer farms is basically the replacement of farmers by bigger equipment and technology; so any subsidy which results in the purchase of more big farm technology results in fewer farmers."

This tax-subsidized move to larger machinery and higher technology encourages investors and large-farm operators to use their tax savings to expand their land base so as to match the capacity of their bigger equipment. This in turn inflates land prices, raises production costs, and forces small farmers off the land. According to 1979 U.S. Department of Agriculture figures, 5% of the nation's farms control 51% of all farmland.

Corporate moves to "vertically integrate" also have profound displacement effects on the small farmer. As farm production is increasingly controlled by companies engaged in non-production aspects of agriculture — sell-

ing farm supplies, processing farm products — once independent farmers are effectively turned into sharecroppers or wage- and piecework laborers for the company. That development has essentially taken place already in the poultry industry, and is advancing in the livestock business and other agricultural sectors. U.S. Department of Agriculture estimates are that the present rate of growth of confinement hog production will require 80% fewer hog farmers in the U.S. over the next 20 years. According to a recent study by the Agribusiness Accountability Project in San Francisco, corporate integrators now control 100% of sugar cane and sugar beets, 98% of fluid grade milk, 97% of broilers, 95% of processed vegetables, 85% of citrus fruit, 80% of seed crops, and 70% of potatoes.

Useful examples of protective strategies exist from various parts of the country, although the broader forces creating these threats to small farmers cannot be stopped on the local level. (This should not deter people from trying to fight for a more equitable federal income tax system, and an end to tyranny by technology and large corporations — people have to act simultaneously on the national and local scene and tie in to groups and reform efforts that are seeking more broad-based change.)

Especially in areas where developers are bidding up rural land prices, one way to deal with the problem is differential, or preferential, tax rates for agricultural land. Differential taxation tries to prevent the notorious skyrocketing of property tax bills when farmland is assessed for its potential value as house lots or shopping center sites. In urban fringe areas, the sale value to developers may be ten times higher than the sale value for use in food

Used by permission of Newspaper Enterprise Association

*"We in Washington see prosperity just around the corner for the family farm. All you have to do is survive until the suburbs reach you, and you'll make a fortune in real estate."*

production. In such situations, farmers can find themselves charged a ruinous tenfold increase in taxes. In 1973, Massachusetts farm advocacy groups pushed through the Farm Value Assessment Act, which established a a Farm Valuation Advisory Committee that assesses farmland based on its agricultural potential, and then applies standard tax rates to that value. All working farms qualify for coverage. The Act includes a proviso that if a farm being protected by differential assessment is offered for sale for non-agricultural purposes, the town in which it is located has a "first right of purchase" — 60 days in which to decide whether to buy the property for agricultural preservation. The Michigan rural "circuit-breaker" described on page 98 of this chapter is another example of how small farmers can be protected against development pressures.

Rural land trusts, as described on page 185, are another way to keep small farmers on their land and facilitate entry of new small farmers.

The National Family Farm Coalition (918 F St. NW, Washington, DC 20004) is lobbying in support of federal legislation to provide financial assistance to new farmers; establish new priorities for federally-funded agricultural research and extension programs; expand direct marketing of food products; and reform tax laws. A Family Farm Development Act, incorporating these provisions, has been periodically introduced in Congress. The Coalition is working now to push through selected portions of that bill, under the title Beginning Farmers Entry Assistance Act.

# REFERENCES

## MORTGAGE FORECLOSURES

"Mortgage Foreclosure Primer," by David Madway and Daniel Pearlman, is a three-part series in the July, August, and November, 1974 issues of *Clearinghouse Review,* available for reading or copying at most Legal Services offices, and university and court law libraries.

## PROPERTY TAX RELIEF

*Property Tax Circuit-Breakers: Current Status and Policy Issues* (1975), a good description of circuit-breaker variations plus other information, is available free from the Advisory Commission on Intergovernmental Relations, Washington, DC 20575.

*Revolt of the Haves,* by Robert Kuttner (Simon & Schuster, 1980), a useful general work on property

tax reform and its relation to progressive goals and citizens' movements, by a former staff member of the U.S. Senate Banking Committee; available at libraries and bookstores.

Massachusetts' statewide campaign for a "split tax roll": for more information, contact Massachusetts Fair Share, 304 Boylston St., Boston, MA 02116.

"Discrimination in Property Tax Assessments Against Low-Income Neighborhoods," by Kenneth Baar, scheduled to appear in the Summer, 1981 issue of *The Urban Lawyer,* available for reading or copying in most law libraries, provides useful background on an important cause of displacement.

## FIGHTING DISPLACEMENT FROM CODE ENFORCEMENT

Community resistance to displacement by code enforcement: a good videotape of the Bois d'Arc Patriots' resistance to Dallas, Texas' CDBG program, titled "The Housing and Community Development Act of 1974," is available from the Southern Governmental Monitoring Project, 75 Marietta St. NW, Atlanta, GA 30303, for a $25 rental fee.

Appropriate and sensitive code enforcement aided by hiring neighborhood residents as inspectors: case study of Paterson, New Jersey, is described in the July, 1969 issue of the *Journal of Housing,* available at most local planning and redevelopment departments, or through NAHRO, 2600 Virginia Ave. NW, Washington, DC 20037.

"Differential Enforcement of Housing Codes — The Constitutional Dimension," by Daniel Mandelker, Julie Gibb and Annette Kolis, a useful reference that explains homeowners' rights in resisting unwanted code enforcement, appears in Volume 55 of the University of Detroit *Journal of Urban Law* (1978), available for reading or copying in most university and court law libraries.

"Municipal Housing Code Enforcement and Low-Income Tenants," by Chester Hartman, Rob Kessler and Richard LeGates, concentrates, as the title indicates, on renters, but much of the material is

useful to homeowner areas as well. The article is in the March, 1974 issue of the *Journal of the American Institute of Planners,* which can be found in most university urban studies and planning libraries, or at local city planning departments; it has also been reprinted in *Housing Urban America* (2nd, 1980 edition only), edited by Jon Pynoos et al.

## MORTGAGE REDLINING AND THE COMMUNITY REINVESTMENT ACT

*Home Mortgage Disclosure Act and Reinvestment Strategies: A Guidebook* (1979), is a good introduction to how neighborhood groups can use HMDA data to analyze real estate loan activity in their neighborhood. It describes the Act, how to use it, and presents a series of case studies on experience neighborhood groups have had using HMDA. It also contains the text of the Act and implementing regulations. Available free from Office of Policy Development and Research, U.S. Department of HUD, Washington, DC 20410.

New HMDA Regulations: A copy of the 1980 Housing and Community Development Act, which (in Sections 304, 310 and 311) extends and amends the Home Mortgage Disclosure Act, is available by writing Information Office, U.S. Department of HUD, Washington, DC 20410. As of this writing, the detailed regulations implementing the 1980 legislation have not been issued, but ask for them when you write HUD.

"A Citizen's Guide to CRA" is available, free, from the Federal Financial Institutions Examination Council, 490 L'Enfant Plaza, 8th floor, Washington, DC 20219.

"Redlining and Disinvestment: Causes, Consequences and Proposed Remedies," by Frances Werner, William Frej and David Madway, a useful overview of the redlining issue, appears as the October, 1976 supplement to *Clearinghouse Review,* available for reading or copying at most law libraries and Legal Services offices.

Community Reinvestment Act challenge strategies: for more information, contact the National Training and Information Center, 1123 W. Washington Blvd., Chicago, IL 60607. The Center publishes a community reinvestment handbook, "Pass the Buck . . . Back" (1979). NTIC and its affiliate, National Peoples Action, publish a newspaper, called *Disclosure,* available for $10 a year, which provides up-to-date information on CRA and HMDA activities by community groups and government agencies.

*The CRA Reporter,* a useful periodical for groups interested in challenge strategies and other CRA activities, is published by the Neighborhood Revitalization Project of the Center for Community Change, 1000 Wisconsin Ave. NW, Washington, DC 20007.

## INSURANCE REDLINING

*Insurance Redlining: Fact Not Fiction* (1979), published by the Midwestern Regional Office of the U.S. Commission on Civil Rights, 230 S. Dearborn St., 32nd Floor, Chicago, IL 60604.

*Insurance Redlining: Profit$ vs. Policyholders* (1978), available from the National Training and Information Center, 1123 W. Washington Blvd., Chicago, IL 60607.

*Insurance Crisis in Urban America* (1978), available from the Federal Insurance Administration, HUD, Washington, DC 20410.

## STOPPING HOMEOWNER RIPOFFS

Information on these practices and what can be done to halt them is available from the Legal Aid Foundation of Los Angeles, 3663 W. 6th St., Los Angeles, CA 90020. The Foundation publishes a good consumer manual, called "Trust Deeds! Watch Out for Foreclosures."

"Home Improvement Frauds: A Preliminary Report," a study prepared for HUD, is available from the Consumer Foundation of America, 1012 14th St. NW, #901, Washington, DC 20005.

## NEIGHBORHOOD SUPPORT FOR LOW-INCOME HOMEOWNERS

For more information on counselling and support services to homeowners, contact:

St. Ambrose Housing Aid Center, 321 E. 25th St., Baltimore MD 21218.

East Side Housing Action Committee (ESHAC), 531 E. Burleigh St., Milwaukee, WI 53212.

An article describing ESHAC and its realty operation appears in the August 10, 1979 issue of *The Neighborhood Works,* a very useful information service published by the Institute for Local Self-Reliance, 1717 18th St. NW, Washington, DC 20009. Subscriptions are $8 per year.

Detroit's Maintenance Central for Seniors, one of the oldest, largest and best of the repair services that can prevent displacement, is reachable at 3750 Woodward Ave., Detroit, MI 48201. They publish a "Handy Manual for Minor Repairs," aimed at older residents, and available for $2.50.

HUD demonstration programs on repair and maintenance aid to low-income homeowners: for information, contact either the Division of Housing Management and Special Users Research (attn: Debra Greenstein), Office of Policy Development and Research, HUD, Washington, DC 20410, or the agencies in the seven cities being financed under HUD's current demonstration:
*Cleveland:* Lutheran Housing Corp. (attn: Kevin McGruder), 1217 Hayden Ave., Cleveland, OH 44112.
*Cincinnati:* People Working Cooperatively (attn: Isabella Healey), 2535 Gilbert Ave., Cincinnati, OH 45206.
*Greensboro:* Greensboro: Greensboro Housing Authority (attn: Deborah Perry), P.O. Box 3115, Greensboro, NC 27402.
*Hot Springs:* Garland County Home Maintenance Advisory Council (attn: Elizabeth Weatherspoon), c/o Judge Bill McCuen, Garland County Court House, Hot Springs, AR 71901.
*Philadelphia:* Philadelphia Corp. for Aging (attn: Susan Gill), Penn Sq. Bldg., 1317 Filbert St., Philadelphia, PA 19107.
*Boston:* Ecumenical Social Action Comm. (attn: Norma Mosley), 62 Atherton St., Jamaica Plain, MA 02130.

*San Francisco:* S.F. Development Fund (attn: Roy Larnders), 315 Granada Ave., S.F. CA 94112.

## HELP FOR OWNERS OF HUD-ASSISTED HOUSING

For information on the outcome of the 1976 HUD settlement and subsequent negotiations regarding anti-displacement aids for owners of HUD-assisted housing under Section 235, 203(b) and 221(d)(2) programs, contact:

The Legal Assistance Foundation of Chicago, 343 S. Dearborn St., Chicago, IL 60604, attn: William Wilen, or

The National Housing Law Project, 2150 Shattuck Ave., #300, Berkeley, CA 94704, attn: David Madway.

HUD-Approved Counselling Agencies: to locate those in your area, write or phone your HUD Area Office (see Appendix A), directing the request to the Neighborhood and Consumer Affairs Representative.

The National Federation of Housing Counsellors, 2451 18th St. NW, Washington, DC 20009, may be another source of assistance.

## PROTECTING SMALL FARMERS

Two key advocacy groups on rural and small town issues are Rural America, 1346 Connecticut Ave. NW, Washington, DC 20036, and the National Rural Center, 1828 L St. NW, Washington, DC 20036.

The Center for Rural Affairs, P.O. Box 405, Walthill, NE 68067, is a good resource on the problems of small farms. They publish *The Small Farm Advocate,* "a newsletter surveying legal and administrative issues affecting small and low-income farmers," available for $7 a year.

The National Family Farm Coalition, 918 F St., NW, Washington, DC 20004, is a lobbying group attempting to get Congress to pass the Beginning Farmers Entry Assistance Act.

*See also the additional rural references at the end of Chapter 4.*

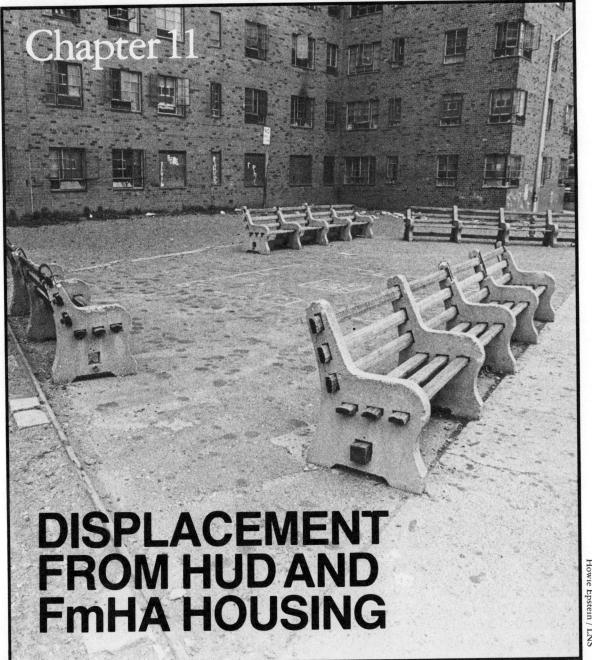

Howie Epstein / LNS

# Chapter 11

# DISPLACEMENT FROM HUD AND FmHA HOUSING

here are several million units of housing around the country subsidized or assisted in one way or another by the U.S. Department of Housing and Urban Development (HUD) and by the Farmers Home Administration (FmHA). They range from single-family houses to huge multi-unit projects, and they provide a critical resource for the nation's lower-income households. These units offer shelter at prices below what the private market demands. Moreover, the fact of government ownership or participation immunizes this housing to a large degree — but not entirely, by any means — from the displacement forces at work in the private sector.

Increasingly, however, especially under the pressures of gentrification, private market displacement is beginning to invade public-sector housing. And there are other displacement forces operating as well within the HUD/FmHA housing system itself.

But government is in many ways a more accessible and responsible landlord than the private-profit kind. And the rules and regulations governing public-sector housing provide some useful means for defending against displacement.

However, readers should be warned that many of the issues discussed in this chapter concerning the protection of government-owned, -subsidized, and -assisted housing and its occupants involve new or changing factors that are somewhat unpredictable. Upcoming Congressional action, HUD regulations, and litigation may significantly affect the picture. Among the more dire predictions is that the government may seek to sell off some or all subsidized housing to private owners, as Great Britain's conservative government is now attempting to do. Groups potentially affected should keep abreast of developments through local Legal Services offices.

# THE GENTRIFICATION OF PUBLIC HOUSING

As people with higher incomes move into parts of the city they formerly rejected, pressures begin to develop for government to do something about the "blighting influence" of public housing located there. Demands begin to be heard to "upgrade" projects by switching from family to elderly occupancy, or by selling off the units as coops or condos, by "thinning out" projects through modernization, or by flat-out demolishing them.

Here are some examples of the results:

• A recent article from the Minnesota *Daily* leads off this way: "In the midst of a severe St. Paul rental housing shortage, eight rowhouses [containing 40 living units] in the city's oldest public housing development are being converted for future sale to private owners . . ."

• A recent news release from the Denver Housing Authority announces a plan to demolish the 184-unit Las Casitas family public housing project and replace it with a medical building and, beginning two years later, housing for the elderly and town-house coops.

• The Elizabeth, New Jersey Housing Authority has announced a plan to renovate its 360-unit Pierce Manor Apartments family project for use as subsidized housing for low- and middle-income elderly persons and other families, a newer version of an earlier plan to convert it to senior citizen housing that was abandoned due to tenant and HUD opposition.

Similar things are happening in Prince George's County, Maryland; Boston; Charles-

ton, South Carolina; New Orleans; Providence; Presque Isle, Maine; Alexandria, Virginia, and many other places. The Alexandria case illustrates particularly well some of the forces at work. A major developer has proposed buying eight of the city's nine public housing projects, and relocating the residents into new and rehabbed units he would provide elsewhere in the city, in exchange for rights to redevelop the project sites — which have become valuable and desirable by virtue of their closeness to the new Washington, D.C. subway line.

Public housing tenants are especially imperiled by displacement in three types of situations: when a project's federal subsidies expire, when local housing authorities decide to disinvest, and when serious renovation is undertaken.

## WHEN FEDERAL SUBSIDIES EXPIRE

Older public housing projects are particularly vulnerable because of the way public housing is financed. Public housing projects are built under federal contracts whereby local housing authorities float the necessary bonds and the federal government supplies an annual contribution, for the length of the bond issue, to cover bond principal and interest repayments. In addition, HUD usually supplies operating subsidies, since rent collections typically fall short of what is needed for utilities, payments in lieu of property taxes, maintenance, insurance, etc. At the end of the bond repayment period, usually 40 years, the locality can own the project and dispose of it — although there are some legal theories that can be used to prevent disposition of these older low-rent housing projects if there still is clear need for them. In some cases bond payments were accelerated in early years, so federal pro-

tection will lapse in less than 40 years. In other places, local use of federal funds for project renovation under HUD's "Modernization Program" may have extended the federal protection past 40 years.

A 1979 Housing Act amendment provides some protections for this valuable housing stock. If a housing authority receives operating subsidies from HUD for a given project after passage of this act, regardless of when the bond repayment period ends, it must commit itself to operate that project as low-income housing for at least ten more years, unless HUD approves an alternate use. Under this amendment, housing authorities also can receive operating subsidies for projects after the bonds are repaid, but in this case too they must make the same ten-year commitment.

Nationwide, some 61,000 units of public housing were built before World War II, and in the 1980s hundreds of thousands more units may come under local control, opening the way for the developers and the demolishers to move in.

## LOCAL DISINVESTMENT IN PUBLIC HOUSING

It isn't just demolition and conversion that take public housing units. Often there is a governmental version of the private disinvestment/abandonment process (see Chapter 7), in which local housing authorities undermaintain units so badly that they become uninhabitable. There are projects all over the country where one-fourth, one-third, or more of all the units are boarded up or otherwise closed down. Sometimes this results simply from lack of sufficient operating funds to maintain the housing. Sometimes it is attributable to incompetent management. But the motivation for this undermaintenance may be more vicious: a conscious first step in the abandonment process, designed to generate negative public opinion about the project as an eyesore and a blight, so as to justify destroying or converting it. As the National Housing Law Project guidebook (cited below) puts it, "Such [public housing authority] practices may reflect . . . deliberate political decisions to close out a project by attrition in order to get rid of it and replace it with something which the power structure and the city consider more desirable."

As an example, it is hard to avoid interpreting the virtual abandonment of Boston's Co-lumbia Point housing project in this light. Built in 1954 on a large garbage-dump/land-fill site jutting into Boston Harbor, this 1500-unit highrise project was a disaster from the beginning. It was stuck in the middle of no-where, with few public services, no stores, and hopeless public transit connections. Residents had to shell out scarce dollars to take cabs for routine shopping and medical trips.

But times change. In the 1970s, Boston discovered that the remainder of the barren spit of land could hold a new University of Massachusetts campus and the John F. Kennedy Presidential Library. And public hous-ing, it seems, was not a desirable neighbor for these prestigious institutions. Malignant neglect of the big project set in: repairs went unmade, vacated units weren't refilled, and it wasn't long before the Housing Authority — with its waiting list of 7,000 — had 1,200 vacant units at Columbia Point. Whole build-ings and floors were abandoned, with no plan or hope of restoring them to low-rent use. (It is not irrelevant to note that the Boston Housing Authority has for several years been under the direction of a court-appointed master and more recently under court receivership, be-cause of the extraordinarily incompetent way it has run the city's public housing program.)

Suddenly came a proposal for "renewal" of the project, a brand new development with community and commercial facilities, de-signed to house people of all income groups together, although only 300 low-rent units were being proposed to replace the 1500 low-rent units originally there. It "made sense" — why not trash the old, mostly abandoned heap and get a spanking new development, a fit companion-piece for a new university and a major tourist attraction? Even the remaining Columbia Point tenants, who would get prior-ity in the new complex, and who were offered no other choice for improving their environ-ment, were for it. But no supplementary plan exists to provide the 1200 lost units elsewhere in the city. So in the process, a big chunk of badly needed low-rent housing will disappear.

Howie Epstein / LNS

There are housing projects all over the country where one-fourth, one-third, or more of all the units are boarded up or otherwise closed down.

**Boston's Columbia Point housing project, given to poor people when the land was regarded as having little value, is to be taken away from them, now that it has become a "hot property."**

And a big tract of land, given to poor people when it was regarded as having little value, is to be taken away from them, now that it has become a "hot property."

## DISPLACEMENT THROUGH RENOVATION

Public housing units also may be lost when older projects receive major renovation funds through HUD's Modernization Program — particularly when it is decided to "thin out" the project in order to improve the residential environment, or in some cases to combine small units to make space for large families. The Modernization Program in San Francisco's Hunters Point project, for example, resulted in demolition of 156 of the project's 993 units. In such instances, displacement issues are complex, since poor site design and excessive density in the original construction may have helped cause a project's rapid deterioration. As in the abandonment process, however, other motivations often are at work as well. The thinning out of Hunters Point, a not very dense project on strict units-per-acre standards, was clearly tied to development of new moderate- and middle-income units on an adjacent site by the city's Redevelopment Agency, which felt that the presence of so large a low-rent public housing project next door would keep away the new development's hoped-for middle-income clientele.

## STRATEGIES TO PROTECT PUBLIC HOUSING

The detailed ins and outs of dealing with public housing depend largely on understanding the laws and regulations governing the various programs that produced it. The fine points of defense strategies, therefore, are too complex and lengthy to be included here — especially since a 550-page legal strategy handbook on precisely this topic has just been published. It is called *HUD Housing Programs: Tenants' Rights,* and should be available at your local Legal Services office, or it can be ordered from the National Housing Law Project, 2150 Shattuck Ave., #300, Berkeley, CA 94704. A parallel handbook on Farmers Home Administration programs, also produced by the National Housing Law Project, should be available towards the end of 1981.

The sections below lay out the basic defensive approaches the handbook deals with. It must be noted, however, that as always the most valuable weapon in any anti-displacement fight is strong organization and a militant action program. Particularly when housing authorities are abandoning or selling projects to facilitate gentrification, a valuable aid in the struggle is a public campaign emphasizing the atrocity of pushing the poor out of housing originally designed for them, just to benefit the wealthy.

## STOPPING DISPLACEMENT WHEN FEDERAL SUBSIDIES EXPIRE

Since this is a relatively recent issue, procedures and protections are still in flux. But setting effective precedents *now* is important: over one million households (some three million people) live in public housing, and over time the existence of every one of those units

will be threatened by the expiration of federal subsidies.

Some local authorities, obviously, will recognize their responsibility to keep on operating public housing for low-income people. Less enlightened housing authorities can be pushed to use the 1979 Amendment allowing extended operating subsidies, or to apply for HUD Modernization funds, both of which require a period of continued low-income operation.

**The Modernization Program in San Francisco's Hunters Point project resulted in demolition of 156 of the project's 993 units.**

In places where local government is actively encouraging gentrification, however, legal arguments may have to be developed, and litigation filed to require the retention of older public housing units. One compelling argument is that the projects were paid for almost exclusively by federal funds and tenants' rents, and that in the face of clear continuing need for these units, a local government should have no right to dispose of this valuable housing resource. State laws, under which local housing authorities are established and operate, may provide additional language that serves to prevent a housing authority from disposing of needed public housing resources.

## FIGHTING DEMOLITIONS AND CONVERSIONS

Of course, even under the 1979 Amendment extending subsidies, a housing authority may push HUD to allow it to demolish or convert a project for "higher and better use." But HUD regulations require the Department

116

to make every reasonable effort to maintain the stock of low-rent public housing. Only if a project is obsolete, no longer suitable for housing purposes, and cannot be returned to useful life, can HUD give such permission, and it must first assess whether the locality's current and projected housing needs require the units in question. It is hard to imagine a place where threatened public housing units are not still needed, and if they are needed, the locality proposing to get rid of them must submit to HUD a one-for-one replacement housing plan. In addition, any families displaced in the process must be relocated into satisfactory replacement housing. But such laws can be interpreted very loosely. Litigation may be required, although even when the court ruling is supportive of the tenants, it may be most useful as a bargaining lever with local housing officials. Arguments that can be used include Section 902 of the 1978 Housing and Community Development Amendments, which requires that "involuntary displacement of persons from their homes and neighborhoods should be minimized" in the administration of federal housing programs.

These protections are not nearly as strong as they might be. There is no flat prohibition against HUD's giving permission for demolition or conversion despite a continuing need for the housing. Nor is there a provision that demolition or disposition is to be allowed only as a last resort, when there are no feasible alternatives. Nor is there an assessment required of the extent to which the local housing authority intentionally allowed the project to deteriorate so as to create a situation of no feasible alternatives. And the relocation and replacement housing provisions are not strong enough either — they should require one-for-

one replacement (rather than the current stipulation that a replacement housing plan of this type be submitted and will be funded *if* HUD has the money available), and they should not allow displacement unless guaranteed relocation housing is available.

## COMBATTING EARLY BOND PAYOFF SALES

When authorities are really eager to make big changes in their projects, they may pay off bond issues early, and then even relatively new public housing can go on the block for conversion or demolition. In one well-publicized instance of this, the Newark, New Jersey Housing Authority sought to demolish the Stella Wright project, as a way of combatting a four-year strike by tenants against substandard conditions. A lawsuit brought by the tenants against this demolition plan forced a negotiated settlement with the housing authority. For a good account of this series of events, see the article by Harris David, "The Settlement of the Newark Public Housing Rent Strike: The Tenants Take Control," in the June, 1976 issue of *Clearinghouse Review*.

## FIGHTING EXCESSIVE VACANCIES

Combatting local housing authority policies and practices that produce excessive vacancies can be hard. Incredibly, the U.S. Housing Act does not anywhere state that housing authorities must operate projects at full occupancy, and HUD has published little in the way of regulations on the subject.

As the National Housing Law Project's guide points out, there are legal provisions that can be used to support the argument that a housing authority is obliged to avoid excessive vacancies. The guide also notes, however, that the law is not enough: "As with the case of

demolition and disposition of public housing, the problem of excessive vacancies is one to be solved by political as well as legal methods and will require the organized effort of the project tenants, of applicants denied admission, and of organizations concerned about the lack of low-income tenants." To date, there has been little effort to organize those on housing authority waiting lists. Vacant public housing units represent a tremendous waste of government money. Filling vacant units makes more housing available to those who need it, and permits more people to remain in the neighborhood. It strengthens projects, also. And it strengthens an important barrier to gentrification.

## HOLDING ON TO SECTION 8 HOUSING

Since 1974, the nation's principal low-rent housing assistance program has been Section 8, with its subsidies to private developers and landlords, on behalf of low-income households, for new, rehabilitated and existing units. Just as in public housing, the expiration of Section 8 subsidies — or the property owner's desire to escape from their restrictions — can have a displacing effect. Section 8 contracts require that rents be kept to a "fair market" level, determined for each area by HUD. That's often pretty high to begin with, but if gentrification begins in the area, something that Section 8 rehab and new construction may help to get going, then owners without Section 8 subsidy restrictions may be able to move ahead of the market in rent increases and profits.

Some Section 8 contracts carry 30-day cancellation notice provisions. Some run for five years, with renewal options up to 40 years.

More recent new housing and substantial rehab projects have 20-year contracts.

Owners and developers trying to get out of these contracts early, or refusing to request renewal, have in effect used public subsidies to obtain financing and lucrative tax write-offs, in order to leverage themselves into a high-profit position in the private market. They do so at the expense of residents of the units concerned, who will be displaced, and at the price of removing needed units from the supply of housing for low- and moderate-income people.

This form of displacement can be fought. Community pressure, as always, is an effective tool. A Section 8 building being gentrified might not look so attractive to the new "class" of tenants if it is surrounded by angry residents and friends. Additionally, the National Housing Law Project guide offers good legal arguments to use in resisting termination of Section 8 subsidies, either by HUD or by private owners.

# PROTECTING FEDERALLY SUBSIDIZED AND ASSISTED RENTAL HOUSING

Displacement causes and remedies are somewhat different in privately owned rental housing that has mortgage interest subsidies or mortgage repayment guarantees from HUD's Federal Housing Administration (FHA), or from the Department of Agriculture's Farmers Home Administration (FmHA). The principal difficulties arise when owners choose to prepay their government-assisted mortgages, in order to free themselves from whatever restrictions go with this assistance, and when owners get into financial difficulties and can't meet their mortgage payment obligations.

## THE MORTGAGE PREPAYMENT PROBLEM

As with public housing and Section 8 subsidies, there is a prepayment problem in federally-subsidized and -assisted projects, with some owners all too ready to shuck off the below-market rents (along with the tenants who pay them) that are made possible by the government's involvement. This problem is compounded by the workings of the IRS' tax shelter provisions, which make it less profitable for the original owners to hold on to their projects after about 12-16 years. Disposition of Section 8 projects (the first of which were constructed in the mid-1970s) for this same reason may become a problem in a few years as well.

Protections and remedies vary according to the particular government aids involved. If the development has received what is known as a "flexible subsidy" (a one-time payment designed to restore the project's financial and physical viability), the owner is legally bound to operate it as low- and moderate-income housing for the full term of the mortgage. If the subsidy comes as "rent supplements," then the Federal Housing Commissioner (a HUD Assistant Secretary) must approve any plan to prepay the mortgage and convert to upper-income use — and there are grounds for challenging such an approval, should HUD give it.

Section 236 and 221(d)(3) projects owned by limited-dividend partnerships which have received neither of these subsidies can prepay their mortgages and convert without FHA approval after 20 years, whereas non-profit owners need FHA approval for such a step throughout the full 40-year life of their mortgages. Section 221(d)(3) projects were built

starting in the early 1960s, so this form of displacement will begin soon in those developments. Section 236 was introduced in 1968, so projects it generated will start joining the displacement line in the late 1980s. As we have emphasized, prepayment is virtually dictated by the workings of current tax laws.

Prepayment-generated displacement is also a serious problem for rental housing produced under two Farmers Home Administration programs. These programs operate in small towns and rural areas. Section 515 provides below market-rate loans, as low as 1%, to non-profit and limited-profit developers, and market rate loans to for-profit developers. The much smaller Section 514 program provides assistance for farmworker housing. Rent supplements or Section 8 subsidies, available to non-profit and limited-profit developers, make the units affordable by lower-income households.

FmHA data show that of the 7,400 Section 515 loans made through 1978, 482 were prepaid, and there has been a recent and dramatic upswing in this activity. (Startlingly, however, FmHA does not know the number of housing units involved, nor how many tenants were displaced when rents went up).

In 1979, Congress passed legislation forbidding prepayment of Section 514 and 515 loans for the first 15 years of the mortgage without FmHA's permission. Although this legislation applied to existing as well as new loans, the retroactive portion was quickly repealed in 1980. Because such prepayment decisions are made largely on the basis of the tax shelter considerations noted above, the new legislation really just fits in with the probable time schedule for the start of conversion and displacement, and we likely will lose close to 10,000 of the pre-1980 units within the next few years.

The prepayment-conversion phenomenon, of course, is just another outrageous example of how public funds are used — under the justification of "incentives" — to enable private operators to get into profiteering situations. Unfortunately, there are real difficulties in trying to interfere with the contractual agreements between project owners and FHA or FmHA which permit this abuse to happen. Nonetheless, the National Housing Law Project guide offers some possibilities to explore in trying to keep this housing for its intended lower-income occupants.

## THE MORTGAGE DEFAULT PROBLEM

Perhaps the greatest displacement threat to tenants in privately owned, federally-subsidized or -assisted rental housing comes when an owner defaults on the HUD-insured mortgage, and the mortgage is assigned to HUD, which then must dispose of the property or foreclose.

After an owner gets seriously behind in payments to the mortgage-holder, an "assignment" period then begins, during which the developer still owns the property but HUD pays off the lender, who assigns the mortgage to HUD. HUD then tries to work out a satisfactory payment arrangement with the developer or tries to find a buyer for the property. If neither is possible, a foreclosure sale ensues.

At a foreclosure sale, either HUD itself or another buyer can purchase the development. HUD is legally limited to bidding no more than the unpaid indebtedness plus certain other costs. Therefore, speculators can easily use such sales to acquire properties they think have potential for higher-rent use. Result: displacement of current tenants and reduction of the lower-income housing supply.

HUD itself becomes the owner at the foreclosure sale if it is the sole or highest bidder. The Department can decide it's easier or less costly to demolish a project it has been forced to take over, which of course means displacement. Or HUD can resell the project or continue to operate it. Some potentially very effective anti-displacement strategies, through continuing HUD ownership or sale to socially-oriented owners-managers, possibly the tenants themselves, are discussed below at pages 121-126.

The potential for displacement in all this is no small-time worry. A large number of developments built under FHA's Section 221(d)(3) and successor Section 236 programs are now labelled "distressed" or "troubled," which means they may soon be headed for default. A 1978 HUD report stated that of the 6700 such projects in the country, only 2000 were financially sound and not in need of further financial assistance; 1700 projects had already received various forms of supplementary Section 8 subsidies, beyond the interest subsidies they originally received on the mortgage loan; and the remaining 3000 projects either "are in the troubled category now . . . [or] probably will require financial assistance in the near future." One hundred and sixty-seven projects were in serious default, 834 had been assigned or were in the process of foreclosure, and 210 already had come into HUD ownership. The report projected that if present trends continued, HUD's inventory of assigned and acquired projects could rise to 3000 by 1982.

HUD studies of the situation have identified the following general factors as contributing to the problem:

**Inadequate subsidies:** rising operating costs, and the increasing gap between tenants' incomes and rents required for financial viability, made the original subsidy formula (either a 1% or 3% interest rate mortgage) wholly inadequate. "In the 83 projects visited by the [HUD] Central Office staff," said the HUD report, "operating expenses increased at an annual rate of 12 percent, but tenant incomes advanced at half that pace." Several attempts to provide additional subsidies, starting in 1974, fell far short of what was needed.

**"Inadequate HUD management of multi-family loans,** including irregular and incomplete physical, administrative and financial reviews due to inefficient management resources. . . ." was another contributing problem, according to the report. "The Department's emphasis on meeting production goals tended to push aside concerns about the success of the projects . . . [and] led field offices to ignore management precautions and prudence, or to overrule them."

**Inadequate on-site project management** with respect to tenant screening, rent collection, and maintenance, due in part to lack of HUD supervision, in part to the limited supply of skilled building managers.

Whatever the cause, however, when a project gets into financial trouble, tenants need to organize themselves quickly and arm themselves with adequate information, if they are going to avoid displacement and get the maximum potential benefits from the situation. Strategies vary depending on the type of transaction. If HUD tries to arrange sale of a distressed project from one private owner to another *before* foreclosure, tenants have fewer legal protections than when HUD itself sells a property after foreclosure. But even in the case of pre-foreclosure sale, political and legal pressure can be applied to force HUD to impose low-income use restrictions on the sale. Useful legal arguments include statutory national housing goals and wording of the Sec. 236 and 221(d)(3) programs; the anti-displacement amendment (Sec. 902) of the 1978 Housing and Community Development Act, referred to above (page 117); Civil Rights Act violations (if racial minorities and other protected groups are involved); violations of regulations pertaining to Community Development Block Grants and Housing Assistance Plans; and even National Environmental Policy Act requirements. (See the National Housing Law Project guidebook for details of these arguments.)

IF HUD has actually foreclosed, different strategies are called for, depending on the type of building and the form of government assistance originally given.

## ONE-TO-FOUR UNIT PROPERTIES

For a long time, HUD insisted on a "vacant delivery" policy when foreclosing on mortgages it had insured for these small buildings: that is, all tenants had to be displaced before the lender would actually be paid. The Department didn't wish to manage occupied buildings and felt it could resell vacant buildings more easily. A series of lawsuits brought by Legal Services attorneys seems finally to have produced a HUD policy that protects rather than harms tenants in such situations. Court rulings have upheld tenants' rights not to be automatically displaced. HUD's final regulations are being drafted at the time this handbook is going to press, but are expected to grant tenants the right to remain, depending on factors such as: ability to pay "fair market" rent; condition of the property; likelihood of vandalism if vacated; and the size of HUD's

Howie Epstein / LNS

inventory of vacant housing in the area. If a new buyer wishes to occupy a unit, eviction would be permitted.

Since exact rules are still being developed, groups fighting displacement from these types of properties should contact the attorneys who are working most closely with the issue: David Madway at the National Housing Law Project, 2150 Shattuck Ave., #300, Berkeley, CA 94704; and William Wilen, Legal Assistance Foundation of Chicago, 343 S. Dearborn St., Chicago, IL 60604.

## MULTI-FAMILY PROJECTS

When HUD comes into ownership of multi-family projects through foreclosure proceedings, the 1978 Housing and Community Development Act (Sections 202 and 203) requires the Department to manage and dispose of such properties in ways that keep them available to, and affordable by, low- and moderate-income families. With few exceptions, foreclosed projects serving lower-income renters must be sold with full Section 8 subsidies. Moreover, the 1978 law requires HUD to maintain foreclosed projects, while it possesses them, in decent, safe and sanitary condition — meaning that prior to any resale they must meet local code standards. The law also directs HUD to minimize tenant displacement and property demolition, and to be responsive to tenants' needs — a provision which includes an implied mandate to work cooperatively with tenant organizations.

Prior to the 1980 Housing Act amendments, multi-family projects that were built with FHA mortgage insurance but without subsidies were given far less protection when they came into HUD possession. But current law requires substantially similar treatment for both unsubsidized and subsidized projects. In the case of subsidized projects, low-income use restrictions and Section 8 subsidy requirements apply to all units; in the case of insured but unsubsidized projects, these protections apply to units occupied by Section 8 eligible households and units vacant at the time of foreclosure, but not to units occupied by higher-income households and units that subsequently become vacant. Some potentially winning legal arguments on why all units in unsubsidized projects should receive such protection are contained in the National Housing Law Project guidebook.

Even with these protections, however, resale to speculative owners could mean subsequent displacement through future mortgage prepayment, rent hikes due to lack of a subsidy commitment for the full length of the mortgage, disinvestment, harassment, etc. Fortunately, recently revised purchaser selection procedures work against that by including considerations of proposed buyers' "track records" in housing matters, especially responsiveness to resident and neighborhood needs. Since the regulations are unclear on how long the property must remain as lower-income housing after resale by HUD, community groups should negotiate for the longest possible period, ideally writing the deed of trust to require this for the full length of the mortgage or 40 years, whichever is longer. As with any such procedure, the only guarantee of effective application is through active monitoring and participation by organized tenants.

Ideally, such projects would be sold to tenant cooperatives, to local housing authorities (possibly for resale to tenants), or to other non-profit owners, providing the units are maintained as low- and moderate-income housing. HUD also can retain a project as low-income rental property under its own ownership and management. If this results in displacement — in order to carry out renovation, for example — the law provides relocation protections for current residents, including a right to return to the renovated unit or to move to a similar HUD-owned unit.

(Displacement protections for *homeowners* in FHA-subsidized housing are discussed on pages 108 and 109. Direct community action to put abandoned HUD-owned housing back into low-rent use is discussed on pages 68-71.)

## THE BOSTON DEMONSTRATION PROJECT

"Distress" in FHA-supported multi-family housing is widespread in Chicago, Newark, New York, Atlanta, Indianapolis, Detroit, Cincinnati, Kansas City, Los Angeles, Cleveland, Hartford, San Francisco, Oklahoma City, and the District of Columbia. But Boston takes the prize. The Section 236 and 221(d)(3) programs have been used extensively there, particularly as relocation housing in urban renewal areas. Nearly 14,000 such units in 115 projects are concentrated in three of the city's central residential neighborhoods: Roxbury, North Dorchester, and the South End. By 1977, an incredible 63% of these projects were in default, either in assignment or already in HUD ownership. Seven thousand families were threatened with rent hikes or outright displacement. A HUD report concluded that the Department "owns or soon may own nearly all of the low-income apartment projects in three inner city areas."

HUD's policy had been to sell these defaulting projects, wherever possible, in "as is" condition. And while waiting for resale, HUD

121

took a "hands off" approach to management: minimal repairs, and low-cost contracts with management firms that were largely incompetent and unresponsive. When new owners took over, needed repairs almost automatically fueled rent increases. Since tenants in these projects were already paying on the average 31% of their incomes for rent, the result was usually displacement.

In response to the extreme situation in Boston, and the 1978 Housing Act amendments referred to on page 121, HUD in 1978 funded a demonstration program there to test a variety of innovative project management and disposition strategies, with emphasis on tenant participation. The HUD Boston Area Office awarded contracts at five projects for technical assistance in management services, as well as for job training and employment for tenants

and neighborhood residents. The basic aim was to plan with the residents for future disposition of each project, including the possibility of resident ownership. Although still in progress as of this writing, the Demonstration Program has produced some useful findings:

**Reduction in project resale price** is a key ingredient in keeping a foreclosed project in lower-income use. Even with the Section 8 subsidies required by the 1978 law, the negative economic dynamics of a "distressed" project are almost certain to reassert themselves unless additional assistance is given. Even though it goes against the grain of traditional market operations, drastically reducing the resale price of foreclosed projects, even to $1, will prove cheaper to HUD in the long run than paying the inflated mortgage costs that go with the Section 8 subsidy formula.

**Section 8 subsidies, although necessary, can contribute to rent increases and displacement.** "Fair market" rent levels required by Section 8 may be higher than rents charged under the Section 236 and 221(d)(3) programs, due to peculiarities in the regulations governing each program. This increase can force out existing tenants not eligible for Section 8 subsidies (unless it is possible to negotiate inclusion of all tenants in occupancy at the time of sale), as well as inflate neighborhood rent levels generally, leading to indirect displacement. And for the tenants saved by Section 8, if subsidy contracts are not renewed at expiration (see discussion of this on pages 117 and 118), the relief may only be short-lived.

**Tenant involvement in disposition planning pays off.** Tenant-management task forces were set up and funded at each of the five

## How the Marion Gardens public housing tenants in Jersey City fought off displacement

Marion Gardens is a 462-unit public housing project in Jersey City, New Jersey. It is also the site of an epic nine-year fight by its tenants — finally victorious — to keep a racist city administration from driving them out so that the project could be upgraded for more "suitable" occupants.

Marion Gardens was built in 1942. It has 15 three-story buildings. It is situated beside a noisy, polluted highway, in the vicinity of trucking terminals, far from shopping and services and public transportation. Constructed next to a lower middle-income Italian neighborhood, Marion Gardens originally housed "submerged middle-class" whites of the Depression and World War II years. As these households moved out during the postwar boom, they were replaced by minority families, many displaced by highway and urban renewal projects. And as racial tension between the project and the surrounding community grew, the Housing Authority's response, encouraged by the financial problems it was experiencing from a growing gap between tenants' rent-paying abilities and project

operating costs, was to undermaintain the project and allow vacancies to build up. As early as the mid-1960s, about 20% of all units were empty.

The future of Marion Gardens became a hot political issue in the early 1970s, when mayoral and city council candidates, seeking support from the Italian community, proposed "phasing out" the project in favor of commercial reuse or senior citizen housing. After the election, the new mayor kept his promises by asking HUD for permission to sell Marion Gardens for rehab and conversion to a moderate-income coop. Among the principal reasons the mayor cited were: bad location of the project, "inability of the Housing Authority to deal with a small group of problem tenants," unsatisfactory management and maintenance by the Authority, and, most important of all, "the concentration of lower-income black families."

It was a description that in fact applied equally to other housing projects in the city, and there were many alternative solutions besides removing the existing tenants. Reorganizing the Housing Authority might

have helped more, as would evicting the problem tenants and constructing sound insulation near the highway.

HUD, to its credit, refused the city's request. Not giving up, the mayor ordered his buildings commissioner to assemble a special task force to inspect Marion Gardens for code violations. More than 2,000 violations were discovered, including such serious ones as water- and garbage-filled basements, leaking steam lines, and exposed electrical wires. Meanwhile, however, inspections of six other housing projects, initiated by the buildings commissioner himself, uncovered similar slum conditions. Revealingly, the commissioner declared four buildings at Marion Gardens "unfit for human habitation," and ordered them vacated, while for the other projects he merely ordered the Housing Authority to submit a program of repairs and improvements within 30 days.

Nothing further was ever done to implement the repair order at the other unfortunate projects. But at Marion Gardens, the commissioner's action was fol-

projects in the Demonstration Program. They were charged with considering various ownership options, including resident-controlled ownership. The results of this process have been highly productive.

At Methunion Manor, a 151-unit project in Boston's South End, tenants are pursuing a careful process of negotiations with HUD, aimed at resident ownership through a non-profit corporation. The Methunion Tenants Council selected an experienced, sensitive management firm (technically on contract to HUD but understood by all parties to be working for the Tenants Council), which supervised major physical improvements under joint resident-management monitoring of the contractors. Residents have been employed in management positions (assistant site manager, chief custodian, maintenance coor-

dinator), and various tenant services have been provided. Tenants are now involved in screening applicants for vacant units. Together, the management firm and Tenants Council have put together a detailed "Disposition Analysis and Recommendations." It contains a Capital Improvements Plan for Repairs and Improvements, both prior to and after sale; a proposed mortgage figure combining acquisition and capital improvements; a projected rent structure based on Section 8 Substantial Rehab Fair Market Rent levels for 100% of the units; a Tenant Services Program to be funded as a project expense; and as the proposed ownership entity, a nonprofit corporation whose membership is composed of the residents of the development.

**Ripple effects of the Demonstration Program.** Other projects in Boston are beginning

to pick up on the lessons of the Demonstration Program. Tenants of the 87-unit Forest Hills Park Apartments organized to stop HUD's sale of their building to a known slumlord, and have since developed a sophisticated disposition proposal based on the Demonstration Program's findings. This is their 11-point statement of objectives:

- To have the complex sold at a reasonable purchase price, which does not create an excessive debt burden for any future owner.
- To reach an agreement with the City of Boston to reduce the tax assessment on the property to a reasonable level.
- To ensure that all back taxes and utility bills are paid before any sales takes place.
- To have all identified rehabilitation and repair work completed before any sale takes place.
- To have the complex sold with sufficient Section 8 subsidy to meet the needs of existing and future tenants.

Jersey City Housing Authority

lowed up by a suspension of new admissions, and a one-year program of "voluntary relocation." City relocation workers tried to persuade as many residents as possible to move, offering them subsidies to get into private units or opportunities to transfer to other projects. As people left, more buildings were boarded up, and conditions worsened in the rest of the project as empty apartments were vandalized, stripped, and illegally occupied. As described by a political scientist at a local college, a "doomsday atmosphere of anxiety" developed. (But those who did leave didn't fare so well either: even with their relocation allowances, the households who opted for private housing wound up paying far more for shelter than they could afford).

As the project shrank, a core group of stable, long-term tenants began to fight to hold onto their housing. (A 1974 HUD survey found that 36% of Marion Gardens tenants had lived there more than ten years, 68% more than five years). The battle, however, had to be fought by a dwindling army: by mid-1975 only 203 families remained, and by February, 1981, that number had shrunk further to a rock-hard 172. But those survivors are the victors whose energy and resistance helped create supportive alliances with other housing

123

- To have the complex sold with a reserve fund adequate for all future repairs, both predicted and unforeseen.

- To ensure that no tenant's monthly rental payments are more than 25% of his or her income, or the present Section 8 Fair Market Rent for the unit, whichever is lower. Any rent increases that result should be phased in over a specified period of time.

- To ensure that the Section 8 Contract Rents set for the complex do not contribute to inflation of other rents in the neighborhood.

- To negotiate an agreement with an interim purchaser that will provide for immediate tenant involvement in decision-making, and conversion to a tenant-controlled ownership structure within a definite time frame.

- To ensure that the interim purchaser uses all income from the complex to meet tenant needs.

- To secure funds from HUD for educational and technical assistance to enable tenants to assume control of the complex within a definite time frame.

In order to implement the last objective and move from an interim purchaser to full tenant control, the Forest Hills Park proposal asks HUD for assistance in setting up a training program for tenants similar to those developed under the Demonstration Program. The aim of the training is to help them develop their organizational skills and their understanding of disposition-related issues. They also seek technical assistance for developing their organization and for detailed disposition planning, including a feasibility study to be done in cooperation with HUD.

It should be noted that HUD regulations now require notice to, and opportunity for comment by, tenants of HUD-owned projects, when the Department is proposing a disposition plan. Where this procedural requirement is violated, which typically is the

case, tenants are afforded good legal grounds to stop the proposed plan and negotiate for one more suited to their needs. The requirements are outlined in the Citizens Housing and Planning Association handbook cited below.

Overall, the strategy of encouraging HUD foreclosure for projects with incompetent and insensitive ownership/management has much to recommend it. It forces out an undesirable owner, forces HUD into the picture, with the various tenant protections HUD must adhere to, and permits extraordinary financial benefits — wiping out the existing mortgage debt and introducing needed operating subsidies. The process also brings real potential for tenant involvement in the disposition planning for rehabilitation, and for new ownership and management entities, including possible tenant ownership. Many of these inadequately

groups in Jersey City, and who filled the room at every monthly Housing Authority Board of Commissioners meeting from 1973 through 1979, keeping the pressure on. "Twenty years ago this was a nice place to live," a local newspaper quoted one tenant as saying. "Most of us have been here that long and we all raised our children here. This is our home. We're not leaving and going anywhere else. No one is going to move us out."

The tenant fightback actually began in 1972, when the first four buildings were condemned. Residents challenged the order to vacate on procedural grounds, but lost that suit in state court. They then tried for a federal injunction against HUD, the city, and the Housing Authority, based on civil rights violations and inadequate maintenance practices. The federal court did not grant the injunction, but did rule that the annual contributions contract between HUD and the Housing Authority obligated the Authority "to maintain the project decent, safe and sanitary," which the judge noted "has obviously not been done."

The effect of the federal court ruling was to create a stalemate: the buildings were saved from demolition, but were not ordered restored to habitable condition.

The court finding also prompted federal and local housing officials to commission a consultant study on alternative uses of the site.

The resulting report was so grossly inadequate that the Housing Authority paid the consultant only $12,500 of the $30,000 contract, but the city moved anyway to implement its predictable recommendation: that Marion Gardens' "image" as an "unsuccessful enclave" be changed by removing the minority population and selling the buildings to a private developer, who would rehab them under the Section 8 program, and would also select future tenants. HUD's Modernization Program was not to be used, even though $1 million in such funds had already been assigned to Marion Gardens. "The adjacent neighborhood views Marion Gardens as a detriment to itself," said the consultant's report, bringing the central issue into the open. "[I]t regards Marion Gardens as a danger and a place to be avoided."

In 1975, the city asked the New Jersey Housing Finance Agency to do a feasibility study of the Section 8 rehab plan, meanwhile rejecting HUD's recommendation that the Modernization funds be spent. But heavy counter-pressure from the tenants caused the

HUD Regional Office to rule that the city could not use Section 8 as a substitute for the Modernization Program. The tenants knew that a shift from public housing to Section 8 funding would remove them permanently from the area.

The tenants also were aided by a July, 1976 ruling by the HUD Regional Administrator, in a Title VI civil rights complaint brought by tenants at another public housing site, that the Jersey City Housing Authority was in "apparent non-compliance" with the Civil Rights Act. HUD's summary of its investigation of that complaint noted:

These apparent non-compliance deficiencies were most reflective at the Marion Gardens project, which is a project that is almost totally minority occupied and is almost completely surrounded by a white moderate-income community. This project has been permitted to deteriorate almost to the point of condemnation.

The HUD report also noted that "apparent discrimination exists based on race in the selection of tenants, the assignment of dwelling units, maintenance and services to projects that are predominantly minority occupied."

In April, 1976, following release of the civil rights

**HUD foreclosures open up a great many opportunities for residents to attack bad conditions, gain security and control, and avoid displacement.**

subsidized projects are facing large rent increases, which surely will displace many of their occupants. Rather than have this happen, the foreclosure-disposition route may be a far more effective anti-displacement strategy.

But there are cautions to be observed, too. While tenant control and tenant ownership may be desirable objectives in many instances, they also offer dangers. Unwary tenants can be left holding the bag for a rundown and still inadequately financed development. Furthermore, as the income-housing cost gap contin-

ues to widen, even the best disposition agreement may spell future distress. Some housing activists argue that a better strategy is to compel HUD to continue ownership of projects it has acquired, and, using a combination of strong tenant organization and existing law, force the government to spend funds to maintain the projects in sound condition, at rents people can afford, with maximum tenant control over management operations. (See the related discussion of "sweat equity"/cooperative ownership vs. public ownership on pages 66-68.)

Whatever route people choose, however, HUD foreclosures do open up a great many opportunities for residents to attack bad conditions, gain security and control, and avoid displacement.

For further information on the Boston

Demonstration, contact the Citizens Housing and Planning Association, 7 Marshall St., Boston, MA 02108. CHPA is assisting in the demonstration and has published a handbook entitled "Planning for the Future of HUD-Owned Housing: A Residents' Guide," by Emily Achtenberg and Ann Silverman (1980, $2.50). An excellent, still highly useful guidebook on background and strategies for tenants in subsidized housing is *Tenants First! A Research and Organizing Guide to FHA Housing* (1974), by Emily Achtenberg and Michael Stone, available for $3 from Urban Planning Aid, 120 Boylston St., Boston, MA 02116. A related project to the Boston Demonstration is the Multi-Family Demonstration Project, 2150 Shattuck Ave., #300, Berkeley, CA 94704, which provides technical assistance in financial and management matters to FHA-

---

investigation and report, HUD assigned $3.4 million in Modernization funds for Marion Gardens, and told the city it had two months to express its intent to use this money. No one was satisfied with this offer. Both the tenants and the city said it was not enough money to do the job, although the city's position apparently was just another attempt to show why getting rid of Marion Gardens was the best course. The tenants wanted a modernization job which would support their desire for a racially mixed project, which they saw as the best permanent defense against continuing threats to abolish their public housing. And on this point the tenants had good backing. They had used the federal Freedom of Information Act to obtain some of HUD's own correspondence, which they shared with the media, revealing that "additional funds [beyond the $3.4 million] are necessary to rehabilitate sufficient units . . . to attract tenants of all persuasions to make it a viable project. . . ." In fact, said HUD, the $3.4 million would rehab only 125 units, meaning that "approximately fifty of the current tenants would have to be relocated. This would allow no room for possibly integrating the project. There would be no available units."

Stepping up the pressure, the tenants called on

HUD not only to increase its Modernization allocation, but to place the Housing Authority in receivership if it continued to resist using the funds assigned to Marion Gardens. In response, HUD announced that refusal to use the Modernization money could result in sanctions related to the city's CDBG grant. So, reluctantly, just before the deadline, the city agreed to accept the $3.4 million.

The city and the Housing Authority then took the incredible step of using public funds to hire a public relations firm to counter the adverse publicity they were receiving over the handling of the Marion Gardens issue. The firm put out press releases blasting HUD's Modernization Program and extolling the virtues of the Housing Authority's Section 8 conversion plan.

In December of 1976, just before the change in administrations in Washington, the tenants informed HUD of their intention to file a lawsuit — and to do it in time to take depositions from departing HUD officials — unless the tenants' requests for increased allocations were met. By this time, the HUD regional office had received another distribution of Modernization funds, and a few days before leaving office the Re-

gional Administrator reserved another $2.6 million for Marion Gardens. This increased the total Modernization funding to $6.4 million ($600,000 of the original $1 million has been subsequently transferred to another project).

This was still not enough to do the entire job. So all through 1977 the tenants continued to press HUD for more. At the same time, they pushed the Housing Authority to make proper use of whatever money it did get. Tenant negotiators won a written commitment so that not one of the 172 rehab work would be phased so that not one of the 172 households would have to move off-site during reconstruction ("We won't move off this site," a local newspaper quoted one tenant as saying. "We're afraid once we get out we won't get back. We're not going anywhere.") The tenants also got the Housing Authority to change the planned distribution of unit sizes to make more units available for large families, including 60 four-, five- and six-bedroom units, and to agree to preserve the four condemned vacant buildings as an environmental noise buffer, and use them for nonresidential purposes. One of these buildings will become the new home of the Housing Authority's executive offices, a move the tenants welcome as likely to

subsidized multi-family projects, to prevent them from becoming "distressed."

## PUBLIC ACQUISITION AS AN ANTI-DISPLACEMENT TOOL

Pushing HUD to take and keep ownership of "distressed" projects is one aspect of a larger public sector housing strategy anti-displacement groups should consider. One of the best ways to protect the housing stock from market forces is to remove it from the private market altogether, via public acquisition. Local public housing authorities and other agencies have the power to acquire property, using federal public housing moneys, state grants, Community Development Block Grant funds, and other resources, either for permanent ownership (with tenant management, where desirable) or for transfer to a limited-equity tenant

cooperative or other non-profit entity. Given the prejudices against public ownership, plus the fiscal constraints many governments are feeling, it will not be an easy task to pressure public agencies into making such purchases. But the advantages are clear: freedom from mortgage payments; less chance of racial and other kinds of discrimination in tenant selection and other management functions; guarantees that rents will be at levels lower-income households can afford; protections against arbitrary eviction; greater obligations to maintain the premises in decent, safe and sanitary condition; and overall, a landlord against whom tenants have relatively greater legal and political leverage. (See Chapter 7, on New York City's programs to reclaim abandoned *in rem* housing, for additional discussion of this point.)

## HOUSING SUBSIDY ALLOCATIONS AND DISPLACEMENT

As we have discussed earlier in this handbook, displacement is a term that applies to neighborhoods and communities as well as to households and the buildings that shelter them. During the past decade several federal policy initiatives have been designed to disperse low-income, particularly minority, households. But these have also developed into displacement dangers for minority communities.

**HUD's "Site Selection Criteria,"** introduced in 1971, is a guidance policy aimed at creating more subsidized low-rent housing in neighborhoods with little of it, and adding less to so-called "impacted areas." It was a policy

insure conscientious maintenance of the site. The other condemned buildings will be adapted for social and recreational services, job training space and tenants association offices, a kindergarten, and a boiler plant. The tenants also successfully insisted that formal review of the Housing Authority's tenant selection plans for all of its sites be included in the Title VI (civil rights) conciliation process.

But the problem of how to get enough money from HUD for effective renovation still remained. In April, 1978, the tenants filed an administrative complaint with HUD, asking that the city's CDBG grant be withheld until the Housing Authority submitted a workable plan for the modernization and marketing of Marion Gardens as an integrated site. They based their case on the still unresolved Civil Rights Act complaint, and on the city's statement, in its Housing Assistance Plan, that the Housing Authority was a "functionary" of the city in meeting its three-year housing goals. While HUD didn't rule for the tenants, the official letter to the city approving the CDBG grant referred to the complaint in a way that created a receptive climate for the tenants' later efforts to get more Modernization funds.

That opportunity came with HUD's July, 1978 an-

Jersey City Housing Authority

long advocated by civil rights groups as a means to enhance racial integration, and it is buttressed by a variety of court decisions won by those groups.

**The Areawide Housing Opportunity Plan (AHOP),** introduced by HUD in 1978, expands the Site Selection Criteria approach to whole metropolitan regions. It calls for cooperative efforts by local governments and planning agencies to expand low-income households' ability to get subsidized Section 8 housing in suburbs as well as cities. The AHOP program gave out $42 million to ten planning groups in metropolitan regions around Baltimore, Hartford, Greenfield (Massachusetts), Eugene (Oregon), St. Paul, the District of Columbia, Springfield (Massachusetts), Seattle, Dayton, and Los Angeles. All told, some 8,000 households will receive aid.

nouncement of a $209 million public housing Urban Initiatives Program (a newer version of the Modernization Program). Marion Gardens tenants and the Housing Authority jointly developed a proposal for the project, which the city's new mayor endorsed. In September, 1978, Marion Gardens received an additional $5 million, raising the total available to $11.4 million. The new grant even included $24,000 to support tenant organizing, the money to be controlled by the tenants' organization, the Marion Gardens Community Association.

Another feature of the Urban Initiatives grant was a written agreement that one of every eight construction jobs for Marion Gardens rehab work would go to a public housing tenant. And the tenants expanded their employment demands to an Urban Development Action Grant (UDAG) proposal for the truck plaza adjacent to the project. They filed an administrative complaint on the UDAG application, and won a commitment for outreach to project residents in job training and permanent jobs, with a goal of placement in 50% of the supervisory and 72% of the non-supervisory jobs. That same administrative complaint — brought when the city reneged on a promise made at a public

**The Regional Housing Mobility Program (RHMP),** introduced in 1979, is a smaller ($3 million) but more aggressive and manipulative evolution of AHOP, designed to use Section 8 housing certificates and counselling services to encourage inner-city residents to move out into the suburbs. Twenty-two metropolitan planning organizations were invited to submit applications showing how they could coordinate activities of local public housing authorities and fair housing groups to administer Section 8 certificates in a way that would promote "regional mobility" (see end-of-chapter references for list of localities receiving grants).

Arguments in support of these policies remain the same as they have been for thirty years or more: racial and economic segregation in the suburbs, and in affluent city neighbor-

hearing in response to Marion Gardens tenants' testimony and requests — resulted in a commitment by HUD to add $300,000 to the UDAG grant to supplement $700,000 in UDAG moneys originally allocated to abate storm sewer problems that were threatening the Modernization program.

An important part of the tenants' anti-displacement fight has been forging links with the surrounding white community. They have begun to meet with neighborhood residents on matters of mutual concern, such as the environmental hazards associated with installation of two 5,000-gallon gasoline tanks near the local elementary school. Marion Gardens tenants also lobbied hard to have CDBG funds allocated to the surrounding neighborhood for home improvement loans. And the successful solution to the storm sewer problem benefits the entire neighborhood by preventing basement flooding in the whole area. The tenants hope that creative and persistent efforts to coalesce around common issues will increase interracial communication and defuse 30 years of fear and distrust.

This "fight back" tale demonstrates the incredible variety of techniques and tools aggressive and creative community groups can use — indeed, must use —

hoods, damages the overall society, curtails the life options of low-income and minority people, and inhibits their attempts to follow the employment trend of industrial relocation out of the cities.

The problem is that HUD's policies are being applied now instead of thirty years ago. "We won't be fooled at this point," said a Black activist at the 1980 National Low-Income Housing Conference, "that they love us so bad they have come up with a wonderful program to expand *our* options, at precisely the same time as the white middle class is expanding *its* options into our community."

If HUD were supplying a steadily increasing amount of inner-city subsidized housing *plus* aggressively developing a similar supply throughout urban regions, these policies would present no problem. But such is not the

to fight displacement. And even then the battle is not over: modernization is underway at Marion Gardens, but tenant vigilance will be required to insure that the $11.4 million is spent properly. Moreover, inflation has made inroads in that money, and it now covers rehab of only 173 units, just enough to house the present minority tenants. No funds are available to rehab and market units to white households. So the tenants will have to continue using the Civil Rights Act as a lever to get more money, to push their goal of an integrated project — an anti-displacement goal for them, but also a necessary step if more housing for low-income families is to be generated in Jersey City.

*This material is drawn from a case study prepared by Steve St. Hilaire of Hudson County Legal Services and from an analysis by Stephen Weissman, then Assistant Professor of Political Science at Jersey City State College. For further information on the Marion Gardens fight, and copies of the various administrative complaints and other documents discussed here, contact the Marion Gardens Community Association, 67 Dales Ave., Jersey City, NJ 07306, or Steve St. Hilaire, Hudson County Legal Services, 574 Newark Ave., Jersey City, NJ 07306.*

case. Now, among other things, the dispersal policy is a reassurance to gentrifying whites that they are not likely to have more subsidized housing in their neighborhoods. More importantly, the failure of government to expand the number of subsidized units in gentrifying neighborhoods accelerates the displacement process.

On the receiving end of HUD's mobility initiatives, the suburbs no longer are the housing havens they once seemed to be. Most have their own fiscal crises now. Much of their post-World War II housing is now deteriorating. Increasing transportation costs make them less viable living places for people with tight budgets. Moreover, traditional inner-city problems of ghettoization and housing abandonment are now appearing in the suburbs too.

"When you only provide the opportunity to move *out* in order to find safe, decent, and sanitary housing," says Philadelphia Congressman William Gray, a member of the Congressional Black Caucus, "then you really are not offering any choice." And in fact, documents relating to the Regional Housing Mobility Program, plus government reports and the writings of influential "urbanists," show that the government's intentions in these approaches are really more to serve the incoming gentrifiers than the low-income households the programs focus on. For example, Anthony Downs (now of the Brookings Institution), a key consultant to HUD during the late 1970s, wrote in his 1973 book *Opening Up the Suburbs: An Urban Strategy for America:* "Middle and upper income households can be brought back into crisis ghettos in sufficient numbers so they become the dominant group there." And at a workshop HUD held in August, 1979, for agencies invited to apply for RHMP grants, a manual prepared under HUD contract and distributed to all attendees described various techniques for "altering people's natural inclinations" to remain in their neighborhoods, by manipulating Section 8 requirements, housing codes, CETA grants, job opportunities, and educational/persuasion programs. (See end-of-chapter references for listing of articles on this subject.)

## COMBATTING HUD'S INITIATIVES

Obviously, HUD's dispersal policies are useful and helpful in some situations. But when their dominant effect — under the supposed intent of giving "freedom of choice" — is to remove the choice to stay in an established neighborhood and community, then anti-displacement groups naturally resist them.

To date, efforts by Black groups in Philadelphia and St. Louis have led these cities to abandon plans to participate in the Regional Housing Mobility Program. Similar campaigns are being mounted in New York and other metropolitan areas. The position of the groups opposed to RHMP is that real choice also requires the option for people to remain in their existing neighborhoods, using Section 8 and other housing and community development subsidies to fix up central city neighborhoods *for* current residents. Only if funds are available to permit either option can a move to the suburbs be regarded as voluntary.

Even more experience has been accumulated in the effort to counter HUD's "Site Selection Criteria." Among the more successful ways of approaching this problem are:

● Treating so-called "impacted areas" as in fact "transitional areas," in which the shift from lower- to upper-income occupancy is well underway and the need for housing subsidies to prevent wholesale displacement is immediate. In Philadelphia, a coalition

WHAT'S THE MATTER WITH YOU, MAN? YOU TRYIN' TO TRAP POOR PEOPLE IN THE INNER CITY?

Nick Thorkelson

of community organizations, Legal Services attorneys, and city officials convinced HUD to allocate 200 Section 8 units to the 90% Black Southwest Center City Area, by citing the rapid gentrification process underway and the fact that unless Section 8 subsidies were given immediately, there would be no available and affordable sites within Section 8 development levels.

• Ensuring that the anti-displacement provisions of the Community Development Block Grant legislation are met, requiring "a reasonable opportunity for residents displaced as a result of activities to relocate in their immediate neighborhoods." (See pages 137-139 for further discussion of CDBG anti-displacement strategies.)

• Making use of the exceptions to site selection standards provided in the HUD regulations. The regulations allow approval of a project in an "impacted area," if sufficient, comparable housing opportunities already exist outside areas of concentration, or if this is necessary to meet overriding needs that cannot feasibly be met elsewhere in the housing market area. (Section 8 substantial rehabilitation subsidies can be given in an impacted area, however, even if neither of these two condi-

tions exist.) Seattle is among the cities that have been able to make effective use of these exceptions. The criteria HUD uses in these guidelines are constantly being amended and clarified, so it is well to inquire at the HUD Area Office about the most recent status of these regulations.

• Litigation — going to court to challenge HUD's refusal to furnish housing subsidies to "impacted areas."

Articles detailing these and other approaches are listed in end-of-chapter references.

## REFERENCES

### HUD & FmHA HOUSING DISPLACEMENT

*HUD Housing Programs: Tenants' Rights,* a 550-page legal strategy handbook for fighting displacement in all kinds of HUD-owned, -insured, and -assisted housing, has recently been published by the National Housing Law Project, 2150 Shattuck Ave., #300, Berkeley, CA 94704. This is an important and useful tool for local anti-displacement groups, as it sorts out programs, applicable regulations and laws, and how to use or defend against them. If not available at local Legal Services offices, it may be ordered direct from the Housing Law Project.

*FmHA Housing Programs: Tenants' and Homepurchasers' Rights,* a parallel handbook, should be available from the National Housing Law Project in the latter part of 1981.

"The Settlement of the Newark Public Housing Rent Strike: The Tenants Take Control," by Harris David, records successful resistance to an attempt to sell off a housing project by early pay-off of the bonds, plus other tenant tactics to improve conditions. It appears in the June, 1976 *Clearinghouse Review,* available for reading or copying at most law libraries and Legal Services offices.

*Tenants First! A Research and Organizing Guide to FHA Housing,* by Emily Achtenberg and Michael Stone (1974), is a still highly useful guidebook on background and strategies for anti-displacement efforts by tenants in subsidized housing. Available for $3 from Urban Planning Aid, 120 Boylston St., Boston, MA 02116.

"Planning for the Future of HUD-Owned Housing: A Residents' Guide," by Emily Achtenberg and Ann Silverman (1980), draws from the Boston Demonstration Program for alternative management approaches to foreclosed HUD-subsidized projects. It is available for $2.50 from the Citizens Housing and Planning Association, 7 Marshall St., Boston, MA 02108. The Association also has other information on the Demonstration Program.

## LOW-INCOME HOUSING DISPERSAL

A useful discussion appears in "Fair Housing vs. Fair Housing: The Conflict Between Providing Low-Income Housing in Impacted Areas and Providing Increased Housing Opportunities Through Spatial Deconcentration," by John Calmore, in the November/December, 1979 issue of the *Housing Law Bulletin.* A review of HUD techniques to encourage dispersal, plus a critique of the Regional Housing Mobility Program, appears in "The Regional Housing Mobility Program: the Government's 'Solution' to the Urban Crisis," by Arlene Zarembka, in the May/June 1980 issue of the *Housing Law Bulletin.* A reply to Calmore's article and other anti-dispersal program arguments, by Harry Berndt, appears in the March/April, 1980 issue of the *Housing Law Bulletin,* along with a brief response by Calmore. Berndt's article stresses the continuing need to promote movement of non-whites to the suburbs, where jobs are and where what is left of the "American Dream" still lives. Issues of the *Housing Law Bulletin,* if not available in local Legal Services offices, are obtainable from the National Housing Law Project, 2150 Shattuck Ave., #300, Berkeley, CA 94704.

Another good article on RHMP, "Low Income Dispersal Plan Stumbles Over Opposition," by Tom Robbins, appears in the May, 1980 issue of *City Limits,* a highly informative housing magazine (New York City-oriented, but with articles of national scope as well), available for $6 a year from 434 W. 33 St., New York City, NY 10001.

For further information on opposition to the Regional Housing Mobility Program, contact Henry DeBernardo of the North Philadelphia Revitalization Coalition, c/o Community Legal Services, Sylvania House, Juniper and Locust Sts., Philadelphia, PA 19107. The Coalition has prepared an extensive, three-volume set of documents supporting their interpretation of the RHMP as racist in intent.

Regional Housing Mobility Program grants in the first round (1980) went to the Association of Bay Area Governments (San Francisco); Metropolitan Dade County Planning Department (Miami); Tampa Bay Regional Planning Council; Atlanta Regional Planning Commission; Kentuckiana Regional Planning and Development Commission (Louisville); Regional Planning Commission for Jefferson, Orleans, St. Bernard and St. Tammany Parishes (New Orleans); Metropolitan Area Planning Council (Boston); Southeast Michigan Council of Governments (Detroit); Tri-State Regional Planning Commission (New York City); Delaware Valley Regional Planning Commission (Philadelphia); Houston-Galveston Area Council; and the Southeastern Virginia Planning District Commission (Norfolk).

The ten Areawide Planning Organizations (APOs) invited to apply for second-round grants are: the Erie and Niagara Counties Regional Planning Board (Buffalo); Indiana Heartland Coordinating Commission (Indianapolis); Mid-America Regional Council (Kansas City, MO); Southeastern Wisconsin Regional Planning Commission (Milwaukee); Southwestern Pennsylvania Regional Planning Commission (Pittsburgh); Genesee/Finger Lakes Regional Planning Council (Rochester, NY); East-West Gateway Coordinating Council (St. Louis); East Central Florida Regional Planning Council (Orlando); Birmingham Regional Planning Commission; and the Mississippi/Arkansas/Tennessee Council of Governments (Memphis).

Chapter 12

# DISPLACEMENT UNDER THE COMMUNITY DEVELOPMENT BLOCK GRANT PROGRAM

Allan Troxler

he Community Development Block Grant (CDBG) Program was introduced in 1974 as an attempt to bring a number of federally-aided renewal/revitalization programs under one funding source, with unified regulations, and with far greater local control over the spending of this money.

Every city in the United States with over 50,000 population, plus qualifying urban counties, is entitled to receive a certain amount of CDBG funding. Grant amounts are calculated on the basis of formulas which take into account a city's total population, its poverty-level population, housing conditions, and growth characteristics in relation to other so-called "entitlement cities." Cities with less than 50,000 population also can get CDBG funds under the Small Cities Program, although on a competitive rather than entitlement basis. With some exceptions, small cities are subject to the same basic laws and regulations that apply to entitlement cities. Effective in 1981, states (rather than HUD) will have the option of administering the Small Cities Program under certain circumstances, and it appears likely that most states will elect to do so.

CDBG-funded activity can take a wide variety of forms, any number of which can result in displacement. But the fact that all these activities proceed from one basic set of program regulations gives an advantage to anti-displacement groups: once it has been established that a displacement-threatening activity is CDBG-funded, there are built-in ways to resist. Two case studies are presented here, one from a small town, one from a city, to show some of the range of CDBG displacement effects, and the ways in which communities can combat them. Following the two stories is an explanation of how to research and contest CDBG-funded activities.

## CDBG IN THE CITY: THE CAMDEN CITIZENS COALITION

The Camden, New Jersey, Citizens Coalition provides a good example of how organized community pressure can shift a city's CDBG allocation toward housing rehab programs that *prevent* displacement.

The Camden Citizens Coalition (CCC) formed to oppose the city's $5.1 million CDBG grant application for fiscal 1979. As in previous years, only a small proportion of the requested funds was intended for housing improvement, and money previously allocated for the purpose had remained largely unspent. Over one-quarter of the requested grant was slated for a small business investment corporation, for landscaping the downtown area, and for more police foot patrolmen. No funds were to be spent on code enforcement. When CCC sued the city to force release of public data on code enforcement operations, the government retaliated with an ordinance allowing the housing inspection department to destroy past records. When CCC got a temporary restraining order against that ordinance, the media picked up the story and the ordinance was rescinded, with officials claiming it was "just a slip-up."

CCC charged the city was attempting to let some of its lower-income neighborhoods deteriorate "naturally" to accelerate abandonment, so that properties there could be taken over through tax sales to facilitate the gentrification process. (See further discussion of this problem in Chapters 7 and 8.) The Coalition also documented numerous civil rights viola-tions, such as disproportionately small amounts of housing rehab money being spent in minority neighborhoods, and dispropor-tionately small amounts of city contracts going to minority firms.

So CCC set out to derail the CDBG award if its uses were not seriously amended. The Coalition filed an administrative complaint with HUD, on the grounds that in a city where 40% of the housing stock is rated "poor condi-tion," the city government was spending its federal funds in ways "plainly inappropriate to meet the needs and objectives included in the application." CCC also filed lawsuits to de-mand proper code enforcement in the city, held hearings and public meetings on the CDBG program, went to Washington to meet with HUD officials, demonstrated at city hall, and brought in activist speakers such as Milton Street, who pioneered the "Walk-In Home-steading Program" in nearby Philadelphia (see pages 68-71) and Henry DeBernardo, who has led the fight against HUD programs that dis-criminate against inner-city minorities (see pages 126-129).

The Coalition demanded that the city in-crease its proposed CDBG housing rehab allo-cation to $2 million of the $5.1 million grant being sought (the original request for this purpose was $750,000), and also fund a neigh-borhood housing development corporation, a revolving rehab loan fund, and an emergency repair grant program. CCC also demanded revamping of the city's urban homesteading program to make sure it would benefit lower-income households instead of gentrifiers.

The outcome was enormously successful. CCC pressure resulted in a massive shift of CDBG funds into anti-displacement housing rehab activities. During the entire 1975-79 period only a little over 11% of Camden's CDBG grants had gone to housing rehab. But in fiscal 1981, rehab work came to $2.5 mil-lion (51%) of the total $4.9 million grant, and 63% of the 1982 grant ($3.4 of $4.8 million) is pegged for housing rehab. For further in-formation about the Camden effort, contact Roy Jones, Chairman, Camden Citizens Coali-tion, 210 S. Broadway, Camden, NJ 08102; or Dennis Rockway, Camden Regional Legal Services, 530 S. Cooper Street, Camden, NJ 08102.

## BEAUTY, KENTUCKY: THE TOWN THAT REFUSED TO MOVE

Community Development Block Grants in small towns and rural areas often cause even more severe displacement effects than in urban areas. Small towns and cities tend to use them in ways not too dissimilar from urban renewal grants in the 1950s and 1960s — moving people out wholesale for projects the power structure wants to carry out. Lesser awareness of rights and fewer legal defense resources in rural areas may make people there even more vulnerable to illegal use of CDBG funds. Rural America's CDBG Rural Monitoring Project (see page 139) has been particularly useful in pointing out certain patterns of abuse, bring-ing about changes in local practices and HUD supervision, and bringing to light specific horror stories.

One such tale is from Beauty, a town of 100 families in Eastern Kentucky coal country that almost was relocated lock, stock and barrel, courtesy of the CDBG program.

The situation was bad from the beginning. Beauty residents first heard that their town was to be removed in January, 1980, when

Joe Szakos

a routine press release from Kentucky's U.S. Congressional delegation announced HUD approval of 23 CDBG "pre-applications" for the state, with invitations to apply for full grants. One of the items in the release, picked up by the Ashland paper, 100 miles away, was a $2.8 million, three-year grant to Beauty for "relocation of families out of the Beauty flood plain, [plus] development of three housing sites."

The official reason given for dispersing the town was repetitive flooding. And flooding was a concern for Beauty, the most recent serious occurrence having taken place in 1977. But less than 20% of the homes in the target area had ever been inundated. Why was the whole town to be moved? As the Concerned Citizens of Martin County (CCMC), a group formed to fight the proposed displacement, put it, "We feel very uncomfortable that plans for highways, railroads, strip mines, or other activities are a possible reason for relocating Beauty." And subsequent evidence indicates that coal company pressure may well have been behind the whole proposal.

## Beauty's residents first heard that their town was to be removed through a routine press release.

The effort to track down, understand, and overturn the CDBG planning process began when one of Rural America's monitoring organizations in the area, the Center for Housing Alternatives and Socio-Economic Options (CHASE-Options), got wind of the plan. A CHASE-Options staff member called the Martin County planner to ask for a copy of the pre-application, only to be told, "It may be a public document but it's not public in Martin County." A copy was finally obtained from the regional planning organization required to review local applications. Attempts to secure the Citizen Participation Plan submitted to HUD as part of the pre-application were unsuccessful. A public hearing on the project was then held, but few townspeople knew of it — the required public notice was printed in the nearby Williamson (West Virginia) *Daily News* rather than in the Martin County paper. And although letters were sent to the 100 households about the afternoon hearing, most residents reported they received them that same morning, and some did not get them until the next day. (The residents finally were able to get a copy of the Citizen Participation Plan — for $1 a page in "copying fees"). When the town government, in February, finally set up a well-publicized hearing on the plan, 73 people showed up out of the 100 resident households. But none of the public officials present could or would answer the basic question of how the plan got started — who decided on Beauty as a CDBG "target area," and why.

Angered, the residents formed CCMC, with an office at the local grocery store, and began making formal contacts with HUD Area Office officials in Louisville and educating themselves in the CDBG process.

CCMC's position was not that Beauty didn't want or need $3 million in community development funds. Flooding was a real problem (although one the town had lived with for a long time), and they could use some financial assistance in dealing with it. But the town definitely wanted a real say in how the money was to be spent. As one resident put it, "I'd rather have my home taken by a flood than

Joe Szakos

give it to the housing agency and the coal companies."

As the battle heated up, the official response (particularly at the county government level, where the plan seemed to have originated) was typically heavy-handed. Concern began to be voiced that "outsiders" were stirring up the community. The area's Congressional delegation was asked to pressure the Community Services Administration to withdraw funds from the monitoring project. But Beauty's home-grown activists persisted. A comment by Bennie Moore, owner of the grocery store, explains why the town had its back so firmly up: "You know," said Moore, "I have never prayed so long and so hard about anything in my life as I have after I heard what they plan to do to Beauty. Why, this is my community. I can go to any door in Beauty and eat supper anytime I want to. You can't buy that with no amount of money."

A second public hearing, held in March, drew 125 people, and, responding to the com-

**"I'd rather have my home taken by a flood than give it to the housing agency and the coal companies."**

munity's fears, county officials told residents they had four choices: have their houses raised above the flood plain; have their houses moved to new property; sell their houses and relocate; or not participate in the program. The officials agreed not to use condemnation powers and pleged not to submit the final plan to HUD until it was approved by CCMC. But despite these pledges, the county Housing Agency continued to withhold information and bypass the residents. And the county commissioners voted against a guarantee there would be no condemnation.

Under CCMC pressure, the HUD Louisville office decided to hold a hearing in the community later in March, and it was then that some of the plan's origins started coming to light.

The HUD field representative informed the community that the original idea had come from the chief county commissioner (the commissioners had eminent domain powers in the area, something they had previously denied to the community). This didn't exactly quiet community anxieties: the chief county commissioner had been convicted in 1963 of embezzling federal funds (later, after serving time in prison, he was pardoned by President Nixon); the housing agency's executive director was his sister-in-law (whose sister and niece also worked for the agency); her son (the commissioner's nephew) was housing agency board chairman and county planner; the commissioner's wife was county treasurer.

At the final public hearing on the application, held the day after the HUD hearing, CCMC had numerous objections to the substance of the plan. They also objected to the fact that they had received it for review just 29 hours before the hearing. Much of the plan was still vague, and there was no guarantee that relocated residents' mortgage terms wouldn't be worsened, a very important consideration

"Why, this is my community. I can go to any door in Beauty and eat supper anytime I want to. You can't buy that with no amount of money."

for the residents. The plan guaranteed only that no one would pay more than 30% of his or her income for housing afterwards, but it would not prevent people who now owned their homes free and clear from being saddled with a mortgage debt again. Citing the continuing vehement objections, the housing agency announced in April it would not submit the application. But residents, wary of continued trickery by the agency, immediately took a delegation to HUD's Louisville office. What they wanted from HUD was an official rejection of the plan in its present form. They were worried that local officials, despite promises and assurances, would sneak the plan in before the upcoming deadline — which in fact is what happened (accompanied by a threat to sue HUD if the plan was not funded).

In response, CCMC filed a formal administrative complaint with HUD, documenting the entire history of the project. Several days later came a letter from Washington signed by the HUD Assistant Secretary for the CDBG program, indicating that because of failure to follow the citizen participation guidelines, the county would be informed that their plan application would be disapproved. Still pressing for the final nail to be put into the coffin, CCMC demanded a formal "letter of disapproval." CCMC's president said: "The letter of disapproval is what we have been working for three months now. Once we get it, we'll give a copy to every family in Beauty so that they can hang it on their wall. It will be a great reminder of how communities can determine their own future."

One month later, in June, 1980, the official disapproval letter from HUD arrived, the first time since the program began in 1974 that a

Joe Szakos

135

CDBG application had been turned down due to lack of citizen participation. The community now hopes to convince the county to throw away the present application altogether, and start from scratch by sitting down with the townspeople and asking them what they want. A series of hearings on the pre-application has just begun, and residents report the citizen participation process is greatly improved. (A more complete account of this victory, from which these pages are drawn, "Beauty . . . The Town That Refused to Move — The Story of an Eastern Kentucky Community's Struggle to Control Its Own Destiny" is available from Joe Szakos, Box 609, Inez, KY 41224.)

## COMMUNITY POLITICS AND CDBG

Political organization and persistence are the common themes linking the success of these citizen groups in two very different communities. At the time this guide is being published, the CDBG program is rapidly undergoing a process of de-regulation and of decentralization from Washington to the local level (and to some extent to the state level, in the case of the Small Cities Program). This process will make local political activity even more central to winning CDBG anti-displacement struggles.

As noted in the opening paragraph of this chapter, the CDBG program originated as an attempt to simplify, decentralize and introduce greater flexibility into the various federally-aided community development programs. Rather than having a raft of small, tightly defined programs, each requiring detailed applications and explanations, the "new federalism" approach of the Nixon-Ford Administrations called for consolidation of these

programs, a reduction in federal regulations, and decentralization of program administration to the local and state levels. Nevertheless, as enacted in 1974, the CDBG program retained a considerable amount of federal supervision, with standards, protections and entitlements clearly spelled out in statutes and HUD regulations, plus some degree of federal monitoring. The current Administration is on its way to eliminating most meaningful federal controls and protections in the CDBG program, which likely will lead to increased displacement for those affected by CD funds. The main changes are as follows:

**A decreased federal role.** Most community groups feel that the explicit statement of federal standards and their uniform application provided greater protection for low- and moderate-income people and their neighborhoods than will occur if the program is left to the discretion of local or state governments. At these levels, city hall and state legislatures tend to speak primarily for the business community and special interests hostile to the poor and their concerns.

**Fewer regulations and entitlements spelled out in the law.** The present Administration's move toward de-regulation means that specific protections will be removed. Already, the requirements for community participation in the community development process have been weakened with Congress' passage of the Omnibus Budget Reconciliation Act of 1981. And regulatory changes already announced by HUD will have similar impact.

**Greater flexibility in use of CD funds.** Almost everyone prefers programs flexible enough to fit local conditions. But the danger of flexibility is that program funds may be wasted by

local governments or scarce resources may be spent for things only dimly related to the program's goals. Too loosely regulated, CDBG funds can be used to benefit developers' interests or affluent neighborhoods, which does little for, or actually hurts low- and moderate-income parts of the city. For example: until July, 1981, CDBG funds could be spent on a defined set of economic development activities, with particular emphasis on neighborhood-based community development corporations. Now the legislation has been made more "flexible" by permitting CDBG funds to be given to private, profit-motivated businesses for economic development activity. For good reason, community groups fear that they will lose out to more politically powerful interests in the intense competition for a shrinking CDBG pot.

**Elimination of detailed application forms and processes.** Introduction of the CDBG program in 1974 greatly reduced and simplified the process by which local governments had previously applied for federal aid under the many different so-called "categorical programs," but still provided for preparation of application documents that permitted adequate review of program activities. The 1981 Omnibus Budget Reconciliation Act has replaced the CDBG application with a statement of the community's development objectives and a description of its projected use of funds. After publishing a draft of the statement for public comment, and holding at least one public hearing, a "final statement" is submitted to HUD and made available to the public, along with certification that the city is complying with various CDBG statutes and "overlay" statute requirements (see below for explanation of what these are).

Previous legal requirements that activities described in the CDBG application not be "plainly inappropriate" or "plainly inconsistent" with needs the city has identified are now gone. HUD's role no longer is to approve applications for projected use of CDBG funds, but merely to monitor their use, for the most part after the fact, and with few standards or data for judging whether the community has met the objectives of the Community Development legislation.

Thus, substitution of this new "final statement" requirement sweeps away a series of entitlements and controls, and much of the information which community groups involved in the CDBG program have become familiar with over recent years. Such standards were critical to the Camden Citizens Coalition and other community groups in fighting to make the program more responsive to the needs of lower-income neighborhoods.

As this goes to press, other written documents formerly required by CDBG guidelines are also being revised. Since 1974, localities have been required to prepare a Housing Assistance Plan (HAP), which had to be consistent with their CDBG program. Recent federal policy changes have eliminated the consistency requirement, leaving the HAP as a free-standing document and breaking the link between a community's housing and community development efforts. The Grantee Performance Report, by which localities annually reviewed how CD funds were spent during the previous year, still holds, and states which become involved with the Small Cities Program will be required to submit one as well. But the detailed forms that have been required doubtless will be altered in a way that will make real review and evaluation more difficult.

Discussion of the contents of Housing Assistance Plans and Grantee Performance Reports and strategies for using them are contained in the various CD handbooks listed in the end-of-chapter references, which remain relevant to date. But changes in administrative regulations in the near future, and likely statutory changes, demand that citizen groups keep informed of the status of these planning and performance documents. In general, as these documents are simplified or eliminated, communities are deprived of the principal data sources they have used to successfully challenge harmful CD programs.

The "bottom line" is this: as a result of loosening federal standards and reduction of information available to community groups, the courts and administrative complaints to HUD probably will be less promising routes for community groups fighting displacement caused by the CDBG program, and local politics will increasingly be the name of the game.

One very new strategy which community groups are developing in the political arena is to get their local government to pass ordinances which parallel all or parts of the former federal protections and standards, and are fashioned to meet the particular needs of the locality. This already has been done in Prince George's County, Maryland, and a community group in Cleveland has drafted similar legislation. Further information on this new approach is available from the Working Group for Community Development Reform, 1000 Wisconsin Ave. NW, Washington, DC 20007.

# HOW TO CHALLENGE CDBG-RELATED DISPLACEMENT

How can community groups and individuals challenge the use of CDBG funds which displaces people rather than helps solve the problem of displacement? What legal standards can they rely on? What are their prospects at the local government level, with HUD, or in the courts? Because of the factors outlined in the preceding section, answers to these questions are changing rapidly. But despite the threats to eliminate many of the handles which have been used in the past by groups like the Camden Citizens Coalition and Concerned Citizens of Martin County, some important legal protections still exist, and HUD's discretion to allow localities maximum leeway is not without limits. Attorneys with local Legal Services offices are available to assist in developing anti-displacement defenses in CDBG situations. And the National Housing Law Project (2150 Shattuck Ave., #300, Berkeley, CA 94704) provides specialized back-up services to local attorneys involved in CDBG advocacy. It is also important to note that, with respect to CDBG funds not yet spent by local governments, the previous more stringent regulations and protections still apply.

Legal strategies for attacking displacement-prone CDBG programs can be intricate. But the following four points are the most basic questions to be raised in challenges at the city, state, HUD, and court levels:

**Is the specific project an eligible activity for use of CDBG funds?** The CDBG statute and HUD regulations define eligible and ineligible activities. These are spelled out in Section

105 of the 1974 Housing and Community Development Act, as amended, and in the Code of Federal Regulations (CFR), Volume 24, Sections 570.201-207. Reference librarians in local court and law school libraries can help you find these statutes and regulations.

Some uses of CDBG funds which might tempt a locality are clearly ineligible. The locality cannot use CDBG funds to pay the mayor's salary, retire sewer bonds, or contribute to the local firemen's ball, regardless of the alleged merits of these activities. On the other hand, within the area of physical community development the list of eligible activities is broad and inclusive. Acquisition of real property, disposition of real property, provision of public facilities and improvements, and physical rehabilitation all are permitted. In addition, economic development and social services activities may be eligible, under intricate and constantly changing rules. Some physical development activities are not eligible because Congress considers them to be covered elsewhere. For example, CDBG funds cannot be used for construction of housing (as opposed to preparing a site for housing construction), because Congress considers that assisted housing construction is adequately covered in the Section 8 new construction and other federal housing programs. (Community-based, non-profit housing developers can, however, use CD funds to construct their own housing.)

Ineligible activities frequently proposed by local governments are described in detail in the Legal Services CDBG Training Advisory Committee material, cited in the references at the end of this chapter. Most, but not all, categories of activities described in these materials are still ineligible at the time of this writing. The Working Group for Community Development Reform has developed worksheets for neighborhood-based monitors to use in classifying activities as eligible or ineligible. These worksheets are a good model of how to approach the problem and, with some revision, remain useful working tools. Write the Working Group for further help.

Definition of eligible activities in statutes and administrative regulations is constantly changing. The current trend is to broaden the number of eligible activities, and to involve the private sector. In the 1981 CDBG amendments, for example, assistance to private businesses in support of economic development projects was made an eligible activity for the first time.

To use ineligibility as a basis for challenging a CDBG activity, local groups and their advocates must have up-to-date statutory and regulatory definitions of eligible activities and a clear definition of the nature of the contested activity. Then they will be in a position to determine whether or not to challenge the activity as ineligible.

## Does the local CDBG program as a whole principally benefit low- and moderate-income persons?
The 1974 Congressional Act that established the Community Development Block Grants requires that the program "principally benefit" low- and moderate-income people. Although Congress has not removed this stipulation, in May, 1981, the new Administration, through a HUD administrative notice, rescinded the "program benefit" regulations the Department had finally issued in 1978 (after considerable pressure from neighborhood groups and national organizations).

At the present time, neighborhood groups face an uphill battle in challenging CDBG programs that do not principally benefit low- and moderate-income people. While the statutory provision still is in place, there are no regulations implementing the statute. Little support from HUD can be anticipated in any dispute over program benefits. The situation is further complicated by the fact that, as noted above, HUD is simplifying data collection and reporting requirements so radically that documenting a case that a local program does not principally benefit low- and moderate-income people will be very difficult and time-consuming.

**Citizen participation.** The CDBG statute requires citizen participation in the program. And as the tale from Beauty, Kentucky, shows, this can be an important tool in challenging CDBG programs.

The 1981 Omnibus Budget Reconciliation Act unfortunately has diluted the statutory standards for citizen participation in the CDBG program. The amendments do mandate at least one public hearing on community development needs, and require that citizens be provided with information on the amount of CDBG funds available and the range of activities that can be undertaken. Citizens must be given an opportunity to comment on needs and on the local government's performance under the program. But both the tone and substance of the new Administration's approach make clear that citizen participation no longer is highly valued. Unlike the older requirements, communities are not specifically encouraged to submit proposals, nor are public agencies required to respond to such submissions; and the precise identification of documents which have to be made public has been deleted.

More generally, and in keeping with other recent HUD actions, the federal Department can be expected to pull back from any strong intervention in local programs simply because there has been inadequate citizen participation. By 1980, after many years of hard battle by community groups and the national organizations representing them, citizen participation requirements under the CDBG program were fairly good. Although still inadequate (HUD enforcement was lukewarm, citizen groups rarely were provided with funding to permit adequate participation, and the requirements never were as strong as under the older Model Cities and OEO programs), they nonetheless represented a significant potential enforcement "hook." A balanced representation of the citizenry had to be included in all phases of CDBG activity, from initial planning through monitoring and evaluation, with adequate public notice and availability of information which citizens needed to gauge the program's impact. It is clear that the de-regulation process currently underway will make the remaining citizen participation requirements harder to enforce.

## "OVERLAY" STATUTES

In addition to standards within the CDBG legislation itself, CDBG program activities are subject to a variety of federal statutes concerning environmental review, labor standards, civil rights requirements, employment requirements, and the Uniform Relocation Act (see Chapter 15). So long as these independent federal statutory protections are not eliminated, they continue to apply to the CDBG program. Even under the simplified administrative procedures of the Omnibus Budget Reconciliation Act, cities must certify that they are meeting the legal requirements of these "overlay" statutes. If these are not complied with, there is a basis for a challenge. Many citizen groups have raised these overlay statute complaints as part of administrative complaints and litigation involving the CDBG program. However, since de-regulation in areas covered by these overlay statutes is high on the current Administration's agenda as well, groups must check the status of these statutes in order to make an informed judgment whether or not to use them.

## SPECIAL CDBG ANTI-DISPLACEMENT GRANTS

In fiscal 1979, special grants were made to twelve cities and counties from the Secretary of HUD's discretionary fund, to carry out projects to counteract displacement. The cities are listed in the end-of-chapter references. In the same year, the HUD Office of Community Planning and Development funded four efforts to develop city-wide anti-displacement strategies. Grants of $60,000 each were made to consultants in Boston, Jersey City, San Francisco and the District of Columbia to develop comprehensive city-wide anti-displacement strategies (contacts for these groups also are listed at the end of the chapter). The results of these demonstrations should be available in 1981, and should offer some useful models of how cities *can* build anti-displacement planning into their CDBG programs.

## NATIONALLY COORDINATED CDBG MONITORING

Actual and potential abuses in the CDBG program led a number of community groups around the country to band together in the mid-1970s to form the above-mentioned Working Group for Community Development Reform. The Working Group operates both as a local information-gathering network and a lobbying force for CDBG reform. Affiliated with the Washington-based Center for Community Change, the Working Group has generated pressure that has helped liberalize CDBG law and regulations in numerous ways. In 1979, the organization got a grant from the Community Services Administration to fund a comprehensive CDBG Monitoring Project, which now has neighborhood monitors in nearly four dozen cities nationwide (see location listings in end-of-chapter references), assisted by a central training and analysis staff in Washington. Parallel network-type CDBG monitoring activities in over two dozen rural areas are carried out by local groups coordinated by Rural America (also listed in end-of-chapter references).

During 1980, the Working Group Monitoring Project focused on five CDBG issues, one of which was displacement. Local monitors can be of invaluable help to anti-displacement groups in their cities, and the Working Group, Rural America, and other monitoring organizations are good references for advice on handling CDBG issues.

# REFERENCES

Due to major legislative changes in the CDBG program contained in the Omnibus Budget Reconciliation Act of 1981, effective July 29, 1981, and sweeping de-regulation of the CDBG program by the Administration, all guidebooks and other materials concerning the program presently in print are to some extent dated and must be used with caution. Much material which refers to legal entitlements, regulations, or patterns of agency practice and philosophy has changed and continues to change.

With these important warnings in mind, the CDBG guidebooks developed by grassroots organizations and advocacy groups may still be very helpful. Many contain important insights about appropriate objectives, strategy, and the CDBG political process which continue to be highly relevant. Among those most useful for community groups are the following:

## UNDERSTANDING CDBG AND HOW TO DEFEND AGAINST IT

*An Advocacy Guide to the Community Development Block Grant Program* (1979), by the Legal Services CDBG Training Advisory Committee, provides excellent background on the program, with hints on what to look for from a neighborhood perspective. The discussion of applicable law and regulations is now dated, however. Available free to Legal Services attorneys, $8.80 to others, from the National Housing Law Project, 2150 Shattuck Ave., #300, Berkeley, CA 94704.

*Community Development Block Grants: A Strategy for Neighborhood Groups* (1978), by Margaret Stone and Barbara Brown, is a 330-page how-to-do-it manual. Contains highly relevant chapters on how to do CDBG-related research, how to develop a proposal, and the politics and litigation aspects of the program. Detailed step-by-step material on HUD forms and procedures is now dated. Available for $3.50 to Legal Services attorneys, $7.50 to others, from the National Economic Development and Law Center, 2150 Shattuck Ave., #300, Berkeley, CA 94704.

*Using Community Development Block Grants for Neighborhood Revitalization* (1978), by Don Borchelt. Not as inclusive as Stone and Brown and not as strongly attentive to displacement issues, but contains useful basic information about how the CDBG program works. Available from the Citizens' Housing and Planning Association of Metropolitan Boston, 7 Marshall St., Boston, MA 02108.

*CDBG Act, Regulations and Explanatory Publications.* The federal statute governing the CDBG program is the Housing and Community Development Act of 1974, as amended, in the United States Codes (available at federal courts and law libraries) at 42 U.S.C. § 5301. The most recent CDBG changes as of early Fall, 1981, are best described in the Conference Report to accompany the Omnibus Budget Reconciliation Act of 1981, House of Representatives Report No. 97-208 of July 29, 1981. This document unfortunately is out of print but should be available, as part of the "Serial Set" at the Federal Depository Libraries located in most cities — phone your local public library to find out the location of your local Federal Depository Library.

Current CDBG administrative regulations are contained in Code of Federal Regulations, 24 C.F.R. § 570 *et seq.* All of these materials are available free from HUD's Office of Community Planning and Development, Washington, DC. CDBG regulations are constantly being revised, so stay in touch with HUD for the latest revisions.

The National Citizens Monitoring Project of the Working Group for Community Development Reform has available their second report (September, 1981) titled *"Community Development" Versus Poor People's Needs: Tension in CDBG.* It's available free to community groups from the Working Group, 1000 Wisconsin Ave. NW, Washington, DC 20007.

*Housing and Development Reporter* is a looseleaf information service, published by the Bureau of National Affairs (1231 25th St. NW, Washington, DC 20037), which maintains a reference file, updated every two weeks, on developments in the CDBG program, among others. Too expensive for most neighborhood groups, it is available in HUD Area Offices and in specialized libraries, such as those maintained by law schools, and many local planning and community development offices.

*The Community Development Digest,* a weekly insiders' news sheet on the CDBG program, is published by Community Development Publications, 399 National Press Building, Washington, DC 20045. The annual subscription cost is $137, but it may be available at HUD Area Offices and at specialized libraries.

A review of how "overlay" statutes have been used by community groups in CDBG struggles is contained in an article by Richard LeGates and Dennis Keating, entitled "CDBG Litigation," which appears in a report, *Decentralizing Community Development,* edited by Paul Dommel et al., available from the Government Printing Office (report #621-944/389, dated June 2, 1978).

## LOCAL CDBG STRUGGLES

"The Housing and Community Development Act of 1974" is a good videotape detailing the struggles of the Bois D'Arc Patriots, a community group concerned with gentrification, displacement and other issues, in the Dallas CDBG program. Available from the Southern Governmental Monitoring Project, 75 Marietta St. NW, Atlanta, GA 30303, for a rental fee of $25. Made during the Ford Administration, this tape is gaining rather than losing relevance as the program is decentralized and deregulated today.

For further information on Camden, New Jersey's fight against CDBG displacement, contact Ray Jones, Chairman, Camden Citizens Coalition, 210 S. Broadway, Camden, NJ 08102, or Dennis Rockway, Camden Regional Legal Services, 530 S. Cooper St., Camden, NJ 08102.

*Beauty . . . The Town That Refused to Move — The Story of an Eastern Kentucky Community's Struggle to Control Its Own Destiny* is available from Joe Szakos, Box 609, Inez, KY 41224. Send a self-addressed envelope with a 37¢ stamp. Copies of the HUD administrative complaint filed by the Concerned Citizens of Martin County are also available from this source.

## CDBG ANTI-DISPLACEMENT DEMONSTRATION PROJECTS

Innovative anti-displacement projects have been funded by HUD in twelve cities, as follows:

**Baltimore:** Establishment of a non-profit real estate corporation to service four neighborhoods. *Contact:* Nancy Steetle, Dept. of Housing & Community Development, 222 E. Saratoga St., Baltimore, MD 21202.

**Brookline, Massachusetts:** Equity assistance to enable renters to purchase their own units. *Contact:* Mark Eldridge, 333 Washington St., Brookline, MA 02146.

**Charlottesville, Virginia:** Deferred and revolving loans, and housing counseling. *Contact:* Glen Larsen, Dept. Housing & Community Development, PO Box 911, Charlottesville, VA 22901.

**Columbia, South Carolina:** Homeowner rehabilitation to create several smaller units out of large houses. *Contact:* Terrance Bott, Community Development Director, 1730 Main St., Columbia, SC 29217.

**Denver:** Non-profit rehab of a downtown hotel; mortgage payment assistance to low-income renters; conversion of a school to low-income housing; public education and technical assistance to encourage formation of housing cooperatives. *Contact:* Lou LaPerriere, Administrator, Denver Community Development Agency, 1425 Kalamath St., Denver, CO 80204.

**Fairfax County, Virginia:** Reconstruction of a mobile home park to reduce overcrowding, improve housing conditions, provide residents with opportunity to own individual mobile homes and own the park itself. *Contact:* Bruce Laval, Dept. of Housing & Community Development, 4100 Chain Bridge Rd., Fairfax, VA 22030.

**King's County, Washington:** Condominium purchase assistance for low-income renters. *Contact:* Tom Phillips, Manager, Housing & Community

Development Div., 1721 Smith Tower Bldg., 506 2nd Ave., Seattle, WA 98104.

**Los Angeles:** Conversion of an industrial loft building to shelter homeless indigents. *Contact:* Kathleen Connell, Dept. of Housing & Community Development, 200 N. Spring St., Los Angeles, CA 90012.

**Minneapolis:** Conversion of lower-rent apartments to homeownership through purchase options. *Contact:* David Niklaus, City Coordinator, 301M City Hall, Minneapolis, MN 55415.

**Seattle:** Rehabbing a vacant hotel for use as a single room occupancy residence. *Contact:* Donald Chin, Dept. of Housing & Community Development, 400 Yesler Bldg., Seattle, WA 98104.

**Washington:** Assistance in giving tenants of units being converted to condominiums "first right of purchase." *Contact:* Marie Nahikian, Dept. of Housing & Community Development, 1133 N. Capitol, Washington, DC 20002.

**Santa Barbara, California:** Conversion of a vacant building into a model low-income cooperative. *Contact:* Carol Galante, Acting Housing & Redevelopment Director, 1235 Chapala St., Santa Barbara, CA 93102.

Citywide anti-displacement demonstration programs were funded by HUD in four cities. Information about them can be obtained from: San Francisco — Patricia Jenny, Berkeley Planning Associates, 3200 Adeline St., Berkeley, CA 94703; Jersey City — Rick Cohen Associates, 904 Hudson St., Hoboken, NJ 07030; Boston — OKM Associates, 148 State St., Boston, MA 02109; and Washington — Washington United Research and Development Corp., 734 15th St. NW, Washington, DC 20005.

## LOCAL CDBG MONITORING ORGANIZATIONS

The following local groups are coordinated by the Working Group for Community Development Reform, 1000 Wisconsin Ave. NW, Washington, DC 20007:

Coalition for Economic Justice
204 East 5th Avenue, #201
Anchorage, Alaska 99501
(907) 272-6113
Contact: Jamie Levine

Bethlehem Area Community Association
1561 Twiggs Street
Augusta, Georgia 30903
(404) 722-5749
Contact: Addie S. Powell

Austin ACORN
503 W. Mary
Austin, Texas 78704
(512) 442-8321
Contact: Mark Shroder

Community Development Coalition of Bergen County
191 Main Street, Rm. 7
Hackensack, New Jersey 07601
(201) 488-0027
Contact: Lolly Burgin

South Bethlehem Coalition
15 W. 4th St.
Bethlehem, Pennsylvania 18015
(215) 866-0740
Contact: Darrell Jordan

Greater Birmingham Ministries
1205 N. 25th Street
Birmingham, Alabama 35234
(205) 326-6821
Contact: Carolyn Crawford/George Quiggle

Massachusetts Community Action
10 West Street
Boston, Massachusetts 02111
(617) 426-4363
Contact: Lew Finfer/Michael Kane

Camden Citizens Coalition
P.O. Box 1021
Camden, New Jersey 08101
(609) 966-0610 or 445-7303
Contact: Roy Jones

Chester Community Improvement Project
229 Norris Street
Chester, Pennsylvania 19013
(215) 876-8663
Contact: Mary Ryan

National Training Information Center
1123 W. Washington Boulevard
Chicago, Illinois 60607
(312) 243-3035
Contact: Ted Wysocki

Commission on Catholic Community Action
1027 Superior Avenue
Cleveland, Ohio 44114
(216) 696-6525
Contact: Tom Gannon

Housing Advocates
717 Citizens Building
Cleveland, Ohio 44114
(216) 579-0575
Contact: Ed Kramer

Inner City Development Corp.
614 Putnam Building, 215 Main
Davenport, Iowa 52801
(319) 322-6216
Contact: Howard Thomas

Michigan Housing Coalition
10 Witherell Street, Suite 2506
Detroit, Michigan 48226
(313) 963-2200
Contact: Frank Steiner

Campana Pro Preservacion del Barrio
P.O. Box 1489
El Paso, Texas 79901
(915) 545-1734
Contact: Juan Montes

Patchwork Central
100 Washington Avenue
Evansville, Indiana 47713
(812) 424-2735
Contact: Judy Skovmand

Community Action Council of Snohomish County
P.O. Box 1185
Everett, Washington 98206
(206) 252-5141
Contact: Carol Cohen

Indianapolis Neighborhood Development, Inc.
936 Prospect Street
Indianapolis, Indiana 46203
(317) 635-2835
Contact: Sarah Knoy

Operation Shoestring
2019 Bailey Avenue
P.O. Box 11223
Jackson, Mississippi 39213
(601) 353-6336
Contact: Elaine Peacock

Peoples' Housing and Community Development Corp.
2100 S. Broadway
Los Angeles, California 90007
(213) 748-0431
Contact: Warren Shahian

Common Space
19 East 26th Street
Minneapolis, Minnesota 55404
(612) 872-1160
Contact: Charlie Warner

Mobile Community Organization
926½ Conti Street
Mobile, Alabama 36604
(205) 433-9502
Contact: Peter Phillips

Cumberland Institute/Nashville
Community Organizing Project
1223 7th Avenue, No.
Nashville, Tennessee 37208
(615) 327-0500
Contact: Ernest Bennett

Newark Coalition for Neighborhoods
38½ Walnut Street
Newark, New Jersey 07102
(201) 643-7711
Contact: Terri Suess

Pratt Center
275 Washington
Brooklyn, New York 11205
(212) 636-3486
Contact: Brian Sullivan

El Centro de Accion Social
37 East Del Mar Boulevard
Pasadena, California 91105
(213) 792-3148
Contact: Nicholas Rodriguez

Tenant Action Group
1411 Walnut Street, #826
Philadelphia, Pennsylvaia 19102
(215) 563-0736
Contact: Eva Gladstein

Portland Community Resource Center
1723 NE Tenth
Portland, Oregon 97212
(503) 284-9465 or 284-9461
Contact: Steve Rudman

Neighborhoods Uniting Project
3501 Bunker Hill Road
Mt. Rainier, Maryland 20822
(301) 277-7085
Contact: Mary Ann Larkin

Committee for the Restoration of Responsive Government
616 W. 24th St.
Pueblo, Colorado 81003
(303) 561-0700 or 544-9230
Contact: Al Gurule/Paul Mora

Chart, Inc.
608 N. 26th Street
Richmond, Virginia 23223
(804) 788-0221
Contact: Collie Burton

Urban League of Rochester
50 W. Main Street
Rochester, New York 14614
(716) 325-6530
Contact: Beverly Jackson

Community Caring Conference
1110 12th Street
Rock Island, Illinois 61201
(309) 786-0345
Contact: Cathy Bolkcom

Metro Housing Resources
734 DeMun
St. Louis, Missouri 63105
(314) 862-4546
Contact: Pete Berndt

Crossroads Urban Center
347 South 4 East
Salt Lake City, Utah 84111
(801) 364-7765
Contact: J. C. May

San Francisco Information Clearinghouse
409 Clayton Street
San Francisco, California 94117
(415) 863-6566
Contact: Rene Cazenave

Pico Neighborhood Association
1804 14th Street, #9
Santa Monica, California 90404
(213) 450-0401
Contact: Susan Mitchnich

Sonoma County People for Economic Opportunity
P.O. Box 1044
Santa Rosa, California 95402
(707) 544-6911
Contact: Andrea Learned

Springfield Project for a United Neighborhood
22 Hancock St.
Springfield, Massachusetts 01109
(413) 781-7720
Contact: Barbara Craig

South Stockton Community Concern
P.O. Box 6114
Stockton, California 95206
(209) 464-4551
Contact: Nate Miley

Washington Innercity Self-Help, Inc.
1459 Columbia Road, NW
Washington, DC 20009
(202) 332-8800
Contact: Don Leaming-Elmer

Citizens for Community Improvement
180 West 1st Street
Waterloo, Iowa 50701
(319) 232-8268
Contact: Eula Harris

Community Action Group
1 E. Second Street
Mt. Vernon, New York 10550
(914) 664-8680
Contact: Tom Sanzillo

Concerned Citizens of Williamsport
416 Pine Street
Williamsport, Pennsylvania 17701
(717) 323-8741
Contact: Bill Miele

Wilmington United Neighbors
1300 N. Broome Street
Wilmington, Delaware 19806
(302) 655-3338
Contact: Kathie O'Toole

**The following local groups are coordinated by Rural America, 1346 Connecticut Ave. NW, Washington, DC 20036:**

Faith, Hope and Charity
P.O. Box 70
Bethel, Vermont 05032
(802) 234-9917
Contact: Helen Chap

Penobscot Area Housing Development Corporation
50 Columbia Street, Room 66
Bangor, Maine 04401
(207) 947-7404
Contact: Al Smith

Rural Development Corporation of Franklin County
58 Federal Street
Greenfield, Massachusetts 01301
(413) 774-5401
Contact: Laurie Meier

North Country Senior Coalition
22 Main Street, Room 4
Massena, New York 13662
(315) 769-2375
Contact: Jewel Euto

Chautauqua County Rural Ministry
Box 362
Dunkirk, New York 14048
(716) 366-1787
Contact: Carol Adams

Central Pennsylvania Legal Services
10 South Prince Street
Lancaster, Pennsylvania 17603
(717) 299-3621
Contact: Randall Chapman

NCALL Research
155 South Bradford Street
Dover, Delaware 19901
(302) 678-8522
Contact: Jeanine Kleimo

Monticello Area Community Action Agency
418 Fourth Street, NE
Charlottesville, Virginia 22901
(804) 295-3174
Contact: Debra Abbott

Scott County Citizens for Better Housing
P.O. Box 416
Gate City, Virginia 24251
(703) 386-3251
Contact: Robert Daley

Wise County Housing Coalition
P.O. Box 1376
Wise, Virginia 24293
(703) 328-2136
Contact: Danny Baker

Assembly of Vance
P.O. Box 1573
Henderson, North Carolina 27536
(919) 438-7319
Contact: Margaret Ellis

CHASE-Options
P.O. Box 57
David, Kentucky 41616
(606) 886-1987
Contact: Joe Szakos

The Youth Project
805 Peachtree #190
Atlanta, Georgia 30303
(404) 872-1311
Contact: Diana Jones Wilson

JONAH
18 South Court Street
Brownsville, Tennessee 38012
(901) 772-5258
Contact: Jo Anne Depweg

United Front
P.O. Box 544
Cairo, Illinois 62914
(618) 734-1502
Contact: Martha Turner

Impact Seven, Inc.
Route 2, Box 8
Turtle Lake, Wisconsin 54889
(715) 986-4171
Contact: Marguerite Donnelly

Minnesota COACT
1216 South Sixth Street
Brainerd, Minnesota 56401
(218) 828-1805
Contact: Denise Scheer

Arkansas ACORN
503 C East Fourth Street
Stuttgart, Arkansas 72160
(501) 673-7776
Contact: Jessie Weiss

Salud y Educacion por el Campesino en Texas
P.O. Box 565
Hidalgo, Texas 78557
(512) 843-8381
Contact: Sandy New

Community Council of Bee County
P.O. Box 1049
Beeville, Texas 78102
(512) 358-1865
Contact: Jessy Garza

Missouri Delta Ecumenical Ministry
Box 524
Hayti, Missouri 63851
(314) 359-1718
Contact: Viola Coleman

South Dakota ACORN
611 South Second Avenue
Sioux Falls, South Dakota 57104
(605) 332-2328
Contact: Phil Moore

Concerned Citizens of Southside
P.O. Box 1642
Rawlings, Wyoming 82301

PPEP
806 East 46th St.
Tucson, Arizona 85713
(602) 622-3553
Contact: Tito Carrillo

Southwest Oregon Community Action Committee
P.O. Box 427
North Bend, Oregon 97459
(503) 756-3176
Contact: Rob Wiener

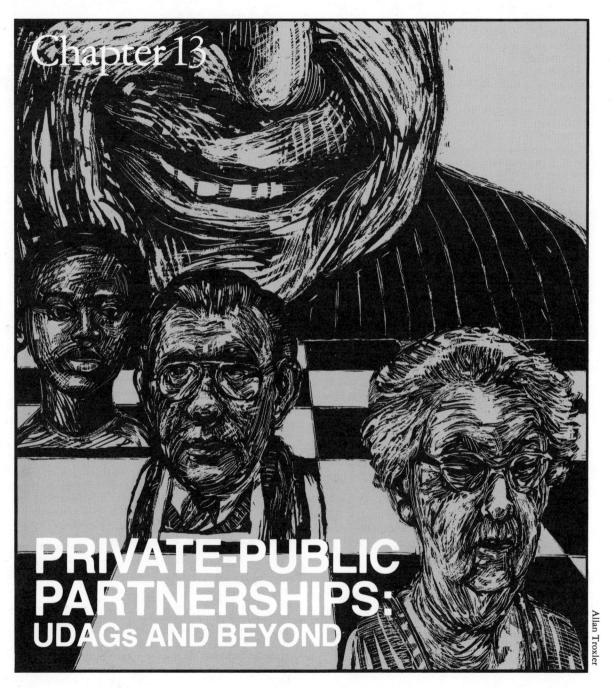

Chapter 13

PRIVATE-PUBLIC
PARTNERSHIPS:
UDAGs AND BEYOND

Allan Troxler

The UDAG Program — Urban Development Action Grants — is only the latest in a sequence of federal-local urban programs designed to directly connect public and private investment, corporate and government planning. Congress recently folded the UDAG program into the Community Development Block Grant program, but with a special UDAG "set-aside" fund. The UDAG philosophy is that the federal government should pass money back to local governments, which in turn will use it as subsidies to "leverage" private development projects that have some beneficial public spinoff, such as job creation or adding to the local tax base. The new proposed "urban enterprise zones," which combine government subsidies with relaxation of various regulations — zoning, minimum wage, environmental protection, health and safety protections, etc. — are yet another variation on the same theme.

UDAGs are competitive grants for "distressed cities," and when a major corporation holds out the prospect of private development in the city, it is certain that federal and local officials' heads will turn. Such "civic improvement" generated by UDAG moneys has also caused displacement of lower-income residents — all for the greater good, as the planners say — and new versions of this approach can be expected to have the same effect. Under UDAG regulations, a city must meet a number of requirements. The applicant city must identify proposed displacement, and priority is supposed to be given to projects that will cause little or no displacement. HUD reviewers are also legally bound to weigh the applicant city's progress in meeting the low- and moderate-income housing and equal opportunity needs of its population. This chapter presents a short case study of a community organization contesting a UDAG backed by the world's largest manufacturing corporation and the government of the nation's sixth largest city, and a look at these same "heavies" at work with UDAG money in another nearby neighborhood.

## DETROIT ACORN VS. "G.M. CROW"

Bob Buchta

UDAG grants often focus on improving corporate properties and the areas around them — construction of a new factory, say, along with park space or some other form of general-use development. In Detroit, the corporate property was the world headquarters of General Motors, and the development plan involved the blighted inner-city neighborhood just north of it. G.M. executives who stray a few blocks from their mammoth new central office complex find themselves in a predominantly Black, low-income area of deteriorated apartment buildings, with a sprinkling of single-family homes. Certainly, to the corporate eye, not an appropriate setting for their world headquarters.

In September, 1978, G.M. announced its intent to buy, rehabilitate and sell 125 single-family homes and 175 apartment units in the neighborhood. At the same time, other private developers, coordinating with G.M., were to construct several new office buildings in the area. And to tie it all together, the city applied for UDAG funds for street widening, park acquisition, and economic development activities in the neighborhood.

No one had bothered to consult neighborhood residents about all this. But ACORN (The Association of Community Organizations for Reform Now), a nationwide association of activist community groups, had just opened an office there, and the shock the G.M. announcement produced in the neighborhood soon turned to a questioning, insistent opposition. The tone was set in an unusual Thanksgiving Day observance. ACORN members paraded the streets with a giant "G.M. Crow," passing out leaflets calling on residents to "Tell G.M. thanks for nothing — displacement with no relocation benefits." The organization had set out to win the maximum it could get for the neighborhood from the giant moving in on it, and that drive evolved into a successful demand that significant amounts of renewal investment be made for the existing residents, rather than simply paying them off to leave.

Many years of intricate corporate-city moves had gone into formulation of the final UDAG-supported plan, and ACORN was up against all that prior preparation in its efforts to work against displacement. As early as the 1960s, G.M. had been candid about its desire that the area provide housing and an attractive close-in community for its management-level employees. Also, the corporation wanted a

well-behaved backyard for its headquarters, where it seems to be consolidating management operations. (In early 1981, G.M. announced it was moving its financing and insurance subsidiaries, employing 700 people, from Manhattan to Detroit.)

The development scenario for this venture was simple: demolish deteriorated buildings, put in better streets, sewer lines, and other capital improvements, and promote new residential and commercial construction. In short, transform the area into a stable, middle-class neighborhood, getting rid of most of the people who already lived there.

If the city had proposed such changes on its own, the resistance could have used numerous legal blocks to force a change. But the private enterprise side of UDAG made the situation much more difficult. (Where is the borderline between public and private responsibility? And how does the community impose its interests on *both* sides of that line?) Some aspects of the plan which contributed most to the gentrification of the neighborhood were to be carried out with purely private money (for example, the purchase of homes by G.M.), whereas many government funded-activities did not directly displace people (for example, new parks and street widening). Determining displacement responsibilities was important because benefits and services under the federal Uniform Relocation Act (URA) are only available for persons and businesses displaced by federal government action. (See Chapter 15 for fuller discussion of the URA). Cities and private developers anxious to pinch pennies, avoid delay, and free themselves from what they regard as burdensome requirements often try to define public activity narrowly. Unless community groups press hard, households and businesses located in such project areas are not likely to receive Uniform Relocation Act benefits.

One of the lessons Detroit ACORN learned is that it is extremely hard to get clear information on what is actually planned in a complex redevelopment program like this. Usually plans are far less clear than what is depicted in the public statements of private sponsors and city agencies — who want the public to believe that funding definitely will be available, that many prospective developers will compete for the opportunity to participate, and that budgets will remain within planned limits. Frequently, neighborhood groups have found that the managers of such large redevelopment schemes want to keep the facts ambiguous, giving alternative versions of what is planned to groups with potentially conflicting interests, in order to keep everyone happy while the project gains momentum.

At times, G.M. appeared to be saying that it planned to purchase, rehabilitate, and resell 150 single-family homes; at other times the number was 125. Ultimately it turned out that they intended to purchase, jointly with other partners, 150 houses, of which only 91 would be rehabilitated, while 59 were to be demolished.

The estimated resale price of rehabilitated homes was almost impossible to pin down. When, under ACORN pressure, G.M. quoted an estimate of $40,000 per house, neighborhood residents protested that few could afford such prices. G.M. then began to speak of a range of prices, including some (unspecified) number of houses at $30,000.

It was even more difficult to pin down plans for the apartment units. Originally the plan proposed that 175 units would be rehabilitated for low- and moderate-income rentals, with first option for neighborhood residents. But when projected rent figures were released, again under ACORN pressure, they were double to triple the existing rents in the area. Originally there was no discussion of subsidies for these units. Then, again under pressure, G.M. began to speak of 50-100 units with Section 8 coverage, but without a commitment. And so it went.

Nick Thorkelson

**The development scenario was simple: transform the area into a stable, middle-class neighborhood, getting rid of most of the people who already lived there.**

Through ACORN, the community fought to make both G.M. and the city specify *precisely* what was planned, adapt the plans to fit the needs of current neighborhood residents, and put forward detailed, written commitments. And there was a fair measure of success in these efforts. Beyond that, the main fight was to force both G.M. and the city to acknowledge that the whole interconnected project was so infused with "public-ness" that the important protections for displacees contained in the federal Uniform Relocation Act should apply to all persons displaced from the area. This effort also was a success.

Ultimately, the UDAG plan was amended to drop its most offensive features and shift $800,000 to relocation benefits. It was agreed that all persons displaced, even by private action, would receive the relocation payments and other benefits guaranteed by the Uniform Relocation Act. Second, G.M. and HUD eventually provided written assurances that 100 housing units would be substantially rehabilitated with Section 8 subsidies, meaning most rehabilitated multi-family units in the area would remain within economic reach of the lower-income residents. ACORN's efforts also won immediate cash-in-the-pocket for some constituents, such as a two-month rent rebate for some of the households in buildings scheduled for demolition.

Against this battery of community action and concrete demand-making, G.M. and the city gave ground grudgingly, seldom acknowledging that their original plans had not called for whatever concession was given. When the commitment to Section 8 subsidies was finally made, for instance, officials claimed "we were planning to do this all along."

Detroit ACORN frequently emphasized

various legal requirements of the UDAG program in political meetings and administrative complaints, and threatened litigation. (Programs that replace UDAG are likely to have at least some similar provisions which community groups and their attorneys will be able to use.) But although legal supports were important, the effect of informed, unrelenting organizational pressure proved most strategic in the end. Creating a community organization sharp enough to get its information in order, and strong enough to make itself felt, was the first objective of ACORN's operations. The next was to ask questions — persistently, frequently, and in many different places. In meetings with G.M., city officials, HUD, the press, and in letters, petitions, and administrative complaints, ACORN asked: how many buildings will be taken? how many rehabbed? which ones? what rents? what evidence is there that plans will materialize? ACORN conducted neighborhood surveys to document actual housing needs, and studied the characteristics of proposed sites. The organization worked with the local neighborhood employment group to identify who the unemployed were and what skills they could offer. Activists both listened to and helped educate and organize neighborhood people.

The community's goals were clear from the start: to get better housing, community improvements, and jobs that would serve existing residents; and if they had to move, they wanted decent affordable housing and relocation benefits. ACORN translated these general goals into specific demands: enough units of appropriate size, properly located, suitable for the households in the neighborhood, and with sufficient Section 8 subsidies. In pushing the issue of employment, they even went so far

as to have residents file application forms with G.M. for the 185 jobs the UDAG proposal claimed would be created for neighborhood people.

ACORN activists feel that if they had been able to get into this battle at earlier stages of the planning, the outcome might have been altered in even more fundamental ways. Experience of other groups confronting large-scale development plans indicates that this is a basic general rule of action: get started as close to the beginning as possible.

There is probably always going to be something like UDAG in the federal repertory of urban programs. Specific regulations will differ, but the intent will be the same — to combine private and public funds in "revitalization" efforts. And when those programs bring displacement to lower-income neighborhoods, they can be fought, with organization, militance, local data research, and knowledge of the law.

For further information on this struggle, contact Detroit ACORN at 2230 Witherell, Detroit, MI 48201.

## POLETOWN: G.M., DETROIT, UDAG STRIKE AGAIN

General Motors, the City of Detroit and the UDAG program are also involved in a much larger controversy, one which likely will displace 3500 residents, demolish 1500 homes, 150 businesses, 16 churches and a hospital.

Bob Buchta

The other side of the coin is a new auto assembly plant G.M. wants to construct on a 465-acre site straddling the Poletown neighborhood of Detroit and the old Dodge Main plant in the adjacent city of Hamtramck, a project that may save 4000-6000 jobs and produce additional spinoff employment. It's a classic confrontation of "reindustrialization" vs. housing and neighborhood values. Poletown is a stable, integrated working-class neighborhood of Blacks and Poles. Detroit and the auto industry need jobs. People need and want their homes and communities. G.M. says it can stay in Detroit only if it builds this new plant. An alternative plan which moves the proposed plant a little to the north, changes the parking plan from vast open lots (the sites of most of the homes to be taken) to rooftop and multi-story structure parking, and makes other changes would save most of the neighborhood. But G.M. says it's not as good a plan, that it will cause too much delay, that they've invested millions in plan preparation, and that they've already acquired 70% of the properties for the proposed project. The properties for the most part have been acquired through the city acting as intermediary, using its eminent domain powers.

Vast public subsidies are involved: the $30 million proposed UDAG grant is less than 1/10 of the total of $320 million in direct government subsidies and property tax breaks estimated in a recent New York *Times* article to be involved in the project. City property tax abatements amount to at least $120 million, and beyond the UDAG, the project is supported by other HUD funds for property acquisition and relocation, CDBG funds, an Economic Development Administration grant for demolition and site preparation (which now seems doubtful due to the Administration's announced intention to abolish the EDA program), state road funds, federal water and sewer grants, plus other public moneys.

Few are opposed to the project per se, given the city's 16% unemployment rate. What is questionable is whether so many homes and businesses have to be taken and whether it makes sense, in a city facing a $230 million budget deficit next year, to give away so many public subsidies and tax breaks to bribe G.M. to stay. The project has been challenged in court by the neighborhood and by Ralph Nader's Corporate Accountability Research Group, which has labelled the project "corporate blackmail." At this writing, both the Michigan and federal courts have refused to stop the project, although further challenges are planned. A major issue is the legality of using eminent domain powers to acquire homes in the area. As the Vice-President of the Poletown Neighborhood Council put it: "If a city can take our homes just because a factory pays more in taxes, what security do any of us have? Are we just pawns? The point is someone bigger than us has walked in and said it wants our neighborhood, and they're using our tax dollars to take it away from us." For further information about the Poletown controversy and the litigation around it, contact the Poletown Neighborhood Council, 3414 Trombly, Detroit, MI 48211, and the Corporate Accountability Research Group, P.O. Box 19312, Washington, DC 20036, which plans to continue the fight nationally to make corporations responsible to their communities.

Bob Buchta

# REFERENCES

Detroit ACORN's address, for further information on the concessions they won, is 2230 Witherell, Detroit, MI 48201.

A good account of the Poletown controversy is the article "Detroit: I Do Mind Moving," by David Moberg, in the February 4-10, 1981 issue of the weekly national newspaper *In These Times* (1509 N. Milwaukee Ave., Chicago, IL 60622).

Further information on the Poletown litigation is available through the Poletown Neighborhood Council, 3414 Trombly, Detroit, MI 48211, or the Corporate Accountability Research Group, P.O. Box 19312, Washington, DC 20036.

An excellent CBS Report on Poletown, "What's Good for G.M. . . . ," is available from California Newsreel, 630 Natoma St., San Francisco, CA 94103.

Robert Goodman's book *The Last Entreprenuers: America's Regional Wars for Jobs and Dollars* (Simon and Schuster, 1979) is a useful study of how state and local governments compete for commercial developments via all manner of concessions and subsidies.

## Chapter 14

## PLUMBING

### WIDE-SPREAD LAV SET

Gleaming white porcelain knobs with polished brass, antique style spout, and porcelain pop-up knob for sinks with hot and cold water pipe holes 8" to 15" apart. Includes a brass pop-up drain. Distance from center of faucet to spigot is 5¼". Diameter of bell under cross handle is 3¼". *P.&L.* (D)

| | |
|---|---|
| 93015 wide-spread lav set | each $278.50 |
| 3 or more sets | each $250.70 |
| 12 or more sets | each $238.10 |

An elegant Roman tub set (not shown) in the style of the above widespread lav sets #93002 and 93013.

| | |
|---|---|
| 93028 Roman tub set-straight handles | each $220.00 |
| 93029 Roman tub set-curved handles | each $220.00 |

### TOILET TANK HANDLES

Brass toilet tank handles in styles matching our brass faucets. *P.&L.* (D)

| | |
|---|---|
| 93021 curved handle | each $24.20 |
| 3 or more | each $22.75 |
| 93020 straight handle | each $24.20 |
| 3 or more | each $22.75 |

### OLD-FASHIONED FAUCETS

This is truly a distinctive set. Old-fashioned solid polished brass faucet set includes hot and cold individual faucets and solid brass center post with chain for rubber sink stopper. Distance from center of faucet to spigot is 5"; 1¼" sink boring required. *P.* (R)

| | |
|---|---|
| 93245 brass faucets | each pair $55.65 |
| 2 or more | each pair $48.95 |
| 8 or more | each pair $41.95 |
| 24 or more | each pair $38.00 |
| 93295 brass center | each $8... |

### VICTORIAN STYLE FAUCETS

Remember the cool, clean style of polished brass and white porcelain found in bathrooms of the past century? These outstanding fixtures are available today in solid brass with beautiful white limoges porcelain. Knobs say "hot" and "cold" exactly as on the old faucets. On all our faucets a minimum 1" hole is needed. All lav sets pictured will fit sink tops up to 2" thick.

### 4" CENTER SET

White limoges porcelain knobs and drain knob mounted on polished brass base and spout. For sinks with 4" between hot and cold water pipe holes. Includes a polished brass pop-up drain. Distance from center of faucet to spigot is 4¾". *P.&L.* (D)

| | |
|---|---|
| 93016 4" center set | each $138.35 |
| 3 or more sets | each $124.50 |
| 12 or more sets | each $118.25 |

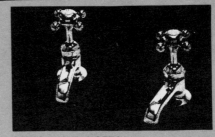

### VICTORIAN FAUCETS

Solid brass hot and cold faucets with porcelain caps labeled "H" and "C" ideal for renovation projects. Especially suited to tubs or other sinks where there is no hole for the spout. 1" sink boring required. Distance from center of faucet to spigot is 3". *P.* (R)

| | |
|---|---|
| 93... victorian faucets | each pair $38.50 |
| 3 pairs or more | each pair $30.00 |
| 8 pairs or more | each pair $24.00 |
| 24 pairs or more | each pair $19.25 |

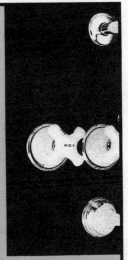

### SHOWER AND TUB SET

Three valve combination tub and porcelain hot and cold knobs, diverter knob, and polished brass head. *P.&L.* (D)

| | |
|---|---|
| 93017 shower and tub set | |
| 3 or more sets | |
| 12 or more sets | |
| 93026 tub set only | |
| 3 or more sets | |
| 12 or more sets | |
| 93027 shower set only | |
| 3 or more sets | |
| 12 or more sets | |

### 4" CENTER SET

DISPLACEMENT DUE TO HOUSING REHABILITATION

149

ousing rehabilitation is one of those deceptive terms that sounds simple but ends up being quite complex. The process can range from reconstructing a vandalized shell to cosmetic refurbishing, and everything in between. Rehab can be done by speculators, by landlords as part of their normal operations, by homeowners, by non-profit groups, by government agencies. It often is spurred and supported by public investments, subsidized by public policy, promoted by code enforcement.

It's almost always aimed at older housing — home for disproportionate numbers of low-income households, who usually get displaced in the rehab process. If the physical work itself doesn't make living there impossible, the increased rent after renovation does.

Often, as we have noted, major rehabilitation efforts are keyed to gentrification — either to take advantage of a process already begun, or as a conscious displacement mechanism en-

gineered by government and developers. So low-income communities get caught on the horns of a dilemma. To want decrepit housing rehabilitated is natural and commendable. But if the price is losing one's home, what course should be followed?

The question becomes more acute as rehabilitation begins to outstrip new housing construction in government programs, and in the private market as well.

Around the country, community organizations have confronted the problem head on. Some of the goals they have fought for are:

● rehabilitation to benefit current occupants and the existing community, rather than for profiteering and gentrification;

● tenants' rights to return to rehabilitated housing;

● staged rehabilitation to enable temporary relocation within the community;

● controlled rents after rehab;

● purchase-price subsidies if the rehab produces condominiums;

● full relocation benefits when displacement is unavoidable.

What prompts rehab, and where the money comes from, will determine community goals. This chapter discusses the main types of housing rehab, and how to guard against the displacement each can cause.

## DISPLACEMENT FROM PRIVATE MARKET REHAB

Rehabilitation is something that kindly landlords do for their grateful tenants, goes the real estate industry myth. Yet consider the Canterbury, a 75-year-old, 90-unit apartment building located in the Hollywood District of Los Angeles. Finally declared a health hazard in 1979 by city inspectors, the Canterbury had been torched by arsonists, was littered with garbage, and had more rats than tenants. Having made all they could out of disinvestment (see discussion of this process in Chapter 7), the owners unceremoniously evicted the mostly elderly tenants, who had to find emergency shelter through charitable groups.

In February, 1980, a rehabilitated Canterbury reopened. The new owners, aiming for an affluent clientele, refused to allow any former tenants to return. Even if they had, none could have afforded to re-occupy the renovated units. A one-bedroom apartment which rented for $185 monthly before rehab was going for $495. As one elderly former tenant said, "They've made it a fancy place for fancy people."

It's a familiar story that should have a happier ending. Indeed, the repairs should have been made — but the beneficiaries should have been the tenants who had been paying for the building with their rents. At the very least, the owners who benefited so handsomely from the rehab process should have been re-

sponsible for relocating and compensating the tenants who were displaced.

Protection and assistance of that sort, however, are hard to come by in the private market. Strategies to prevent tenants from being displaced by private redevelopers, or at least enable them to obtain relocation aid, include:

**Market controls.** Effective local rent, eviction, conversion, demolition and anti-speculation controls (see full discussion in Chapters 4, 5, 6 and 9) can help deal with private rehab displacement. While rent control usually will allow landlords' rehab costs to be passed through to tenants as rent increases, these ordinances require a close relationship between actual expenditures and the amount of the increase. Additionally, landlords may be required to spread (amortize) rehab costs over the expected life of the improvements. But many rent control laws contain some form of exemption for substantially rehabilitated units, in order to encourage upgrading of the housing stock. When this exemption produces de-controlled high-rent units, tenants can challenge it on the grounds that this decreases the supply of low- and moderate-rent housing, which defeats the purpose of rent control. (This type of challenge is discussed in an article titled "Residential Rehabilitation and Rent Control: The Massachusetts Priority" in Volume 11, 1976, of the *Urban Law Annual,* available for reading or copying at most law libraries.)

Similarly, many of the "just cause" eviction statutes discussed in Chapter 9 permit a landlord to evict a tenant in order to carry out rehabilitation. But limits can be placed on use of this just cause — allowing eviction only for code-related improvements and not for luxury rehab, giving tenants who must move a first

**A one-bedroom apartment which rented for $185 monthly before rehab was going for $495.**

right to return, and requiring relocation payments to tenants displaced when landlords choose to upgrade their properties. Washington, D.C.'s rent control ordinance contains these last two provisions.

Local ordinances preventing or limiting conversion of rental units to condominiums or non-residential use, protecting the stock of single-room occupancy (SRO) hotels, regulating demolition, or discouraging housing speculation also serve to discourage the kind of profit-oriented private housing renovation that causes displacement.

**Establishing the program connection.** If it can be demonstrated that the rehabilitation is being undertaken because of a public investment or program, even if it is not part of that program, there may be a basis for winning the protections and compensations of the Uniform Relocation Act or equivalent benefits (discussed in Chapter 15). Chapter 13 described the success of Detroit ACORN in having privately rehabbed housing covered by good relocation, right-to-return, and subsidy provisions because the renovations were being carried out in coordination with a federal Urban Development Action Grant.

**Making "private rehab" public.** In the long run, anti-displacement groups must find a way to make government take responsibility for private rehab displacement at a level which matches the level of public subsidy involved in generating that rehab in the first place. Since 1969, landlords have been able to take acceler-

ated depreciation benefits up to $20,000 per unit rehabbed for low- and moderate-income use, which gives them an enormously valuable tax shelter (see further discussion of tax shelters in Chapter 4). But the displacement this indirect government incentive produces is called a "private" process, with the existing tenants paying the displacement consequences. Abolishing the false division between public and private responsibility might get Uniform Relocation Act benefits for "private" rehab displacement. Or to qualify for tax shelter subsidy, landlords could be required to provide right-of-return and to accept rent controls. Clearly, basic reforms are badly needed and long overdue.

## DISPLACEMENT FROM MUNICIPAL CODE ENFORCEMENT

As discussed in Chapter 10, housing and health codes are mixed blessings for lower-income households in deteriorated dwellings. The codes are intended to ensure safe and sanitary housing and as such are useful weapons against callous landlords. But while these codes set out what the society regards as minimum standards for habitation, we do not at the same time provide people with the resources that enable them to pay for meeting these standards. Code enforcement can require owners of sub-standard housing to lay out so much money that displacement results. In rental housing, this can come from improvement costs being added to existing rents, if straight "pass through" is allowed, or from abandonment or demolition if owners choose not to make improvements. Code officials generally take a very narrow view of their

Photograph © 1978 Ken Light

## DISPLACEMENT FROM FEDERALLY-AIDED REHABILITATION

While the rehabilitation of rental housing has not been a major goal of federal programs in the past, this is changing as rehabilitation becomes economically a more necessary and feasible approach to providing housing. In the near future, displacement threats from federally-aided housing rehab are likely to come from the Section 8 substantial rehab and moderate rehab programs, the Section 312 low-interest rehab loan program (evein in its new curtailed form), the Section 223 (f) refinancing program, and the Community Development Block Grant and Urban Development Action Grant programs. The Neighborhood Housing Services (NHS) program of the Neighborhood Reinvestment Task Force, a joint creation of HUD and the Federal Home Loan Bank Board, is emerging as an influential force promoting private-public partnerships to foster rehabilitation, and this too may be a source of displacement.

## SECTION 8 SUBSTANTIAL REHABILITATION

The Section 8 Substantial Rehabilitation program gives subsidies to developers for major renovation jobs. HUD's rules for this program offer better, but still inadequate, defenses against displacement than did past programs. Two different sets of protections are involved: the stronger applies when Section 8 substantial rehab funds come from a special HUD account for use within Neighborhood Strategy Areas (NSAs); the other applies where local allocations of Section 8 substantial rehab money are used, even if the use occurs within

work: it is a matter of indifference to them whether violations are removed by fixing the building up or by removing the building itself. Tenants who complain about code violations face retaliatory evictions. And those who are displaced by "private" response to public code enforcement are eligible for none of the compensations or protections provided for those displaced directly because of public programs.

Community groups working to prevent displacement must therefore be wary of code en-

forcement unless it is part of a comprehensive package — including carrots *and* sticks — which insures that current residents will be around to benefit from the improved conditions. This package must include rehabilitation and rent subsidies, controls on rents and other market forces, tenants' right to return to the rehabilitated units, and changes in ownership where needed — all in the context of a code enforcement program planned and implemented with the full participation of the affected community.

an NSA. HUD Area Offices — see Appendix A for a list of these — or local Community Development agencies can identify the precise funding sources for various Section 8 rehab projects.

## SPECIAL-FUNDED SECTION 8 SUBSTANTIAL REHAB WITHIN NSA'S

Official designation of an NSA gives cities access to a special HUD set-aside fund of Section 8 substantial rehab money. Within NSAs, community groups should press for use of these special funds rather than local Section 8 allocations, because only tenants affected by this specially funded Section 8 rehab are given the full protections and benefits of the Uniform Relocation Act (discussed in Chapter 15).

These displaced tenants must receive written notice of their right to continue in occupancy in the rehabbed building, or in comparable replacement housing, for four years. This is, in effect, a right-to-return provision when rehab work requires temporary displacement. Such displacees have the right to temporary or permanent relocation assistance from the local government. In their post-rehab housing, such tenants are also guaranteed they will not have to pay more than 25% of their income for rent, the right to a Section 8 Certificate, if they are eligible, and the right not to be displaced unless a move is required for rehab or demolition. These protections apply to tenants only, not to displaced homeowners.

## OTHER SECTION 8 SUBSTANTIAL REHAB

Substantial rehab projects funded by local allocations of Section 8 money are not given full Uniform Relocation Act coverage. But the Section 8 program regulations give displaced tenants (again, not homeowners) the following protection:

• Tenants are not to be displaced unless "this is necessary to carry out the project." And unless evicted for a "good" cause, unrelated to the rehabilitation, displaced tenants are eligible for both temporary and permanent relocation assistance from the developer.

• If tenants must be displaced temporarily, they are entitled to "actual reasonable out-of-pocket expenses, including moving costs and rent increases for a maximum of one year."

• The owner, not the local government, is responsible for providing relocation assistance. Any tenant who believes that s/he is not receiving proper relocation payments or opportunities to relocate is entitled to appeal to the local HUD Area Office.

• If tenants are permanently relocated, the owner must provide them with a "reasonable choice of opportunities to move to a suitable replacement dwelling." If suitable replacement housing is not available because the tenant cannot afford it and HUD subsidies are unavailable, then the owner must provide a four-year rent subsidy, up to $4,000, to ensure that the displaced tenants pay no more than 25% of their income for the replacement housing.

• Displaced tenants must be provided with a written explanation "that is sufficient to enable them to understand fully the reason for their displacement and the relocation opportunities and assistance . . . available to them," with 90 days advance written notice prior to the displacement, and with appropriate relocation advisory services.

• All lower-income tenants who are single persons, even if they are not elderly or handicapped, may return after rehab if they are eligible for the Section 8 program.

• Once rehab is completed, the Section 8 regulations cover all subsidized tenants, whether they live in the building prior to rehab or not. This includes protection against eviction except for good cause.

Although these Section 8 displacement protections are reasonably strong, the past history of HUD's rehab programs suggests that tenants cannot depend on either local housing agencies or private developers to implement full protections and compensations. Tenants must organize to ensure that they are not illegally displaced, that they do receive Section 8 benefits, and, if they are displaced, that they receive the relocation benefits to which they are entitled.

## SECTION 8 MODERATE REHABILITATION

The Section 8 Moderate Rehab program, which subsidizes building owners for smaller renovations, includes HUD's strongest relocation protections for tenants. On the other hand, this program is far less likely to cause displacement than Section 8 substantial rehabilitation and the Section 312 program (described below). It involves generally smaller expenditures, meaning smaller rent increases needed to cover rehab costs, and is less likely to require tenants to move while repairs are being made. Local public housing agencies administer this program, and its protections apply to rehab both inside and outside NSAs.

Tenants cannot be permanently displaced under this program unless the rehab work is reducing the number of units, or a family is too large for the rehabilitated units. Owners

153

must certify that they have not evicted tenants in the year preceding the submission of their application to the local public housing agency. Tenants who are temporarily displaced during rehab have a right to return. And any tenants who are displaced are eligible for Uniform Relocation Act benefits (discussed in Chapter 15).

## SECTION 312 REHAB LOANS

The Section 312 program provides direct low-interest federal rehab loans through local public agencies. The program is usually administered by a local community development, redevelopment, or code enforcement agency. It is one of the very few direct housing loan programs of the federal government — as opposed to insuring or subsidizing the interest rate on private loans or subsidizing rents. As such, it appears very expensive on any one federal budgetary year, since the entire amount of loans made that year are a cost to the federal treasury, although the loan repayments are additions to the federal treasury over the life of the loan, and the ultimate cost of direct loans is far cheaper than subsidizing interest costs on private loans. Largely because of "budget politics," the new Administration and Congress recently cut back sharply on the Section 312 program, eliminating all new funding, which leaves paybacks of already outstanding loans as the sole source of new Section 312 loan money. Because the program will continue, albeit at a far lower level of activity, and because similar approaches may be funded under local CDBG programs, we will describe some of its features.

In the past, Section 312 focused mainly on single-family homes, but that emphasis has

been shifting toward apartment buildings. In 1980, 4,500 rental units were eligible for $60 million in rehab funds, twice the total of rental units rehabbed during the entire previous decade.

Under Section 312, landlords who own buildings with between 5 and 100 units, either located in low- or moderate-income

*"Oh, Pete, what fun we could have doing over one of those brownstones!"*

Drawing by B. Tobey; © 1969 / *The New Yorker Magazine,* Inc.

neighborhoods or initially occupied after rehab by a majority of low- or moderate-income tenants, are eligible for 20-year loans of up to $32,000 per unit at only three percent interest.

Fifty-six percent of the buildings selected for the Section 312 program thus far have been occupied. But the displacement impact may have been higher. Landlords may be displacing poorer tenants prior to the final selection of buildings for rehab under the program, and there is no obligation to account for prior tenants. HUD says available evidence shows that "very little displacement has occurred as a *direct* result of Section 312 multifamily rehabilitation [and] relatively little displacement is expected in the near future." Given the fact that prior to rehab 92% of the tenants were low- and moderate-income, it is hard to accept HUD's conclusion that very little direct Section 312 displacement has occurred. And HUD's 1980 report to Congress on the program admits: "Given data constraints, there is no way to ascertain the amount of displacement *indirectly* resulting from Section 312 rehabilitation activities."

## RENT CONTROLS

Landlords who receive Section 312 subsidies are no longer free to charge market rents after the completion of federally-subsidized rehab: for five years, their rents are controlled by HUD. The federally-imposed ceiling allows landlords to cover all operating expenses, however, with Section 312 loan and any other mortgage debt service costs included among them, plus a "reasonable return on investment" (generously defined as up to 20 percent annually).

Landlords participating in the program

must sign a "Rent Regulation Agreement" with the HUD Area Office, notify tenants in writing of its terms, and notify the local agency administering the program of any rent increases and the reasons for them during this five-year period. However, neither the local agency nor HUD has to give official approval for a rent increase, nor do the Section 312 regulations even have a formal procedure for tenants to challenge such increases. Assumedly, their only legal route would be the courts.

This limited rent control only covers tenants who remain after rehab and receive a notice of "right to continue in occupancy." Landlords may offer their tenants inducements to sign a waiver of this right, and it is important that tenants realize they are giving up some important protections if they agree to sign such waivers.

## RELOCATION BENEFITS

Since 1978, tenants displaced by the Section 312 rehab program have been entitled to the benefits provided under the Uniform Relocation Act, but only if the Section 312 loan to the landlord exceeds $2,500 and the tenant is required to move. Tenants who were already paying in excess of 25% of their income for rent prior to rehab, and who can't afford post-rehab rents, are not considered to be displaced if their post-rehab rents go up only by the amount of the landlord's increased utility and property tax costs, plus 5%. This stipulation overruled a prior HUD policy which said that tenants in buildings rehabbed with Section 312 loans did not have to pay more than 25% of their income for rent, regardless of what they paid before rehab. As HUD explained in announcing this regulation: "the application of a mandatory 25% income ceiling on rents

makes many needed rehabilitation projects infeasible." So much for low-income tenants.

## SECTION 8 SUBSIDIES

Any tenant displaced from a Section 312 rehab project who is eligible for a Certificate of Family Participation for existing Section 8 housing is supposed to receive such a subsidy. But this benefit depends on whether the public housing agency which administers the Section 8 program has sufficient units available. Section 312 displacees receive no special priority for Section 8 Certificates under HUD's rules. However, HUD announced a demonstration program in 1980 combining the Section 312 program, Section 8 subsidies, and the CDBG program, designed to prevent the displacement of poor tenants because of the Section 312 program.

## PROGRAM PROTECTION SHORTCOMINGS AND TENANT RESPONSE

By far the most glaring weakness of Section 312's tenant protections is that the program's rent control ends after five years, and then landlords can boost rents, whether occupants can afford them or not. Because of this and the other shortcomings in the regulations which we have mentioned, tenants dealing with Section 312 rehab obviously are well-advised to organize to gain maximum enforcement benefits, and to challenge the displacement which the program — especially after its five-years' "good behavior" — may produce.

## SECTION 223(f) REFINANCING

HUD's Section 223(f) mortgage insurance program is intended to enable landlords to get refinancing in order to be able to do moderate

rehab without significantly increasing rents. ("Refinancing" means that the landlord takes out a new loan to cover both rehab costs and existing indebtedness on the property, replacing the former mortgage with a new all-inclusive mortgage. Frequently, if that earlier loan had a short payback period or high interest rate, the monthly repayments required for the new loan can remain at the old level.)

A detailed explanation of the Section 223(f) program appears in "Housing and Central Cities: A Conservation Approach," by Kenneth Phillips and Michael Agelasto, in Volume 4 of the *Ecology Law Quarterly* (1975), which is available for reading or copying at most law libraries. Section 223(f) may be used to finance subsidized conversion of rental units into cooperatives and condominiums for lower-income households in order to prevent displacement. It may also be used together with HUD's Section 8, Section 312, and CDBG programs. HUD plans a Target Area Preservation demonstration to test this concept on a neighborhood level. (For further information on this new rehab program, contact the Housing Conservation Project, Earl Warren Legal Institute, 396 Boalt Hall, University of California, Berkeley, CA 94720.)

## REHAB DISPLACEMENT FROM CDBG AND UDAG FUNDS

Localities have spent more Community Development Block Grant (CDBG) funds for housing rehab than for any other purpose. Mostly, these expenditures have gone to homeowners, but they also are used for rental property rehab. (CDBG and how to deal with it are discussed in Chapter 12.) Urban Development Action Grants (UDAGs, discussed in Chapter

13) also have been used for rehab projects. Both have caused displacement, and neither brings with it much in the way of special protections or compensations for displacees. But given effective public pressure, both CDBG and UDAG programs can have anti-displacement provisions attached to them. And funds from either can also be used to pay relocation costs and compensations, if the community demands it.

The following are two cases in which effective community pressure altered the displacement impact of UDAG/CDBG rehab programs.

## SALEM, MASSACHUSETTS

Salem received a UDAG of $1.9 million in August, 1978, for industrial development and neighborhood rehabilitation. When industrial developers withdrew from the project, HUD agreed in March, 1979, to modify the UDAG contract to provide $1.3 million for neighborhood rehab only.

The focus was on 300 substandard apartments, almost half of the rental housing in the Point neighborhood, where about 40% of the residents are low-income Hispanics. The plan called for the Salem Housing Authority to subsidize renovation of 50 units through HUD's Section 8 Moderate Rehab program, and also to use Massachusetts' Section 705 state program for the rehabilitation of large, low-income family housing. In addition, 100-140 units were to be rehabbed and converted to condominiums for purchase by "moderate-income" neighborhood residents. Meanwhile, CDBG funds were targeted for associated neighborhood improvements.

When the plan was explained to Point neighborhood residents in a series of meetings

in February and March, 1979, they became alarmed at the possibility of the displacement of low-income tenants. When the Salem Planning Department failed to respond satisfactorily to neighborhood requests for plan changes, the Salem Housing Alliance and Salem Spanish-American Association filed an administrative complaint with HUD in April, 1979. (See end-of-chapter references for how to get a copy.) They charged that the proposed rehab work would displace 450 low-income tenants. Except for households eligible for Section 8 subsidies in the 50 apartments rehabbed under that program, most tenants living in target buildings were sure to be forced out by higher post-rehab rent increases and condominium prices they could not afford. The complaint cited Salem for failing to have an adequate relocation plan; failing to meet its Housing Assistance Plan goals for renter rehabilitation; using available housing subsidies disproportionately to benefit homeowners; not having adequate citizen participation; and discriminating against low-income Hispanics, who would be disproportionately displaced by the proposed UDAG/CDBG rehab.

The two community groups proposed extensive changes and conditions in the UDAG contract (which was more a part of the rehab plan than was the CDBG agreement), including: collection of new base data on rents, family size, ethnicity, and housing needs of neighborhood residents; a more accurate estimate of displacement; controls to ensure that rent increases do not exceed actual rehab costs; requirements for participating banks to refinance existing loans along with their rehab mortgages, in order to lower post-rehab rents; property tax exemptions or deferrals to prevent rehab-induced tax hikes from raising rents;

programs for adequate relocation and replacement housing; withholding of condo conversion funds until low-income families were assured they could buy them; Uniform Relocation Act benefits for all displacees; creation of a community center; hiring of neighborhood residents for program jobs; and creation of effective fair housing and affirmative action plans.

They didn't get all they asked for, but they did win some significant concessions. Salem's mayor appointed a Citizens Advisory Committee for the rehab program. In March, 1980, after consultation with this Committee, the city adopted the following guidelines to avoid displacement from UDAG and related private-market rehab:

• The city will provide relocation counseling and, if necessary, temporary relocation housing. Landlords participating in the program must also agree that post-rehab rents will be increased by only enough to cover operating cost increases. (Private landlords who do not receive UDAG assistance, however, are not regulated.)

• The condo conversion program was modified to require approval of any conversion-related rehab by at least 75% of present tenants. In structures with five units or more, only those buildings where a majority of existing tenants can afford to purchase their units will be converted to condos. Present tenants in buildings to be converted cannot be evicted prior to rehab without just cause. Post-rehab monthly condo payments must not exceed the prior rent by more than 5%. And priority in condo sales is to be given to displacees, Point neighborhood residents, tenants living in substandard housing, and low- and moderate-income tenants.

• In order to allow moderate-income neighborhood residents to buy rehabbed condo units, Salem will provide interest-free loans for up to 25% of the purchase price and will use the Massachusetts Housing Finance Agency below-market interest rate loan program to reduce financing costs. Sliding-scale downpayments will be based on tenant-purchaser income.

• Present tenants of units rehabbed into condos who do not purchase can stay. Their future rent increases will be based only on increased operating costs, and they can only be evicted for just cause.

Obviously, if these guidelines are forcefully applied, displacement caused by Salem's rehab program will be significantly reduced. (Further information on this successful struggle can be obtained from North Shore Community Action Programs, 17 Sewall Street, Peabody, MA 01960, and the Massachusetts Law Reform Institute, 2 Park Square, Boston, MA 02116.)

## JERSEY CITY'S MONTGOMERY GATEWAY: THE RIGHT TO RETURN AFTER REHAB

When the rehab process causes temporary displacement, the right of tenants to return to the unit they inhabited becomes a crucial issue. Landlords have little reason to ensure that this happens, and the experience of most federally-subsidized renewal and rehab programs has been that few such displacees do get to return.

Community pressure brought this issue to a head in Jersey City, New Jersey, an old industrial city, now in decline due to corporate disinvestment, with much deteriorated housing and a high rate of housing abandonment.

Low-income minority households dominate in the downtown area; forty percent of residents there are Hispanic.

In the last four years, rehab and renewal activity in downtown Jersey City, mainly gentrification-oriented, has given the city one of the nation's highest rates of households displaced by public action. CDBG and Section 312 rehab moneys have been directed toward four "historic district" Neighborhood Strategy Areas, where "brownstones" are being reconverted for a wealthier clientele, with an eye to Manhattan just across the Hudson River.

Private investment activity has been closely related to public activity in the center city area. In the Montgomery Street part of downtown, a $7 million UDAG, $1 million in CDBG funds, and an estimated $31 million of private investment funds are supporting extensive development just west of Van Vorst Park. In the 15-square block segment known as "Montgomery Gateway," the city's goal is to remove barriers to private development, through creation of a "more marketable development climate." Concretely, this means replacing concentrations of poor people with controlled occupancy by a "better" segment of the lower-income population. The plan is to use UDAG funds to help rehabilitate and construct some 700 housing units, 489 through Section 8 new construction and substantial rehab. The city Housing Authority is to create 120 of these through the "turnkey" process. The New Jersey Housing Finance Agency is to commit $25 million in below-market interest rate mortgages.

In other words, the Gateway area should end up with a lot nicer housing than it has now, courtesy of a massive outlay of public

funds. And the current residents reasonably began to ask — why not for us?

The Jersey City Redevelopment Agency, using UDAG, CDBG and state funds, was responsible for site acquisition and household relocation for the Gateway project. The redevelopment plan originally provided for the relocation of 225 residents from substandard housing slated for demolition and rehabilitation. After residents organized the Montgomery Gateway Residents' Committee (MGRC) to oppose displacement, they discovered that in fact 360 households and 83 individuals were to be displaced. All were poor, 98% were minority, and 97% were tenants.

With the assistance of the Legal Services office and local community organizations concerned about displacement, approximately 120 of the households to be displaced were contacted. The survey revealed that 88% wanted to return to former housing after rehabilitation because of their ties to the neighborhood.

The city's relocation assistance program merely provided "assurances" from the private developers that displaced residents would have "top priority" on occupying the rehabilitated apartments, if they were eligible for the Section 8 program. The city was responsible for finding replacement housing for the displaced residents and providing relocation assistance. $1.2 million was reserved in CDBG and UDAG funds for relocation costs for displaced residents.

But all the signs indicated that the real interest of the city was to clear the neighborhood as cheaply as possible, and get it ready for a new population. The Redevelopment Agency cut off heat and water in most of the apartments it acquired, and refused to provide

# Gentrification Blues

Judith Levine and Laura Liben ©
*written for the Anti-Displacement Committee of Boerum Hill/Gowanus, Brooklyn, New York*

3. When the brownstoners came, they said they liked integration,
To live with other races and have neighborly relations.
I got the gentrifi---, gentrification blues.
Now it's to hell with good relations
If it doesn't raise the property values.

*Refrain*

4. They say that a brownstone is the people's housing,
But what about the folks who can't afford a hundred thousand?
I got the gentrifi---, gentrification blues.
They're living somewhere else now,
They're the many who've been kicked out by the few.

*Refrain*

5. I woke up this morning, I looked next door —
There was one family living where there once were four.
I got the gentrifi---, gentrification blues.
I wonder where my neighbors went 'cause I
Know I'll soon be moving there too.

*Refrain*

6. Somebody said, "Where will we go?"
There ain't no places left around here no more.
I got the gentrifi---, gentrification blues.
Guess we gotta fight back
'Cause we ain't got nothin' to lose.

*Refrain*

1. I woke up this morning, I walked out my door,
I noticed my neighbors weren't there any more.
I've got the gentrifi---, gentrification blues.
When I asked where they gone to,
That's when I heard the bad news.

*Now we've got Häagen-Dazs ice cream and the New York* Times
*'Cause the real estate agents brought in their own kind.*
*But good-bye to Bustelo and the people who drink it,*
*Good-bye to integration and the people who think it.*

2. Well, I looked in the windows, I looked in the doors —
They were hanging up the chandeliers and sanding the floors.
I got the gentrifi---, gentrification blues.
The rent sign said "five-hundred fifty dollars, one floor through."

*They call it Boerum Hill to make it sound classy;*
*Used to be Gowanus and they said it was trashy.*
*But some folks still remember this neighborhood*
*When the rents were lower and the living was good.*

building security or board up vacant units. There were 22 fires in 16 Agency-acquired buildings. Adding insult to injury, the Agency filed massive eviction suits against on-site tenants, and continued to do so despite promises to stop.

And when it came to possibilities for returning to the neighborhood, the development plans did not provide sufficient four- and five-bedroom apartments to meet the needs of displacees. Moreover, the private developers insisted they would screen out "undesirable" tenants, and residents believed this would be used to exclude displacees despite their "priority to return" status.

So MGRC fought to make sure that displaced residents could get back to the neighborhood. The organization wanted *guarantees* that displacees would have the *right* to return and to be eligible for Section 8 certificates for the new and rehabbed units. Additionally, MGRC demanded two major changes in the rehab plan. One was the creation of more large-family units. The second was "phased" development: rehab of vacant buildings first, so that residents could move temporarily within the neighborhood while their own premises were being rehabbed. And families not accommodated by that approach were to be given priority in subsidized units no more than five blocks from their current address.

MGRC and its attorneys filed an administrative complaint with HUD which challenged the relocation planning for Montgomery Gateway. (See end-of-chapter references for how to get a copy.) The organization lobbied city, state, and federal officials to ensure that displaced tenants would be able to return. It demonstrated to protest the ongoing displacement.

Pressure on the Housing Authority yielded an increase in the planned number of three-bedroom apartments in the Section 8 turnkey plan from 85 to 103, and in the number of four-bedroom apartments from 10 to 52. Meanwhile, however, families continued to be forced out of the neighborhood, or lured to relocate by city promises of relocation benefits. Most were not even receiving the lump-sum four-year relocation assistance payments guaranteed them by the Uniform Relocation Act. A showdown meeting in Washington, involving MGRC, the Jersey City mayor, the Secretary of HUD, and a staff aide to one of New Jersey's U.S. Senators, started the delinquent money flowing.

But the drain of continued displacement undercut the possibilities for winning an agreement on phased development. By the summer of 1980, when MGRC finally got a signed agreement with the city, only 14 of the original Gateway households remained in the center of the UDAG project area. The resistance of these few residents, however, was still holding up the works. So the city, the state Housing Finance Agency, and the developers signed a memorandum of understanding with the holdout families and MGRC, guaranteeing that the families would have their apartments fixed up in the interim, that they would not be moved off the site during the rehab project, and that there would be an on-site security force during the redevelopment work.

MGRC also got a written guarantee that developers could not refuse to accept former residents arbitrarily or on the basis of hearsay, and that refusal to accept a former tenant back into the neighborhood must be based on documentation of a substantial likelihood that the household would be harmful to the property or

to other tenants. The agreement also includes a local civil rights organization in the tenant selection procedure to ensure integrity in the screening. MGRC plans to try and strengthen this agreement into an absolute right to return, through further political pressure on the city government, and possibly by filing another administrative complaint with HUD. MGRC also persuaded the city to allocate $60,000 to the organization for tracking displacees from private projects elsewhere in the city, in order to get them into other Section 8 units being developed in Jersey City. (A copy of MGRC's innovative tracking proposal is available through Hudson County Legal Services, 574 Newark Ave., Jersey City, NJ 07306.)

The upshot is that, although unable to win an absolute right of return for Montgomery Gateway displacees, MGRC was able to negotiate some significant gains that likely will lead to the return of a substantial number of former residents.

An ironic epilogue: press reports quoted the State Community Affairs Commissioner at the September, 1980 groundbreaking ceremonies for the Gateway project as telling how "his grandfather literally died 'of a broken heart' when he was forced to leave his Jersey City home years ago because the New Jersey Turnpike Extension was coming through the neighborhood."

## GATEWAY OFFSHOOTS: NEW STATE LAW, NEW CITY STRATEGY

One of the side effects of the Gateway struggle was the introduction of a bill in the New Jersey Legislative Assembly which would require — as a condition of state Housing Finance Agency assistance to projects involving

50 or more units — phased development and the guaranteed right to return for anyone displaced by such projects. Hearings were held in December, 1980, and the bill has received support from the New Jersey Tenants Organization and the Puerto Rican Congress of New Jersey. (Copies are available from Hudson County Legal Services.) And Jersey City, with the participation of community groups, is now developing a comprehensive anti-displacement strategy. The process is supported by a HUD grant to a private consulting firm. The grant resulted from pressure by a broad private-public sector coalition that analyzed the recent history of displacement pressures in Jersey City, and revealed an overall pattern of poor people being moved out of areas ripe for residential and commercial gentrification by affluent river-crossers from New City. (For further information, including a detailed case-study of the Jersey City anti-displacement strategy, contact Rick Cohen & Associates, 904 Hudson Street, Hoboken, NJ 07030.)

## STATE AND LOCALLY SPONSORED RENTAL REHABILITATION

In addition to federally-sponsored rehabilitation, some state and local governments also subsidize private rehabilitation through low-interest loans or tax abatements. Relocation protections and assistance for tenants displaced by these programs are weak. Two examples of this part of the rehab displacement problem are San Francisco's Rehabilitation Assistance Program (RAP) and New York City's J-51 Tax Abatement program.

## SAN FRANCISCO'S REHABILITATION ASSISTANCE PROGRAM

The RAP program is San Francisco's adaptation of the statewide California Residential Rehabilitation Program, which authorizes local governments to use tax-exempt revenue bonds to subsidize rehab in designated neighborhoods. The local government must take "every possible action" to prevent the displacement of residents due to post-rehab rent increases, and it may impose rent controls on rehabilitated buildings to protect tenants.

But those provisions of the law have not proved reassuring. There has been considerable opposition to the RAP program out of fear of the displacement it might cause. Tenant and neighborhood groups in the Haight-Ashbury area even sued to prevent its use. They claimed that the city's environmental impact statement was deficient under federal and state law because it underestimated RAP's probable direct and indirect displacement impact on poor and minority renters. Although this federal lawsuit was dismissed, anti-RAP organizing has continued in that neighborhood and others targeted for rehab. For a critique of this local approach to rehab and recommendations as to how rehab displacement could be avoided, see the report by the San Francisco Bay Area Planners Network, *RAP in the Tenderloin: The Dangers We See and Our Recommendations for Revising the Program* (1977), available from the Planners Network, 360 Elizabeth Street, San Francisco, CA 94114.

## NEW YORK CITY'S J-51 TAX ABATEMENT/EXEMPTION PROGRAM

Property tax abatements and exemptions, especially when combined with other housing rehabilitation subsidy programs, have proven increasingly popular. In effect, the city subsidizes the rehab by permitting partial or full relief from increased property taxes the landlord would have to pay after rehab has increased the building's value. Cities find this method attractive because it requires no direct cash subsidy — rather, the cost is in foregone taxes the city might otherwise receive. (Other property owners, of course, must fill the revenue gap that results).

New York City pioneered in providing tax breaks to encourage rehab of substandard housing and conversion of non-residential buildings to residential use, when it passed its "J-51" program (named after the section of the Administrative Code that established it) in 1955. Under J-51, the city offers two kinds of property tax inducement. One is total exemp-

Becket Logan / Metropolitan Council on Housing

tion from the property's assessed value, for up to twelve years, of the increased value caused by the rehab work. The other is abatement of whatever taxes are due on the property, in an amount equal to 90% of the rehab costs for non-luxury items. This abatement can be taken for 12-20 years, with a maximum of 8⅓% of the total cost written off in any one year. The post-rehab rents of buildings which receive the rehab tax abatement are controlled under the city's rent stabilization ordinance for the length of the abatement period. But the abatement provision pushes owners to overspend on their renovation work, which leads to higher rents. And there is no protection for tenants who are displaced as result of this locally-subsidized rehabilitation. Since one of the major uses of J-51 has been to convert single room occupancy (SRO) hotels into luxury apartments and coops, displacement of lower-income people is built into the program. Developers harass the elderly and poor who live in these hotels, trying to push them out so that conversion and rehab can move ahead. A New York City Councillor, as reported in the New York *Times,* cited the case of "an 89-year-old woman living in a [SRO] hotel in Greenwich Village . . . on the fifth floor, [who] had been left without heat, running water or elevator service for two months. He asserted that her toilet had been deliberately stuffed with newspaper, the electricity had been sporadic and the landlord's agents had set off the fire alarm almost every night."

Property tax abatement and exemption programs of this sort can easily get out of hand. In New York City, much is given to subsidize rehabilitation in upper-income areas that would have been undertaken without this subsidy. In one well publicized example, a build-

ing right across from City Hall was converted from offices to coops selling for $72,000-$112,000 and received an abatement on rehab costs amounting to $276,000 a year, $3.3 million over the 12-year life of the abatement. "Tax expenditures," as these are known, tend not to be scrutinized closely and just mount up: a recent report by the New York City Council President showed the total value of J-51 abatements to date is over $1 billion. Loss of this tax revenue means reduced municipal services and increased financial burdens on those who do not receive such benefits.

If these programs are to benefit lower-income households, they must be accompanied by displacement controls and a pinpointing of benefits to lower-income neighborhoods. Their help to low-income tenants in taking over landlord-abandoned tax delinquent buildings, as described in Chapter 7, has been one effective example of how this subsidy has been used.

Recent amendments to the J-51 program passed by the New York City Council eliminate its future use in some of Manhattan's "hot" real estate districts. But the Council would not eliminate its use throughout Manhattan for conversion of SRO hotels. It did, however, require that SRO tenants be given a lease, and agreed to finance a legal advocacy and education program to assist SRO tenants in resisting illegal eviction attempts by converters. The severity of the SRO displacement problem due to use of J-51 tax abatements was such that Terence Cardinal Cooke of New York took the unusual step of overtly intervening in a City Hall political matter by urging passage of protective legislation.

(See the related discussion of SRO hotels in Chapter 6.)

## HISTORIC PRESERVATION

Historic preservation through neighborhood conservation and rehabilitation has enjoyed increasing popularity in recent years. The National Historic Preservation Act of 1966 established an Advisory Council on Historic Preservation to coordinate federal historic preservation activities, which include placing buildings and sites on the protective National Register of Historic Places. Additionally, preservationists have relied heavily on the National Environmental Policy Act (NEPA) to challenge the destruction of historic buildings and districts.

On the whole, historic preservation laws are far more protective of buildings than of the tenants inside them. Thus, it is not surprising that, unless carefully structured, these efforts to conserve our historical heritage may wind up imposing severe displacement costs on the lower-income people to whom these buildings have "trickled down."

The Tax Reform Act of 1976 gives "accelerated depreciation" tax shelters for rehabilitation by owners of historic properties, regardless of what income group is being served by the rehabbed units, and no anti-displacement protections or compensations whatsoever accompany work encouraged this way. Add on the special state and local property tax abatements often given for historic preservation activities, and all the speculative benefits of quick repair and resale (see discussion in Chapter 4), and it becomes clear that historic preservation can easily generate profiteering displacement. An historic rehabber can get a building certified as an historic structure, evict low-income tenants, convert the building into luxury rental housing, condos or

today.

Next door, near where the Hells Angels once lived, Fitzpatrick remembers, lived Diane, the "den mother" of the street, who handed out petitions for tree plantings and worked in the city's low-cost-rehabilitation-loan program. Last year she was evicted.

As he talked, a Volvo pulled into a nearby driveway shaded by trees planted through Diane's efforts. Someone with a briefcase walked into a home rehabilitated with a low-cost loan Diane helped administer.

Last Christmas, Fitzpatrick went to a party given by the philosophy professor who evicted Diane, and he wandered to the flat where she once lived.

"I remembered how it had been," he said, "with kids' drawings on the wall and the whole place falling down through a combination of her own incompetent housekeeping and landlord neglect. I couldn't recognize it. There were gallery lights everywhere, Italian tile and copper fixtures. Diane read *House and Garden;* she had bourgeois dreams. If she could have seen it, she would have sat on the floor and cried.

"Buying a Victorian for $21,000 was like picking up a bargain at a garage sale. Plus, I had some hippie idea I didn't want to live in a house with a garbage grinder and a washing machine. But I remember when black kids used to play on this block. What have we done?"

*From "Up and Coming Amid the Down and Out," by Katy Butler. Reprinted with permission from* **Mother Jones** *magazine, © 1980, the Foundation for National Progress.*

Bennett Hall / *Mother Jones*

## "What have we done?"

Between 1970 and 1978, according to economists Barry Bluestone and Bennett Harrison, about 15 million jobs were lost due to industrial plant closings. Steel making and car manufacturing — the heart of urban centers in the Midwest — lost out to advanced technology and the fuel-efficient marketing strategy of Japanese multinationals. Other heavy industry across the country followed shoemaking, textile manufacturing, dressmaking and television assembly to Asia and Latin America, attracted by cheaper labor.

In San Francisco, the flight of heavy industry began early. The city lost 11,933 — a fifth — of its manufacturing jobs between 1962 and 1972. Small foundries, breweries and printing shops closed down, driven out by the cheaper, nonunion labor of foreign competitors, or crippled by rising land costs as large corporations competed for space. With the decline in jobs, San Francisco lost part of its connection with a gritty union past that kept things from becoming too clean and precious. . . .

On upper Ashbury Street one recent night . . . Joe Fitzpatrick, a city planner, sat drinking a glass of excellent California Zinfandel in the renovated back parlor of his home — an unpainted $100,000-plus Victorian he bought for $21,000 in 1967.

The house was once a home for old Latino ladies and later a hippie crash pad. Now, Fitzpatrick lives here alone. The Hells Angels used to shoot off guns across the street, and the Grateful Dead once practiced down the block, where a wine merchant lives

commercial use, and enjoy substantial tax shelter and resale profits.

The National Commission on Neighborhoods recognized the displacement problem posed by federal tax policies which ". . . created incentives for historic district restoration . . . often . . . at the expense of low and moderate income residents of those newly discovered historic neighborhoods, many of whom have been displaced by more affluent homeowners." The majority of the Commission recommended to Congress:

> While the Commission would not end the movement of affluent people back into the cities, it does not believe that the Federal Tax Code should give special benefits to those who eject the poor from their neighborhoods under the banner of historic preservation. The Commission therefore recommends that § 191 of the Code be allowed to expire in 1981. Removal of this special tax benefit for restoration by the affluent would not put an end to displacement but it would at least put an end to an important incentive to the displacement presently in the Tax Code.

(The National Commission on Neighborhoods' 1979 Final Report, *People, Building Neighborhoods,* is available for $7.50 from the U.S. Government Printing Office, Washington, DC)

## SAVANNAH LANDMARKS: TRYING TO MINIMIZE DISPLACEMENT

Like preservation laws, preservationist organizations traditionally have been concerned about the fate of buildings rather than their occupants. In many situations, preservationists have ruthlessly removed low-income tenants in the course of saving the architecture of the past. A 1971 study of the preservation activities of the Pittsburgh History and Landmarks Foundation by Arthur P. Ziegler, Jr., concluded:

. . . preservationists have been as indifferent (perhaps even more indifferent) to community self-determination as have redevelopment authorities. Historic preservation groups across the country from the 1930s up until today remorselessly removed neighborhood residents regardless of their longevity in the proposed historic district or their commitment to that area. They simply replaced them with well-to-do residents who could understand the value of the structure and who could afford to restore and maintain them.

Some shifting in that attitude is beginning to appear, however. As one example, the National Trust for Historic Preservation and the Interior Department have recently put together a small ($1 million) fund to help non-profit groups in historic neighborhoods develop low-income rental housing. The National Trust will select groups in 10-12 neighborhoods which either are listed or eligible for listing on the National Register of Historic Places, and will offer low-interest loans and grants, on a matching basis, to acquire and rehabilitate multi-family housing for rental to low-income households. The Trust also will work with the Federal Home Loan Bank Board in locating mortgage funds. For more information on this program, contact the Inner Cities Ventures Fund, National Trust for Historic Preservation, 1785 Massachusetts Ave. NW, Washington, DC 20036.

Perhaps the most notable example of this change in consciousness is Savannah Landmarks, a reformed offshoot of the Historic Savannah Foundation which restored the Historic District in that Georgia city in the early 1970s. Currently, the Savannah Landmarks Rehabilitation Project is restoring 1,200 units in the Victorian District — 89% Black and mostly lower-income in population — and is trying to guarantee that at least half the rehabbed units are kept available for current residents. The effort relies on a variety of rehab subsidy programs — HUD's Section 8 and 312 programs and Savannah's Homeowner Rehabilitation Program — in combination with UDAG money and private foundation funds. Without the subsidies, rent and mortgage increases resulting from rehab costs would probably displace most of the residents.

It is too early to tell if this benevolent approach can succeed in promoting historic preservation without displacement. Shortages in the availability of subsidy funds are likely to grow worse, and the limitations of the subsidy programs themselves may cripple the attempt. Moreover, since the other half of the units in the District will be rehabbed without subsidy, and since the neighboring Savannah Historic District has been largely gentrified through rehab, uncontrolled market forces may undo what good Savannah Landmarks does accomplish. There are no municipal rent, eviction, and resale controls. There are no guarantees that Section 8 contracts will be renegotiated when they expire. So it is a question of wait-and-see whether the Landmarks approach establishes a precedent for combining anti-displacement goals with large-scale historic preservation rehab programs. (For more information on the Savannah experience, contact the Savannah Landmarks Rehabilitation Project, Box 8801, Savannah, GA 31412.)

## STRATEGIES FOR RESISTING DISPLACEMENT FROM HISTORIC PRESERVATION

Historic preservation situations call for the same anti-displacement strategies as other rehab threats to lower-income residents: market controls, rent subsidies, and the right of former residents to return. Where CDBG funds are used to support preservation rehab — a use specifically allowed in the 1974 Housing and Community Development Act — then the general anti-displacement strategies and defenses outlined in Chapter 12 come into play. Because historic preservation laws and their users usually differ somewhat from other rehab situations, however, resistance often must take slightly different forms. One thing that remains constant, of course, is the need for organization and information. The sub-sections below suggest some additional tactics to employ — along with whatever responses are appropriate to the government programs which the preservation effort may use. Following those suggestions are two cases of creative use of preservation laws to prevent displacement.

**Form alliances.** Alliances between anti-displacement groups and preservationist organizations can be important. Even if preservationists are not at first sympathetic to neighborhood demands, they may be persuaded to assist residents who are well organized, because the coalition can prove mutually beneficial. Neighborhood groups could offer to support litigation to prevent demolition of historically or architecturally valuable buildings, or to cooperate with historic designation applications sponsored by preservationists, but only on condition that the preservationists agree to do whatever proves necessary to prevent displacement once rehab begins. Preservation groups, which often have prestigious and powerful memberships, may prove influential in obtaining displacement protection as well as rehab funding from government and private foundations.

**Demand participation.** Community groups should use their political prowess and pressure to get adequate representation on all preservation planning committees, both neighborhood-level and citywide. Even with "friendly" preservationist groups, quite a struggle may be needed to gain effective participation in planning and guiding anti-displacement aspects of rehab projects.

**Challenge historic designations.** If a proposed historic designation seems likely to invite speculators and preservationist rehab specialists, and thus cause displacement, neighborhood groups can oppose the site designation and its listing on the National Register of Historic Places and parallel state and local registers. While displacement is not a factor normally considered in the designation process, it may be productive to try to make this an issue. After a building or neighborhood has been nominated, opponents can file comments, first with state historic preservation officials, and then with the Office of Archeology and Historic Preservation of the National Park Service (U.S. Department of the Interior) and the Advisory Council on Historic Preservation. For the details of the certification process, contact a local historic preservation society. The National Trust for Historic Preservation (1785 Massachusetts Ave. NW, Washington, DC 20036) and their 1980 *Directory of Private Nonprofit Preservation Organizations* should be helpful resources.

On the building-by-building level, opposing historic structure certification can delay and frustrate the tax shelter the owner almost certainly wants to get. Tenants can use this tactic as a basis for negotiations — agreeing to support the certification application in exchange for legally binding and recorded covenants by the owner recognizing tenants' rights to remain or return, limiting rents and/or promising to apply for rent subsidies, agreeing to pay any temporary moving expenses, etc. Revised federal rules for certifying buildings eligible for historic preservation rehab tax breaks, together with review and appeals procedures, were published in the December 19, 1980 *Federal Register*.

**Take to the streets.** Often, public protests against the gentrification-oriented activities of historic preservationists can be quite effective. As an example, the Anti-Displacement Committee of Boerum Hill/Gowanus in Brooklyn, New York, mounted a demonstration against the 15th Annual Boerum Hill House Tour. The tour is supported by the real estate brokers, the Brooklyn Union Gas Company and various banks, and is an event whose overt purpose is to show off the neighborhood's architectural gems, but which serves as well to arouse gentrifiers' instincts among the house tourists. The neighborhood group rented a flatbed truck, decorated it with banners and signs and travelled through the neighborhood, leafletting. They also held a speak-out on the displacement problem and how such house tours added to gentrification pressures. Events of this type can serve to prick the consciences of some tourists, scare others away, and assist in building a local anti-displacement movement. (For further information on this approach, contact the Anti-Displacement

Committee of Boerum Hill/Gowanus, 151 Bond St., Brooklyn, NY.)

# CREATIVE USE OF HISTORIC PRESERVATION LAWS TO PREVENT DISPLACEMENT

## COLONIAL VILLAGE, VIRGINIA

Colonial Village is a huge (1,095 unit) rental complex in Arlington County, Virginia, the initial section of which was built in 1935 as the nation's first FHA-insured large-scale housing complex. In 1977, the 42-acre complex, along with some surrounding land, was purchased by a subsidiary of Mobil Land Development Corporation, triggering fears by residents that the complex would be demolished for other development, condominiumized, or otherwise drastically changed. The Village's prime location — near a new Washington subway line and between a commercial district and some high-rise offices — gave ample cause for such fears.

Because of the age and significance of the complex, tenants decided to try a defense through Arlington County's recently enacted historic preservation ordinance. Among other protections, this law requires an owner who wishes to demolish an historic structure to first offer the property to any interested group that would preserve it. The tenants of Colonial Village immediately formed a tenants' association to be that purchaser, if need be. The County's Historical Landmark Review Board unanimously accepted the tenants' petition that the Village be accorded landmark certification, based on its historical status with respect to FHA programs, its status as the first large-scale rental complex in Arlington County, and its widely copied architectural features — low-densities, staggered setbacks,

separation of pedestrian and auto traffic, undeveloped interior greenbelts and clustering of apartments in courtyards, all features previously found only in single-family home developments.

In the face of threatened legal action by the new owner, a compromise was worked out that includes the following elements:

• Acceptance of the original 276-unit section of the Village as an historic district.

• Retention of 951 of the units, under the following plan: 75 are to be sold to a quasi-public housing corporation, which is seeking Section 8 subsidies to convert them into moderate-income cooperatives; 74 are to be sold to a limited-equity cooperative sponsored by Colonial Village tenants; 100 will be sold as condominiums to existing occupants at below-

market prices; 114 will be kept as rental units until at least 1994; and 588 will be kept as rental units until at least 1984, at which time they can be sold as condos. One hundred and forty-four of the units will be demolished for an office complex, and 500-600 new units will be built on a site adjacent to the Village.

• Assurances that no one who wants to stay will be displaced from the Village, and that those whose units are being torn down or sold will be relocated as renters in other parts of the Village.

While clearly not an all-out victory for the residents, the story does show some of the ways historical preservation laws can be imaginatively used to protect needed housing. Nor is the battle over. The Colonial Village tenants' association continues to press for greater protections. It has just persuaded the Virginia Register of Historic Places to designate all of Colonial Village, except the portion nearest the subway stop, an historic landmark. While only an honorary designation that cannot change the local government's decision, this step makes the property eligible for the National Register of Historic Places, which in turn creates tax disincentives for an owner who wishes to tear such a structure down.

## THE INTERNATIONAL HOTEL, SAN FRANCISCO

Another instance where historical preservation laws have been used to combat displacement occurred in San Francisco, during the effort to protect the International Hotel (see page 56 for further description of this struggle). Aided by the local office of the National Trust for Historic Preservation, those fighting to save this residential hotel succeeded in having it placed on the National Register of Historic Places, not because of any architectural merit but strictly because of social considerations — its long-term history as a home for immigrating Filipinos, and its function as communal housing for these immigrants on their periodic returns to the city from agricultural, mining, and maritime work. While this designation did not prevent eventual eviction of the tenants and demolition of their building, it did pave the way for a grant from the National Trust, joined by a local foundation, to develop a plan for new low-rent housing and community facilities on the site of the demolished hotel. This plan is now working its way slowly through the city's bureaucratic machinery.

# REFERENCES

## LOCAL REHAB DISPLACEMENT STRUGGLES

Salem, Massachusetts' Point Neighborhood: Information on the Salem community campaign can be obtained from North Shore Community Action Programs, 17 Sewall St., Peabody, MA 01960; and the Massachusetts Law Reform Institute, 2 Park Sq., Boston, MA 02116.

A good report on the Salem challenge and its successes is contained in issue #4, 1980, of *Shelterforce*, available from 380 Main St., East Orange, NJ 07018.

Jersey City, New Jersey — the Montgomery Gateway struggle: Further information and copies of relevant documents are available from the Montgomery Gateway Residents Committee, c/o St. Bridget's Convent, 370 Montgomery St., Jersey City, NJ 07302; and from Hudson County Legal Services, 574 Newark Ave., Jersey City, NJ 07306, attn: Steve St. Hilaire.

Jersey City's Anti-Displacement Strategy: a detailed case study is available from Rick Cohen & Associates, 904 Hudson St., Hoboken, NJ 07030.

## REHAB DISPLACEMENT PROTECTION THROUGH RENT CONTROL AND OTHER TYPES OF LEGISLATION

"Residential Rehabilitation and Rent Control: The Massachusetts Priority" examines challenges to rehab exemptions in rent control laws on the grounds that they controvert the laws' basic purpose. It appears in Volume 11 of the *Urban Law Annual* (1976), available for reading or copying at local law libraries.

Washington, D.C.'s "Right to Return" clause under rent control: Section 707 of the city's rent control ordinance, entitled "Tenant's Right to Re-rent," is worth examining for groups seeking similar legislation. The District of Columbia Rental Housing Act of 1977 can be found in Volume 24 of the District of Columbia Register, available at most law libraries.

Proposed new law on displacees' right to return and requirement for phased development: copies of a New Jersey bill on these matters are available from Hudson County Legal Services, 574 Newark Ave., Jersey City, NJ 07306.

## SECTION 223(f) MORTGAGE REFINANCING

"Housing and Central Cities: A Conservation Approach," by Kenneth Phillips and Michael Agelasto, offers a detailed explanation of the Section 223(f) program. It appears in Volume 4 of the *Ecology Law Quarterly* (1975), available for reading or copying at most law libraries.

Further information on Section 223(f) and its applications is available from the Housing Conservation Project, Earl Warren Legal Institute, 396 Boalt Hall, University of California, Berkeley, CA 94720.

## MUNICIPAL REHAB TAX EXEMPTION AND ABATEMENT PROGRAMS

San Francisco's Rehabilitation Assistance Program (RAP): a critical analysis of this program appears in a report by the San Francisco Bay Area Planners' Network, *RAP in the Tenderloin: The Dangers We See and Our Recommendations for Revising the Program* (1977), available from the Planners Network, 360 Elizabeth St., San Francisco, CA 94114.

New York City's J-51 Program: a good description of this program appears in "Revitalization of Inner City Housing through Property Tax Exemption and Abatement: New York City's J-51 to the Rescue," by Janice Griffith, in Volume 18 of the *Urban Law Annual* (1980), available for reading or copying at most law libraries.

## CODE ENFORCEMENT REHAB DISPLACEMENT

"Municipal Housing Code Enforcement and Low-Income Tenants," by Chester Hartman, Rob Kessler and Richard LeGates, addresses this issue. It appears in the March, 1974 issue of the *Journal of the American Institute of Planners,* available for reading or copying in most university city planning or urban studies libraries, and in the Second Edition of *Housing Urban America,* edited by Jon Pynoos et al. (Aldine, 1980), available in bookstores and libraries.

## MANUALS ON REHAB PROGRAMS AND DISPLACEMENT PROBLEMS

*Innovations in Housing Preservation: Techniques for Financing the Moderate and Substantial Rehabilitation of Multifamily Buildings* (1979), discusses rehab financing, including HUD's Section 8 and Section 312 programs. $15.

*Saving Rental Housing: Strategies for Preserving Older Residential Buildings* (1980), discusses tax policies, code enforcement, social services, refinancing, and alternative forms of ownership and management in rental rehab programs. $15.

Both of the above are available from The Center for Community Development and Preservation, 180 S. Broadway, White Plains, NY 10605.

*Guide to Housing Conservation in Urban Neighborhoods: A Practitioners' Handbook* (1980), by Pat Jenny, Dennis Keating and Ken Phillips, focuses on how to accomplish rehab in rental properties without displacement of tenants. Available from the Housing Conservation Project, Earl Warren Legal Institute, 396 Boalt Hall, University of California, Berkeley, CA 94720.

Two periodicals covering the rehab displacement issue, one local, the other national, are:

*Chicago Rehab Network Newsletter,* published monthly by neighborhood groups fighting displacement. Available free from the Chicago Housing Resource Center, 343 S. Dearborn Ave., Suite 1508, Chicago, IL 60604.

*Neighborhood Conservation and Reinvestment,* a bimonthly published by Preservation Reports, 1016 16th St. NW, Suite 275, Washington, DC 20036. Very expensive ($90/year), but should be available at many HUD Area Offices and local community development departments.

HUD has funded the Community Rehabilitation Training Center (operated by the University Research Corporation, 4340 East-West Highway, Suite 900, Bethesda, MD 20014) to provide rehab training and technical assistance to public agencies and community groups. Neighborhood organizations interested in sponsoring rehab without displacement should contact this Center for information on HUD's rehab policies and programs.

## HISTORIC PRESERVATION

The National Trust for Historic Preservation, 1785 Massachusetts Ave. NW, Washington, DC 20036, has available several useful publications:

*Historic Preservation Law: An Annotated Bibliography* (1976), by Ellen Kettler and Bernard Reams, $6.

*Tax Incentives for Historic Preservation* (1980), by Gregory Andrews, $12.95.

*Directory of Private Nonprofit Preservation Organizations* (1980), useful in locating local preservation organizations regarding certification process, $6.95.

*Conserve Neighborhoods,* a bi-monthly newsletter, available for $2.50/year.

The Trust's Inner Cities Ventures Fund provides low-interest loans and grants to selected neighborhood groups, to acquire and rehabilitate multi-family housing for rental to low-income households.

The Conservation Foundation, 1717 Massachusetts Ave. NW, Washington, DC 20036, has published a useful study, *Neighborhood Conservation and the Elderly* (1978), by Phyllis Myers.

*American Preservation: The Magazine for Historic and Neighborhood Preservation* has published several excellent articles discussing the displacement problem caused by historic preservation in cities such as Seattle, Chicago, Louisville, Detroit, and Philadelphia. Published bimonthly by Briggs Associates, P.O. Box 2451, Little Rock, AR 72203. $12/year.

*The Contribution of Historic Preservation to Urban Revitalization* (1979) is a study which analyzes the renovation of four historic districts in Seattle, Savannah, Galveston, and Alexandria (Virginia). The case studies include discussion of the displacement issue. Produced by the Advisory Council on Historic Preservation, available for $4.75 from the U.S. Government Printing Office, Washington, DC 20402.

*From Historic Preservation to Urban Conservation: Urban Revitalization Displaces The Poor — A Working Paper* (1978), by Gretchen Klimoski, presents a comprehensive analysis of this issue and also offers evidence of the shift of some preservationists toward concern for anti-displacement goals. Available from the Ohio Historic Preservation Office, I-71 and 17th Ave., Columbus, OH 43211.

*People, Building Neighborhoods* (1979), the Final Report of the National Commission on Neighborhoods, contains various evaluations and recommendations on the historic preservation issue, especially the need to get rid of accelerated depreciation for historic rehab. The report is available for $7.50 from the U.S. Government Printing Office, Washington, DC 20402.

Colonial Village, Virginia: An account of this successful use of preservation laws to prevent displacement appears in "Historic Preservation: A Stay of Execution?", by Nadine Huff, in the October, 1980 issue of *Urban Land,* published by the Urban Land Institute (1090 Vermont Ave. NW, Washington, DC 20005), available in many planning and urban studies libraries.

Savannah Landmarks, one of the largest and best known attempts to do historic preservation with a minimum of displacement, can be reached at Box 8801, Savannah, GA 31412.

The Anti-Displacement Committee of Boerum Hill/Gowanus, which organized protests against gentrification-oriented "historic house tours" of the neighborhood, can be reached at 151 Bond St., Brooklyn, NY.

In the late 1950s, urban renewal bulldozers demolished the West End — a 7500 person, largely Italian community in Central Boston. The neighborhood's close-knit character was captured in Herbert Gans' sociological study The Urban Villagers. In its place stands Charles River Park, a luxury high-rise and town house complex. Recently a budding artist of the people took some spray paint to a sign there and added a little historical reminder to the public.

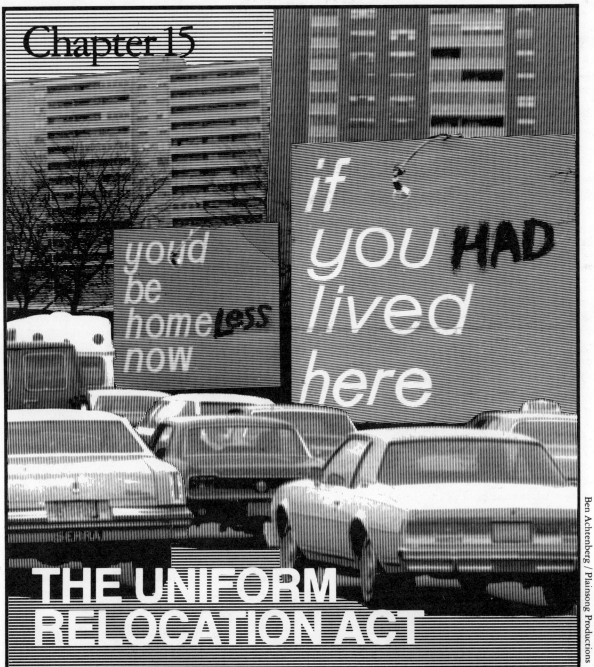

Chapter 15

you'd be homeless now

if you HAD lived here

THE UNIFORM RELOCATION ACT

Ben Achtenberg / Plainsong Productions

169

No War Declared
No Storm Had Flared
No Sudden Bomb So Cruel
Just A Need For Land
A Greedy Hand
And A Sign
That Said
"URBAN RENEWAL"

Rick Stafford / Three Cats Photos

If you can't stop displacement, the obvious next step is to get the maximum compensation for the dislocation which is being imposed.

As previous chapters have indicated, sometimes, with solid and militant organization, it's possible to negotiate relocation benefits from private developers operating in the private market (see, for example, the discussion of condo conversions, Chapter 5). But the principal source of such benefits is government — either directly or through requirements it can place on private developers as a condition for getting subsidies or permits.

Sometimes state or local governments take steps in this field. But the foremost supplier of relocation benefits is the federal government, primarily through the Uniform Relocation Assistance and Property Acquisitions Act of 1970 (known as the Uniform Relocation Act, or URA).

Federal relocation assistance began in the 1950s in response to massive, direct displacement by the "federal bulldozer" under the highway and urban renewal programs. But the federal response was a failure. Frequently, it was a grotesque joke, as government relocation workers guided displacees into worse housing at higher rents. Community anger and pressure forced a series of reforms, each insufficient but at least offering more concrete aid.

The URA was the most recent of these reforms. Like the others before it, URA is tied exclusively to displacement caused by direct government action. So, as government aid has shifted more and more toward support of private development, the increase in benefits the URA brought has been offset by a reduction in the number of situations where it applies. Now it's more often *indirect* rather than direct government action that causes the problem.

The Anti-Displacement Project regards this private/public distinction as misleading and dangerous. As noted in Chapter 2 and elsewhere, an important goal of the anti-displacement movement should be to gain public acceptance of the extent to which the government, through its tax policies, permit processes and expenditure programs, supports and triggers the actions of private entrepreneurs. Such extensive government involvement, without which most private development would not occur, should logically lead to providing expanded URA-type coverage.

But there is also another battle on the same front: the fight to improve the URA itself, to make it a truly effective and humane form of aid to those displaced households it does cover.

## WHAT THE URA PROVIDES

In adopting the Uniform Relocation Act, Congress had two main purposes: first, to make relocation policies and assistance uniform among the various federal property-taking agencies; and second, to increase levels of assistance to people displaced by federally-funded property taking. In brief, the major provisions of the 1970 Act called for:

● A moving allowance of up to $300, and a "dislocation allowance" of up to $200, per household.

● "Replacement housing payments" to homeowners of up to $15,000 above the fair market value, primarily to cover higher interest costs, since many owners had mortgages written at earlier and far lower interest rates.

● Rent supplement payments to tenants of up to $4,000 to cover the cost of obtaining decent replacement housing. These payments are meant to cover the difference between actual rent levels and what the displacee can afford by paying 25% of his/her income. Such payments also can be used as downpayments in purchasing a home, so long as the displacee matches with his/her own money any downpayment in excess of $2,000.

● Guarantees of decent replacement housing and adequate relocation services.

● Direct construction of housing by the taking agency as a "houser of last resort" where replacement housing resources are inadequate.

Following passage of the 1970 URA, many states passed related laws, to cover displacement caused by actions of state and local government agencies. Some offer virtually the same protections and aids embodied in URA, some are far weaker. Consult with your local Legal Services office to find out whether your state has its own version of URA and what it covers.

One of the potentially most important, but least used features of the Uniform Relocation

Act is its replacement housing provision. It stipulates that where there is insufficient relocation housing to meet the needs of displacees from a URA-covered operation, project funds may, and in some instances must, be used to rehabilitate or construct homes for those displacees. Needless to say, most property-taking agencies are highly reluctant to use funds that otherwise could build highways or convention centers for something as mundane as low-rent housing. But a sharp and ready community can make them act otherwise.

Consider, for instance, the happy example of the McDaniel-Glenn public housing project in the Mechanicsville section of Atlanta. One hundred twenty-eight of the project's units were scheduled for demolition as part of the construction of Atlanta's new subway system. The residents' tenant association, backed by staff of a local community center, with some help from Atlanta's Community Design Center, insisted: 1) that the government follow through on its legal obligation to replace the lost units; 2) that the new units be constructed in the immediate vicinity; 3) that the displacees themselves be consulted about the design of the replacement units; and 4) that no one would have to move until the replacement units were ready for occupancy.

The result: 128 very attractive new housing units, with the same mix of apartment sizes as the original units, were built on four scattered sites within a few hundred yards of the original location. They are designed to specifications the residents developed in a series of community workshops. The displacees moved in in early 1981, and only then was the transportation agency permitted to tear down the old units in the path of the new subway.

Of course, even with this apparently ideal outcome, there are a few problems. For instance, some families have outgrown (by housing authority standards) their old units, and will not be allowed to move to their equivalent-size replacement unit. Instead, they will be placed in larger units in another housing project. But by and large, this is a relocation story with some good results and important lessons, the most important of which is this: wherever possible, insist that housing scheduled for demolition be replaced on a one-for-one basis, and without loss of large, family-sized units, and that no one moves *until* replacement housing suitable to everyone's needs is ready for occupancy.

Louis Dunn

## WEAKNESSES IN THE URA

Problems began to appear with the Uniform Relocation Act almost immediately after its passage. By now there are so many holes and weaknesses in it that even the government admits it needs strengthening. The main gaps and flaws are as follows:

**The URA is not uniform.** Incredibly, the Act permitted each of the 13 federal agencies that displace people to write their own regulations. Since detailed regulations are the key to how laws are carried out, it is no surprise that a 1978 report by the U.S. Government's General Accounting Office found "an inconsistent, inequitable, and confusing array of differing formats, terminologies, and guidelines in the 13 Federal agencies' regulations, resulting in people being treated differently when displaced by these agencies."

**The URA's intended area of coverage has been severely narrowed.** Many, perhaps most, persons displaced as a result of expenditure of federal funds are not even covered by the Act. In large part, this is because in 1974 various federally-funded, locally-administered programs such as urban renewal, model cities, and concentrated code enforcement, all covered by the URA, were replaced by the Community Development Block Grant Program (see Chapter 12). As a result of the way the URA is worded, people displaced by CDBG funds did not fall under its narrowly defined protections.

To give one example of the absurd situations this gives rise to: a person displaced by housing code inspection activity carried out under a Concentrated Code Enforcement program, funded by urban renewal funds, would have received URA benefits. But a person displaced by housing code inspection activity carried out under the city's CDBG program would not. HUD has even (successfully) fought neighborhood residents and Legal Services attorneys in court when they tried to win relocation aids and protections for those displaced under these new federally-funded programs. It is not surprising that during the 1970s the number of displacees from HUD-assisted programs who got URA assistance went down considerably. But the total number of persons displaced as a result of government assistance and programs did not decline at all.

Another coverage gap is that, with one exception (see page 154), residents of privately-owned buildings, who are evicted when the owner receives HUD funds and commitments in order to build a Section 8 low-rent development, are not given URA coverage because the displacement itself is "private" activity by the landlord.

ORGANIZE – AND LEARN THE LANGUAGE!

Louis Dunn

Perhaps the most shocking fact is HUD's own insistence on interpreting the URA as narrowly as possible, in order to save itself money. There are instances where HUD has taken over a nursing home or a Section 236 moderate-income housing development following mortgage default (see Chapter 11 for further discussion of this phenomenon), after which it makes a business decision to close down the nursing home or project, because to keep it running would cost too much in subsidy funds and a new purchaser cannot be

found. HUD then evicts all the occupants, elderly frail people from the nursing home, lower-income families from the 236 development, and refuses to provide any moving expenses, relocation assistance or replacement housing, maintaining that their business decision is not a "project" as defined under the Uniform Relocation Act. Sadly, the courts generally have upheld HUD in such instances.

**The URA was never aimed at the true scope of the displacement problem.** The URA doesn't even pretend to apply to displacement either by projects that combine private and public funds, or by "purely private" actions which in fact are happening only because publicly funded development is underway nearby. Such situations, as we have indicated elsewhere in this guide, are likely to become increasingly prevalent. In the energy field, for example, new Department of Interior policies encourage energy conglomerates to exploit subsurface resources on Native American reservation land, a move that already has produced substantial displacement among a population historically maltreated by displacers, and a trend that can only increase in the 1980s as these policies are expanded.

## PROPOSED AMENDMENTS TO THE URA

Congressional hearings on amending the 1970 Act were finally held in late 1979, although no bill has yet been passed. These amendments have been widely supported by Legal Services clients and attorneys, the National Low Income Housing Coalition, the National Urban Coalition, and other groups, and have even found partial support from HUD, the U.S. Department of Transportation, and other government agencies. In brief,

the most important of the proposed changes would:

● Create a central authority to issue truly uniform regulations implementing the Act.

● Extend coverage to all persons displaced by a federal or federally-assisted project, even where there is a private sponsor of a government-subsidized venture (such as a privately sponsored Section 8 development), or where the agency's original intention in acquiring the property was not for the purpose of a federal "project."

● Protect displacees' benefits against the ravages of inflation, 1) by raising the $4,000 rental adjustment payment maximum to $8,000, and annually updating the figure to reflect changes in the Consumer Price Index; 2) by increasing the maximum allowed for moving expenses and the displacement allowance from $300 and $200, to $600 and $400, respectively; and 3) by removing the limit of $15,000 above the fair market price on payments to displaced homeowners, and allowing such payments to be used to cover additional property tax payments as well as additional mortgage interest payments.

There are many other changes and improvements proposed in the amendments, some of which affect business displacement. See the references at the end of this chapter for information on obtaining transcripts of the hearings on these amendments, which contain much useful information on the URA.

Most anti-displacement organizations feel that, while a clear improvement, these amendments do not go far enough in revamping the URA. Testifying before the Senate Intergovernmental Subcommittee, the National Housing Law Project and the National Low Income Housing Coalition proposed that the Act needs

the following additional changes to become
truly effective:

**Increase moving expense and dislocation
allowances.** The present limits should be
upped to $750 (minimum) and $1,000 (maximum) and the dislocation allowance should be
raised to $500.

**Tie homeowner payments to housing
costs.** Payment levels to displaced homeowners should be set so as to insure they don't
have to pay more than 20% of their income for
housing (the same standard the government
uses in its Section 235 subsidized homeownership program).

**Establish a special relocation assistance
compliance office** to oversee the Uniform
Relocation Act. The proposed amendments
call for the President to select an existing
federal agency to establish uniform regulations. It is likely the President would designate
the General Services Administration or the
Office of Management and Budget, both of
which at different times during the 1970s
were responsible for administering the URA,
and both of which carried out their tasks poorly.

**Demand local anti-displacement analysis
and strategy.** As a condition for receiving federal funds, localities should be required to
"analyze the causes and estimate the scale of
displacement now occurring, regardless of
cause; and propose and carry out an effective
strategy for ending displacement from residential neighborhoods. Just as no one should
be *kept* out of any neighborhood because of
race, creed, nationality, or household composition, no one should be *pushed* out of any
neighborhood because of circumstances beyond his or her control."

## NEGOTIATING RELOCATION SETTLEMENTS BASED ON THE URA

As several community groups have shown,
it's possible to use the URA as a negotiating
base, either to secure some benefits when the
applicability of the Act is disputed, or to gain
benefits higher than those the law mandates.

In San Francisco, the Redevelopment
Agency took possession of the Planters Hotel
in the mid-1970s as part of its Yerba Buena
Center renewal project. Those living there at
the time were given URA benefits, but the

Just as no one should be *kept*
out of any neighborhood because of race, nationality or
household composition, no one
should be *pushed* out of any
neighborhood because of circumstances beyond his or her
control.

Agency subsequently leased the hotel to a private operator pending designation of a developer. New residents were not informed by the
hotel operator or the agency that they were
moving to a hotel scheduled for delivery to
a redeveloper. When they received eviction
notices in the summer of 1980, the residents,
through their Legal Services attorneys, claimed
they were covered by the URA, a claim the
agency and HUD denied. When the residents
decided to litigate the issue, based on their
reading of the statute, as well as on alleged
violation of an agreement the Redevelopment
Agency had signed several years before, settling the major relocation lawsuit against the
Yerba Buena project, the agency decided to
enter into settlement negotiations. An important bargaining consideration was the agency's
commitment to deliver the hotel vacant to the
redeveloper by February 1, 1981, with a possible $105,000 penalty if the deadline could
not be met.

The final agreement amounted to a
$101,000 package of benefits for the Planters
tenants and the city's low-income housing
stock. Some 50 tenants received up to $1,000
each in dislocation allowances and rent supplements, with the actual amount dependent on
when they moved out and other factors. The
remaining money, $55,000, was placed in a

housing replacement fund, with the Legal Services attorneys as trustees, to be used to assist in purchasing, rehabbing or leasing replacement housing for the units lost at the Planters. The tenants are now negotiating with the neighborhood housing development corporation that emerged from the prior Yerba Buena relocation lawsuit settlement (see page 55) to use these funds as part of a larger financial package to purchase and rehab another nearby hotel for low-rent use, with ex-Planters residents having admissions priority. For further details on this innovative agreement and how it was won, contact Fred Feller, S.F. Neighborhood Legal Assistance Foundation, 870 Market St., #1103, San Francisco, CA 94102.

A second San Francisco story also shows how URA standards should not limit the demands community organizations make as part of a bargaining process.

In 1979, the Hastings Law School announced plans to expand into the Tenderloin neighborhood around it, occupied mainly by elderly low-income people. (This is the neighborhood where the SRO hotel stock is under attack by luxury hotel developers and the tourist industry generally; see the discussion on pages 57 and 194.) The move was opposed by neighborhood residents who were supported by Legal Services attorneys.

Because it is a state institution, supposedly training attorneys to work for the public good, Hastings was particularly vulnerable to community pressure to make it act responsibly towards its neighbors. So community negotiations with Hastings officials produced an agreement that displacees would receive up to $6,000 as a rent adjustment payment over a six-year period (although the maximum re-

Gary Kell / Tenderloin Times

quired under California's state version of the URA was only $4,000 over four years); that replacement units would be provided equal in number to the units being taken, by converting two transient hotels to permanent low-rent use; and that elderly displacees who moved into other Hastings-owned buildings in the area would receive a guarantee of no rent increases for the rest of their lives. Hastings also agreed to set up a legal clinic for the elderly residents in the neighborhood (although the school currently is being sued by a public interest law group for reneging on this part of the agreement).

The Detroit ACORN group described in Chapter 13 also used the negotiation process to secure URA benefits for persons who probably would not have qualified under current narrow interpretations of the law's coverage.

## RAISING RELOCATION BENEFIT LEVELS AS AN ANTI-DISPLACEMENT TOOL

It can be argued that as the amount of relocation compensation required goes up, the likelihood goes down that displacement-causing projects will be carried out, because of the increase in project costs. HUD officials and others think that the measurable reduction of URA-covered displacement activity that appeared in the early and mid-1970s was in part due to reluctance of government officials to pick up the tab.

HUD also likes to caution against "excessive" relocation benefits because they may get in the way of urban "revitalization" activities. Testifying on the proposed Uniform Relocation Act amendments, HUD's Assistant Secretary for Community Planning and Development expressed the Department's opposition to extending URA coverage to households displaced indirectly by federal programs and funds. He voiced concern that anyone who felt his or her displacement was linked in any way to public actions could bring a claim. "This would have a generally negative effect," he concluded, "on those very neighborhood preservation programs designed to assist low- and moderate-income persons." But given the fact that those "preservation" programs generally are displacing the poor as part of the "urban renaissance" that is bringing the middle class back to the city, it seems more accurate to suggest that what HUD really fears is a slowdown of its urban revitalization programs if better protection is afforded to those displaced in the process.

## THE STRATEGIC PROBLEM: FIGHT FOR MORE RELOCATION BENEFITS? FIGHT DISPLACEMENT? FIGHT FOR BOTH?

Demands for increased relocation benefits are clearly in the community's interest. But increased money payments also may occasionally undercut individual and collective resistance to displacement. It has happened that relocation cash payments in the thousands of dollars have been offered, in effect, as bribes to get households to move. Hard-pressed low-income families particularly may find this sort of blandishment difficult to resist. But the seemingly enormous cash grant usually erodes within a year or two, leaving them, and others, faced with inadequate incomes to cope with a growing housing shortage and rising rents.

What goals to set in anti-displacement struggles, and how to pursue them, are organizing and educating problems that must be dealt with in each community. Even in the most successful anti-displacement battles, some households may have to move, and they should get the maximum in relocation benefits. But deciding how to divide organizational energies between getting those benefits, and continuing to hold the line against any further displacement, can be a crucial decision.

The Anti-Displacement Project believes that the larger and more basic fight is to stop displacement altogether in its present forms, and to win the right to residential stability as well as to decent, affordable housing for everyone. The second line of defense is economic protection and acceptable replacement housing for those who do get displaced. And toward that end, an improved and expanded Uniform Relocation Act and other guarantees of sufficient displacement compensation are necessary goals for the anti-displacement movement. No matter what strategy is chosen, a cohesive community is essential to win and enforce victories, as illustrated by the fight against luxury hotel expansion in San Francisco's Tenderloin (see page 194); the fight to save Beauty, Kentucky, from extinction (see pages 132-136); the fight to save the Marion Gardens housing project in Jersey City (see pages 122-127); and the People's Firehouse struggle in Brooklyn (see pages 74-78).

## REFERENCES

### UNIFORM RELOCATION ACT: PROPOSED AMENDMENTS

*Senate Hearings on Proposed Amendments.* The record of these hearings contains excellent material on the shortcomings of the 1970 URA. To get a copy of the record, write to Senator Jim Sasser, U.S. Senate Subcommittee on Intergovernmental Relations, Washington, DC 20013, and ask for a copy of the September 5 and November 6-7, 1979 hearings on S. 1108.

### URA INTERPRETATIONS

"Preventing or Ameliorating Displacement in Connection with Section 8," by Florence Roisman, offers arguments about why presently non-covered Section 8 displacees should be given URA protection. The article appears in the July, 1980 issue of *Clearinghouse Review,* which should be available for reading or copying at most law libraries and Legal Services offices.

### LOCAL STRUGGLES

Atlanta — McDaniel-Glenn housing project. For more information on this effective use of the replacement housing provision of the URA, contact Houston Wheeler, Wesley Community Center, 159 Ralph McGill Blvd. NE, Atlanta, GA 30365.

### PROPOSED STATE LEGISLATION

A strong state anti-displacement bill, titled the Neighborhood Stabilization Act, has been introduced into the Massachusetts legislature by Rep. Mel King of Boston. It would require that, where displacement is occurring as a result of investment of state funds, a Neighborhood Stabilization Plan be included as part of the Environmental Impact Report. The Plan would set forth specific remedial actions by state agencies, with respect to housing subsidy allocations, permanent and construction jobs, and contracts. At least 2% of the total public and private cost of each project would be set aside as a Community Assistance Fund, for loans and grants to prevent displacement of neighborhood residents. And a Neighborhood Review Committee would be established to oversee the planning and implementation of the plan. For further information and a copy of this bill, write Rep. Mel King, State House, Boston, MA 02133.

# Chapter 16

*I was terrified. I felt very much alone. I couldn't afford to move, and neither could most of the people.*

# BEATING THE MARKET WITH COOPERATIVE HOUSING AND COMMUNITY LAND TRUSTS

Allan Troxler

In the long run, forced displacement is not likely to be stopped, nor the general housing crisis resolved, without replacement of the private market system — without progress, that is, toward social ownership of housing, and social control over its production and maintenance. This chapter examines two ways to move toward this goal: limited-equity cooperative housing, and community land trusts.

## COOPERATIVE HOUSING

Housing cooperatives are a form of collective property ownership by residents themselves. Coops differ from condominiums, in which individual living units are individually owned, with areas outside the units (hallways, entrances, exterior walls, roof, and land) owned in common by all the unit owners. In a cooperative, all the residents of the building or development are shareholding members of a cooperative association which owns the entire property, and their shares represent the value of the space they occupy and use. Members' shares give them the right to exclusive use and occupancy of the space they live in, and access to common spaces.

Cooperatives are potentially an effective anti-displacement device, since they do not permit outside control — only those who live there are members of the cooperative association. New housing can be built on cooperative principles from the outset. Alternatively, existing multi-family rental structures, and even free-standing single-family homes, can be bought by tenants or others and converted to cooperatives. Coops are beneficial in rural as well as urban areas — a set of handbooks on the operations, legal issues, and financing/acquisition of rural cooperative housing, recently prepared for Rural America by the Cooperative Housing Foundation, is listed in the references at the end of this chapter.

But it's necessary to pick the right kind of coop and start it in the right way, if the purpose is to prevent displacement. As discussed in Chapter 5, cooperatives pushed on renters as conversions can be as disruptive as involuntary condominium conversions. Of the two basic forms of housing cooperatives, only one — the limited-equity coop — offers a true defense against market-generated displacement.

**Stock cooperatives.** In this approach, each occupant (shareholder) is allowed to sell his or her share in the cooperative for whatever the market will bear at the time the resident moves out (although the cooperative association retains the right to approve the buyer). This arrangement of course feeds housing speculation and means the cost of housing will continue to spiral.

**Limited-equity (or low-yield) cooperatives.** This form of coop seeks to keep housing costs permanently low by retaining the economic benefits of the arrangement for the entire cooperative, rather than for individual shareholders. The limited-equity coop prevents coop share values from inflating along with the general market, guaranteeing that any public subsidies the coop may have used, and the savings it has generated, are passed on to new members as they join. Of course, members are allowed to sell their shares when they want to relocate, but the cooperative membership agreement has built-in restrictions governing how much a share may be sold for.

Several types of restrictions are possible. The agreement may stipulate that members who move out are entitled only to the equity they originally put into the property — that is, the purchase price of membership shares in the cooperative association. Under other agreements, relocating members are entitled to the amount of their original cash payment plus any portion of their monthly payments that went for principal repayment on the coop mortgage. In another version, sellers are permitted to retain their dollar share of the coop's equity buildup (original membership share price plus mortgage principal repayments), increased by some annual percentage to cover all or part of inflationary value increases over the period of residence. Yet another possibility is for the individual and the cooperative association to split, under a predetermined formula, any increase in the market value of the shareholder's interest. Improvements made to the property by the resident are also covered by such agreements.

The underlying principles of limited profit-taking are: 1) that the housing the cooperative owns is viewed as a resource for *use*, rather than for money-making; 2) that its housing is collective property rather than a collection of private investments; and 3) that the overall social benefit of keeping housing costs low outweighs any individual's need or desire to make a profit.

Limited-equity cooperative membership provides the traditional benefits of homeownership: security, the right to use or fix up one's space as one wishes, the right to deduct mortgage interest payments and property taxes from one's federal and state income tax, access to homeowners' property tax exemptions and property tax rebates for the elderly (in states where these exist), etc. Furthermore, transfer of ownership in a coop is usually far easier and cheaper than selling a house. Shares in a cooperative which has a single, blanket mortgage usually can be transferred without the costs of a real estate agency, refinancing, and new title insurance.

Beyond these practical, financial advantages, cooperative-building and living can engender a sense of community, as neighbors share decision-making, property care and repair responsibilities. This growth of communal spirit often leads to the organization of cooperative support services for members, such as child care, food-buying clubs, and recreation.

**Cooperative-building and living can engender a sense of community, as neighbors share decision-making, property care and repair responsibilities.**

**Determination of housing payments in a cooperative.** The housing payments made by a coop resident reflect the resident's proportional share of the cooperative's mortgage payments, taxes, and operating expenses. (Residents may pay differing amounts, depending on the quantity and quality of the space they occupy.) While these monthly payments may fluctuate, depending on changes in operating costs, there are important limits to how much and how quickly they will rise:

• Cooperatives are nonprofit corporations, so there are no costs to members from profiteering by owners.

• Cooperatives generally are not bought and sold, so there are none of the huge jumps in financing costs — higher mortages at higher interest rates — which accompany property sales and account for the lion's share of most monthly housing bills. (Where cooperative associations have to take shorter-term "balloon mortgages," however, this stable financing advantage is considerably reduced. In New York City, for instance, coops are having to take ten-year loans which have to be renegotiated at the new prevailing interest rate — certain to be higher — when they come due).

● All management decisions in a cooperative are made by the coop members themselves, usually through a democratically elected board of directors. So any operating cost increases that do occur are tied directly to residents' wants and needs, rather than to outsiders' standards and profit desires.

**Forming coops in existing housing.** Conversion of rental units into lower-income cooperatives by existing tenants has wide potential, but should be explored with particular energy in communities that have adopted rent control and related regulations (see Chapter 9). Landlords whose profits have been regulated by rent limits, or by taxes assessed on speculative sales (see Chapter 4), may be willing to sell buildings at reasonable prices to their tenants. Community groups in cities with rent control should consider pushing for additional legislation to facilitate such conversions. Washington, D.C., for instance, has passed a so-called "right of first refusal" ordinance (discussed in detail below) which gives a big boost to tenant-initiated coop conversion possibilities. Under this law, any landlord who wants to sell

**Operating cost increases are tied directly to residents' wants and needs, rather than to outsiders' standards and profit desires.**

Metropolitan Council on Housing

a building must offer it first to the occupants, who have over a year to arrange to buy their building.

A recent handbook produced by Community Economics, Inc. for the California Department of Housing and Community Development (see end-of-chapter references for how to get it) outlines the process of converting an existing rental building to a cooperative. The first step is to form a tenant association to plan the switchover. Financing alternatives have to be explored. Rules and guidelines have to be devised, tenants must be informed and educated. A cooperative corporation must be established to go through various governmental application and approval processes, and to actually assume ownership and management control of the building. The process is complex, but has been successfully followed by many groups. Barring unusual problems, it all takes about a year, and there are many community-oriented consultants and organiza-

tions available to provide help. Good starting points for information and referral to sources of assistance are the National Association of Housing Cooperatives, 1012 14th Street NW, #805, Washington, DC 20005, and the national and regional offices of the National Consumer Cooperative Bank (see page 187).

Financing assistance is available through a variety of sources, including Community Development Block Grant and Section 8 housing subsidy funds. Government construction and rehabilitation loans at below-market interest rates may be available, plus loan guarantees for mortgages up to 100% of total development costs, which removes the need for downpayment. The new National Consumer Cooperative Bank (2001 S Street NW, Washington, DC 20009) is another possible source of funding and technical assistance, although it will have only limited funds available for housing cooperatives.

Prior to getting mortgage financing to purchase the property, a tenant association will need "seed money" for consulting, legal and architectural fees, to pay for permit applications, and to cover any purchase "options" required. (An option gives an exclusive right to buy property within a specified period of time, and usually costs about 5% of the purchase price. It generally gives a tenant association six months to a year to decide whether it can or wants to buy the property.) The amount of seed money needed may range from a few thousand to tens of thousands of dollars. Part of this may be raised from potential cooperative members, in the form of loans, contributions, membership fees, etc. Other sources include state and local housing and community development agencies, and various private foundations and organizations, such as the Housing Assistance Council, 1828 L Street NW, Suite 606, Washington, DC 20036, and Rural America, 1346 Connecticut Avenue NW, Suite 500, Washington, DC 20036, both of which limit their assistance to rural groups.

Not all rental housing is appropriate for conversion to coops — particularly buildings for which the sales prices is too high, or which are so deteriorated as to make it too costly or difficult to put them into decent shape. Resident-initiated cooperative housing also involves considerable work and dedication by members in order to succeed. And although they are intended to bring out the best in human relationships, coops also can produce internal tensions. Even in a highly supportive coop, failure of a member to meet monthly payment obligations, even if it's due to causes beyond the member's control, can result in financial strain on other members, leading to an uncomfortable eviction process.

At the lower income levels, coops are difficult to begin because of purchase and rehab cost factors. It takes extra pressure and commitment, and sometimes special programs, to make such coops a viable alternative. In New York City, Columbia University professor Robert Kolodny researched the experience of low-income tenant groups creating coops in housing their landlords had walked away from (discussed in Chapter 7) and found the following five ingredients essential to their success:

## A COMMITTED TENANT ORGANIZATION

The groups Kolodny studied had very strong impetus to organize, being "largely self-generated, with the tenants coalescing around the crisis of their orphaned buildings."

They were moved by "a sense of desperation and an absence of other housing options." But once started, says Kolodny, "the effort involved in hanging on and successfully operating a de facto cooperative [after the landlord had abandoned the property but before the tenants had title] brought cohesion and confidence to the tenants and helped develop skills that they would need to oversee the property's rehabilitation and long-term management."

## SUBSIDIES FOR PROPERTY ACQUISITION

"In part," Kolodny found, "the New York coops worked financially because the acquisition costs were so low . . . in most cases the buildings were already owned or taken by the city . . . with the intent of transferring title to the residents," and the transfer price averaged about $250 per unit. For market-rate properties, cost-reducing subsidies would be essential.

## SUBSIDIES FOR REHAB AND REDUCED REHAB STANDARDS

Lowered acquisition costs were not enough, says Kolodny, pointing out that the successful New York low-income coops

also required rehabilitation financing at below market interest rates. The majority of the projects used the city's municipal loan program, whereby funds borrowed by the city at a tax exempt rate are passed through to the borrower, subject only to an administrative surcharge. One advantage of municipal financing was that less exacting physical standards had to be met than would have been required if FHA or conventional financing had been used. Almost inevitably, the scope of upgrading was determined by 1) establishing the minimum housing code [requirements] and basic considerations of health, safety and welfare, and then 2) figuring what was left for "optional" expenditures by working backwards from the rents residents could reasonably be expected to afford. This

method often dictated patching instead of replastering; retaining old tubs, sinks and basins; buying appliances second hand, and so forth. The involvement of the tenants in the process made such tradeoffs possible because there was a direct and visible relationship between the costs of rehabilitation and their eventual monthly charges. With an in-place tenantry, the usual cosmetic improvements designed to aid marketing were of less importance.

## TAX BREAKS

Another "critical subsidy" for the successful coops, Kolodny found, was

relief from tax liens accumulated during the abandonment process, [which] was usually handled by having the city take the property. Relief from real estate taxes following rehabilitation and conversion was provided by the city's very generous J-51 program . . . which generally exempts and abates all taxes for the first 12 years after rehabilitation [see discussion on pages 161 and 162].

## TECHNICAL ASSISTANCE

Kolodny pointed out that a variety of professional support groups, some private-nonprofit, some municipal, were crucially involved in teaching inexperienced tenant organizations rehab planning and supervision and housing management. For groups seeking to set up limited equity coops, there is a list of resources at the end of the chapter.

Even amidst the difficulties, however, the benefits of the cooperative approach were evident. "What really induces the residents to invest their energy (which, rather than cash, was their primary contribution)," wrote Kolodny, "was their interest in gaining control over their residential circumstances. . . ." Subsidies and "the substitution of labor for cash" were the main buffers against escalating costs. Although coops weren't much cheaper than other housing to operate, it did seem that they increased "the level of services and satisfaction for the same housing dollar."

The most important factor is that control gives residents greater opportunity to make trade offs. They can lower the thermostat to an agreed upon temperature if they decide that the cost of the fuel is more onerous than the increased chill inside their apartments in cold weather. Cosmetic work can be deferred because there is much less of a marketing problem than might be encountered by a private landlord. By the same token, where incomes permit, tenants can assess themselves in order to improve services or facilities.

With the proper kinds of assistance, conversion of existing housing to limited-equity coops is a viable and valuable alternative to excessive rents and displacement for low-income families. A closer look at the process and its pitfalls is provided below in the case study of the Beecher Coop.

## WASHINGTON, D.C.'S "RIGHT OF FIRST REFUSAL" LAW

**Under Washington, D.C. law, any landlord who wants to sell a building must offer it first to the occupants, who have over a year to arrange to buy their building.**

Since 1977, 15% of the District of Columbia's rental stock has either been converted to condos or stock coops or is in the conversion process. So the D.C. government has recently developed some highly useful protective ordinances, along with financial and technical assistance programs, to aid transfer of housing ownership from absentee landlords to tenant cooperatives.

The basic legislation is what is known as a "right of first refusal," or "first opportunity to

How D.C. tenants become homeowners:

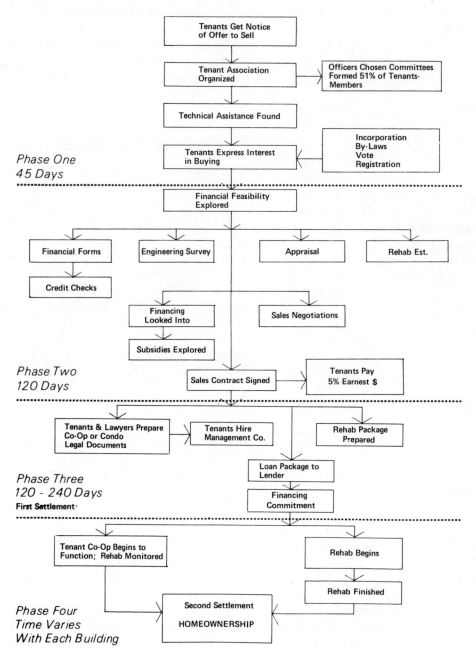

purchase." An owner wishing to sell or demolish a rental structure of any size, or convert it to non-residential use, must officially notify the tenants, stating the purchase price a tenant group would be asked to pay if interested.

## ORGANIZING FOR RESPONSE

Tenants then have 45 days to organize and incorporate a tenant association and respond to the offer (30 days, if there already is an incorporated tenant association). In order to qualify under the law, at least 51% of the tenants must join. The association must then register with the city, and express an interest in purchasing the building.

## NEGOTIATIONS

The tenants' formal expression of interest triggers a 120-day exploration and negotiation period. The tenant association must get an engineering survey, rehab estimate, and appraisal on which to base analysis of the financial feasibility of purchasing the building, calculating mortgage costs to cover purchase and rehab, plus operating expenses. Financing alternatives are explored, negotiations are undertaken with the owner, and a sales contract signed. A refundable earnest-money deposit of no more than 5% of the purchase price is given to the owner.

## SETTLEMENT

Next comes a 120-240 day settlement period (180 days minimum if the tenants are planning to establish a limited-equity cooperative). Extension to 240 days is given if the lender agrees in writing to make a decision on financing within that time. During this period, the legal documents are drawn up, including those for formal establishment of the cooperative association. A management company is hired in almost all cases, at least for the first few years; this is something most lenders will insist on. The rehab package and interim loan application are prepared, and the operation moves to first settlement (property transfer). After that, rehab work is carried out with the interim loan, and a second settlement occurs, with permanent mortgage financing. (See chart on opposite page.)

## PROGRAM ASSISTANCE

The District of Columbia government also provides a variety of services and financial aids for the formation of a limited-equity coop. The D.C. law defines this kind of coop as one in which the sale value of shares is limited to a 10% annual compounded rate of return, plus the value of the member's improvements, minus the costs of preparing the unit for the next occupant. These program aids include:

**Coop seed money loans** to tenant associations where at least 50% of the member households are under Section 8 income limits. The loans can be used to cover lawyers', architects', appraisers', engineers', consultants', and organizers' fees. An initial retainer money loan of up to $5,000 is available, and then a comprehensive seed money loan — which can cover loan processing fees, closing costs, marketing and other fees — can be obtained for up to 8% of total project costs. Both are made at no interest and are due when the project receives permanent financing.

**First right of purchase loans,** available to tenant associations establishing low-yield cooperatives in which at least 50% of the member households are under Section 8 income limits. These are made on a matching basis to assist in the earnest-money deposit, where members cannot themselves come up with the 5% through their own savings, and to provide "gap financing" to make up the difference between the amount of the interim mortgage and the amount needed to buy, rehab, and market the housing. The earnest-money assistance loan bears no interest.

**Home purchase assistance loans,** available to households meeting Section 8 income guidelines, to be used to finance their coop membership shares at a level which assures they will not have to devote more than 28% of their household income to housing costs. These are deferred payment loans and have a $11-16,000 maximum, depending on the type of unit being purchased.

**Rehabilitation loans,** short- and long-term, for tenant-purchased buildings located in Community Development and Neighborhood Strategy Areas.

**Technical assistance** to prospective tenant purchasers. Most notably, the city funds several organizations, listed in the end-of-the-chapter references, to advise and work with tenant groups.

The Washington program has evolved and expanded in response to the way speculative owners were reacting to the city's rent control legislation. In the last two years, some 50 buildings, containing nearly 6,000 units, have been converted to limited-equity coops.

But the program is far from perfect. Major problems include: inadequate time allowed to form a tenant association and respond to a landlord's sudden demand to buy or get out —

In the last two years, some 50 buildings, containing nearly 6000 units, have been converted into limited-equity coops.

## THE BEECHER HOUSING COOPERATIVE, WASHINGTON, D.C.

On Christmas Eve, 1977, 95 tenants living in a ten-building, three-story apartment complex located in the Glover Park neighborhood of Washington, D.C., received eviction notices from the new owner of their building. Condo conversion was coming. Esther Siegel, a tenant who was to become a leader in the struggle to prevent eviction, said later: "I was terrified. I felt very much alone. I couldn't afford to move, and neither could most of the people."

Siegel and the other tenants decided to fight the eviction by forming a limited-equity cooperative. They established the Beecher Low-Rise Tenants Association (BLTA) and immediately sought help from the surrounding community and city officials. They held a "We Shall Not Be Moved" block party and went door to door to get support from their neighbors. Neighborhood residents were asked to write the owner urging him to sell to the tenants. The Glover Park Citizens' Association put further pressure on the owner and made a sizeable donation to the Tenants Association. The City Council member representing the neighborhood and the District's Congressional representative also helped out. A $1,000 contribution to assist the organizing campaign was obtained from the Advisory Neighborhood Commission, a city-created planning group which serves as an intermediary between the D.C. government and local neighborhoods. Help and advice were received from other coop groups in the area.

By April, 1978, the BLTA was able to announce it had reached an agreement with

*District of Columbia Mayor Marion Barry, Jr. (right) joins William Walker and Burnette Johnson, officers of the 15th Street Tenant Association, in celebrating the purchase of their 51-unit apartment complex. The city helped the mostly elderly tenants convert the four buildings into a limited-equity cooperative.*

District of Columbia Department of Housing and Community Development

particularly true for larger buildings; limited resources under the city's financial aid program; and the shortage of financing from private lending institutions to provide permanent mortgage loans. The city is trying to get banks and savings and loans to establish a lending pool for such mortgages. In other localities, state housing finance agencies, if available, or city mortgage bond programs (see page 103) may be the most promising source of financing.

Further information about Washington's approach to converting rental units into low yield tenant cooperatives is available through the D.C. Department of Housing and Community Development, 1133 N. Capitol, Washington, DC 20002.

the owner to buy six of the ten buildings, containing 63 units. The other four he insisted on keeping for sale as condos. (These events took place before the city passed its "right of first refusal" ordinance.) An initial sales price of $961,606 was set, and the tenants were given 18 months to arrange financing. During that period, BLTA had to pay the landlord $200 per month per unit, occupied or not, and for each month the tenants failed to reach a closing, the sales price would increase by $10,000.

## "I was terrified. I felt very much alone. I couldn't afford to move, and neither could most of the people."

Rents up to that point had been $140-150 a month (all units in the complex had only one bedroom), so the $200 monthly payment per unit, when vacant units were added in, translated into an immediate $100 rent increase for each household. As soon as the option was signed, tenants assumed management of the property, doing a lot of the labor themselves to save money. They also developed an "internal subsidy" program, which enabled some residents to stay who otherwise might have been forced to move.

Towards the end of the option period, BLTA found a savings and loan willing to give them permanent financing — a 30-year mortgage at 11¼% interest. But as a condition of the loan, they were required to rehab the units substantially. To finance the rehab, they obtained a $767,000 loan from the D.C. government — $609,500 at a 3% interest rate, amortized over 20 years, plus $157,500 for which repayment was waived as long as the property

was kept available for low- and moderate-income households.

The final stumbling block was money for the downpayment, and the tenants decided to raise this themselves. In three days, they collected $63,000, enough to cover the initial closing: each tenant put in $1,000, in some cases by borrowing from friends, relatives, or other tenants. On June 5, 1978, the closing occurred — an event featured in the Washington *Star*. With the pre-existing vacancies and a few added during the negotiation period, those tenants living in buildings which the owner retained for condo conversion were able to move into the tenant-run buildings.

Once the purchase was completed, rehab began. BLTA renovated one building at a time, with tenants continuing to live in the apartments, even though water and heat had to be turned off in the process. "We had a lot of cookouts," said Esther Siegel. Coop members also set up a "buddy system," in which units already rehabbed played host to units undergoing rehab.

During the rehab period, however, it became clear to the tenants that they would need additional working capital. The acquisition loan had not fully covered the purchase price, and various closing costs — legal fees, the D.C. real estate transfer tax, bank finance charges — which had been deferred to allow the closing to go through on the basis of the $63,000 downpayment, had to be raised in cash. Having pretty much exhausted their own resources, they devised an unusual scheme: they decided to turn Beecher into a "leasing cooperative." Under this financing method, a group of high-income investors, seeking tax shelters through rapid-depreciation tax deductions available from this sort of

extensive rehab work, purchase the property and lease it back to the tenant cooperative. The coop then assumes the role of "managing general partner," while the investors are "limited partners" who have no operational control over the project. This sale/leaseback arrangement is common in commercial real estate developments, but the Beecher case may be the first time in the U.S. that it has been used to assist moderate-income tenants in retaining their homes.

The sale/leaseback deal, involving six limited partners and a six-year lease — the length dictated largely by tax shelter law considerations — was completed in November, 1979. Management control of the complex remained with the coop, which hired its own residents for most of the managerial and custodial positions. A good deal of voluntary labor by the highly motivated coop members keeps maintenance costs down.

But the sale/leaseback arrangement, while providing the tenants with needed capital they could not otherwise obtain, has some disadvantages. One is that residents cannot take tax deductions for mortgage interest payments and property taxes, since the limited partners, as legal owners, now have the right. (Not that many lower-income homeowners are in a position to take advantage of this tax provision, however.) Most problematic, however, is that at the end of the six-year lease period, BLTA must exercise its option to purchase full ownership in the buildings, if the complex is to remain a limited-equity coop. This may be both perilous and expensive. The purchase price for the transaction will be based on the new appraised value, with all the rehab included. The residents will have to refinance the project at its new value in order to pay the limited partners the 50% of the value increase they are entitled to under the partnership agreement. (Since the six limited partners are somewhat committed to the coop and are not merely hard-nosed investors, these problems may not be fatal, but the arrangement builds in far less long-term security than is desirable.) Members may have difficulties refinancing the coop, and they almost certainly will wind up with higher monthly payments. Since these already are $330—far higher than previous rents — it is likely that some members would have to move.

This higher housing cost structure resulting from previous finance and rehab costs, plus the cost-accelerating dilemma of the leaseback deal, reemphasize researcher Robert Kolodny's findings in New York City (page 66): without subsidies, coops do not work well for low-income families. Beecher's current $330 monthly cost, assuming a 25% ratio of housing cost to income, translates into an annual income requirement of $15,800, and that does not include the $1,000 needed to buy into the coop in the first place.

To help overcome this economic barrier to membership, BLTA has secured 26 Section 8 certificates, aiming for a 40% level of lower-income occupancy. As present tenants move out, only applicants eligible for Section 8 will be accepted until that goal has been reached. (Among other things, the coop's loan agreement with the D.C. government provides that Beecher will take displacees from other conversions in the city). There is some concern in the BLTA that the Section 8 residents, being insulated by their subsidies from cost inflation in the monthly payment (Section 8 fills the gap between 15-25% of income, and whatever the "fair market rent" is) may be less receptive

to stringent expenditure controls, voluntary labor, self-maintenance requirements, etc. But new residents are being selected with an emphasis on commitment to coop principles, and a considerable amount of education and orientation work is done with newcomers.

All in all, the story of the Beecher Coop offers an example worth study by other groups interested in limited-equity coop formation. Further information is available through Peter Behringer of Multi Family Housing Services, 518 N. Charles Street, Baltimore, MD 21201, which provided much of the essential technical assistance to the BLTA.

*(The Beecher Coop material was drawn from a case-study prepared in the Summer of 1980 by Max C. Ludeke, a research intern for the National Consumer Cooperative Bank.)*

# ANTI-DISPLACEMENT CONDOMINIUMS

The condominium form of ownership — individual ownership of the residential unit and joint ownership by all individual owners of areas outside the living unit — has been generally associated with upper-income households. But it also may have potential benefit for lower-income households. With some imagination, it may even be used as an anti-speculative device, particularly when linked with appropriate "deed covenants" — agreements made between the buyer and seller, which can be written so as to also obligate any future buyers to use and sell the property in non-profiteering ways.

A condominium association is in essence an agreement to "bind" the land on which the condominium sits, and therefore is similar to the land trust concept described below. It is a voluntary agreement by all member-owners

about how the land can and cannot be used. Condominium associations have boards of directors elected by the members, and the associations function as mini-governments. They have the power to perform services, such as maintenance, trash collection, security, water and sewer services; to tax their members in the form of assessments for services; to create and enforce rules and regulations; and to plan for the future of the area owned by the association. It is a form of community for which housing has provided the common starting point.

On this foundation, it is possible, using covenants, to create and enforce anti-displacement principles — prohibiting purchase of units by speculators, limiting unit resale prices, etc. The laws on what can be done by condominium associations through covenants vary from state to state, and still are evolving. But in general the courts have given wide latitude to such voluntary agreements — excluding, of course, any that discriminate on racial or religious grounds.

Although to date there has been little experience with the use of condominium associations and covenants as anti-displacement devices, the potential is there. And the condominium ownership form has a few advantages over the cooperative. For one, it has proven more acceptable in this country, where there are over three times as many condo owners as coop owners, which means that it also finds greater acceptance among mortgage lenders. Also, the condominium form may be less conducive to discriminatory behavior, since each owner has the right to sell to whomever he or she wants, whereas in a cooperative a purchaser must be approved by the association board of directors, which raises the possibility of veiled, illegal discrimination. On the other hand, condominium purchase involves less social motivation than does coop membership, so condominium residents are less likely to pursue community goals such as preventing displacement. And federal Section 8 subsidies are not available for condominiums, although they are for cooperatives.

Nonetheless, the condominium form should be explored for its anti-displacement potential. Some of the more creative work in adapting the condominium form of ownership to socially creative ends has been done by a private law firm, Hyatt and Rhoads, 2200 Peachtree Center Harris Tower, Atlanta, GA 30303.

## COMMUNITY LAND TRUSTS

One of the principal underlying causes of displacement is speculation on land and buildings. People buy real estate, wait for its value to rise, and then sell for a quick, often huge, profit. This in turn raises the cost of any housing involved, because the new owner has to make enough to pay for the speculator's profits out of income from the property.

This profiteering process injures the society as a whole by causing inflationary pressures

> "Man did not make the earth, and though he had a natural right to *occupy* it, he had no right to locate *as his property* in perpetuity any part of it; neither did the Creator of the earth open a land-office, from whence the first title deeds should issue."
>
> Thomas Paine

and displacement, as previous chapters have discussed. It also perverts the meaning of "value" in real estate. Any real increase in property value occurs because of the usefulness and attractiveness of land, or its improvements, to society. But the present system of buying and selling real estate gives all increases in that value to individual speculators, rather than to the society that created it.

Recently, there has been increasing interest in community land trusts, legal creations designed to alter the way land is held so as to place social needs rather than individual profit at the forefront. Land trusts keep down prices so that property can more easily be used to meet people's needs. They also offer a mechanism by which communities can decide collectively how land will be used.

The land trust idea is not completely in opposition to private ownership. Rather, it makes an important and useful distinction between the kinds of personal property that human beings create through their own efforts — homes, crops, goods, businesses — and resources that were created without human intervention — land, minerals, air, water — and which therefore ought to be held in trust by and for the community.

Concretely, the community land trust is a nonprofit corporation chartered to hold land in the best interests of the community — the future community as well as the present. Land that a trust purchases or receives by donation is never again resold: it is permanently taken off the speculative market.

The directors of the land trust are elected by the community concerned. They decide how that land is used — housing vs. farmland, for instance — and by whom. Those who obtain the right to use the land are exactly that —

*"Religious freedom is my immediate goal, but my long-range plan is to go into real estate."*

Drawing by Donald Reilly; © 1974 / *The New York Magazine*, Inc.

users, not owners. They get a lease, usually for 99 years, that is renewable, and also inheritable: the lease/use rights can be passed on to children, other relatives, friends, or anyone else when the lessee dies. But the person leasing the right to use the land must be the actual user of the land. He or she cannot be an absentee, subleasing it or otherwise controlling how another uses it. The amount paid by the user to the community land trust under the lease is

185

**Land that a trust purchases or receives by donation is never again resold: it is permanently taken off the speculative market.**

determined by a combination of what the land is being used for, the costs the trust incurred in acquiring the land, and other ongoing costs, such as property taxes.

This concept of "leasehold" is, of course, not new. It is being used increasingly in commercial real estate transactions in urban areas (most skyscrapers in New York City, for example, are built on leased ground) and has even been adapted for land acquisition for entire "new towns" such as Irvine, California. In its commercial uses, the leasehold device enables landowners to maximize their profits. In land trusts, however, the leasehold is a way to ensure socially beneficial use of land, to limit profits, and to use whatever profits exist for the good of the community as a whole.

Beyond the land leasing arrangement, the user of the land has all the other rights and security that an owner traditionally has in our society. Users may remain as long as they want, and be free of interference from the community land trust, so long as the use restrictions and other conditions set forth in the lease agreement are not violated. When leaseholders want to relocate, they can sell, or move, the buildings and other improvements on the property. Often these human-made items will be bought by the land trust, which leases them to the new leaseholder.

Individual donations of land to trusts also have increased in recent years. The Internal Revenue Service has accelerated this by recognizing an increasing number of trusts as deductible "charities," especially those that emphasize land conservation or aid low-income people. But even trusts without formal exemption status can offer donors tax breaks. If donors give their land to the Trust for Public Land, the Institute for Community Economics, or comparable tax-deductible organizations (see end-of-chapter references), the gift can then be channeled to its intended recipient. Most trusts offer arrangements that allow donors to use the gift land for their own purposes until their death.

Many land trusts have been formed in rural areas, mostly as a means to preserve farmland and make land available to beginning farmers. A few of these rural land trusts are including housing in their activities. A list of some of the more successful rural land trusts appears in the references at the end of this chapter.

## LAND TRUSTS AND HOUSING

There are few large-scale or long-established examples of community land trusts in urban areas of the U.S. One group with some practical experience to share is the Community Land Cooperative of Cincinnati, an interdenominational church-community effort in the city's West End that has already purchased several buildings, with assistance by the Institute for Community Economics and the Cincinnati Legal Aid Society. Further information about their efforts is available from CLCC at 932 Dayton St., Cincinnati, OH 45214, and from Patrick Hornschemeier, Cincinnati Legal Aid Society, 901 Elm St., Cincinnati, OH 45202.

The Cedar-Riverside PAC/Westbank CDC in Minneapolis is attempting to acquire a large block of land and housing from the city (which recently acquired it from HUD, as part of a long-standing urban renewal controversy), and is seeking to have the community land trust model incorporated into their development plans. They already have established a land trust, and if successful in their negotiations with the city's Housing and Redevelopment Authority and City Council, they will have the largest urban land trust in the country. Further information on this venture is available from the Cedar-Riverside PAC/Westbank CDC, 2000 S. 5th St., Minneapolis, MN 55454.

**Neither traditional "private" nor "public" housing, the community land trust incorporates some of the best features of each.**

Land trusts are completely compatible with housing cooperatives. As non-profit corporations, they are well situated to obtain loans and grants to support cooperative housing ventures. The use agreements for trust land can also be written to prohibit speculation and displacement in whatever improvements are made. Resale controls for housing, for instance, can obviously be included in the lease. It also would be possible to modify and expand the trust concept to include housing as well as land.

Land trusts are one of the few ownership mechanisms around which ensure that public housing subsidies, once given, are passed on to user after user, rather than being absorbed as profit by non-user owners. The benefits of low-interest Farmers Home Administration loans and HUD Section 8 subsidies, when allocated to land trust properties, are not deleted or lost when there is a transfer of leaseholders. Whatever benefits they gave the original user families are retained in reduced property prices that perpetuate access for future lower-income families.

The idea of community land trusts is just taking root in this country. The main obstacle to the spread of land trusts so far has been lack of financing for initial land purchases. There are signs that private lending institutions are shifting away somewhat from their unwillingness to fund land trusts. Government policy also has been changing for the better: the Farmers Home Administration has now opened its Section 515 Rural Rental Cooperative Loan program to land trusts as owner/developers, as well as allowing land trust leaseholder families to apply for Section 502 Rural Housing Loans. Several state housing finance agencies have followed HUD's decision to make Section 8 subsidies available for rental housing on land trust property. And Boston has become the first city to channel CDBG funds to a community land trust.

With regard to their specific relevance to the problems of gentrification and displacement, Chuck Matthei, director of the Institute for Community Economics in Boston, one of the leading land trust proponents and technical assistance providers in the country, has written as follows:

1) The core of our practical argument for CLTs is that while many traditional land and housing strategies have limited their efforts to one principal goal — providing initial access to decent housing to low-income people — this is, while still an important objective, no longer adequate by itself to meet growing needs and the current economic pressures. A strategy for today must include at least three elements. It must:

  ● provide and preserve land and housing, with security and equity, for low-income people today;

  ● provide for the transfer of land and housing from one user to the next, to insure that the same property will still be available for low- or moderate-income families, despite the rising prices of a speculative market, tight credit, and high interest rates; and
  ● create a mechanism to enable communities to develop an indigenous economic base and a capacity to meet a larger share of their own land, housing and service needs.

2) Neither traditional "private" nor "public" housing, the CLT incorporates some of the best features of each, with considerable flexibility in adapting to the various social, economic and land use units in the community. The CLT strikes a fair balance between the legitimate interests of the individual citizen or family (lifetime security of tenure; fair equity for actual earned investment; and a reasonable legacy for use of descendants) and the legitimate interests or responsibilities of the community as a whole (to ensure that these individual rights are fairly available to all of its citizens; to exercise the principal voice in long-term land use planning and the future evolution of the community; and to retain the incremental increase in the value of the land — the value created through common effort or larger economic forces — for the community, building an indigenous economic base and capacity.)

3) Adoption of the CLT model does not require a local community or community organization to alter or discard any of its previous development plans (for housing, commercial development or whatever); rather, the CLT simply adds another dimension to those plans, often increasing their long-term impact and benefit. Thus, it can be adapted to virtually any situation, preserving its character and uniqueness, but establishing an important structural, economic and political link between the various residents, businesses, and land uses in the community.

Excerpts from "Community Land Trusts" by Chuck Matthei, a chapter from the forthcoming book, *Financing Community Economic Development,* appear as Appendix C in this guide.

## REFERENCES

### HOUSING COOPERATIVES

Good starting points for information and referral to sources of assistance are:

National Association of Housing Cooperatives, 1012 14th St. NW, Suite 805, Washington, DC 20005. They have produced a technical manual, titled *Cooperative Conversion Handbook,* which HUD is scheduled to print and distribute, but when this will occur is unknown at this point. A draft copy is available from NAHC but is quite expensive ($25 for members, $50 for nonmembers); contact them for information on obtaining it or the HUD edition.

National Consumer Cooperative Bank, 2001 S St. NW, Washington, DC 20009, and its regional offices:

89 Broad St., Room 1116
Boston, MA 02110
Director: Harriet Taggart
(617) 223-5234

110 S. 4th St., Room 117
Minneapolis, MN 55401
(612) 725-2305
Director: Ann Waterhouse

1330 Broadway, Suite 1017
Oakland, CA 94616
(415) 273-7576
Director: David Thompson

c/o NY Bank for Savings
1238 Ave. of the Americas,
3rd flr.
New York, NY 10036
(212) 841-7212
Director: Philip St. George

PO Box 2730
315 King St., Suite 210
Charleston, SC 29403
(803) 724-4113
Director:
Thomas Barnwell, Jr.

221 W. Lancaster
Suite 301
Ft. Worth, TX 76102
(817) 870-5587
Director: Rene Martinez

815 Airport Way S.
Rooms 416C&D
Seattle, WA 98134
(206) 442-0706
Director: Darel Grothaus

144 W. Lafayette Blvd.
Suite 608-612
Detroit, MI 48226
(313) 226-2400
Director: Dave Friedrichs

Funding information for rural housing coops: the Housing Assistance Council, 1828 L St. NW, Suite 606, Washington, DC 20036; and Rural America, 1346 Connecticut Ave. NW, Suite 500, Washington, DC 20036.

"Operations Handbook — Rural Cooperative Housing" is one of three handbooks prepared in connection with the National Rural Cooperative Housing Demonstration, funded by HUD, the Farmers Home Administration and the National Consumer Cooperative Bank. The others deal with the legal issues involved in developing and managing rural cooperative housing, and with financing and acquiring cooperative construction and rehab. The "Operations Handbook" also lists technical service organizations for coops and national and regional coop federations and associations. The handbooks are available from the Cooperative Housing Foundation, 2501 M St. NW, 4th floor, Washington, DC 20037.

*An Introduction to Cooperative Conversions,* by Community Economics, Inc., outlines the process of converting an existing rental building to a coop. Available free from Business Services, California Dept. of Housing and Community Development, 921 10th St., Room 102, Sacramento, CA 95814. Community Economics, Inc., a highly competent community-oriented consulting firm, is located at 1904 Franklin St., Oakland, CA 94612. CEI has been involved as a technical consultant to an unusual project in Oakland, in which a group of homes were moved from the Grove-Shafter Freeway route and relocated nearby as a scattered-site cooperative, using Highway Trust Fund money from the state's department of transportation.

*Multi-family Housing: Treating the Existing Stock,* by Robert Kolodny, contains conclusions about New York City's experience with low-income tenant conversion of landlord-abandoned buildings cited in this chapter. It is available from the National Association of Housing and Redevelopment Officials, 2600 Virginia Ave. NW, Washington, DC 20037.

## WASHINGTON, D.C.'S PROGRAM OF ASSISTANCE TO HOUSING COOPS

For general information and the contents of the "right of first refusal" law, contact the Tenant Purchase Assistance Office, 1133 N. Capitol, D.C. Department of Housing and Community Development, Washington, DC 20002.

City-funded groups that advise and work with tenant groups forming coops: University Legal Services, 324 H St. NE, Washington, DC 20001; Ministries United to Support Community Life Endeavors (MUSCLE), 680 Eye St. NW, Washington, DC 20024; Metropolitan Washington Planning & Housing Association, 1225 K St. NW, Washington, DC 20005. (MWPHA has produced a well-done booklet describing the conversion process, titled "From Rental to Co-operative: A Tenant Initiative.")

## THE BEECHER HOUSING COOPERATIVE

For more information, contact Multi Family Housing Services, attn: Peter Behringer, 518 N. Charles St., Baltimore, MD 21201. They provided much of the essential technical assistance to the Beecher Low-Rise Tenants Association.

## SOCIALLY RESPONSIBLE CONDOS

Some of the more creative work in adapting the condominium form of ownership to socially useful ends has been done by the Atlanta law firm of Hyatt & Rhoads, 2200 Peachtree Center Harris Tower, Atlanta, GA 30303.

## COMMUNITY LAND TRUSTS

*The Community Land Trust: A Guide for a New Model for Land Tenure in America* (1972), is one of many informative and useful publications from the Institute for Community Economics, 120 Boylston St., Boston, MA 02116. The Institute should be considered a good general resource for groups interested in land trusts. The *Guide,* 117 pages, costs $7.50. Other items available from ICE include:

*A Model Lease Agreement* for urban community land trusts, 50¢.

*Model Community Land Trust Corporation By-Laws,* $3.

*Citizens Action Manual: A Guide to Recycling Vacant Property In Your Neighborhood* (1979), explains how community land trusts can get vacant property for use as parks, gardens, recreation areas, etc. It also

offers a step-by-step explanation of the tax advantages from donation of land or sale at reduced price to land trusts. Additionally, the *Manual* contains a good listing of resources for funding and technical assistance. It is available, free, from the Trust for Public Land, 82 Second St., San Francisco, CA 94105. TPL also has regional and field offices at 254 W. 31 St., New York, NY 10001; 219 E. 5th Ave., Tallahassee, FL 32303; Rt. 2, Box 37A, Burton, WA 98103; 401 Euclid, Room 342, Cleveland, OH 44114; 320 Paseo de Paralta, Suite I, Santa Fe, NM 87501; and 5848 Foothill Blvd., Oakland, CA 94605.

TPL is also a good general resource for information on land trusts, and offers a variety of useful publications and services:

Regional Technical Assistance Program of TPL's Urban Land Program has produced training units for use by community groups, including Neighborhood Inventory and Assessment; Neighborhood Real Estate Primer; Neighborhood Land Trust Handbook; Tax Benefit Analysis Guide; Surplus Public Land Acquisition Techniques; Participatory Open Space Planning; Participatory Site Development Guidebook; and Site Management and Maintenance Issues.

TPL also is able to provide neighborhood groups with workshops on innovative land use planning, neighborhood land-banking programs, and other topics, and can assist neighborhoods in preparing CDBG applications related to land acquisition projects.

Economic Development Strategies, a consulting group at 15 Marie Ave., Cambridge, MA 02139, has also developed some useful approaches to rural land trusts, working with the Montana Land Reliance.

The Community Land Cooperative of Cincinnati, one of the few urban land trusts involved in housing, can be reached at 932 Dayton St., Cincinnati, OH 45214, or through Patrick Hornschemeier, Cincinnati Legal Aid Society, 901 Elm St., Cincinnati, OH 45202.

The Cedar-Riverside PAC/Westbank CDC, which is seeking to acquire part of an urban renewal area in land trust form, may be reached at 2000 S. 5th St., Minneapolis, MN 55454.

Some of the more successful rural land trusts are: The Ottaquechee Regional Trust, 39 Central St., Woodstock, VT 05091, attn: Richard Karbin.

Information on agricultural trusts in Marin County, California, Mesa County, Colorado, and Jackson Hole, Wyoming, all of which emphasize purchase of easements rather than outright ownership, to make limited funds go farther, is available through the Trust for Public Land, 82 2nd St., San Francisco, CA 94105, attn: Jennie Gerard.

The Appalachian Regional Trust (officially, the Regional Land Trust for Appalachian Communities) seeks to establish an umbrella trust to spin off community trusts whose main purpose is rural housing and economic betterment. Their headquarters is Clairfield, TN 37715.

Chapter 17

Neil Miller

A FEW FURTHER IDEAS

The campaign against displacement evolves with each skirmish. In localities across the country approaches are being tried that may become familiar weapons in the near future. This chapter reviews a new legal theory and some other useful litigation steps; a program of direct financial assistance to reduce displacement; use of zoning and planning powers to require downtown commercial developers to provide housing to mitigate the increased housing demand their new projects create; and direct housing construction by community groups to make sure housing for lower-income households remains in the area.

## THE "AVERY THEORY": AN INNOVATIVE CHICAGO LAWSUIT

*Avery vs. Landrieu* is a class action anti-displacement suit brought against HUD, local government agencies, and a private developer by residents of Chicago's Uptown community. (Avery is the name of one of the plaintiffs, a community resident. Moon Landrieu was Secretary of Housing and Urban Development at the time Uptown added HUD to its list of targets). The suit challenges gentrification in the Uptown area on the grounds of economic and racial discrimination.

The Uptown neighborhood is a 20-square block area in Chicago's mid-North side. Its east and west fringes are strips of expensive high-rise condominiums and single-family homes. But the interior, known as the Heart of Uptown, houses poor white families from Appalachia, Blacks, Latinos, and Native Americans. Its location and housing stock make the Heart of Uptown a likely victim for gentrification.

The *Avery* lawsuit was triggered by a developer's proposal to build an enormous shopping-residential complex, called "Pensacola Place," on a five-acre site at the eastern edge of the Heart area. The development plan featured 100,000 square feet of expensive shops, topped off with two 40-story towers of high-income apartments. In preparation for this project, the developer (Mayor Daley's ex-son-in-law) had already destroyed a low-income residential apartment hotel and some stores, and had bought up a 120-unit building housing low- and moderate-income Black families, whose leases he terminated after announcing the building would be completely rehabilitated.

The lawsuit sought to halt all this, by pointing to "the existence of a historic conspiracy by which the city and private developers, acting in concert, fulfilled the demand for upper- and middle-income housing by the destruction of low-cost housing in 'target areas,' the expulsion of the poor persons (many of whom are racial minorities) from the target area, and the construction of expensive housing occupied by well-to-do persons, most of whom are white; [and] that this conspiracy was now being extended into the Heart of Uptown through Pensacola Place."

Furthermore, the suit charged that as a result of displacement, "the members of the plaintiff class will be forced to live in racially segregated slums," and in the process Heart of Uptown "will be changed from a racially integrated neighborhood to a neighborhood occupied almost exclusively by affluent residents who are predominantly white and do not presently live in the community." The work of the City Planning Commission and City Council in amending Chicago's zoning code to permit Pensacola Place, and to allow, even encourage,

Tony Heriza / Community Media Productions

"I have never felt comfortable anywhere else," said Sharon Agnew, a 27-year-old mother of two who has lived in the neighborhood for 20 years. "The people who live here now don't want to go anywhere else. They just want decent, affordable places to live in. It is the people with money who are trying to destroy us. They are behind all the arsons that make it impossible to find apartments you can afford. They want to turn it into a neighborhood for the rich and the collegiate."

*from "Redevelopment Stirs Fear in a Chicago Community," New York Times, February 2, 1981*

destruction of minority-occupied low cost housing, the suit charges, are sufficient "state action" to bring the matter under the coverage of federal civil rights law and the Fourteenth Amendment of the U.S. Constitution.

As James Chapman, one of the chief lawyers in the *Avery* suit, put it in an interview in the April, 1980 issue of *Chicago Lawyer*,

We said that [Pensacola Place] was part of a plan to destroy the racially integrated nature of the community. The developer could not afford to build a very expensive high-rise building and have poor black people half a block away. . . . The city and the developers want poor people and minorities out of there. The land, from their point of view, has a much higher and better use and will return large tax revenues for the city if redeveloped.

In May, 1978, the Federal District Court refused to dismiss the case, as had been requested by the developer and city officials involved in the project. Instead, the court found that the Uptown plaintiffs had both a legitimate cause of action and a basis to sue under federal law. Subsequently, the suit was expanded greatly in scope, when Uptown added HUD to the list of defendants, charging that the federal agency had acquiesced in the city's decision to withhold Community Development moneys from the area, even though it had been officially designated a Neighborhood Strategy Area (NSA). NSAs are proposed by cities and approved by HUD as priority areas for expenditure of federal housing and Community Development funds. By contrast, in Pittsburgh, Philadelphia, and elsewhere, HUD had imposed sanctions on city governments for refusing to use Community Development funds in NSAs. The Uptown plaintiffs charged that HUD's failure to take similar action in Chicago constituted an agreement to hold back public investment benefitting existing lower-income residents, and thereby aided the transformation of the neighborhood.

Subsequently, the Chicago Housing Authority was added as a defendant in the suit because of its historic refusal to provide public housing in areas of the city like Uptown (a pattern which has made CHA and HUD the subject of protracted litigation, called *Hills vs. Gautreaux*).

In early 1979, the developer offered to settle out of court, in order to avoid the delays the suit was obviously going to cause. In exchange for letting the developer off, the community's negotiators demanded — and won — important concessions and basic changes in the project plan. As approved by the court, the final

settlement agreement with the developer required:

● At least 21% of the planned new units to be subsidized Section 8 housing, with preference for occupancy given to former tenants and persons who live in the Heart area.

● Affirmative action programs to hire minority contractors and community residents for the construction work.

● Substantial modification of the original project, including reduction in the number of apartments from 1,100 to 250, and the installation of a large food market — desperately needed by the community — in place of specialty stores.

● A commitment by the supermarket to hire 60% of its 140 expected employees from the community.

● Money damages amounting to $60,000, to be allocated among former tenants who had been ejected from already acquired properties, and to a fund for costs of litigation.

The settlement with the private developer did not affect the community's suit against the city and HUD. That part of the case was referred for mediation to the Community Relations Service for the U.S. Department of Justice. After a series of meetings between the plaintiffs and the public defendants — HUD, the City of Chicago, and the Chicago Housing Authority — the mediator suggested that the plaintiffs draw up a draft consent decree, setting out the kind of settlement they would like to have. All parties reached basic agreement on the terms of a settlement, with some details still to be worked out. But just at the time of this writing, Chicago's Mayor Jane Byrne suddenly announced the city was backing out of the agreement, which, even though it had not

yet been signed, had been orally approved in open court by the city. Community residents interpret this turnabout in light of political wheeling and dealing around Chicago's ward politics, and the final outcome cannot now be predicted. The community will now press its suit before the court once again, unless an acceptable consent decree can be won.

As originally agreed to, the resolution was as follows:

● That HUD and the Housing Authority commit themselves to provide approximately 1,200 Section 8 or public housing units in the Heart of Uptown area over the next five years — about two-thirds through rehab, one-third through new construction.

● That the community have substantial control over design, production, and management of this housing.

This second point — viewed by Uptown plaintiffs as vital to the community's survival — caused some controversy. At first, HUD held out for a completely open competition in selection of Section 8 developers, ruling out direct commitment of funds to specific Uptown organizations. The community argued that standard bidding procedures would favor experienced construction and management firms over community-based developers.

The compromise reached was that the city would assist the plaintiffs to set up a land bank cooperative. The coop, acting either on its own or as the general partner to a developer, would submit proposals for projects to use the Section 8 housing allocations. Any resident of the Heart of Uptown would be able to buy a share in the coop for $6, and would then have a vote in directing the land bank's activities. A committee consisting of five representatives of the plaintiffs and five representatives of the city would screen and select proposals submitted for the Section 8 unit allocations, using criteria including the degree of community support for the proposal, whether the developer is community-based, how the proposal fits into an overall anti-displacement strategy, etc. These provisions, if eventually agreed to, seem likely to ensure a high degree of community control over future development in the Heart of Uptown.

## FURTHER USE OF *AVERY*

In the Spring of 1980, a neighborhood savings and loan association bought up 18 properties in a four-block area of Uptown, intending to convert them into high-rent apartments or condominiums. When it became apparent that there was no immediate market for such units, the bank applied for Section 8 financing, all the while investing no money in maintenance, and evicting occupants as well. Tenants organized to negotiate with the bank, but the talks quickly stalled. The tenant group then asked to join in the *Avery* suit, charging the savings and loan with participation in the same large-scale conspiracy to kick current residents out of the neighborhood, and the community agreed. Faced with this threat, the bank has reconsidered its negotiating posture and is beginning to work out an agreement with the tenant group. The experience shows again the usefulness of legal actions in giving community residents the leverage they need to bring powerful agencies and institutions to the bargaining table.

Whether the *Avery* theory and approach are useful to other communities depends in large part on the particulars of each case. Uptown activists view the following factors as important in making such a decision:

Tony Heriza / Community Media Productions

**Strong and well-organized community backing** for the litigation, especially when it comes to the need for a united front during settlement negotiations.

**Skillful attorneys** with a firm commitment to, and understanding of, the community.

**Money.** Such litigation is extremely costly, even if attorneys contribute their services or work solely for possible court-awarded fees.

**Public education** to inform both the community and the city at large about the theories and issues raised in the suit.

**Expert help** — sociologists, city planners, demographers, etc. — from universities and elsewhere.

The *Avery* attorneys and their community clients are also putting together a national network of similar cases and resources. For further information and materials about the *Avery* case and related efforts, contact the Avery Anti-Displacement Clearinghouse, 1218 W. Wilson, Chicago, IL 60640.

## A RELATED CASE IN BOSTON

A similar challenge, involving development which would break up an integrated neighborhood through displacement, has recently been filed in Boston. The suit, *Munoz-Mendoza vs. Pierce,* aims to stop the award of a $19 million Urban Development Action Grant for Copley Place, a project to be constructed on vacant land and air rights over the Massachusetts Turnpike. The development plan calls for nearly 800,000 square feet of office space, luxury hotels, luxury stores, a parking garage, and 100 housing units, 25 of which will be available to low-income households. The ripple effects of the project will displace an estimated 600-1,000 families from the nearby neighborhoods of Chinatown, the South End, and South Cove. The plaintiffs in this class action are all minority households, including a 69-year old blind Black woman who has lived in the same apartment since 1954; a Puerto Rican family of five; a Cape

Tony Heriza / Community Media Productions

Verdean woman who has lived in the neighborhood for 42 years; a Chinese-American widow who arrived from China two years ago, speaks no English, and lives around the corner from her mother. They claim that in a city which has experienced much racial tension and violence in recent years, these neighborhoods are among the very few racially integrated living areas left. And they claim that the UDAG award will intensify the essentially all-white gentrification these neighborhoods have undergone in recent years, that it will directly lead to the plaintiffs' displacement, and that it will thereby deprive them of their rights under the 1964 Civil Rights Act and the 1968 Fair Housing Act. (Further information about this suit is available from Greater Boston Legal Services, 793 Tremont Street, Boston, MA 02118, attention: Albert Wallis).

## A USEFUL MODEL CONSENT DECREE IN PHILADELPHIA

The settlement decree in *Fox vs. HUD* relates to Philadelphia's Washington Square West urban renewal area, and offers a good example of how the courts can be used to assure housing rights not only for displacees, but for the remaining residents of a disrupted area. In this case, the right to continue living in an area that is racially integrated, and not to be displaced into a segregated area, was central to the court's supportive ruling. The resolution of the litigation calls for HUD to make available Section 8 subsidies for 20 new and 111 substantially rehabilitated units, of specified sizes, with the rehab subsidies to apply only to a specific group of buildings, and the new units to be constructed on specific parcels within the renewal area. The consent decree also gives priority for occupancy of these units to the class of plaintiffs who brought the suit. Additionally, it forbids the Philadelphia Housing Authority — which is not trusted by the community — from developing or operating the housing, and requires either HUD or city funding of $147,000 for a community-based nonprofit housing development corporation in the renewal area.

(Copies of the *Fox vs. HUD* consent decree are available through Community Legal Services, Sylvania House, Juniper and Locust Streets, Philadelphia, PA 19107, attention: Harold Berk).

## EQUITY PARTICIPATION FOR LOWER-INCOME HOMEBUYERS

*Equity participation* is a program that eases purchase of houses, condominiums, or coop shares by lower-income households. It can be carried out by either a public agency or a nonprofit community support group.

Basically, equity participation is a co-purchasing arrangement, in which the sponsoring organization takes over part of a household's housing cost outlay, in exchange for an equivalent financial interest in the housing unit. Downpayment and mortgage payments are shared proportionally according to the agreement; if and when the unit is sold, any value increase (or decrease) is also shared in the same proportion.

The benefits are direct: if a sponsoring agency takes a 25% interest in a unit, for instance, the downpayment and mortgage payments the participating household will have to make will be only about three-fourths of the normal amount. (Under most such arrangements, however, 100% of property taxes, insurance, utilities, and maintenance are paid by occupants). The sponsoring agency has no decision-making power over the occupant household, being a silent partner only.

A program of this type can be amplified through built-in subsidies: tax-exempt state or local government revenue bond financing, to lower basic interest costs, or direct assistance through public grants. (A recent city-wide UDAG project application by the City of San Francisco, available through the Mayor's Office, contains such a proposal). Equity participation operations also can be pinpointed to assist specific types of households (via income limits, for example) or specific types of home purchases (rental units being bought as condos by their occupants, for example).

Tony Heriza / Community Media Productions

The State of California has recently established the Homeownership Assistance Program, to be run through local government agencies as a demonstration. The program offers equity participation to tenants wanting to purchase their units as condominiums or cooperatives, and to certain categories of mobile home owners — particularly those buying into condominium or cooperative mobile home parks. Under the program, the state will co-invest up to 49% of the purchase price, reducing downpayment costs as low as 3%. The occupant's share of the loan will be fully amortized, while the state's share will be repaid when the property is sold, thereby reducing the household's monthly mortgage payments as well. For further information about the program, contact the California Department of Housing and Community Development, 921 10th Street, Sacramento, CA 95814.

While equity participation can help prevent displacement of specific households, its overall effect raises some troublesome issues. Sponsoring agencies in essence become partners in speculation, with as much to gain from value increases as any other investor or owner. And since no additional housing is being created by these programs, the additional housing demand they create among families otherwise shut out of the market may bid up housing prices generally and fuel speculation. For an equity participation program to be an effective anti-displacement tool, it must include price and resale controls on the properties it subsidizes. And ideally, sponsoring agencies should have first option to repurchase the units in which they own shares, to ensure that they are then passed on to households that need these benefits.

## REQUIRING DOWNTOWN COMMERCIAL DEVELOPERS TO PROVIDE HOUSING, TOO

One of the serious causes of displacement, as described in the Seattle and Boston analyses in Chapter 2, is the gentrification of central business districts, when skyscrapers, hotels, convention centers and high-class shops replace older office buildings, warehouses, factories, and other less intensively used commercial space. This type of development brings in thousands of white-collar jobs, creating a tremendous additional demand for housing, which in turn pushes older residents out of

the city. In San Francisco, downtown development creates about 10,000 new jobs a year, but fewer than 1000 new housing units are built each year. While not all downtown workers live in the city, estimates from San Francisco are that the total of new units built is less than half the number of new households entering the city annually.

An obvious answer is to make those who profit so handsomely from downtown development assume some of the responsibility for the housing demand their activities create. In San Francisco, this now is being done, through use of the zoning and permit process and the powers of the Planning Commission. Under state environmental impact laws, the city is required to deal with its housing problems and can, as part of its mitigation measures, require developers to meet housing demands their building projects cause.

In the Tenderloin area, luxury hotels are building additions, and vacant and non-residential sites are being bought up for new hotels. When the Hilton, Ramada and Holiday Inn all came to the San Francisco Planning Commission around the same time, in 1980, for permission to build some 2400 units all told, the neighborhood saw the forces gathering to push them out. They also saw the possibility of using the permit process to wring maximum concessions from the hotel corporations.

Neighborhood pressure on the hotels and the Planning Commission resulted in a remarkable agreement, whereby the Ramada and Holiday Inn will create a housing subsidy fund for the neighborhood, by adding 50¢ per room per night onto 80% of the new hotel rooms (the assumed average occupancy rate for the hotels) over the next 20 years. The fund will produce $270,000 a year, or $5.4 million

over the life of the agreement. (Alternatively, if a $2.5 million federal Urban Development Action Grant for rehabbing four hotels in the area comes through, the Ramada, instead of making the 50¢ per room contribution, will provide a $3 million fund to subsidize rents in these hotels — hopefully down to $150 a month — for 15 years, and one of the four hotels will be given to a non-profit community group after 15 years.)

The two hotels also will each pay $50,000 a year for the next four years — $400,000 in all — to fund neighborhood-designated social services. And priority in 50% of the jobs at the new hotels will be given to Tenderloin residents. (The Hilton, for the moment at least, has decided to hold off on its building application.)

The agreement was completed at the end of a 12-hour Planning Commission meeting, attended at times by more than 250 Tenderloin residents, and it culminated a long and well-orchestrated community effort. According to the San Francisco *Chronicle* report, the Holiday Inn attorney (who until recently had been the long-time chairman of the city's Redevelopment Agency) "said his hotel chain had initially resisted the housing payment trade-off out of fears that its future projects in San Francisco . . . or others nationally would be held to similar requirements." Those fears, we hope, will be fully justified. Neighborhood groups in other cities should not underestimate how much protection and compensation can be squeezed out of high-profit enterprises, providing there is a strong community effort and a reasonably sympathetic public body in the middle.

It is important, too, to note the cumulative effects even partially successful neighborhood and housing preservation struggles can have. The San Francisco *Chronicle's* editorial on this agreement noted (bitterly, since, like most major dailies, it is on the side of the big developers) that "the city was prompted to action because it was still smarting from the memory of how Yerba Buena's opponents managed to cost San Francisco millions of dollars by stalling the project for years in the courts." That distorted historical reference was to a series of tenant lawsuits which led a federal court to enjoin the entire $385 million project, because the city had made inadequate provision for those being displaced, and to force a settlement on the city, the "cost" of which was a requirement that it provide over 2000 permanent low-rent units through rehabilitation or new construction. Lessons of this type are useful all around. The innovative neighborhood-hotel agreement is all the more remarkable since this time only indirect displacement is involved.

**The San Francisco Planning Commission is requiring the developer of a 43-story office tower to build 550 residential units over the next 5½ years.**

In another instance, the San Francisco Planning Commission voted to require the builders of a 43-story, $115 million office tower that will house 2500 employees to mitigate the project's impact on local housing needs by building 550 residential units over the next 5½ years. The Commission uses a formula based on employees per square foot and the presumed proportion of commuting office workers, to arrive at its mitigation figure. Half of the required units will be for low- and moderate-income tenants.

The Planning Commission initiated this approach in the Summer of 1980, and to date

has imposed housing requirements on nine downtown commercial development plans that have come before it. Nearly 1700 housing units are promised under these approved plans, although, with the one exception just cited, all will be market-rate units. One weakness of the approach is implied in the word "promised" — whereas these housing commitments are legally binding in theory, there is no time period set forth for producing the housing, and the enforcement mechanism is unclear. Assumedly, the Planning Commission or a public-interest group could sue the developer to require performance. And the fact that the same developers may again come before the Planning Commission for approval of future projects may be a spur to compliance. But the system does not hold the desired downtown development "hostage" until the housing commitment is met, or even require simultaneous work on both. It remains to be seen just how much developers will honor their legal commitments.

Up to this point, the Planning Commission has been applying these conditions on a case-by-case, discretionary basis. The City is now seeking to amend its zoning laws to make provision of housing by downtown developers a general requirement. Options for mitigating measures may also be offered: providing rent subsidies for housing in other neighborhoods, renovating existing housing, or paying money into a city housing development fund. For further information about these innovative San Francisco approaches, contact the S.F. City Planning Department, 100 Larkin St., San Francisco, CA 94102, attn: George Williams.

(Related material on "inclusionary zoning" techniques successfully employed by the California Coastal Commission is cited on page 49).

## THE COMMUNITY AS HOUSING DEVELOPER

### INQUILINOS BORICUAS EN ACCIÓN, BOSTON

Inquilinos Boricuas en Acción (Puerto Rican Tenants in Action), or IBA, is a community-based housing development and service provider group that dates from mid-1960s' resistance to Boston's massive South End urban renewal project. Parcel 19 of that project, some 30 acres containing 2,000 people, mainly Puerto Rican but with a large number of Blacks, Asian-Americans and elderly whites, was the focus of a great deal of effective protest over displacement of existing residents, including a well publicized "Tent City." IBA (under its original name, the Emergency Tenants Council — they changed their name in 1975) was formed in 1968 to develop an alternative to the Boston Redevelopment Authority's plan for Parcel 19, which would have meant destruction of the existing community and displacement of its residents, 90% of whom had low or moderate incomes. Under the motto "No nos mudarmos de la Parcela 19/We shall not be moved from Parcel 19," they put forth the following specific objectives for the area they renamed Villa Victoria:
- prevent the displacement of the residents (mainly low and moderate income) of Parcel 19, now Villa Victoria;
- develop family and elderly housing with low rents and unit sizes compatible with the needs of residents;
- create an exciting neighborhood with quality design work providing attractive and usable open spaces and a sensible traffic pattern;
- develop cultural activities to strengthen the identity of the community;
- provide support services to ensure the success of the residents in the new living environment;

• promote improvements in the economic standard of living of the residents of Villa Victoria as well as overall economic activity and commercial services;
• develop a total neighborhood with residential, institutional and commercial activities;
• guarantee long term community control over the entire area;
• mobilize public and private resources in the area to build new community facilities (schools, clinics, etc.) to benefit existing residents.

To date, IBA has achieved remarkable success in meeting these goals. They have six housing developments to their credit, plus a wide range of related community projects:

**Tremont-Shawmut:** The Emergency Tenants Council (ETC) was designated developer for Parcel 19 by the Boston Redevelopment Authority in 1969. Using an array of subsidies — the federal Section 236 mortgage interest-subsidy program, the federal rent supplement program, leased public housing funds, and proceeds from the sale of syndicated tax shelters (see more detailed discussion of this below) — they moved immediately to renovate 71 apartments in 13 rowhouses for family occupancy. ETC set up a management firm to oversee tenant selection, rent collection and maintenance, and was able to ensure that the majority of units went to former Parcel 19 residents and to other Parcel 19-ers slated for displacement. The project was completed in 1971.

**West Newton Street:** In 1969, ETC and a Black South End community group, the South End Tenants Council, helped organize tenants of a slumlord on West Newton Street to withhold rents and demand city intervention to bring the buildings up to code. Under city and community pressure, the landlord finally sold the properties to the Boston Housing Authority. The 136 units in the 25 West Newton Street buildings were finally rehabbed in 1973

Nick Thorkelson

under a "Turnkey II" agreement with the Housing Authority. The rehab was not done by ETC, which did not have jurisdiction outside their Parcel 19 area, but by another community-oriented development entity. The buildings were turned over to the developer for rehab, and the rehabbed buildings were then sold back to the Housing Authority. Subsequently, under an additional, precedent-setting agreement, ETC's management firm, rather than the Housing Authority, took over tenant selection and management, a move which again ensured that the original residents could return to their renovated buildings.

**Torre Unidad:** With two development projects under their belt, mainly for Puerto Rican and Black families, ETC/IBA set out on an ambitious project to build new housing, to meet the needs of elderly white residents of the neighborhood. The result was a new 19-story

tower, containing 201 apartments, completed in 1974. The project used seed money from local non-profit groups and construction financing from the Massachusetts Housing Finance Agency. Once built, Torre Unidad (Unity Tower) was sold to the Boston Housing Authority under a "turnkey" agreement, with ETC's management firm continuing to run the project.

**Viviendas La Victoria I:** This was IBA/ETC's first attempt at building new family housing. The development, completed in 1976, includes 73 apartments and 108 townhouses (with 54 three-, four- and six-bedroom houses among them). Financing was provided through the federal Section 236 interest-subsidy program and through proceeds from syndication of the tax shelters, and the Section 8 program provides long-term operating subsidies. The quality of IBA/ETC's work, com-

bined with Boston's low-rent housing shortage, generated 1300 applications for the 181 units.

**Casa Borinquen:** IBA/ETC's fifth project, completed in 1977, was rehabilitation of 36 family apartments in nine scattered-site rowhouses. Financing and subsidization were accomplished through the Massachusetts Housing Finance Agency and the Section 8 program.

**Viviendas La Victoria II:** This project, delayed for a couple of years by lawsuits filed by a neighborhood pro-gentrification organization which opposes more subsidized housing in the area, will consist of 31 renovated apartments, in eight rowhouses, and 159 new townhouses, again with lots of large units. It will be largely completed by the end of 1981. A low-interest $250,000 loan from the Ford Foundation's Local Initiatives Support Corporation is part of

the initial financing, which also includes Section 8 and so-called Section 11(b) bonds issued by the Housing Authority. This project will complete revitalization of the old Parcel 19. Five thousand applications have been received for the 190 units.

In total, IBA/ETC over the past 13 years has built or renovated 489 units of low- and moderate-income housing, and 190 more are nearing completion. All the housing, plus another 164 units developed by others (the West Newton Street project and a 36-unit HUD-owned "distressed" project, of the type discussed on pages 118-126) are managed by IBA's management subsidiary. Some 3,000 people now live on what was Parcel 19, nearly 50% more than its population at the onset of urban renewal.

The diversity of financing mechanisms, development approaches and building types that comprise Villa Victoria, as well as the

groups served by it, are overwhelming. The housing is sensitively designed, around a Spanish-style plaza with trees and an arcade. As the Boston *Globe's* architectural critic described it in 1977:

> There is a sense of neighborhood focus . . . Villa Victoria comes to an intense focus at its center, where a covered, arched shopping arcade and several pedestrian streets meet at a plaza that is obviously where the action is. As you approach, you begin to feel you're on someone else's turf and had better watch your behavior . . . Part of Villa Victoria's strength is its ethnic solidarity. No one pretends that Puerto Ricans don't run the place, though many other groups share it.

The Boston *Herald-American* characterized Villa Victoria as "a first-class and very sophisticated piece of development," and it won an award from the Boston Society of Architects.

In line with its original goals statement, IBA has gone beyond the provision of satisfying, affordable shelter. In the office building they developed and own, they operate a wide range of community-oriented programs: social services to families and the elderly; day care for 58 children; residential security and crime prevention; cultural/educational programs (music, visual arts, a summer program for children, festivals, and communications, including a small cable TV station); technical assistance to other community housing developers, and commercial development.

The social services program includes translation, information, one-to-one counselling, and advocacy work for residents. Social therapy also is available through social workers on the IBA staff and workers from the Family Services Association of Greater Boston who are placed at IBA. It also coordinates services with other providers in the area and maintains a referral and follow-up system in the areas of health, education, welfare, and legal services. Special services aimed at the elderly include

197

recreation, homemaking, a visiting nurse, medical checkups, hot lunch and nutrition, and occupational therapy. Services are adapted to the variety of ethnic and racial backgrounds of the resident population, which includes significant numbers of Puerto Ricans, Asian-Americans, Blacks and whites. One of the initial commercial development ventures was the opening of a laundromat.

Funding sources for IBA's non-housing programs are as varied as the source of its housing subsidies: CDBG funds, United Way, CETA, private foundations and corporations, the Department of Education's Bureau of Nutrition, Title XX, the Massachusetts Council for the Arts and Humanities, the National Endowment for the Arts, the Law Enforcement Assistance Administration, and service fees.

All in all, Inquilinos Boricuas en Acción and its various subsidiaries are a $3-million-a-year operation, with nearly 100 full- and part-time employees, the majority of whom are Villa Victoria residents. Construction and rehabilitation activities have created nearly 1,000 temporary jobs. In 13 years, IBA has grown into New England's largest Hispanic-controlled private non-profit organization.

One of the more remarkable features of this thoroughly remarkable venture has been the true community control that has characterized all of IBA's work. Membership in IBA is restricted to area residents. This membership elects a board of directors, also restricted to residents, at an annual community congress. IBA's two subsidiary corporations — one a non-profit that engages in the initial stages of housing development, the other a for-profit corporation that undertakes the bulk of housing development efforts and property management, and is the general partner of the syndi-

Inquilinos Boricuas en Acción

cated partnership that owns the housing — have interlocking boards composed of IBA board members and outsiders with technical skills and relevant experience.

IBA has drawn on a wide variety of architectural, legal, economic, and housing consultants throughout its work. One key group has been Greater Boston Community Development (GBCD), which as development consultant to IBA has helped identify the most appropriate subsidy program for each phase of housing, prepare applications for public agencies, and negotiate subsidy commitments. GBCD has also helped structure and market one of the most significant features of IBA's operation, its form of ownership. All of IBA's

housing (except Torre Unidad, which, as noted, was conveyed to the Housing Authority under a "turnkey" arrangement) is owned by limited partnerships, with IBA as managing general partner, making all decisions regarding management and investment in upkeep. The other "silent" partners are wealthy private investors seeking to shelter otherwise taxable income from taxation, through rapid artificial "paper" depreciation the tax laws allow housing and other capital goods. Through a process known as "syndication," such investors will pay lots of cash in order to join the partnership and become eligible for a share of this depreciation shelter.

IBA has used the money raised in this manner to invest in programs for the community and special amenities for its housing: landscaped yards, parquet wood flooring, a roof garden, wall-to-wall carpeting, the plaza that is the social and architectural focus of Villa Victoria. The use of these tax shelters by and for community groups is a difficult, two-edged issue. Used creatively, they obviously provide substantial benefits to community groups, and in some cases represent the only way a housing venture can move ahead. On the other hand, they are a major loophole in the tax system, enabling doctors, dentists, lawyers, and others with overblown incomes to escape their rightful share of taxes, which, if paid, could provide the money communities need for housing and other programs. Something clearly is wrong with a system that permits communities to meet their needs only if they sell tax avoidance schemes to the rich.

This (non-trivial) problem aside, IBA represents perhaps the most successful community-based housing development venture in the country. For more information, contact them at 405 Shawmut Ave., Boston, MA 02118.

## THE BERNAL HEIGHTS COMMUNITY FOUNDATION, SAN FRANCISCO

At a very different scale from Inquilinos Boricuas en Acción is the much newer Bernal Heights Community Foundation (BHCF), located in an area at the southern end of San Francisco's Mission District. BHCF has undertaken a more modest housing effort, in the context of an overall plan for community control in this mixed neighborhood of 7,000 households.

Bernal Heights is basically a low- and moderate-income neighborhood, about one square mile in size and very hilly: it rises from a sea level base to a 400-foot elevation at its highest point. It is largely a family community, with lots of seniors and children, and is evenly split between renters and homeowners. The city's diverse ethnic population is blended in Bernal Heights, not in separate enclaves, but in very fine grain house-by-house integration. Thirty-nine percent of the neighborhood's population is Latin, 31% white, 12% Black, 9% Filipino, 3% Chinese, and 1% each Japanese and American Indian. As with many of the city's in-lying and topographically and architecturally interesting neighborhoods, the gentrification pressures are mounting.

Bernal Heights has a long history of struggling to preserve itself. In the mid-60s and early 70s, residents successfully fought off an effort by the San Francisco Redevelopment Agency to bulldoze hundreds of Bernal homes. They later fought to preserve the open space atop Bernal hill, in the face of threatened industrial development.

It was a move by development speculators in the northwest part of the area that began the recent community control campaign in 1976. Developers and a bank applied for permits to build eleven shoe-box style houses on one block of Elsie Street, a steep and narrow substandard street. If implemented, the development would have created a 275' × 50' wall on the downhill side and a threat to the lives and property of nearby residents, due to inadequate fire and emergency vehicle access on the block. A further peril was the prices at which the proposed houses were to be marketed, well beyond existing price levels, thereby pushing the speculation spiral on the hill.

The residents' response was to reorganize the Northwest Bernal Block Club to fight the proposed development. When the speculators refused to modify their plans, the block club carried the battle to the sympathetic City Planning Commission, and won a moratorium on further development in the area, plus the right to put forth a non-threatening development proposal through a process of grass-roots organizing. The result was the highly sophisticated, 140-page *Elsie Street Plan,* which lays out detailed design, cost and energy guidelines to ensure that new construction on the hill will be affordable as well as compatible with existing patterns, preserving the rich architectural variety and human scale of the current neighborhood. The Plan also contains a street improvement plan for the safe development of the Elsie Street block that had been the subject of so much controversy.

In July, 1978, the San Francisco City Planning Commission took the remarkable step of passing the *Elsie Street Plan* into law, and establishing a unique model of neighborhood government to go with it, the Neighborhood Building Review Board. The Board, elected by neighborhood residents, holds statutory power over future development of a portion of Bernal Heights. While the Planning Commission rejected the neighborhood's proposed guidelines for controlling speculative profits, it formally accepted their design and energy guidelines as the criteria by which the Board would judge development plans, and these were instituted as the operating rules for Planning Commission determinations in the area. It is believed to be the first instance of such decentralized neighborhood planning powers in the nation. In 1979, the Northwest Bernal Block Club expanded its guidelines to propose the concept of inclusionary zoning, requiring that 25% of all new development on the street be affordable by low- and moderate-income residents.

Since its inception, the Review Board has functioned effectively, securing beneficial changes in developers' proposals, and has approved ten of eleven development projects brought before it. The *Elsie Street Plan* and its spinoffs struck a very responsive chord in the city bureaucracy and in the media, and the group's work in general has been highly and favorably publicized in the city.

The success of the Northwest Bernal Block Club triggered more block clubs in the neighborhood and rejuvenated old ones. Fights against speculative, unsafe development were launched by other block clubs, and several other sub-neighborhood plans were produced by these groups, including the *East Slope Plan,* which also has been officially adopted by the San Francisco Planning Commission, and the Powhattan Strip Plan, now in process.

The *Elsie Street Plan* called for formation of a community development corporation to enable direct neighborhood involvement in the preservation and construction of low- and moderate-income housing and the provision of community services in Bernal Heights. In late 1978, the Bernal Heights Community Foundation was founded to meet this need. The Foundation's board represents all parts of the

Neil Miller

neighborhood. In three years it has grown from an organization with one paid staff member, and an annual budget of $5,000, to a staff of twelve, including eight VISTA volunteers, and a budget of $563,000. Like IBA in Boston, funding comes from a wide variety of sources, eliminating a vulnerability that characterizes many neighborhood organizations dependent on a single funding agency or pot of money. Apart from VISTA support, BHCF has received Section 8 housing subsidies, city CDBG, open space, cultural and senior program funding, and numerous private foundation grants for preparation of plans and implementation of specific neighborhood improvement projects.

One of the Foundation's major projects is development of a new Bernal Heights Neighborhood Center, in two adjacent buildings acquired with a $500,000 CDBG grant. The center, now being rehabbed, will house a range of community services. Another major Foundation project is neighborhood organizing and planning, aimed at expanding membership in various organizations in the area and completing grass-roots sub-area plans for other parts of the hill. The Foundation also has sponsored and provided technical staff to a variety of neighborhood improvements by Bernal residents. Neighborhood volunteers have built mini-parks and playgrounds, planted trees and community gardens, constructed step-walks on the steep hills, and organized hill-wide cleanups.

The Foundation's housing work has three elements: small-scale new construction, capital improvements necessary before large-scale housing production can begin, and rehabilitation. In 1979, BHCF acquired a 11,000-square foot lot, and by the end of 1981, using California Housing Finance Agency financing

Janet Fries © 1980

*Model of proposed solar houses on the slopes of Bernal Heighs in San Francisco.*

and Section 8 subsidies, construction should be completed on four low-income units. A non-profit corporation, with residents of the units holding a majority of seats on the board of directors, will own and manage the project. The Foundation also holds an option on a single-family house and adjacent lot as its next construction/rehab project, and is investigating acquisition of some of the 150 neighborhood sites they have catalogued as suitable for small-scale development. If the City of San Francisco's UDAG proposal for equity participation financing (discussed earlier in this chapter) is implemented, that would give the Foundation the ability to carry out in-fill construction for lower-income households on a broader scale. BHCF also is working on the possibility of a scattered-site coop as a means of facilitating development through amalgamation of the large number of dispersed in-fill lots on the hill.

The Foundation also is looking at the possibility of large-scale new construction on two sites. One is appropriate for about 25 single-family housing units for low- and moderate-income families. The other is suitable for

mixed use development of 40-50 units of low- and moderate-income family and senior housing, plus open space, recreation facilities, and commercial storefronts. In both cases, development is being thought of as part of an overall neighborhood plan, with major capital improvements, in the one case to ensure safe vehicular and pedestrian access and sufficient city services, in the other to demolish a vacant bowling alley and initiate the development over an existing underground parking facility. An active block club in that part of the neighborhood has begun to pressure the owner to allow interim neighborhood development and community use of the open portion of the site for recreation activities. They also have written a set of guidelines for development of the site. The City Planning Commission, when it formally adopted the *Elsie Street Plan,* also mandated production of a Bernal Heights Capital Improvement Plan, focusing on improvements necessary for the development of affordable housing in the area, including streets, sidewalks, step-walks, utilities, parks, drainage, etc. Preparation and implementation of this plan is a necessary precondition to larger housing development in the area.

The third component of the Bernal Heights Community Foundation's housing program is self-help rehab. The group plans to use the city's $1.6 million rehabilitation finance pool to establish a $150,000 revolving loan fund, from which they will make 10-20 loans, ranging from $3,000-12,000, to low- and moderate-income homeowners and renters. The fund will offer sliding scale low-interest and deferred payment loans (not due until the building is sold), to correct real hazards, such as crumbling foundations, faulty wiring, leaky roofs and poor plumbing, encourage long-term energy efficiency through weatherization and solar retrofitting, and make improvements to adjust for increased family size. In addition, the Foundation will establish a self-help weatherization and solar retrofitting counselling service. A door-to-door survey in one part of the hill indicated that 52% of the households interviewed were ready to participate in such a program. The Foundation's position is that the inability of current residents to pay for such repairs often causes them to sell and move off Bernal Heights, and that programs to reduce energy costs also can result in neighborhood stability.

Unlike previous code enforcement efforts, the program will be strictly voluntary. And any rehab package for rental units would require approval from both landlord and tenants, and would include rent control and lease-eviction protections.

How to develop innovative financing and ownership forms to combat pressure on housing costs, and ensure permanent affordability, is one of the Foundation's central concerns. BHCF will be exploring joint ventures with private developers, limited-equity and scattered-site cooperatives, use of special assessment districts, deed restrictions to limit resale profits, equity participation, syndication, and joint ownership by residents and a neighborhood nonprofit corporation.

Operating carefully, building their base, and integrating housing, planning and social service programs, the Bernal Heights Community Foundation offers a useful and successful model for other neighborhoods. For further information, they can be reached at 399 Cortland Ave., San Francisco, CA 94110.

## REFERENCES

The Avery Anti-Displacement Clearinghouse is a national network of cases and resources similar to the *Avery vs. Landrieu* case. They can be reached at 1218 W. Wilson, Chicago, IL 60640.

Information about the Boston case, *Munoz-Mendoza vs. Pierce,* which challenges displacement that disrupts racially integrated neighborhoods, is available from Greater Boston Legal Services, 793 Tremont Street, Boston, MA 02118, attn: Albert Wallis.

*Fox vs. HUD,* the consent decree issued in Philadelphia, is available from Community Legal Services, Sylvania House, Juniper & Locust Streets, Philadelphia, PA 19107, attn: Harold Berk.

Equity participation information is available from the California Department of Housing and Community Development, 921 10th Street, Sacramento, CA 95814. San Francisco's to date unfunded UDAG proposal for equity participation subsidies is available through the Mayor's Office, City Hall, San Francisco, CA 94102.

Information on San Francisco's innovative requirement that downtown office developers provide housing is available from the S.F. Planning Department, 100 Larkin St., San Francisco, CA 94102, attn: George Williams. Specific information on the housing agreements signed with the hotel developers, and related "downzoning" efforts to limit the invasion of the tourist industry into this residential hotel neighborhood, is available from the North of Market Planning Coalition, 295 Eddy St., San Francisco, CA 94102.

For further information on community-based housing developers, contact Inquilinos Boricuas en Accion, located at 405 Shawmut Ave., Boston, MA 02118. A good background document on the important issue of how ETC/IBA got organized and how it is run, is the June, 1979 case study, "Community Control Model," HUD Technical Assistance Control No. H-4370, available from IBA.

The Bernal Heights Community Foundation is located at 399 Cortland Ave., San Francisco, CA 94110.

Chapter 18

WRAPPING IT ALL UP

The principal lessons we hope this guidebook has provided for community groups are:

**1.** Make sure you have analyzed fully and correctly the displacement problem you are facing. The reasons displacement pressures are building up usually have to do with broader economic, social and political forces affecting your area, which often are region-wide in scope. Unless you begin to understand those forces and root your anti-displacement work in that analysis, it is unlikely that you will be able to develop effective and durable strategies to counter the displacement push. The kind of background analysis undertaken by local groups in Seattle and Boston, outlined in Chapter 2, should be done in all communities.

**2.** Build coalitions and alliances. Displacement rarely is an isolated phenomenon, affecting only one block or even one neighborhood. An understanding of the forces underlying displacement pressures necessarily implies the need to link up with other neighborhood and housing groups, and with city- and region-wide and national groups, such as trade unions, religious organizations and social action agencies which share your concerns and can join the fight. References to state-wide housing organizations in California, New Jersey, and Massachusetts are given at the end of Chapter 9. Some helpful experience in building city-wide coalitions may be available from the Seattle Displacement Coalition (619 N. 35 St., Seattle, WA 98103), which consists of city-wide and neighborhood housing groups, individuals, and sympathetic church, labor, and civil rights organizations. SDC began as an anti-redlining group, then moved to broader activities, with city-wide housing forums and conventions. It works to shift CDBG funds to housing, amend land-use and zoning ordinances to encourage more housing construction for lower-income households and prevent housing demolition, pass condominium conversion restrictions, and enact tenants' rights legislation.

**3.** Act now! Unless displacement forces are countered early, fighting them may be impossible or unnecessarily difficult. One problem in developing a quick response is that, unlike earlier forms of displacement from the 1950s and 1960s, where the "federal bulldozer" came in and uprooted whole areas for urban renewal and highway projects, newer forms of displacement are less dramatic, with a less visible cause. Undermaintenance, abandonment, and gentrification all creep in slowly, largely unannounced. And so it is harder to rally people and to grasp what is happening. One of the values of coalition work and linkage with other groups is being able to learn from each other's experience and be able to read the handwriting on the wall. There is no substitute for timely action.

**4.** Employ a wide variety of strategies. As the previous chapters have shown, there is an enormous range of strategies community groups can use: drafting and passing legislation, bringing lawsuits and administrative complaints, demonstrating, negotiating, lobbying, building/rehabbing/managing their own housing, doing research and surveys, counselling, and many others. And these strategies must be pursued, as appropriate, on the local, state and national levels. Particularly effective is forceful, direct action, either in holding on to one's turf or taking over resources the community needs to maintain itself. The People's Firehouse group in Brooklyn (Chapter 8) and Milton Street's "walk-

*City Life / Vida Urbana, Boston*

*Boston*

*You are not alone. Across the country, people just like you carry on the anti-displacement campaign. Sometimes, leaning out your window, with a sign telling the landlord you're as important as he is, or spreading the word from the front porch, with only your cat for company, it gets lonely. Look around. Take a step forward. There are your neighbors — insisting on safe living conditions, united for low-income housing, and fighting for your community.*

*Shelterforce*

*Cleveland*

*Metropolitan Council on Housing*

*New York City*

GERAGHTY
WE WANT
DECENT LIVING
CONDITIONS
JUST LIKE
YOU!

*Boston*

NO MORE
EVICTIONS
FIGHT FOR
OUR HISTORIC
JAPANESE
COMMUNITY

*San Francisco*

*Washington, D.C.*          *Portland, Oregon*

LET US
DECIDE
WHAT'S BUILT
IN OUR
NEIGHBORHOOD

in homesteaders" in Philadelphia (Chapter 7) show the power of people dealing with their own problems directly.

**5.** Finally, to repeat a point made at several places in the guidebook: ultimately, displacement of people who lack economic and political power will not be halted without a major shift in the society's priorities. We believe that people have a *right* not to be displaced from their homes and neighborhoods, and that *decent, affordable housing is a human right.* As such, it must take precedence over the "right" to profit from housing. As long as profit-making is paramount in the development, ownership and management of housing, and it is more profitable for those who own property to undermaintain or abandon it, speculate in housing, convert their rental units into condominiums, raise rents to "what the market will bear," undertake luxury rehabilitation, or evict tenants arbitrarily, people will be displaced. Aggressive action by community groups can in some cases stop these forces or slow them down, as we have shown. But the only truly effective anti-displacement measures, the only ones that can stop our national scandal of 2½ million displacees annually, must get to the root of the problem. And that means *control* over our housing and communities, not by outsiders looking to maximize their profits, but by the people who live there.

Gaining acceptance for a *right* to decent, affordable housing will be a long haul, of course. What such a program might look like is suggested in the document prepared by Boston's All City Housing Organization, titled "Toward a Housing Platform for the People of Boston." ACHO grew out of that city's rent control and anti-displacement movement

205

and quickly realized the need to broaden their analysis and program. While it is not a document that any major U.S. city is likely to enact in the immediate future, the ACHO draft platform represents the kind of visionary, comprehensive, detailed program needed to ensure an end to forced displacement and assurance of housing rights for all Americans. (Those wanting further information about ACHO and its platform should contact Kathy Gannett, 38 Lindsay St., Dorchester, MA 02124.)

## ALL CITY HOUSING ORGANIZATION
## TOWARD A HOUSING PLATFORM FOR THE PEOPLE OF BOSTON

The members of the All City Housing Organization (ACHO) believe that all people have a right to:
- decent, affordable, and secure homes
- stable (not static or exclusionary) neighborhoods
- adequate portions of society's wealth for improving our housing
- a safe and open city
- control of their homes and their neighborhoods.

Yet thousands of Boston's residents are being forced to pay more than they can afford for housing, to leave their homes, to live in substandard conditions, or to leave the City completely. When the economic interests of the housing and financial industries conflict with the rights of the people to housing, these rights are denied. Government, which should protect the people, protects the economic interests instead. [The details of this conflict between people's needs and the powers of industry and government are presented in ACHO's background paper, "Boston's Housing Crisis," portions of which are excerpted in Chapter 2.]

Since private industry and the present government refuse to plan for the needs of the people for housing, we must ourselves build a comprehensive housing platform. This document is a first step toward that goal. This draft platform recognizes and deals with the interrelated forces that lead to displacement, and unites the diverse constituencies that must work together to stop it. The platform proposes a unified group of measures to protect our homes, protect our neighborhoods, improve our housing, build a safe and open city, and increase

popular control of our homes and neighborhoods. It recognizes that the struggle for housing cannot be fought in isolation, but must be waged together with fights for jobs, for community development that benefits community residents, and against discrimination.

Even those in government admit that the private housing market cannot provide us with our rights to housing. Ultimately housing must be owned by and for the people. Present forms of public management and control of housing clearly will not meet our needs. As a first step in the continuing struggle to obtain our rights to housing, this platform calls for improved management of public housing and increased reliance on housing that is "socially owned" by the public or by community development corporations, tenant unions, non-equity co-ops, or neighborhood councils. Regardless of the owner, though, "socially-owned" housing must be owned by those direclty accountable to the residents, operated solely for the benefit of the residents, restricted to permanent use by low- and moderate-income families, and prohibited from resale on the private market. This platform also calls for devoting an adequate portion of society's resources to the people's needs for housing, and allocating such resources on the basis of need.

### I. PROTECTING OUR HOMES

Few Bostonians can afford the cost of new housing. Thus existing affordable housing, whether privately or publicly owned, must be preserved, despite the economic interests that would in some neighborhoods abandon it, and in others convert it to high-priced housing for those returning to the "New Boston." Tenants and homeowners need protection both from these economic forces and from the increasing costs of energy and inequitable taxation that beset us all.

### A. MAKE MULTI-FAMILY HOUSING AFFORDABLE FOR TENANTS

All privately-owned multi-family housing should be treated as a "public utility" and strictly regulated to prevent gentrification, disinvestment, and displacement. If privately-owned housing cannot meet the people's needs for housing, it should be converted to a form of social ownership.

1. Strengthen rent and eviction controls
   — end "vacancy decontrol" in Boston, and roll back rents on decontrolled apartments
   — extend coverage of Boston's rent control system to include all multi-family housing

— extend coverage of rent control to so-called "luxury" housing
— allow rent increase only for unavoidable, proven increases in operating costs and property taxes, with automatic decreases for cost reductions or for failure to provide services, maintain the property, or meet tax payments
— prohibit rent increases for luxury renovations unless agreed to by tenants in advance
— allow evictions only for just cause; prohibit evictions for non-payment of rent due to lack of job or income
— provide landlords the opportunity to turn their housing over to a form of social ownership, if they do not choose to or cannot provide adequate housing under these conditions.

2. Control condomania
   — ban evictions for condo conversions
   — ban conversions when the vacancy rate of rental housing is below 8%
   — provide present tenants (first as a group, then

individually) with the first option to purchase in all sales of multi-family buildings.

3. Step up code enforcement

— vigorously enforce housing and building codes, rent withholding, repair-and-deduct, and receivership laws, to ensure safe and sanitary housing

— have the City correct major code violations, recovering costs through direct collection of rent payments or liens on property

— vigorously enforce existing methods of taking buildings for back taxes

— enact new programs to enable the City to immediately acquire vacant properties or properties in substantial violation of regulatory measures, to assume existing mortgages, and to repay the owner over time for a negotiated equity value.

4. Stop arson-for-profit

— require smoke detectors in all dwelling units and common areas

— authorize immediate cancellation of insurance

Nick Thorkelson

City Life / Vida Urbana, Boston

on arson-prone buildings owned by absentee landlords

— require arson-related costs (relocation, boarding, demolition) to be financed from insurance proceeds.

5. Fight discrimination in housing

— discrimination and racism are rampant throughout our housing system. Our unified program for combatting racism and discrimination is detailed below under "Building a Safe and Open City."

6. Strengthen disclosure and enforcement of controls on multi-family housing

— require all owners of multi-family housing to register with and be licensed and approved by a City "Home Protection Board," responsible for overall enforcement of regulatory measures, and authorized to revoke licenses for non-compliance

— require public disclosure of all registration and compliance information (including data on rent control, code violations, condo conversion status, fair housing practices, tax delinquency, and fire insurance).

### B. *GUARANTEE HOMEOWNER SECURITY*

Resident homeowners with low or moderate incomes should be encouraged and assisted to maintain and improve their properties, provided that the benefits of such improvements accrue to the residents of the buildings and to the neighborhoods. Residents who meet with economic hardship should have the right to stay in their homes and neighborhoods if they so desire.

1. Stop real estate speculation

— require public disclosure of all private offerings of houses for sale

— implement a speculation tax to discourage rapid resale by absentee owners (with a high tax rate on briefly-owned property, falling to zero over a period of years, and with an increasing rate with increasing profit)

— require full disclosure to a prospective buyer of the previous selling price and the documented cost of repairs.

2. Encourage home improvement

— expand and revise home improvement programs for repairs to bring the property to adequate standards of habitability, or for improvements to decrease energy consumption, to provide direct government grants or loans at low or zero interest to resident homeowners with low or moderate incomes, in exchange for voluntary participation in the Home Protection Board's regulations described above for multi-family dwellings.

3. Provide freedom from default
— enable homeowners, long-term residents of their neighborhoods, who default on mortgage payments because of loss of jobs paying low or moderate wages, to turn their houses voluntarily over to the City, in return for the ability to remain as tenants in their homes.

4. Stop redlining and other discrimination in lending
— strictly enforce the Community Reinvestment Act
— require community reinvestment to benefit low- and moderate-income residents of the community
— closely monitor lending practices of banks and other financial institutions with regard to discrimination on the basis of geographical location, race, sex, or marital status.

5. Strengthen rights to home insurance
— require insurers to cover at least 80% of the replacement cost of a home.

6. Reduce the burden of regressive property taxation
— recognize the hardship placed by property taxes on people with low or moderate incomes by granting them abatements based on need
— support and strengthen the principle of "tax classification" that lowers assessments on residential property vs. those on industrial or commercial property.

## C. IMPROVE AND PROTECT PUBLIC AND SUBSIDIZED HOUSING

Almost 20% of Boston's residents live in publicly-owned, Boston Housing Authority housing, or in privately-owned, publicly-subsidized apartments under state or federal programs. Existing public housing should be upgraded and preserved as a major resource for people with low and moderate incomes. Existing privately owned, publicly-subsidized multi-family housing should be upgraded and preserved as an additional resource for these people.

1. Rebuild Boston's public housing
— create a massive public housing rehabilitation and reconstruction program to provide jobs and

*City Life / Vida Urbana,* Boston

decent housing. Obtain funds as outlined under "Improving Our Housing Supply" below.

2. Eliminate vacancies
— eliminate deferred maintenance; modernize and rehabilitate vacancies to return all units to habitable condition
— encourage "sweat equity" and tenant control of repairs.

3. Stop resale for profit
— forbid private resale to profit-making landlords of public and FHA housing
— turn public housing over to forms of "social ownership" if, in the short run, the Boston Housing Authority is not able to provide necessary services
— restrict deeds to subsidized housing to ensure continued use as lower-income housing; prohibit private resale
— provide public and community-based groups with the first option to purchase.

4. Stop demolition
— do not demolish structurally sound units
— provide one-to-one replacement of public housing units when demolition is unavoidable.

5. Strengthen control by tenants; encourage community-based ownership
— strengthen tenant input at all levels of decision-making
— prohibit discrimination against subsidized tenants in mixed-income buildings
— eliminate mortgage debts for existing community-based owners who are willing and able to maintain their properties and be accountable to

project residents, in exchange for social ownership of the property.

6. End discrimination and racial violence in public housing
— see "Building a Safe and Open City" below.

7. Control rents and profits on subsidized housing
— strictly enforce regulations on rents, conditions, and profits in subsidized housing
— require capital contributions from private owners in exchange for tax shelter or syndication benefits they already received
— foreclose immediately in case of default on mortgage or regulatory commitments.

8. Repair and maintain, and renegotiate the cost of, publicly-acquired housing

For all housing acquired through tax and code enforcement proceedings or bought through the Neighborhood Stabilization Fund (see below), the City should:
— repair and rehabilitate the units to achieve decent, safe, and sanitary conditions
— renegotiate mortgage terms with private lenders to reduce interest rates, extend repayment terms reflecting lower market values (where the market is depressed), and require lenders to absorb losses out of reserves as a business risk
— maintain the housing in public ownership or transfer it into social ownership at no costs (and debt-free) to community-based, non-profit organizations.

9. Provide adequate housing subsidies; favor grants in place of subsidies
— provide subsidies so that no one must pay more than he or she can afford for housing
— calculate subsidies to reflect true ability to pay, based on income and family size
— include all utility costs in rent payments, or subtract utility costs from tenants' shares of rent payments
— tie future use of housing subsidies to forms of socially-owned housing
— gradually phase out subsidy payments in favor of direct grants for socially-owned housing.

## D. REDUCE THE BURDEN OF ENERGY COSTS

1. Protect those who can't afford to pay
— prohibit shut-off of electricity, phone, gas, oil, to people who cannot pay their bills.

2. Encourage conservation and self-reliance
— provide financial and technical assistance for weatherization and conversion to "alternative" energy sources
— require owners of multi-family housing to undertake weatherization programs.

3. Build community self-reliance in energy
— promote municipal utilities
— organize small-scale energy production for localities (windmills, water power)
— increase research on renewable energy sources.

4. Control the major providers of energy
— strictly regulate or nationalize all private utilities and energy companies
— pay special attention to "padding" of costs by "construction work in progress" and similar charges
— oppose nuclear power as too costly and too unsafe a "solution" to our energy problems.

## II. PROTECTING OUR NEIGHBORHOODS

The choices of locations for major capital investments by government, big business, and institutions are the principal causes of massive displacement. With $10 billion in major projects eventually planned for downtown, the Southwest Corridor, Mission Hill and Tufts medical centers, and all sections of Boston's Waterfront, the issue will soon no longer be whether people with low and moderate incomes can remain in their neighborhoods, but whether there will be room for them anywhere in the "New Boston." By the end of the decade, Boston's residential patterns may approach those of many Third World or European cities, with the poor and minorities commuting from their homes in outlying slums to low-wage service jobs in the gentrified inner-city "core."

To counter this trend, low- and moderate-income residents of neighborhoods must gain increased control over major development and land use decisions, to prevent destruction of viable neighborhoods and to maximize benefits to the residents.

### A. *OPPOSE DESTRUCTIVE PROJECTS*
— provide no public assistance (UDAG, CDBG, tax breaks, zoning changes) to any development . . . which will cause substantial displacement, job loss, or other negative effects (e.g., noise or air pollution) on low- or moderate-income communities.

City Life / Vida Urbana, Boston

### B. *PROVIDE NEIGHBORHOOD CONTROL*
— give democratically-elected neighborhood organizations veto power over large-scale development or institutional expansion planned for their neighborhoods. These groups should be involved in every step of planning and implementation of large-scale development, as in the Southwest Corridor Project currently in construction.

### C. *NEIGHBORHOOD STABILIZATION PLAN*
— require a Neighborhood Stabilization Plan from city, state and federal governments to offset potentially negative effects on residents with low and moderate incomes, including specific mandatory provision of housing subsidy funds, jobs and training commitments, plus set-aside of development profits, construction costs, or tax revenues to fund anti-displacement programs.
— ensure community approval of the Neighborhood Stabilization Plan.

### D. *USE PUBLIC LAND AND BUILDINGS FOR PUBLIC PURPOSES*
— require development and reuse of publicly-owned land and buildings to be consistent with community needs and to provide maximum benefit to people with low and moderate incomes, such as reusing schools and other public facilities for socially-owned housing, and redeveloping industrial sites to provide stable jobs at prevailing union wages for residents with low and moderate incomes.

### E. *CREATE OR RETAIN UNION-WAGE JOBS*
— use public regulation and incentives such as CETA and UDAG funds to encourage urban location or expansion of firms providing stable jobs at prevailing union wages for people with low and moderate incomes
— discourage or prevent plant closings and relocations which threaten the viability of low- and moderate-income communities
— require all publicly-assisted housing and community development to provide a definite proportion of construction and permanent jobs at prevailing union wages for low- and moderate-income residents of the locality, minorities, and women.

### F. *PUT THE NEEDS OF THE COMMUNITY FIRST*
— allocate community development funds to particular neighborhoods based on need, with specific uses to be determined by residents of the community
— provide housing options in other communities, for families with low or moderate income, to provide advantages in jobs, location, and services, without diminishing the prior commitment to preserve and improve existing working-class neighborhoods.

209

## III. IMPROVING OUR HOUSING SUPPLY

The coming of age of the "baby boom" generation and the continued loss of existing housing require expanded construction and rehabilitation of housing for poor and working people. Yet this new housing is held hostage to demands of developers and financial institutions for maximum profits and to monetary, fiscal, and social policies of government.

Furthermore, the cost of new housing . . . is beyond the reach of most people. Resources exist in this society to provide this housing. For example, a transfer of 10% ($15 billion) of the national Defense budget to the construction of new housing would provide 300,000 units of *debt-free* housing nationally, including 8-10,000 for Massachusetts. The State tax on high incomes proposed below could provide $1 billion in direct public grants for housing construction, providing an additional 20,000 units in Massachusetts, doubling the present rate of construction and meeting the state-wide

*City Life / Vida Urbana, Boston*

shortfall in new housing construction estimated by the state Dept. of Community Affairs. By providing direct grants instead of loans for new housing, one of the largest costs of new housing could be avoided — the "middleman" costs of interest paid to private financial institutions.

### A. *CONSTRUCT NEW AND REHABILITATE OLD HOUSING*

New construction and rehabilitation of housing for families with low or moderate incomes should be provided, and financed in ways that reduce the dependence of housing on credit and the control of private financial institutions.

1. Meet the people's housing needs
   — ensure that all publicly-assisted housing production is for the exclusive benefit of people with low or moderate income
   — provide funding and units on the basis of housing need and non-exclusionary principles
   — plan housing to meet the special needs of families, children, the elderly, and the handicapped
   — allocate sufficient resources to family housing, traditionally ignored in Boston's housing policies.

2. Phase out banking "middlemen"
   — phase out current mortgage credit and tax-exempt bond financing for new construction and rehabilitation
   — create a program of direct public grants and direct loans at zero or low interest rate
   — channel funds through public agencies (like the Massachusetts Housing Finance Agency or the Boston Housing Authority), to developers of community-based, non-profit housing.

### B. *USE A FAIR SHARE OF SOCIETY'S WEALTH TO MEET OUR HOUSING NEEDS*

Adequate funds will be needed for: new construction and rehabilitation grants; extra rent subsidies; public acquisition of foreclosed housing; repair and rehabilitation costs for homeowners, FHA, and public housing; adequate funds for city housing enforcement agencies, such as the Home Protection Board. To provide these increased funds for housing and community development programs:

1. Start a Neighborhood Stabilization Fund
   — A Neighborhood Stabilization Fund (NSF) should be established. (Such legislation has already been submitted to the state legislature.) The principal source of funds for the NSF should be from capital investment, profits, and tax revenues generated by major development projects costing over $10 million. Any major project would be assessed a percentage of the front-end construction cost; profits generated by the development or its lessees; state tax revenues (sales, hotel, meals taxes, etc.)

generated by the project; any money paid to the State Dept. of Corporations and Taxation as part of a 121A special tax agreement
   — Boston should also apply for a special UDAG grant of at least $20 million to initially fund the NSF, as a 1-to-2 match for private, state, and city funds set aside or assessed from major development projects.

2. Restrict use of UDAG funds
   — restrict the City's UDAG applications to neighborhood-oriented jobs and housing development that will benefit poor and working people
   — the City should not apply for, nor should HUD approve, UDAG funds for downtown commercial,

*City Life / Vida Urbana, Boston*

luxury housing, or hotel development such as Copley or Lafayette Places, or the Immobilare luxury housing complex on the Charlestown Waterfront
   — no UDAG money should be given to any developer unwilling to guarantee the Boston residents' job policy at prevailing union wages for any construction or permanent jobs generated by the proposed development.

3. Use CDBG funds to strengthen the neighborhoods
   — a percentage of CDBG funds equal to the percentage of Boston's low- and moderate-income residents living in public housing should be directly

provided to maintain and improve public housing

— a fair proportion of CDBG funds should benefit tenants as well as homeowners

— housing and community development planning should reflect the priority of enabling people with low or moderate incomes to remain in stable, viable, but non-exclusionary communities with adequate services and public facilities that are responsive to the community's needs.

— give priority in allocating all housing funds and only allocate community development funds (e.g., CDBG and UDAG) for preventing displacement (caused by gentrification and disinvestment) and for improving the viability of communities for those with low and moderate incomes. Funds should be used for rehabilitating existing housing, building new low- and moderate-income housing, and upgrading public facilities and services (e.g., mass transit, police, schools, day care, commercial facilities) that serve the needs of the community.

4. Use public employee pension plan funds

— require investment of a portion of public employees' pension funds in publicly-assisted housing production, through existing public finance agencies or a newly-created state housing development bank

— use UDAG or CD money to ensure an adequate return to the pensioners.

5. Reform property taxes

— oppose extreme tax-cutting measures like Proposition 2½ that will hurt lower-income people by forcing drastic cutbacks in the state and local services on which they rely

— reduce the regressive residential property tax and replace it with progressive state taxes on wealth, business, and the banking and insurance industries, thus requiring no cuts in the existing level of local government expenditures and services

— close the loopholes in the regressive property tax system by eliminating:

— property tax breaks for developers

— property tax and interest deductions for *high-income* homeowners

— real estate depreciation deductions for developers

— place new progressive taxes on income, wealth, and corporate profit, such as an additional tax of

5% on after-tax incomes greater than $25,000 in Massachusetts.

6. Reallocate currently available federal tax revenues away from socially harmful or wasteful spending priorities to housing and other socially necessary priorities.

— cut defense spending by 10% and use the proceeds to build new housing.

## IV. BUILDING A SAFE AND OPEN CITY

Discrimination in housing, arising from racist policies ignored by the government, of insurance companies, the real estate industry, and banks, has limited housing choices for people of color and controlled the

*City Life / Vida Urbana*, Boston

areas in which they can live. Other people are often discriminated against because of their age, sex, family or marital status, or sexual preference. Control of people's lives, because of their color or otherwise, must end, and active steps must be taken to reverse this history of repression. At the same time, viable neighborhoods of people of color must be protected from gentrification.

### A. *END DISCRIMINATORY HOUSING PRACTICES*

To end block-busting and reverse block-busting, steering, and denial of housing:

1. Improve enforcement of current civil rights laws

— simplify the complaint process for discrimination

— establish an aggressive investigative team that will not only respond to complaints but will also "police" real estate companies.

2. Strengthen laws and regulations

— provide stronger punishment and higher (than the present $1000 maximum) damages for those found guilty of discrimination

— require real estate agencies to publish listings to be distributed, and to keep uniform listing books for all customers

— eliminate the exemption of owner-occupied dwellings from the Fair Housing Law of 1964

— include marital status and discrimination against children in federal law.

### B. *PROTECT NEIGHBORHOODS OF PEOPLE OF COLOR*

1. Support neighborhoods of people of color as viable places to live

— ensure that "redevelopment" benefits current residents

— enforce affirmative action in hiring.

### C. *PROTECT PEOPLE OF COLOR IN ALL NEIGHBORHOODS*

1. Actively oppose violence against people of color

— provide adequate protection

— require prompt and accountable responses from police in case of trouble.

— have public officials immediately decry acts of violence against people of color.

2. Remove support from those who discriminate

— withdraw all federal funds from communities that have exclusionary zoning

— withdraw funds from community organizations

that endorse violence against people of color or that ignore civil rights laws.

3. Take affirmative action to create housing opportunities

— support the Tenants' Policy Council plan for voluntary desegregation of public housing
— increase low- and moderate-income housing in equal proportions in the cities and in the suburbs.

## V. INCREASING POPULAR CONTROL OF OUR HOUSING AND COMMUNITIES

No single community or neighborhood can hope to come to grips with the overall housing needs of society. The government can best determine these needs and ensure that they are met. But past experience with public housing has shown that centralized control over the operation of housing is prone to political favoritism, mismanagement, and eventual decay. Providing all residents of the City with more immediate control over their homes through social ownership will be the surest safeguard that Boston's housing stock is adequately maintained. Similarly, since the neighborhoods are recognized as one of Boston's greatest strengths, the residents who have made the neighborhoods great must have maximum control over the future of their neighborhoods, consistent with the overall needs of society.

A. *STRENGTHEN CONTROL BY RESIDENTS OVER THEIR HOUSING*

— establish the right of tenants to collective bargaining with their landlords
— provide financial assistance to tenant groups

B. *INCREASE COMMUNITY CONTROL OVER CDBG AND OTHER FUNDS*

— establish locally-elected councils to determine how CDBG funds should be spent in each neighborhood
— guarantee minimum allocation of funds to each neighborhood
— provide for a City-wide Neighborhoods Council

C. *PROVIDE NEIGHBORHOOD HOUSING TO MEET A NEIGHBORHOOD'S NEEDS*

— allocate funds for housing construction on a priority basis to public and community-based developers of socially-owned housing; private developers must be approved by residents of the project and/or neighborhood, with strict regulation of profits and requirement of option to purchase by public or community-based groups for

social ownership, after construction is completed
— ensure that all publicly-assisted housing production meets community needs and standards for design, unit size, site location, construction, and management, and is approved by poor and working-class residents of the housing or neigborhood.

D. *PROVIDE ADEQUATE FINANCIAL AND TECHNICAL ASSISTANCE TO COMMUNITY GROUPS*

— guarantee a core of staff to locally-elected councils
— provide adequate financial support of and technical training for community groups planning to develop or operate socially-owned housing.

*City Life / Vida Urbana*, Boston

## REFERENCES

Three excellent visual presentations on the displacement problem, available for rent or sale, are:

*We Will Not Be Moved,* a 30-minute slide show, with sound, about Cincinnati's Over-The-Rhine area, produced by the Community Media Workshop, 125 Superior Ave., Dayton, OH 45406.

*It's Not a House . . . It's My Home,* a 30-minute videotape documentary about the Boston area, available from the Urban Planning Aid Media Group, 120 Boylston St., #523, Boston, MA 02116.

*Mission Hill and the Miracle of Boston,* a 60-minute film on how the "New Boston" and some of its major medical complexes have displaced old-time residents. Available from Cine Research Associates, c/o Richard Broadman, 28 Fisher Ave., Boston, MA 02120.

*Neighborhood Self-Help Case Studies* (1980). This book contains abstracts of 54 case studies written by neighborhood organizations about projects they have successfully undertaken to revitalize their communities. An order form is provided to get free copies of each of the case studies. Available from HUD Office of Neighborhoods, Voluntary Associations and Consumer Protection, Washington, DC 20410; order by HUD's number HUD-NVACP-618.

HUD, through the Urban Institute, is evaluating the 125 neighborhood organizations that received grants under the first two rounds of the Neighborhood Self-Help Program, with 15 being looked at intensively to see what are the characteristics that enable them to carry out projects and function well internally. Interim reports on this two-year study should be available by late 1981. For further information, contact the Div. of Community Conservation Research, HUD, Washington, DC 20410, attn: Joel Friedman.

*The Politics of Rural Housing: A Manual for Building Rural Housing Coalitions* (1980), available from the Housing Assistance Council, 1025 Vermont Ave. NW, #606, Washington, DC 20005.

The Planners Network is a nationwide organization of progressive urban planners, community organizers and academics that may be able to provide help to community groups facing the threat of displacement. Contact them at 1901 Q St. NW, Washington, DC 20009.

Two national organizations that have been active in anti-displacement work are:

The National Urban Coalition, 1201 Connecticut Ave. NW, Washington, DC 20036. Among their recent useful publications are *A Compendium of Anti-Displacement Strategies* (1981) and *Neighborhood Transition Without Displacement: A Citizens' Handbook* (1979), $6.

The National Association of Neighborhoods, 1651 Fuller St. NW, Washington, DC 20009.

Boston's All City Housing Organization can be reached through Kathy Gannett, 38 Lindsay St., Dorchester, MA 02124.

The Seattle Displacement Coalition can be reached at 619 N. 35 St., Seattle, WA 98103.

photograph © 1978 Ken Light

# Appendix A
## AREA OFFICES:
### U.S. DEPARTMENT OF HOUSING AND URBAN DEVELOPMENT

15 New Chardon St.
Boston, Mass. 02114
(617) 223-4111

1 Financial Plaza
Hartford, Conn. 06103
(203) 244-3638

Statler Bldg.
107 Delaware Ave.
Buffalo, N.Y. 14202
(716) 855-5755

Gateway 1 Bldg.
Raymond Plaza
Newark, N.J. 07102
(201) 645-3010

666 5th Ave.
New York, N.Y. 10019
(212) 399-5290

Federico Degetau Federal Bldg.
Chardon Ave.
Hato Rey, P.R.00918
(809) 753-4201

Two Allegheny Center
Pittsburgh, Pa. 15212
(412) 644-2802

Universal North Bldg.
1875 Pennsylvania Ave. NW
Washington, D.C. 20009
(202) 673-5837

Two Hopkins Plaza
Baltimore, Md. 21203
(301) 962-2121

Curtis Bldg.
625 Walnut St.
Philadelphia, Pa. 19106
(215) 597-2645

701 E. Franklin St.
Richmond, Va. 23219
(804) 782-2721

230 Peachtree St. NW
Atlanta, Ga. 30303
(404) 221-4576

Daniel Bldg.
15 S. 20th St.
Birmingham, Ala. 35233
(205) 245-1617

Children's Hospital Foundation Bldg.
601 S. Floyd St.
Louisville, Ky. 40201
(502) 582-5251

Jackson Mall
Avenue West
Jackson, Miss. 39213
(601) 969-4703

415 N. Edgeworth St.
Greensboro, N.C. 27401
(919) 378-5363

1801 Main St.
Columbia, S.C. 29201
(803) 765-5591

1111 Northshore Dr.
Knoxville, Tenn. 37919
(615) 637-9300

Peninsular Plaza
661 Riverside Ave.
Jacksonville, Fla. 32204
(904) 791-2626

Patrick McNamara Federal Bldg.
477 Michigan Ave.
Detroit, Mich. 48226
(313) 226-7900

1 N. Dearborn St.
Chicago, Ill. 60602
(312) 353-7660

151 N. Delaware St.
Indianapolis, Ind. 46207
(317) 269-6303

6400 France Ave.
Minneapolis, Minn. 55435
(612) 725-4701

200 N. High St.
Columbus, Ohio 43215
(614) 469-7345

744 N. 4th St.
Milwaukee, Wis. 53203
(414) 291-1493

2001 Bryan Tower
Dallas, Tex. 75201
(214) 749-1601

410 S. Main Ave.
San Antonio, Tex. 78285
(512) 229-6800

1 Union National Plaza
Little Rock, Ark. 72201
(501) 378-5401

Plaza Tower
1001 Howard Ave.
New Orleans, La. 70113
(504) 589-2063

200 NW 5th St.
Oklahoma City, Okla. 73102
(405) 231-4891

2 Gateway Center
4th and State Sts.
Kansas City, Kans. 66117
(816) 374-4355

Univac Bldg.
7100 W. Center Rd.
Omaha, Nebr. 68106
(402) 221-9301

210 N. 12th St.
St. Louis, Mo. 63101
(314) 425-4761

Executive Towers
1405 Curtis St.
Denver, Colo. 80202
(303) 837-4513

300 Ala Moana Blvd.
Honolulu, Hawaii 96850
(808) 546-2136

1 Embarcadero Center
San Francisco, Calif. 94111
(415) 556-2238

2500 Wilshire Blvd.
Los Angeles, Calif. 90057
(213) 688-5973

520 SW 6th Ave.
Portland, Oreg. 97204
(503) 221-2561

403 Arcade Plaza Bldg.
1321 2d Ave.
Seattle, Wash. 98101
(206) 442-7456

334 W. 5th Ave.
Anchorage, Alaska 99501
(907) 272-5561

# Appendix B
# PROPOSED AFFORDABLE HOUSING ORDINANCE FOR SAN FRANCISCO

The following ordinance was placed on the November, 1979 ballot, through the initiative process, by a coalition of housing-concerned organizations called San Franciscans for Affordable Housing. It was an attempt to draft and enact a comprehensive local approach to meeting the city's housing needs. Proposition R, as it was labelled on the ballot, contained controls over rent increases and conversion of rental units into condominiums; limited eviction of tenants from rent-controlled units to "just cause"; controlled housing speculation through specific anti-speculative provisions in the rent control mechanism; and provided mechanisms for increasing the supply of housing (by shifting a portion of the hotel tax to a housing subsidy fund; creating a municipal bond program to assist in the development, rehabilitation and purchase of low- and moderate-income housing; shifting Community Development Block Grant funds to housing production; and using surplus city land and buildings for housing — all to be produced by neighborhood-based housing development corporations). The processing of building permits was expedited, and "in-law apartments" encouraged. The city's Board of Supervisors (city council) was directed to take further steps to control housing speculation. Homeowners' improvements were also encouraged by limiting verification inspections on permit work to the work for which the permit was taken out.

The ordinance was defeated 41%-59%, in large part because several months before the election the City acted to head it off by passing weak rent control and condo conversion control ordinances. An analysis of the Prop. R campaign may be found in the Fall, 1979 issue of *Shelterforce,* available from 380 Main St., E. Orange, NJ 07018.

**Be it ordained by the people of the City and County of San Francisco:**

**TITLE I: STATEMENT OF PURPOSE**

The purpose of this ordinance is to remedy serious housing problems which endanger the public health and welfare of the people of San Francisco, especially senior citizens, people on fixed incomes, and people with low and moderate incomes who are forced to spend an excessive percentage of their income for housing.

This ordinance will address these housing problems in a unified and comprehensive manner, ease the hardship caused by these serious housing problems, protect and provide housing for low- and moderate-income persons, increase new housing construction, preserve the character of the existing housing stock and assure that housing costs are at fair and reasonable levels which, in the case of rental housing, allow landlords a fair and reasonable return on investment.

**TITLE II: DEFINITIONS**

In this ordinance:

A. The **Base Rent** for any controlled unit is the lowest rent charged for that unit between November 1, 1978 and October 31, 1979, plus that percentage of the rent charged on November 1, 1978 equal to the percentage increase in the Rental Component of the Consumer Price Index from November 1, 1978 to October 31, 1979. If no rent was in effect on November 1, 1978, the base rent shall be the rent first charged for that unit after November 1, 1978, plus that percentage of the rent first charged after November 1, 1978 equal to the percentage increase in the Rental Component of the Consumer Price Index from the date the rent was first charged to October 31, 1979. In no case, however, shall the base rent be greater than the rent in effect for the controlled unit on November 1, 1979.

B. **Board** means the Rental Housing Board established by this ordinance.

C. **Commissioners** are the members of the Rental Housing Board.

D. A **Controlled Unit** is any residential rental unit except:

1. A unit used primarily for non-residential purposes;

2. A unit which is governmentally owned, operated or managed or in which a governmentally subsidized tenant resides if state or federal laws or regulations exempt that unit from municipal rent control and an actual conflict exists;

3. A unit in a hotel where that hotel was as of June 1, 1979, and still is, operated primarily for transient guests staying less than 30 days and the unit is not the tenant's primary residence. Once a tenant has resided in the hotel for 30 days or longer, and the hotel is the tenant's primary residence, the unit occupied by the tenant shall be controlled for the tenant's remaining length of stay in the hotel, notwithstanding that the hotel may be operated primarily for transient guests. No landlord shall attempt to recover possession of such unit in order to avoid having the unit defined as a controlled unit.

4. A unit in a hospital, convent, monastery, extended-care medical facility, asylum, non-profit home for the aged, dormitory owned and operated by an educational institution for the housing of students, or a non-profit stock cooperative unit occupied by a shareholder of the cooperative whose total stock is substantially equivalent to the proportion of total building space occupied by the shareholder's unit;

5. A unit subject to a fixed term rental agreement in effect on the effective date of this ordinance, until the rental agreement expires or is terminated, except that any unit having a fixed term rental agreement entered into between April 15, 1979, and the effective date of this ordinance shall be controlled unless the landlord of the unit, on petition to the Board, can show that the lease was not entered into to circumvent the provisions of this ordinance, Chapter 37 of the Administrative Code or Ordinance No. 181-79 of the City and County of San Francisco;

6. A unit in a two- or three-unit structure in which at least one unit is owner-occupied; and

7. A newly constructed unit which is completed and offered for rent for the first time after the effective date of this ordinance, except for new units constructed on land where formerly stood a residential building demolished pursuant to a permit applied for between June 1, 1979 and the effective date of this ordinance.

E. A **Disabled Person** is any person who has a physical impairment which substantially limits one or more major life activities, such as caring for oneself, performing manual tasks, walking, seeing, hearing, speaking, or breathing.

F. **Financing Costs** are the entire amount of loan costs, including interest, principal payments and all other fees and expenses associated with the loan.

G. **Hotel** is any hotel, motel, inn, roominghouse, boarding house, or tourist home.

H. **Housing Services** are those facilities and services which enhance the use of a residential rental unit, including but not limited to repairs, replacement, maintenance, painting, heat, hot and cold water, utilities, elevator services, locks, patrols and other security devices, storage, janitorial services, refuse removal, pest control, furnishings, and kitchen, bath, laundry, and recreational facilities in common areas.

I. A **Landlord** is an owner, lessor, sublessor, or any other person or entity entitled to receive rent for the use of a residential unit, or his, her or its agent, representative or successor.

J. A **Low-Income Person** is a person whose income meets the U.S. Department of Housing and Urban Development guidelines under Section 8 of the Housing Act of 1937, 42 U.S.C. § 1437f(f)(2).

K. A **Moderate-Income Person** is a person whose income meets the U.S. Department of Housing and Urban Development guidelines under Section 8 of the Housing Act of 1937, 42 U.S.C. § 1437f(f)(1).

L. A **Neighborhood-Based Housing Development Corporation** is a non-profit corporation the majority of whose membership or governing body are residents of the neighborhood where activities assisted by the Housing Development Corporation are to be carried out.

M. **Net Cost Increase** is a unit's proportionate share of increases in costs of maintenance and operating expenses, property taxes and fees, and the cost of capital improvements including financing costs for each improvement (amortized over the useful life of each improvement), minus any decreases in these costs, except that only half of the registration fee imposed by the Board may be included.

N. **Refinancing Costs** are those financing costs for a loan secured by the property containing the controlled unit, where the loan was not obtained pursuant to a sale of the property.

O. **Rent** is the consideration demanded or received for the use of a residential rental unit, including but not limited to that demanded or paid for use, occupancy, parking, pets, furnishings, housing services, subleases, or deposits.

P. A **Rental Agreement** is any verbal, written, or implied agreement between a landlord and a tenant for the use or occupancy of a residential rental unit.

Q. **Rental Component of the Consumer Price Index** means the Residential Rent Component of the Consumer Price Index for All Urban Consumers for the San Francisco/Oakland Standard Metropolitan Statistical Area issued by the United States Department of Labor, Bureau of Labor Statistics.

Computations of the increase in the Consumer Price Index for any time period shall be made using the most recent index issued before the beginning of the time period and the most recent index issued before the end of the time period.

R. A **Rental Vacancy Survey** is a survey of all residential units in San Francisco that are decent, safe and sanitary and immediately available to the general public for non-transient rental occupancy. This survey shall be done by or on behalf of the Board, according to generally accepted statistical procedures, and shall make use of all available relevant data.

S. A **Residential Rental Unit** is any unit in San Francisco rented for residential use, together with the land, buildings, and housing services supplied in connection with its rental.

T. A **Sale** is:

1. Any conveyance, transfer or grant of title to real property;

2. Any contract or lease which has substantially the same effect as a conveyance, transfer or grant of title; or

3. Any contract for such conveyance, transfer or grant under which possession of the property is given to the buyer, or any other person designated by the buyer.

U. A **Tenant** is any renter, successor to a renter's interest or any other person entitled to the use or occupancy of a residential rental unit.

**TITLE III: RENTAL HOUSING BOARD**

A. ***Composition.*** There shall be a Rental Housing Board with the same number of members as the Board of Supervisors. It shall be elected by district in the same manner as the Board of Supervisors, except that there shall be no runoff election. The members shall be subject to the same eligibility, disclosure and recall provisions as the Board of Supervisors. Every year the Rental Housing Board shall elect one of its members to serve as chair.

B. ***Term of Office.*** Except as provided below, each member of the Board shall be elected to serve a four-year term to run concurrently with the term of the Supervisor in the district from which the member is elected. The first election for the Board shall be held at the June, 1980 election, and each member's initial term shall expire on the expiration date of the term of the Supervisor from that member's district. Thereafter, elections for members of the Board shall be held at the same time as the elections for the members of the Board of Supervisors.

C. ***Interim Board.*** Within 14 days of the certification of the election results for the November, 1979 general municipal election, each member of the Board of Supervisors shall appoint one person residing in his or her district to serve as a member of an interim Board. The interim Board shall act as the Board, and shall be subject to the same eligibility and disclosure provisions as the Board of Supervisors. Its members shall serve until the first election of the Board. All actions of the interim Board, except for final actions on petitions, shall be temporary and interim and subject to approval by the first elected Board.

D. ***Powers and Duties:*** The powers and duties of the Rental Housing Board shall include but not be limited to the following:

1. To require and administer registration and reregistration of all controlled units and charge fees for registration and other services provided by the Board;
2. To oversee and administer the stabilization of rents, the setting of base rents, the rent adjustments based on net cost increases and the civil remedies provided for in this ordinance;
3. To adjudicate petitions concerning whether or not a unit is controlled, excess rent payments, the base rent for a controlled unit and any other matters authorized by the Board;
4. To promulgate rules and regulations reasonably necessary to the execution of its responsibilities under this ordinance;
5. To permit individual rent adjustments either upward or downward, as are shown to be fair and equitable, either on an individual or consolidated basis;
6. To preserve low- and moderate-income housing through the control of demolition;
7. To delegate its powers to hearing examiners and individual Commissioners except as otherwise provided;
8. To determine if a residential rental unit is a controlled unit or not;
9. To make such studies, surveys and investigations, and to conduct hearings to obtain information necessary to carry out its responsibilities;
10. To administer oaths, subpoena witnesses and documents, seek civil and injunctive relief and enforce the spirit and provisions of this ordinance;
11. To reinstate rent controls suspended pursuant to Section I(2) of Title IV; and
12. To take such other actions as are necessary and proper to the execution of its powers and responsibilities and to further the purposes of this ordinance.

E. ***Financing:*** In order to help pay for its operations, the Board shall charge fees for the registration of all controlled units and fees for the filing of petitions before the Board and other services provided by the Board, except that filing fees may be waived on a declaration under penalty of perjury of inability to pay. The Board for the first year of its operation may impose on each landlord a registration fee of up to $5 a year for registration of each controlled unit. The Board may adjust registration fees annually to reflect any increased or decreased costs of operation. The City and County of San Francisco shall advance and guarantee the Board's operating costs for the first year, but the Board shall fully reimburse the City and County of San Francisco out of its revenues.

F. ***Rules and Regulations:*** The Board, after prior public notice and at least one public hearing, may adopt, amend, repeal and supplement rules and regulations. In the absence of such rules or regulations the business of the Board shall be conducted in accordance with generally accepted principles of administrative law, with special regard to preserving the rights of all parties. Rules and regulations regarding petitions brought pursuant to this ordinance shall include, but not be limited to the following:

1. ***Hearing Examiners:*** The Board shall appoint hearing examiners to conduct hearings on petitions. Hearing examiners shall have the power to administer oaths and affirmations.
2. ***Notice and Right to be Heard:*** When a petition is filed by a landlord or tenant the Board shall send a copy to the opposing party within 10 days. The hearing officer shall notify all parties as to the time, date and place of hearing. Both the landlord and the tenant of a controlled unit shall have the right to be heard at the hearing. All hearings shall be open to the public.
3. ***Right of Assistance:*** All parties to a hearing may have assistance from anyone of their choice.
4. ***Records:*** The hearing examiner may require any party to the hearing to produce any relevant books, records, papers, or other documents. All documents required under this Section shall be made available to the parties involved at the office of the Board prior to the hearing.
5. ***Hearing Record:*** The Board shall compile an official record which shall constitute the exclusive record for decision on the issues at the hearing. The record of the hearing shall include: all exhibits, papers and documents required to be filed or accepted into evidence during the proceedings; a list of participants present; a summary of all testimony accepted in the proceedings; a statement of all materials officially noticed; all recommended decisions, orders and/or rulings; all final decisions, orders and/or rulings, and the reasons for each. Any party may have the proceeding recorded or otherwise transcribed at his or her expense.
6. ***Quantum of Proof and Notice of Decision:*** No decision shall be issued unless supported by a preponderance of the evidence. All parties to a hearing shall be sent a timely written notice of the decision and a copy of the findings of fact and law upon which the decision is based. At the same time, parties to the proceeding shall be notified of their right to appeal and to judicial review.
7. ***Consolidation:*** Petitions concerning units in the same building or development may be consolidated for hearing.
8. ***Appeal:*** Any person aggrieved by the decision of the hearing examiner may appeal to the Board. On appeal, the Board may conduct a new hearing, may rule on the basis of the official record without holding a hearing, or may take any other appropriate action.
9. ***Timing of Decision:*** The rules and regulations adopted by the Board shall provide for action by a hearing examiner on any petition within 90 days following notice to the opposing party by the Board of the filing of the petition.
10. ***Finality of Decision:*** The decision of the hearing examiner shall be the final decision of the Board unless timely appeal is made to the Board. The decision of the hearing examiner shall not be stayed pending appeal. In the event that the Board on appeal reverses or modifies the decision of the hearing examiner, the parties shall be restored to the position they would have occupied had the hearing examiner's decision been the same as the Board's.

G. ***Publication:*** Rules, regulations, forms and pamphlets issued by the Board shall be written in an easily understood manner and published in English, Spanish and Chinese.

H. ***Public Records:*** All documents of the Board or its subordinate officers shall be public records and open to inspection at the Board's office, except that the Board shall keep confidential from anyone other than parties to an action income tax records and other personal financial information the disclosure of which would constitute an invasion of privacy. Board documents may be copied for the cost of the copying, but anyone may copy documents involving a case to which he or she is a party without payment on declaration under penalty of perjury of inability to pay.

I. ***Rent Control Docket:*** The Board shall maintain a Rent Control Docket at its office, which will contain listings of all actions taken by the Board and of all petitions filed with the Board and the action taken on them.

J. ***Publicity:*** The Board shall provide adequate publicity concerning the provisions of and the rights provided under this ordinance. That publicity shall include, but is not limited to, periodic distribution of information concerning the Rental Component of the Consumer Price Index and the distribution of a pamphlet which sets forth the rights of landlords and tenants under this ordinance in a brief and easily understood manner. The Board shall make this pamphlet available to landlords of controlled units, and each landlord shall be obligated to provide it to his or her tenants as soon as practical.

K. ***Meetings:*** The Board shall meet as often as necessary, in public and according to a published schedule; a substantial portion of these regular meetings shall be held on evenings and weekends. Additional meetings of the Board shall be on the demand of five Commissioners. Seven Commissioners shall constitute a quorum for all business, and all decisions except as otherwise specified shall be taken by a majority of those present and voting.

L. ***Compensation:*** Each Commissioner shall receive $50 for every meeting attended which lasts for five hours or more in a single day. The Board shall not meet more often than necessary to carry out its duties and responsibilities under this ordinance. The Commission shall adopt rules to allow for payment of an appropriate portion of this compensation for meetings lasting less than five hours.

M. ***Staff:*** The Board may employ on a temporary or permanent basis consultants, legal counsel and staff, including an executive director, hearing examiners and inspectors, as necessary to perform its responsibilities and to fulfill the purposes of this ordinance. The executive director, hearing examiners and inspectors may, to the extent allowed by law, be exempt from the civil service provisions of the Charter of the City and County of San Francisco.

**TITLE IV: RENT CONTROL**

A. ***Temporary Rent Stabilization:*** Rents for controlled units shall not be increased between the effective date of this ordinance and February 1, 1980.

B. ***Registration:*** By February 1, 1980, landlords of controlled units shall register such units with the Board on forms provided by the Board. The form shall include: the current rent for the unit; the rent in effect for the unit on November 1, 1978, and any lower rent charged between November 1, 1978 and October 31, 1979; the rent in effect on November 1, 1979; the housing services provided; the address of the rental unit; the name and address of the landlord and agent, if any; the name and address of someone residing within the City and County of San Francisco authorized by the landlord to accept notices, orders, petitions or subpoenas from the Board; and such other information as the Board deems appropriate. No landlord may increase rents for any controlled unit unless it is registered.

C. ***Maximum Rent:*** Beginning on February 1, 1980, the maximum rent on any controlled unit shall be the base rent, unless the landlord has made a rent adjustment based on net cost increases under Section D of this Title or has received an individual rent adjustment under Section E of this Title.

D. ***Rent Adjustment Based on Net Cost Increases:***

1. Beginning February 1, 1980, the maximum rent on any controlled unit may be increased to cover net cost increases since November 1, 1979 not already passed on to the tenant in a rent adjustment under this Title. This rent increase may not be more than the percentage increase in the Rental Component of the Consumer Price Index since the last rent adjustment. Rents may only be adjusted under this Section if no other rent adjustment under this Title was made in the preceding 12 months. If a landlord wishes to increase rent more than the amount allowed in this Section, the landlord may request an individual rent adjustment under Section E of this Title.
2. Rents may only be increased under this section if the tenant is given 30 days written notice. The notice shall contain the following information:
   (a) the base rent;
   (b) the nature and amount of net cost increases;
   (c) whether or not the unit has been properly registered in accordance with this ordinance and other rules and regulations promulgated by the Board;
   (d) a statement that, upon the tenant's request, the landlord will make available for inspection, at a reasonable time and place, documentary evidence of the net cost increase;
   (e) a statement of the tenant's right to petition the Board under Section E of this Title to contest the landlord's figures;
   (f) a statement of the percentage increase in the Rental Component of the Consumer Price Index since the last adjustment of rent under this Title; and
   (g) any other information required by the Board.
3. The landlord must furnish documentary evidence of the net cost increase to the tenant within 10 days of a tenant's written request. If the request is made more than 14 days before the effective date of the increase, it shall not become effective until such evidence is furnished.

E. ***Individual Rent Adjustment:*** The Board, on the petition of a landlord or a tenant of a controlled unit, may make an upward or downward adjustment of the rent. In making such an adjustment, the Board shall provide that the landlord receive a fair and reasonable return on investment. In making an individual rent adjustment, the Board may consider, but is not limited to, the following factors:

1. The purposes of this ordinance;
2. The amount of property taxes;
3. Operating and maintenance expenses;
4. The addition of capital improvements, including the reasonable value of the landlord's labor and the useful life of the capital improvements;
5. The amount of living space and services;
6. The condition of the unit, and the level of compliance with applicable housing, health and safety codes;
7. Whether the property has been purchased and held as an investment for a long or short period of time; and
8. The landlord's actual cash investment and the return on that investment, including rents received, appreciation in the value of the property, benefits from federal and state income tax provisions, and all other relevant factors.

The Board need not consider all of the listed factors in each individual rent adjustment, but, on its own motion or the motion of a party, it shall consider any or all of the listed factors,or additional factors considered appropriate by the Board.

F. ***Sham Transactions:*** In considering a request for a rent adjustment, the Board may disallow costs associated with sham transactions.

G. ***Anti-Speculation Provision:*** No rent increase shall be authorized under this Title to compensate for a reduced cash flow due to increased financing costs, if at the time the landlord acquired the rental unit it was reasonably foreseeable that the reduced cash flow would occur based on the rental schedule in effect at the time of the sale. This Section shall apply only to units acquired after the effective date of this ordinance.

H. ***Refinancing Costs:*** In considering a request for an individual rent adjustment, the Board shall not take into account refinancing costs except to the extent the proceeds of the refinancing were used to make improvements to the controlled unit or the building or property containing that unit.

I. ***Decontrol:***

1. ***Decontrol.*** In January, 1982 and every second January thereafter, the Board shall hold hearings to determine if serious housing problems still exist in the City and County of San Francisco. If the Board finds that serious housing problems no longer exist, it shall conduct a rental vacancy survey. If the survey shows that the vacancy rate is at 5% or above, the Board shall conduct another survey twelve months later. If the vacancy rate has remained at 5% or above, this shall be reported to the Board of Supervisors who shall place a measure suspending, but not repealing, the rent controls in Title IV on the ballot at the next general election.

2. ***Reinstatement hearings.*** If controls are suspended, beginning one year after the date of such suspension, and every twelve months thereafter, the Board shall hold hearings to consider the reinstatement of rent controls. The Board shall reinstate rent controls if it finds one or more of the following:

(a) There are serious housing problems in San Francisco;
(b) A substantial number of tenants have received excessive rent increases since decontrol;
(c) Tenants are spending an excessive portion of their income for rent; or
(d) The vacancy rate for rental housing has dropped below 5%.

If the Board holds reinstatement hearings for five consecutive years without reinstating rent controls, the Board shall be dissolved after the fifth set of hearings.

**TITLE V: REMOVAL OF UNITS FROM THE RENTAL HOUSING MARKET**

A. ***General Provision:*** In order to protect the supply of rental housing, any landlord who wishes to remove a unit from the rental housing market by conversion to condominium or stock cooperative, by demolition, or by conversion to non-residential use must comply with the provisions of this Title as well as any other applicable ordinance or regulation of the City and County of San Francisco not inconsistent with its provisions.

B. ***Conversion to Condominium:***

1. The City Planning Commission may approve the removal of a unit from the rental housing market by conversion to condominium or stock cooperative only when:

(a) It has determined that the tenants in not less than 80% of the units of the conversion project have indicated their intent to purchase a converted unit by the signing of unit reservation forms and intent to purchase forms and by making a deposit of 15 times the monthly rent into an interest-bearing neutral escrow depository. This deposit shall not be provided from funds under the control of the landlord; or

(b). The rent controls under Title IV have been suspended pursuant to Section I of Title IV and the City Planning Commission has determined that the tenants in more than 50% of the units of the conversion project have indicated their intent to purchase a converted unit by the signing of unit reservation forms and intent to purchase forms and by making a deposit of 15 times the monthly rent into an interest-bearing neutral escrow depository. This deposit shall not be provided from funds under the control of the landlord.

2. Prior to approval of the conversion project, the City Planning Commission must also determine:

(a) That the landlord has not, for the purpose of preparing the building for conversion, evicted tenants, engaged in misrepresentation or coercive practices to cause tenants to purchase units, raised rents, or evicted tenants for the purpose of rehabilitating or reconstructing their units and failed to offer them the opportunity to return to their units after rehabilitation or reconstruction is completed. These factors may be judged by an examination of the monthly vacancy factor and rent schedules over the preceding two years, as well as other practices;

(b) That the landlord has not denied or attempted to deny any tenant a right or benefit under this ordinance or other applicable law for the purpose of conversion;

(c) That the landlord has complied with all applicable provisions of the City's housing, building, planning and subdivision codes or that adequate funds have been escrowed or bonded to assure compliance prior to the close of escrow on any converted unit; and

(d) That the conversion project is consistent with the objectives of the San Francisco Master Plan and any federal, state or local housing program applicable to any part of the conversion project.

3. If approval of the conversion project is denied under Sections 2(a) or (b) of this Title, then the landlord may not again seek approval for a conversion of that project until 18 months from the date of denial.

4. Notwithstanding the above provisions, the City Planning Commission shall not approve the conversion of more than 700 rental units to condominium or stock cooperative in any calendar year.

C. ***Demolition or Conversion to Non-Residential Use:***

1. No unit, except those defined under Sections D(1) or (4) of Title II, may be removed from the rental housing market by demolition or conversion to non-residential use unless a certification has been received from the Board. The Board shall not issue such a certification unless it finds that:

(a) The rental unit is vacant and uninhabitable, with substantial violations of the housing or other applicable codes, and is not capable of being made habitable in an economically feasible manner that can result in a fair and reasonable rate of return for the landlord; or

(b) The rental unit is on a site that will be developed so as to include at least the same number of units and at least the same amount of living space affordable by low- and moderate-income persons as were available before the proposed demolition or conversion. Units added to the low- and moderate-income housing stock elsewhere in the City and County of San Francisco may be used to satisfy this provision. The Board shall promulgate regulations and take all other necessary action to enforce this provision.

2. No demolition or other permit necessary to accomplish demolition or conversion to non-residential use shall be issued unless the Board has first issued its certification.

D. ***Applicability.*** The provisions of this Title shall apply to all applications for conversion to condominium or stock cooperative or for demolition or for conversion to non-residential use which have not received final approval as of the effective date of this ordinance.

**TITLE VI: PROTECTION, ENFORCEMENT, AND JUDICIAL REVIEW**

A. ***Just Cause Eviction:*** No landlord shall recover possession of a controlled unit unless he or she shows the existence of one of the following grounds:

1. The tenant has failed to pay the rent to which the landlord is legally entitled, unless the tenant has in good faith withheld rent pursuant to state law or this ordinance.

2. The tenant has continued, after a reasonable time following written notice to stop, to be so disorderly as to destroy the peace and quiet of the other tenants or occupants of the premises.

3. The tenant has willfully or by reason of gross negligence caused or allowed substantial damage to the premises.

4. The tenant has continued, after a reasonable time following written notice to stop, to breach substantially any reasonable written rules and regulations.

5. The tenancy is conditioned on employment of the tenant as manager of the building, and that employment has legally terminated or otherwise expired.

6. The owner or lessor seeks in good faith to recover possession for his or her own use and occupancy.

7. The landlord, after having obtained all proper permits from the City and County of San Francisco, intends to undertake substantial and material remodeling or reconstruction which cannot be done while the tenant resides in the premises. In such cases, including those in which the remodeling or reconstruction is being done in preparation for converting the units to condominiums or stock cooperatives, the tenant shall be offered the opportunity to move back into the premises as a tenant upon completion of the work.

8. An owner-occupant of a building seeks in good faith to recover possession of a unit in that building for use and occupancy of his or her child, parent, brother, sister, grandparent or grandchild, provided that the tenant has resided in the building less than one year and is not disabled, and provided that no substantially equivalent unit is vacant and available in the same building.

9. The landlord seeks to recover possession to demolish or otherwise permanently remove the unit from use after having obtained all proper permits from the City and County of San Francisco. In the event that new housing is built on the same site, the tenant shall be offered the opportunity to move into that housing upon its completion.

B. ***Relief for Eviction:***

1. The reasons enumerated in Sections A(6) and (8) of this Title shall not be grounds for evicting a tenant when the landlord is seeking to convert all or part of the building into condominiums or stock cooperatives or is the purchaser of a condominium or stock cooperative unit who wishes to evict a tenant who was living in the unit prior to conversion.

2. In the case of those grounds for eviction not the fault of the tenant (grounds described in Sections A(6), (7), (8), and (9) of this Title), the landlord shall pay to the tenant, prior to his or her moving if requested by the tenant, either the tenant's actual moving expenses not to exceed $1,000, or at the tenant's election, a payment based on the number of rooms in the apartment: $275 for a one room apartment, $300 for two rooms, $350 for three rooms, $400 for four rooms, $450 for five rooms, and $500 for six or more rooms. The Board may adjust this payment schedule to account for inflation and other relevant factors. This section shall not apply when a tenant rents from a landlord who has occupied the unit and it is understood between the parties at the time of rental that the landlord wishes to reoccupy the unit at a definite future date, or the landlord resides in the same unit as the tenant.

3. If the event claimed as grounds for eviction under Sections A(6), (7), (8), and (9) of this Title is not substantially initiated within six months after the tenant moves, and the landlord's conduct is willful, the tenant shall be entitled to a further payment of $1,000 or three times actual damages sustained, whichever is greater, plus reasonable costs and attorneys' fees.

4. If the tenant is evicted under Sections A(6) or (8) of this Title and the owner or relative who moves into the tenant's former unit resides there less than six months, the eviction shall be rebuttably presumed not to have been in good faith and the tenant may recover the damages specified in Section B(3) of this Title.

C. ***Retaliatory Eviction Protection:*** Notwithstanding the existence of any of the above grounds, no landlord may retaliate against any tenant for using or asserting any rights under this ordinance, or for organizing others to use or assert these rights. Such retaliation shall be subject to suit for actual and punitive damages, injunctive relief, and reasonable costs and attorneys' fees. Such retaliation shall be a defense to an eviction action. In any action in which such retaliation is at issue, provided that the act alleged to have been retaliatory occurred within one year of the protected conduct, the burden shall be on the landlord to prove that the dominant motive for the act alleged to be retaliatory was some motive other than retaliation.

D. ***Civil Remedies for Excess Rent:***

1. ***Relief From Excess Rent Payments:*** A tenant from whom a payment of rent in excess of the maximum rent authorized by Title IV of this ordinance is demanded, accepted or retained may petition for relief from the Board. The Board, after notice and a hearing, shall determine whether a violation has occurred, and, if so, the extent of the excess payment. The Board may order the landlord to pay a refund directly to the tenant or may allow the tenant to deduct the sum from his or her rent payments.

2. ***Willful Demand for Excess Rent:*** A landlord who willfully demands, accepts or retains any payment of rent in excess of the maximum rent authorized by Title IV of this ordinance shall be liable to the tenant from whom such payment is demanded, accepted or retained for

damages in the amount of $300 or three times the amount by which the payment demanded, accepted or retained exceeded the maximum lawful rent authorized by Title IV, whichever is greater, plus reasonable costs and attorneys' fees.

3. *Board Action:* If the tenant from whom such payment is demanded, accepted or retained in violation of this ordinance fails to bring an action under this Section within ten months after the date of occurrence of the violation, the Board may bring its own action to recover such payment. Thereafter the tenant on whose behalf the Board acted is barred from also bringing such an action against the landlord based on the same violation. In the event the Board prevails, it shall be entitled to retain the costs incurred in the settlement of the claim, and the tenant against whom the violation has been committed shall be entitled to the remainder.

4. *Deduction of Excess Amounts from Rent:* A tenant who has paid more than the maximum rent authorized by Title IV shall be entitled to a refund in the amount of the excess payment. A tenant may elect to deduct such amount of the refund due from his or her future rent payments, rather than pursuing the remedy provided in Section D(1) of this Title, provided that the tenant informs the landlord in advance in writing of his or her intention to do so. A tenant shall not be penalized by his or her landlord for deducting refunds pursuant to this Section.

5. *Judicial Relief:* The Board and tenants and landlords of controlled units may seek relief from a court of appropriate jurisdiction to enforce this ordinance and the rules, regulations, orders and decisions of the Board.

6. *Judicial Review:* Any party aggrieved by a final action of the Board may seek judicial review in a court of appropriate jurisdiction.

## TITLE VII. INCREASING HOME OWNERSHIP OPPORTUNITIES AND EXPANDING THE SUPPLY OF RENTAL HOUSING FOR LOW- AND MODERATE-INCOME PERSONS

A. *Housing Development Opportunities Fund:*

1. *Establishment:* There is established a Housing Development Opportunities Fund, hereinafter called the Fund, for the purpose of increasing the supply of owner-occupied, cooperatively owned and rental housing affordable by low- and moderate-income persons. The Fund and allocations from the Fund shall be administered by the Office of Community Development of the City and County of San Francisco, or the successor office or agency performing the same or related functions, subject to the advice and prior approval of the Mayor's Citizen's Committee on Community Development. In the event that the Mayor's Citizen's Committee on Community Development ceases to exist, the Board of Supervisors shall establish a committee composed primarily of low- and moderate-income persons to replace it.

2. *Allocation of Funds:* Money deposited in the Fund shall be allocated to neighborhood-based housing development corporations, or their designees, and to other eligible recipients as provided for in this Title. The units assisted by the Fund shall reflect the proportionate housing needs of low- and moderate-income families, elderly, and disabled persons in the City and County of San Francisco. All newly constructed housing units assisted by the Fund shall be accessible to and suitable for occupancy by disabled persons as required by federal law and regulations, but under no circumstances shall common space be inaccessible or less than 5% of family units or 10% of other units be suitable for occupancy by disabled persons. A maximum of 25% of the Fund may be used to improve existing residential units, and a minimum of 10% of such units shall be accessible to and suitable for occupancy by the disabled. Resale restrictions shall be imposed on the sale of all housing units assisted by the Fund in order to ensure that such units will continue to be occupied by low- and moderate-income persons.

B. *Allocation of Resources to the Housing Development Opportunities Fund.*

1. *Allocating Part of the Existing Hotel Tax for Citywide Housing:* The Board of Supervisors shall retain without modification Part III, Article 7, of the San Francisco Municipal Code, Subsections 502 and 515, paragraphs (2), (3), (4) and (5), which establish the Hotel Tax rate and how it is collected, and provide for the allocation of a portion of Hotel Tax revenues to meet replacement housing obligations associated with the Yerba Buena Center urban renewal project; except that, in order to make available revenues from the Hotel Tax for expansion of the supply of housing, on a citywide basis, affordable by low- and moderate-income persons, Subsection 515(2) shall be amended to add the following paragraph:

"(h) The balance of the funds in excess of the amounts required for the purposes described in paragraphs (a), (b), (c), (d) and (e) above shall be used to facilitate the development or improve-

ment of housing throughout San Francisco affordable by low- and moderate-income persons and to supplement the rent of low- and moderate-income tenants in such newly developed or improved housing. That balance shall be deposited in the Housing Development Opportunities Fund and administered in accordance with Section A of this Title by allocation to neighborhood-based housing development corporations or their designees. That balance shall be used for the costs associated with site acquisition, pre-development and construction of new units, the improvement of existing structures, and rent supplements for tenants in such newly developed or improved housing."

2. *Revenue Bonds to Provide Below-Market Rate Loans for the Purchase or Improvement of Owner-Occupied Housing:* The Board of Supervisors shall take all steps necessary to issue tax-exempt mortgage revenue bonds for the purpose of making below-market rate loans. All such loans shall be affordable by low- and moderate-income persons for the purchase or improvement of residential property which will be owner-occupied. Mortgage revenues shall be the sole source of funds pledged for repayment of the bonds, and the bonds shall be issued at no cost or risk to the City and County of San Francisco. The proceeds of the bond issue shall be deposited in the Housing Development Opportunities Fund and administered in accordance with Section A of this Title.

3. *Revenue Bonds to Develop Housing Affordable by Low- and Moderate-Income Persons:* The Board of Supervisors shall take all steps necessary to issue tax-exempt mortgage revenue bonds for the purpose of making below-market rate loans to neighborhood-based housing development corporations or their designees for the development or improvement of units affordable by low- and moderate-income persons. Mortgage revenues shall be the sole source of funds pledged for repayment of the bonds and the bonds shall be issued at no cost or risk to the City and County of San Francisco. The proceeds of the bond issue shall be deposited in the Housing Development Opportunities Fund and administered in accordance with Section A of this Title.

4. *Allocation of Community Development Block Grant Funds to Produce Low- and Moderate-Income Housing:* Each year the Board of Supervisors shall allocate 25% or more of San Francisco's entitlement grant of federal Community Development Block Grant funds to assist in the development or improvement of housing units affordable by low- and moderate-income persons. These grant funds shall be deposited in the Housing Development Opportunities Fund and administered in accordance with Section A of this Title by allocation to neighborhood-based housing development corporations or their designees for site acquisition, pre-development and construction costs or for the costs of improving existing structures.

The Community Development Block Grant funds allocated to the Housing Development Opportunities Fund shall be those Community Development Block Grant funds which traditionally have been and would be allocated to the Redevelopment Agency; provided, however, that in no event shall the Housing Development Opportunities Fund receive less than 25% of each annual entitlement grant.

C. *Using Surplus City-Owned Land for Housing.* The Board of Supervisors upon the recommendation of the administrators of the Housing Development Opportunities Fund specified in Section A of this Title shall make available, at the lowest feasible price, city-owned surplus land and buildings to neighborhood-based housing development corporations, or their designees, suitable for housing units affordable by low- and moderate-income persons.

D. *Stabilizing Housing Costs by Discouraging Housing Speculation.* The Board of Supervisors shall adopt further legislation beyond that contained in this ordinance, to discourage housing speculation, defined as the rapid turnover of residential property, not for the dominant purpose of living in it or renting it to others on a long-term basis, nor for the dominant purpose of improving the property, but for the dominant purpose of making excess or windfall profits from holding the property for a short period of time.

E. *Facilitating the Planning and Permit Process to Encourage Expansion of the Housing Supply.*

1. *Expanding the Housing Supply through the Development of Minor Second Units:* The Board of Supervisors shall take all steps necessary to implement the provisions in the Planning Code that provide for "minor second units," commonly known as "in-law apartments," in existing residential structures. Such provisions shall be implemented only with the consent of the neighborhood affected. The City Planning Commission shall establish procedures for determining whether such consent exists.

2. *Speeding Up the Processing of Construction Permits to Encourage Additions to the Housing Supply:* The Board of Supervisors shall develop a system for expediting the processing of permits necessary for the development of new housing.

3. *Setting Reasonable Limits on Code Inspections to Encourage Home Improvements and Repairs:* The Board of Supervisors shall amend the relevant codes to provide that when an owner-occupant of a single-family home has been issued a permit for improvement or repair of the property the City and County of San Francisco shall limit its inspection to the repairs and improvements undertaken pursuant to that permit. Nothing in this provision shall limit the right or obligation of the City and County of San Francisco to require the removal of immediate and serious hazards to the health or safety of the occupants.

## TITLE VIII: GENERAL PROVISIONS

A. *Non-Waiverability:* Any provision in a rental housing agreement which waives or modifies any provision of this ordinance is against public policy and void.

B. *Partial Invalidity:* This ordinance shall be liberally construed to achieve its purposes and preserve its validity. The provisions of this ordinance are severable. If any of its parts or applications are held invalid, that shall not affect the other parts or applications, which are intended to have independent validity. If this ordinance or any provision of this ordinance is held invalid, the Board of Supervisors shall enact a substitute ordinance or provision which to the extent legally possible has the same effect as the provision ruled invalid by the court.

C. *Remedies Non-Exclusive:* The remedies of this ordinance are not exclusive and shall be in addition to any other procedures or remedies provided for in any other law.

D. *Repeal of Inconsistent Legislation:* Chapter 37 of the San Francisco Administrative Code, also known as Ordinance No. 276-79, is hereby repealed.

# Appendix C
# COMMUNITY LAND TRUSTS

## "Sell the earth? Why not sell the air, the clouds and the great sea?"

**Tecumseh** (1768-1813), Shawnee chief, considered to be the most effective native opponent of U.S. expansion

No element of a local economy is more fundamental to it than the land and natural resource base on which and from which the wealth of the community and of most of its individual members is produced. Central to North American culture has been the concept and legal institution of private ownership of land. That institution is intended, in the minds of most, to provide security and a means of preserving wealth to individual families and stability to local communities. Often, however, the land and resources and their economic value have been rendered unavailable to the communities and to many of their members. In some cases it has even been taken directly from and forever lost to them, or used to their detriment. A comprehensive and successful approach to community economic development must include a reassessment of the relative needs and rights of local communities and individuals in relation to those of private corporate interests. It must also include a redefinition of "property" and a mechanism for permanently returning the value or use of the land and natural resources to the local community and its members, together with equal justice in access.

## THE PROBLEM: LAND AS A COMMODITY

The dream of land ownership motivated many nineteenth-century North American immigrants. Through ownership they expected to build security, equity, and a legacy for their descendants. These are legitimate aspirations and should be recognized.

The institution of private ownership, however, did not simply provide for secure individual possession and use. It transformed land and resources into marketable commodities, leaving a wide opening for speculation,

monopolization, absentee ownership and control, and profit-motivated planning and development. The effects of such practices had long been felt, but the increasing political and economic complexity of the twentieth century and the rapid development of technology have made the problems much worse.

Between 1976 and 1978, for instance, the value of an average acre of farm land increased 26 percent nationwide and far more in some areas. The United States has lost more than 4 million family farms since the 1930s, with minority-owned farms particularly hard hit. Ownership of farm land has become significantly concentrated, and corporate holdings have increased. Young would-be farmers are often unable to finance acquisition. Production has seriously declined in some regions. New England, for example, must import more than 80 percent of its food.

Rising fuel costs, transportation problems, and changing lifestyles and family structures bring thousands of upper-income residents back to the center cities, accelerating the process of "gentrification" and reducing the number of low-income rental housing units. Housing prices in affected neighborhoods may double in a matter of months. Since most housing stock in low-income neighborhoods is owned by absentee landlords, the residents are unable to exert any meaningful control over neighborhood development or over their own personal futures. Although gentrification holds the attraction of increased property values and tax revenues for municipal governments, it also increases the burden on public assistance and rent or acquisition subsidy programs. The social cost to individual families and neighborhoods is devastating.

Nowhere is the economic impact of private ownership on local communities (and states) more obvious than in the virtual corporate monopoly of productive timber and mineral resources. Seven corporations own 32 percent of tree-covered Maine, absentee landlords control at least two-thirds of the privately-held land in West Virginia. Through a long history of privilege and political influence, corporate owners have received extraordinary tax advantages while realizing enormous profits from the minerals and timber. If the value of these states' resources is compared to the numbers of their populations, they would seen to be two of the most prosperous areas in the world. But if you look in the back hills and hollows, or at the statistics describing average income and available services in Maine or West Virginia, you will encounter some of the most abject poverty in the United States.

## PROPERTY VERSUS "TRUSTERTY"

Governments at every level have made efforts to respond to these problems, with zoning, land-use planning, purchase of development rights, limits on corporate land ownership, and special loan funds. The actions taken to date have been far from adequate, however, while financial pressures and probable budget cuts may well limit the future effectiveness of many of these programs. Above all, there is little indication that legislators or government agencies are willing to confront the serious inequities of distribution of land and resources; nor will they address the basic concepts and issues of private ownership and "property rights" and return the control and use of these basic economic resources (the original "commonwealth") to the local communities.

It is in this redefinition of the concept of "property" that the beginnings of a solution may be found. An appropriate and important distinction can be made between "property" and what might be called "trusterty." Property consists of things human beings bring about through their own efforts—manufactured goods, homes, cultivated crops, enterprises—any of which might be owned either individually or cooperatively. Trusterty, on the other hand, would include the land, its natural resources, the oceans, and the atmosphere, which were created without human intervention and should be held in trust by the community for its people, present and future.

It is this critical distinction that the institution of private ownership fails to make. "Real estate" routinely includes both land and constructed improvements, without differentiation. Once understood and applied through objective legal and organizational tools at the local level, however, this simple distinction could form the basis for altering the land-holding practices that concentrate ownership in the hands of a few and deprive local communities of their indigenous wealth and their rightful control over their own development.

## COMMUNITY LAND TRUSTS

Such an alternative is beginning to emerge from grassroots initiatives in a number of rural communities and urban neighborhoods across the country. This alternative is called the Community Land Trust (CLT), which attempts to guarantee the legitimate aspirations of private ownership while blending them with the needs and inherent interests of the local community.

A CLT is a democratically structured nonprofit corporation with an open public membership and an elected board of trustees. The board includes leaseholders of trust-owned lands, other community residents, and public interest representatives. The trust acquires land through purchase or donation with an intention to retain title in perpetuity, thus removing the land from the speculative market. Appropriate uses for the land are determined, a process comparable to land-use planning or zoning, and it is then leased to individuals, families, cooperatives, or businesses or for public purposes.

Typically the trust offers a lifetime (or 99-year renewable) lease, which may be transferred to the leaseholder's heirs if they wish to continue the use of the land. Leaseholders must use the land in an environmentally and socially responsible manner, but the trust may not interfere with their personal beliefs, associations, or activities. Leases are given only to those who will make use of the land, and priority in leasing may be given to those whose needs are greatest. Leaseholders pay a regular lease fee, but need no down payments, credit, or conventional financing to gain access to the land.

While leaseholders never own the land, they do own buildings, improvements, and the fruits of their own labor. Should they leave the land and terminate the lease, they may sell or remove their possessions and improvements, but they cannot sell the land itself. In such an event the trust often retains the first option to purchase improvements, for resale to the next lessee. Purchase is made at the owner's original invested cost, adjusted for inflation, depreciation, and damage. The leaseholder/property owner is thus guaranteed a real dollar equity in improvements but is prevented from making indirect speculative gains from the increased value of the land.

The CLT offers a number of short- and long-term advantages to individual members and to the community as a whole. By joining together, families establish collective credibility and assemble resources far greater than the individual families can muster. The CLT provides lifetime security of use equal to that of private ownership, and use of the land may be passed on to heirs without the imposition of federal or state estate taxes, which force many heirs to sell all or a portion of the family land for payment. The community of land and people created by the CLT can also give support and assistance in daily land use and in times of special need.

The CLT gives the local community greater power to shape its own future. While the leaseholders have secure tenure and considerable freedom in their use of the land, decisions about redistribution and long-term commu-

nity planning and development are made by the community from a firm economic base.

The most direct economic resource created through the CLT is the income from lease fee payments. Those who use the land and resources of the "common trust" have a responsibility to give a fair return to the entire community for the use of its land. The lease fee is based on the full value of the land alone, without considering the value of the improvements the leaseholders construct on it. Typically, the CLT makes an effort to distinguish between the "use value" of the land — the income or equivalent value the lessees can reasonably expect to derive from the intended use of the land, as provided in the purposes of the lease — and its "full market" (or speculative) value. Land use fees are based on the use of the land, adjusted to account for inflation or deflation. The CLT can use the income from lease fees to finance further land acquisitions, land-use planning, management and administrative activities, or for other community development or service programs.

## BENEFITS TO COMMUNITY RESIDENTS

Through full value lease fees, the trust retains the unearned increment in the market value of the land for the community, since the increased value of community land is usually the product of the efforts or investments of community residents. We see the opposite situation in many existing low-income communities: residents who labor to improve their community and the quality of their own lives in it also enhance the value of land in the community and its attractiveness as a speculative investment. By improving their circumstances, they may actually initiate or accelerate the market forces that will ultimately drive them from their homes and neighborhoods. If the land base in the neighborhood were held in a CLT, these residents would retain the value of their labor for themselves, their neighbors, and their heirs.

Through the authority of a CLT to grant or withhold leases, charge full value lease fees, and exercise the first option on improvements in the event of a sale, local communities are given powerful control over their own development. The trust can encourage and plan for development to meet community needs and interests, discourage or actually prohibit development motivated by the expectation of speculative gains, and insure that the community receives direct financial benefits from the development and economic activity on its common landbase.

The CLT may also choose to lease tracts of land for less than their full value fee to facilitate access to the land by low-income families or to respond to personal hardship or incapacity of the lessees. This reduced fee represents an implicit subsidy — the use of local community economic resources to meet the particular needs of individual members.

## RESOURCE MANAGEMENT

Several alternatives are available for management of a community's timber and mineral resources. As one of these alternatives, resources owned directly by the CLT may be leased on terms that allow the lessees to earn a fair return on their labor but retain the inherent value of the resources for the community.

Efforts are now under way in one New England community to develop a model forest land trust, integrating elements of the prevailing private ownership structure with a CLT model. Development pressures and the need for wood as an alternative energy source pose serious threats to New England's forests. A considerable percentage of the region's extensive woodlands is divided into small private holdings. Most of these are presently unmanaged and economically unproductive. Their owners lack management capability, and it is often neither practical nor economical to contract for responsible, professional management of such small tracts. The twofold danger is that these woodlots will continue to be unproductive, depriving the region of badly needed resources, or that they will be damaged by careless, once-through cutting. The challenge is to aggregate the small woodlots into parcels large enough to sustain long-term, careful management programs.

In the forest trust model, as now proposed, individual land-owners will donate the development rights to their forested land to the trust, receiving a tax credit for the gift. The landowners would then form a partnership, with the trust also participating as a partner, and pool the value of their timber in a long-term forestry program managed by the partnership and/or by the trust. Such management can increase the value of the forest several times and bring additional income to the landowners and to the trust itself. In this particular example, state-owned lands located in the local community may be included in the program through involvement of the state as a partner or through a gift of the lands by the state to the local forest trust.

For the individual landowner this model offers economic advantages through the gift tax credit, property tax reductions for forest land in management, direct income from the management program, and reduction of estate tax liabilities. For the local community, state, and region, the model offers the development of new industries appropriate to the character of the community, jobs for both skilled and unskilled workers, an increased supply of valuable resources, reduced energy costs from the use of "waste" wood to replace fossil fuels, and increased revenues (directly, in cases in which the community or state is a participant; indirectly through taxes on income generated). The model offers environmental advantages by reducing pressure for development and by increasing forest yields while improving aesthetic conditions and wildlife habitat.

## FUNDING

To date the lack of acquisition financing has been the greatest barrier to the growth of CLTs. Considerable progress was made in 1978-1979 in the development of new financing sources and strategies, and several important precedents were established.

In the public sector the Farmers Home Administration (FmHA) agreed, after more than a year of negotiations, to open its Section 515 Rural Rental Cooperative Loan Program to CLTs as landowners/developers. Ownership of housing units may be transferred to resident families at the end of each mortgage period; thus the CLT acts as a financing vehicle for family home ownership. The leaseholders are eligible for the FmHA Section 502 Rural Housing Loan program, with the leasehold interest, but not the title to the land, included in the security for the loan. The CLT retains an option to buy out the remainder of the loan in case of default.

The U.S. Department of Housing and Urban Development (HUD) and several state housing finance agencies have offered to make Section 8 rent subsidies available to land trust developments. Section 8 payments are made to the CLT as owner of the land and, initially, of the housing units. The trust enters into an agreement with the families that lease the units that allows them to purchase their homes through rental payments. The CLT retains the first option on the units. Boston has become the first city to give a HUD Community Development Block Grant to a neighborhood land trust.

In 1979 the federal Appalachian Regional Commission (ARC) funded a land trust/land banking feasibility study for that region. Based on the positive conclusions of the study, an Appalachian Land Bank has been established, and ARC has promised to provide its initial operating and acquisition capital. This is the first institution of its kind in the United States (there is a success-

ful provincial land bank in Saskatchewan, Canada).

These developments represent a growing awareness of the advantages of the Community Land Trust model on the part of public officials and agencies. This awareness is matched by interest and support from private, nonprofit funding organizations and individuals. With increasing frequency CLTs are receiving grants and loans from foundations, churches, and national low-income housing assistance organizations. Financial assistance has come in the forms of gifts, direct loans, loan guarantees, and certificates of deposit to leverage loans from local banks. The Institute for Community Economics, a nonprofit organization that provides organizational, legal, planning, and financial counseling to CLTs, has established a revolving loan fund to provide short-term (5 years or less) start-up loans to CLTs and related projects.

As the CLT model becomes more widely recognized and understood, for-profit lending institutions and real estate development companies are showing a greater willingness to enter into business agreements with local trusts. A number of local banks have now made construction or mortgage loans directly to CLTs. In a recent development, the Institute for Community Economics in Boston formed a partnership with a for-profit development corporation to purchase an 85-unit low-income housing project that had defaulted to HUD. The institute will participate in the general partnership in trust for the tenants, organization and the neighborhood land trust, which is to be formed with financial assistance from the proceeds of the project. The institute's ownership share will transfer automatically to its partners when they have developed the necessary management capability. The project will be syndicated to include a number of tax-shelter investors as limited partners; however, first options on the limited partners' ownership shares and a set-aside fund from the proceeds of the syndication will give the tenants the option of establishing full cooperative ownership of their buildings by the end of the mortgage period. The land is conveyed to a neighborhood trust of which the tenants or tenant organization are members. This project is the first major example of a partnership between a CLT and a for-profit business organization. It gives the CLT access to much-needed financial resources and business management skills.

Of course, the CLT may use its own revenues (from leases or timber management) for land acquisition or developing financing. While these are quite limited in the early stages of a trust's development, they do represent significant long-term potential.

Some CLTs have chosen to increase or accelerate lease fee payments to meet mortgage payments for land acquisition. Typically, the family that pays this rate, which is higher than the normal use value fee, receives a reduction or suspension of land use fees when purchase of the land by the trust has been completed.

The CLT may have certain indirect resources and advantages, through the use of nonprofit land acquisition or bargain sale techniques. In such a transaction the CLT acquires land and/or improvements as a gift or at a price considerably below their full market value. The donor/seller receives a tax credit for the gift and a reduction of capital gains tax liabilities. For many potential donors these savings will equal the foregone cash return. A CLT can only offer such tax advantages if it is recognized as a 501(c)(3) organization by the Internal Revenue Service. To date the IRS response to applications for 501(c)(3) classification from local CLTs has been inconsistent. A non-exempt CLT, however, may partake of the benefits of these techniques, through the assistance of the Institute for Community Economics, the Trust for Public Land, or comparable 501(c)(3) organization, which would resell the land to the local CLT on terms that allowed the CLT to purchase it without outside financing (through lease fees from its use or other income). The 501(c)(3) organization would use its revenue from the sale to support its educational, advocacy, and technical assistance programs for local CLTs or to expand the capital base of its revolving loan fund.

Whatever the means of financing, acquisition of land by a CLT represents the creation or re-creation of a stable, accessible economic base in and for the local community. The trust can provide justice to community members in the distribution of land and housing, and security in their use. It can give the community far more effective control over its evolution and economic development. It can make indigenous natural resources once again available to the community, with opportunities for economic development and the creation of additional jobs. It can provide direct and indirect revenues and a credit base to finance development, and it can guarantee that the incremental value created by that development and by the efforts of local citizens will be retained by and for the community. The financial, political, and educational barriers to significant CLT development are real, but if CLTs continue to make progress their potential is also very real — and the need for them is increasingly urgent.

*This is a chapter by Chuck Matthei, Director of the Institute of Community Economics, from a forthcoming book,* Financing Community Economic Development, *available from the Program in Urban and Regional Studies, Cornell University, Ithaca, NY 14853.*

# INDEX OF PLACES, ORGANIZATIONS AND AGENCIES